16e

S0-BRJ-916

Brief Course

Contemporary Business Mathematics

for Colleges

16e

Brief Course

Contemporary Business Mathematics

for Colleges

James E. Deitz, Ed.D.
Past President of Heald Colleges

James L. Southam, Ph.D.
San Francisco State University

SOUTH-WESTERN
CENGAGE Learning·

Australia · Brazil · Japan · Korea · Mexico · Singapore · Spain · United Kingdom · United States

SOUTH-WESTERN
CENGAGE Learning·

**Contemporary Business Mathematics
for Colleges, 16e**
James E. Deitz, Ed.D., and James L. Southam, Ph.D.

Senior Vice President of Editorial, Business:
Jack W. Calhoun

Senior Acquisitions Editor: Charles McCormick, Jr.

Developmental Editor: Daniel Noguera

Editorial Assistant: Courtney Bavaro

Marketing Manager: Adam Marsh

Senior Marketing Communications Manager:
Elizabeth Shipp

Senior Content Project Manager: Cliff Kallemeyn

Rights Acquisition Specialist, Text: Amber Hosea

Rights Acquisition Specialist, Image: Deanna Ettinger

Media Editor: Chris Valentine

Frontlist Buyer, Manufacturing: Ron Montgomery

Senior Art Director: Stacy Jenkins Shirley

Cover Designer: Lou Ann Thesing

Cover Images: ©iStock Photo

For product information and technology assistance, contact us at
Cengage Learning Customer & Sales Support, 1-800-354-9706
For permission to use material from this text or product,
submit all requests online at **www.cengage.com/permissions**
Further permissions questions can be e-mailed to
permissionrequest@cengage.com

Exam*View*® is a registered trademark of eInstruction Corp. Windows is a registered trademark of the Microsoft Corporation used herein under license. Macintosh and Power Macintosh are registered trademarks of Apple Computer, Inc. used herein under license.

Library of Congress Control Number: 2011942779

ISBN 10: 1-133-19114-2

ISBN 13: 978-1-133-19114-8

South-Western Cengage Learning
5191 Natorp Boulevard
Mason, OH 45040
USA

Cengage Learning products are represented in Canada by Nelson Education, Ltd.

For your course and learning solutions, visit **academic.cengage.com**

Purchase any of our products at your local college store or at our preferred online store **www.ichapters.com**

Printed in the United States of America
1 2 3 4 5 15 14 13 12 11

To the Student

Contemporary Business Mathematics for Colleges, Edition 16, presents an arithmetic-based, basic approach to business mathematics. It emphasizes a practical, skill-building approach to prepare you for future careers in business through step-by-step development of concepts, numerous practice exercises, and a focus on business applications of techniques. It will also provide you with business vocabulary, practices and valuable background information for future business courses such as bookkeeping, accounting or finance. The text progresses from basic to more complex business mathematics topics.

During its previous editions, *Contemporary Business Mathematics for Colleges* sold more copies than any other business mathematics textbook. As always, the goal of this new sixteenth edition is to make a successful book even better. This edition continues to maintain its coverage of practical business mathematics problems and offers step-by-step solutions to help you solve these problems. The content of the new edition continues to be focused entirely on business mathematics with its emphasis on both the needs of contemporary business students and the requirements of shorter regular and online courses. *Contemporary Business Mathematics for Colleges* presents the basic principles of mathematics and immediately applies them in a series of practical business problems. This new edition continues to provide a balance among conceptual understanding, skill development, and business applications.

In the modern business environment, managers, employees, and consumers all need knowledge of and skill in business mathematics. Although computers and calculators are used to do many of the calculations, it is important to understand the concepts behind the mechanical computations. The purpose of this business mathematics textbook is to increase your mathematics knowledge, to develop your skills at applying this knowledge, and to introduce you to business application areas. This will make you more valuable employees, wiser consumers, and more prepared for your future business studies.

KEY FEATURES

Integrated Learning Objectives: These icons identify the sections of each chapter where each specific Learning Objective is addressed. The Learning Objectives are there to remind the students of the organization of the chapter.

Concept Checks: At the end of the section for each Learning Objective is a Concept Check to reinforce students' understanding of that particular Learning Objective.

Step-by-Step Problem-Solving Approach: Short, concise text sections are followed by examples with step-by-step solutions. Students learn mathematical concepts by immediately applying practical solutions to common business problems, and they gain confidence in their own problem-solving skills by learning the way example problems are solved and then practicing these techniques in the assignments.

Business Examples and Applications: Every mathematical technique is introduced and/or followed by a relevant business-related example. These business problems and examples from a variety of business applications help students better relate to the material as they learn how it is successfully applied.

Bottom Line: This end-of-chapter feature ties each Learning Objective to self-test problems (with answers). Students have the opportunity to check immediately whether they have mastered the chapter's key skills before moving on to the assignments.

Self-Check Review Problems: Located at the end of each chapter, the self-check review problems provide yet another opportunity for students to reinforce their understanding before completing the end-of-chapter assignments. Answers are provided at the end of the text.

End-of-Chapter Assignments: Every chapter has a minimum of two assignment sets. These provide students with many hundreds of problems to enhance their mastery of the mathematical concepts and business-related applications.

Methodology for Solving Word Problems: Chapter 3 contains a time-tested methodology for solving various types of word problems and also an introduction to some algebraic concepts. These items are presented at this early point in the text so that students will have important basic tools as they begin their study of business mathematics.

Video Icons: Video icons are placed where appropriate throughout the text to direct students to the video clips that are available on the companion website.

Microsoft® Excel Templates: Spreadsheet templates give students practice with both mathematics and spreadsheet software. The Excel templates were prepared by Adele Stock, faculty, Minnesota State Colleges and Universities, and are available on IRCD and companion website.

Product Website: The text website at www.cengage.com/bmath/deitz provides financial calculator material from Chapter 23, online quizzes, Internet links for the text, teaching resources, and more.

SUGGESTIONS TO IMPROVE YOUR STUDY

The special features in *Contemporary Business Mathematics for Colleges* are meant to help you focus your study. Keeping up with the coursework and making consistent use of the features will improve your performance on homework assignments and exams.

1. Read the text and study the step-by-step illustrations and examples carefully.
2. Work the Concept Check and the Bottom Line problems. These features will give you a comprehensive review of the problems in each chapter, before you get to the assignments.
3. Read the instructions carefully for each assignment before solving the problems.
4. Your instructor may tell you whether you are to work in groups or by yourself. However, you will not have learned until you can do the calculations yourself. Ask your instructor for help if you have difficulty understanding what you are asked to do, or how to do it.
5. Before working a problem, try to estimate your answer. The early chapters present methods for doing this.
6. Use shortcuts in your calculations to increase your confidence. Shortcuts are presented in several chapters.
7. Write numbers neatly and clearly, and align them in columns to help avoid errors.
8. Space is provided on the assignment sheets to compute most problems. Show each step in the solution so that if you make an error, your instructor can help you locate the cause.
9. Record your scores for each assignment on the Progress Report at the end of the book.

Acknowledgments

We would like to acknowledge the work of reviewers and verifiers who provided suggestions about ways to continually improve our text.

Allan Sheets, International Business College, Indianapolis
Amy McLaughlin, Utica School of Commerce
Brenda Rudolph, Flathead Valley Community College
Cheryl O'Berry, Pasco Hernando Community College
David Heilman, Ohio Business College
Dawn Stevens, Northwest Mississippi Community College - Desoto Center
Debra Kayser, Sheridan College
Diane Hagan, Ohio Business College
Dr. Wanda J. Flowers, Enterprise State Community College
Emma A Faulk, Alabama State University
Gale Sheppeard, Holmes Community College
Gerald Sweeney, Ventura College
Jeff Davis, Stevens-Henager College
John Donnellan, Holyoke Community College
Judy Hurtt, East Central Community College
Julia Angel, North Arkansas College
Kara Ryan, College of Notre Dame of Maryland
Karla West, Flathead Valley Community College
Kathy H. Scott, Western Piedmont Community College
Kelli Butler, Mid Michigan Community College
Leasa L. Davis, Mountain State College
Linda Davis, Copiah-Lincoln Community College
Mahmudul Sheikh, Rust College
Mary Dombrovski, St Cloud Technical and Community College
Mauritia Dodson, Ivy Tech Commuity College
Monill McClure, Spoon River College
Paula Luft, Black Hawk College-East Campus
Rhonda Posey, Copiah-Lincoln Community College
Richard Rhoads, West Hills Community College
Sherry Harris, UAM College of Technology, Crossett
Steve Hixenbaugh, Mendocino College
Thomas Burzycki
Tiffany Harrison, Stevens-Henager College

We also thank the staff at South-Western who worked to make this new edition the best business mathematics text possible: Sr. Acquisitions Editor, Charles McCormick, Jr.; Marketing Manager, Adam Marsh; and Developmental Editor, Daniel Noguera.

James E. Deitz
James L. Southam

About the Authors

JAMES E. DEITZ
PAST PRESIDENT OF HEALD COLLEGES

Author *James E. Deitz* brings both a thorough understanding of effective education today and a practical business knowledge to the latest edition of this leading text. Dr. Deitz earned his bachelor's degree in accounting from Memphis State University and doctorate of education from UCLA. Dr. Deitz has been an educator for more than 35 years, including professorships with UCLA and Los Angeles State College and a long-standing position as President of Heald Colleges. An active member of the business community, Dr. Deitz is a recognized international speaker and has served on regional educational accrediting commissions. Dr. Deitz serves currently on the Executive Committee and Board of Trustees of Dominican University of California and as a member of the Board of Directors of Bank of Marin. He has authored several texts in addition to this best-selling *Contemporary Business Mathematics for Colleges*.

JAMES L. SOUTHAM
SAN FRANCISCO STATE UNIVERSITY

Author *James L. Southam* has a diverse background of professional, educational, and teaching experience in business and mathematics. Dr. Southam holds bachelor's and master's degrees in mathematics education from Southern Oregon College, a Ph.D. in mathematics from Oregon State University, an MBA in finance from University of California, Berkeley, and a law degree from University of California, Hastings. Dr. Southam's 40 years of teaching experience include San Francisco State University College of Business, California State University, Stanislaus, Southern Oregon College, Oregon State University, and the University of International Business and Economics in Beijing. Both domestically and internationally, Dr. Southam has participated in business ventures, has been a business consultant, and is a successful author. He is a member of the San Francisco State University Athletics Hall of Fame.

BRIEF CONTENTS

CONTENTS

CONTENTS

CONTENTS

CONTENTS

Contemporary Business Mathematics

for Colleges

Part 1

Fundamental Applications

Fractions

1

Learning Objectives
By studying this chapter and completing all assignments, you will be able to:

Learning Objective 1   Change improper fractions and mixed numbers.

Learning Objective 2   Change fractions to lower and higher terms.

Learning Objective 3   Add fractions and mixed numbers.

Learning Objective 4   Subtract fractions and mixed numbers.

Learning Objective 5   Multiply fractions and mixed numbers.

Learning Objective 6   Divide fractions and mixed numbers.

Mathematics is a subject used in almost every phase of business. You have been exposed to business-related mathematics at least since your first visit to a store as a child. Some of business mathematics is the arithmetic of whole numbers which you started learning before you entered school. But most of business mathematics involves other additional numbers: fractions, decimals, and percents. In Chapter 1 we study fractions; in Chapter 2, decimals; and in Chapter 5, percents. (*Note:* A review of vocabulary and basic operations of whole numbers is available in Appendix C.)

Fractions are a natural part of cultures around the world. Very young children who cannot yet read learn simple fractions such as one half and one third when their parents teach them about sharing a candy bar or a pizza. Before the development of inexpensive handheld calculators, fractions were more important than they are today because they permitted shortcuts in arithmetic. However, fractions are still important in some industries. Moreover, the rules of fractions will always remain very important in algebra and higher mathematics.

Notation and Vocabulary of Fractions

Ristorante Porta cuts its medium-sized pizzas into six pieces. Each piece is "*one sixth*" of the pizza. If you take two pieces of pizza, you have "*two sixths*" of the pizza. Using numbers, two sixths can be written as $\frac{2}{6}$. If you buy two medium-sized pizzas and cut each pizza into six pieces, you will have twelve pieces, or *twelve sixths,* written as $\frac{12}{6}$. If you eat one of the twelve slices of pizza, eleven pieces remain, or *eleven sixths,* written as $\frac{11}{6}$.

In the three fractions $\frac{2}{6}$, $\frac{12}{6}$, and $\frac{11}{6}$, the bottom number (6) is called the **denominator.** The top numbers (2, 12, and 11) are called **numerators.** The horizontal line that separates the numerator from the denominator is called the **fraction bar.** $\frac{2}{6}$ is called a **proper fraction** because the numerator (2) is *smaller than* the denominator (6). $\frac{12}{6}$ and $\frac{11}{6}$ are called **improper fractions** because the numerators are *greater than, or equal to,* the denominators. Notice that $\frac{11}{6}$ represents one whole pizza plus $\frac{5}{6}$ of the second pizza. $\frac{11}{6}$ can be written as $1\frac{5}{6}$ which is called a **mixed number** because there is a whole number part (1) and a proper fraction $\left(\frac{5}{6}\right)$.

Figure 1-1 illustrates these concepts. Diagram b represents a proper fraction. Diagrams a, c, and d all represent improper fractions. Diagram d also represents a mixed number.

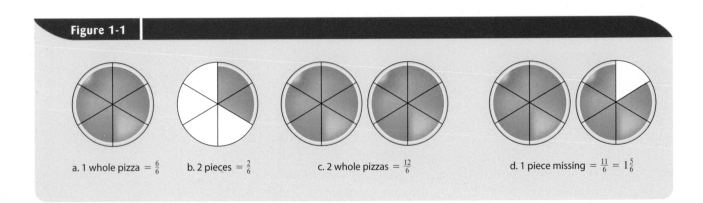

Figure 1-1

a. 1 whole pizza $= \frac{6}{6}$ b. 2 pieces $= \frac{2}{6}$ c. 2 whole pizzas $= \frac{12}{6}$ d. 1 piece missing $= \frac{11}{6} = 1\frac{5}{6}$

Changing Improper Fractions and Mixed Numbers

In Figure 1-1(d), the diagram shows that the improper fraction $\frac{11}{6}$ is equal to the mixed number $1\frac{5}{6}$. With any fraction, you can interpret the fraction bar as the division symbol so that $\frac{11}{6} = 11 \div 6$. In whole-number arithmetic, $11 \div 6$ equals a *quotient* of 1 with a *remainder* of 5. Therefore, using simple arithmetic, we can change improper fractions to mixed numbers and mixed numbers to improper fractions.

Learning Objective **1**

Change improper fractions and mixed numbers.

> **STEPS** to Change an Improper Fraction to a Mixed Number
>
> 1. Divide the numerator by the denominator.
> 2. The quotient is the whole-number part of the mixed number.
> 3. The remainder is the numerator of the fraction part.
> 4. The original denominator is the denominator of the fraction part.

EXAMPLE A

Change $\frac{11}{8}$ to a mixed number.

STEP 1   STEPS 2, 3, & 4

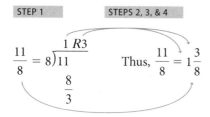

Thus, $\frac{11}{8} = 1\frac{3}{8}$

Note: Refer to Point A in Figure 1-2 to see where these numbers appear on a ruler.

Figure 1-2

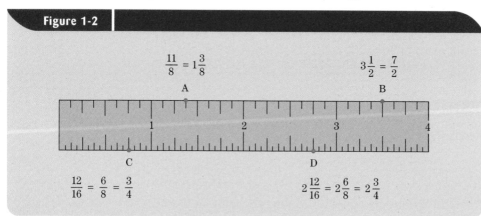

> **STEPS** to Change a Mixed Number to an Improper Fraction
>
> 1. Multiply the denominator of the fraction part by the whole number.
> 2. Add the numerator of the fraction part to the product of Step 1. The sum is the numerator of the improper fraction.
> 3. The denominator of the fraction of the mixed number is the denominator of the improper fraction.

Change $3\frac{1}{2}$ to an improper fraction.

STEP 1   STEPS 2, 3

$2 \times 3 = 6$ Thus, $3\frac{1}{2} = \frac{6 + 1}{2} = \frac{7}{2}$

Note: Refer to Point B in Figure 1-2 to see where these numbers appear on a ruler.

Changing Fractions to Lower and Higher Terms

Learning Objective **2**

Change fractions to lower and higher terms.

Read Point C on the ruler shown in Figure 1-2. Point C marks the distance $\frac{12}{16}$ of an inch, but it could also be read as $\frac{6}{8}$ or $\frac{3}{4}$ of an inch. Thus $\frac{12}{16}$, $\frac{6}{8}$, and $\frac{3}{4}$ are three ways to write the same value. We say that $\frac{6}{8}$ is in **lower terms** and $\frac{12}{16}$ is in **higher terms** because 8 is a smaller denominator than 16. We also say that $\frac{3}{4}$ is in **lowest terms** because it cannot be changed to any lower terms. When we change a fraction to lower terms, we say that we are *reducing* the fraction to lower terms. If we change a mixed number such as $2\frac{12}{16}$ to $2\frac{3}{4}$, we say that we have reduced the mixed number to its lowest terms. When we change fractions to higher terms, we say that we are raising them to higher terms.

STEPS **to Reduce a Fraction to Lowest Terms**

1. Divide both the numerator and the denominator by a common divisor greater than 1 to arrive at a reduced fraction.
2. If necessary, repeat Step 1 until the fraction cannot be reduced any further.

Note: If a fraction's numerator and denominator have no common divisor greater than 1, the fraction is already in lowest terms.

● **EXAMPLE C**

Reduce $\frac{12}{16}$ to lowest terms.

$$\frac{12}{16} = \frac{12 \div 2}{16 \div 2} = \frac{6}{8} = \frac{6 \div 2}{8 \div 2} = \frac{3}{4} \qquad \text{or else} \qquad \frac{12}{16} = \frac{12 \div 4}{16 \div 4} = \frac{3}{4}$$

Note that dividing by 4 once is faster than dividing by 2 twice. Always use the greatest common divisor that you can find.

STEPS **to Raise a Fraction to Higher Terms**

1. Divide the new denominator by the old denominator. The quotient is the *common multiplier.*
2. Multiply the old numerator by the common multiplier.
3. Multiply the old denominator by the common multiplier.

EXAMPLE D

Raise $\frac{3}{4}$ to twenty-fourths.

STEP 1

$$\frac{3}{4} = \frac{?}{24} \qquad 24 \div 4 = 6$$

STEPS 2 & 3

So, $\frac{3}{4} = \frac{3 \times 6}{4 \times 6} = \frac{18}{24}$

STREAMING VIDEO

Reducing and Raising Fractions

Adding Fractions and Mixed Numbers

Fractions and mixed numbers are all numbers, so they can be added and subtracted just like whole numbers. However, when you add fractions and/or mixed numbers, you must first find a **common denominator.** This is a denominator shared by all the fractions and it also will be the denominator of the fraction part of the answer.

The smallest common denominator possible is called the **least common denominator.** If the least common denominator is not easily apparent, it may be quicker to use the first common denominator that you can discover and then reduce the answer to lowest terms. The product of all the denominators always will be a common denominator, but very often there will be a smaller common denominator.

Learning Objective **3**

Add fractions and mixed numbers.

STREAMING VIDEO

Adding and Subtracting Fractions and Mixed Numbers

STEPS to Add Two or More Fractions and/or Mixed Numbers

1. If necessary, change the fraction parts to fractions with common denominators. The common denominator is the denominator in the fraction part of the answer.
2. Add the numerators to make the numerator of the fraction part of the answer. If there are any whole-number parts, add them to make the whole-number part of the answer.
3. If necessary, change an improper fraction to a mixed number and mentally add any whole-number parts.
4. Reduce the fraction part of the answer to lowest terms.

EXAMPLE E

Add $2\frac{7}{8}$ and $4\frac{3}{8}$.

The fractions already have a common denominator of 8.

$$
\begin{array}{r}
2\dfrac{7}{8} \\[2mm]
+\,4\dfrac{3}{8} \\[2mm]
\hline
6\dfrac{10}{8} = 6 + 1\dfrac{2}{8} = 7\dfrac{1}{4}
\end{array}
$$

STEP 2   STEP 3   STEP 4

EXAMPLE F

Add $\frac{5}{6}$ and $\frac{3}{4}$.

A common denominator is $6 \times 4 = 24$.

$$
\begin{array}{r}
\dfrac{5}{6} = \dfrac{5 \times 4}{6 \times 4} = \dfrac{20}{24} \\[3mm]
+\,\dfrac{3}{4} = \dfrac{3 \times 6}{4 \times 6} = \dfrac{18}{24} \\[3mm]
\hline
\dfrac{38}{24} = 1\dfrac{14}{24} = 1\dfrac{7}{12}
\end{array}
$$

STEP 1

STEPS 2, 3, & 4

● EXAMPLE G

Add $3\frac{5}{8}$ and $7\frac{5}{6}$.
The least common denominator is 24.

STEP 1

$$3\frac{5}{8} = 3\frac{15}{24}$$

$$+7\frac{5}{6} = +7\frac{20}{24}$$

$$10\frac{35}{24} = 10 + 1\frac{11}{24} = 11\frac{11}{24}$$

STEP 2   STEP 3

✔ CONCEPT CHECK 1.1

a. Add $\frac{4}{5}, \frac{2}{3},$ and $\frac{5}{9}$.

The least common denominator is 45.

$$\frac{4}{5} = \frac{4 \times 9}{5 \times 9} = \frac{36}{45}$$

$$\frac{2}{3} = \frac{2 \times 15}{3 \times 15} = \frac{30}{45}$$

$$+\frac{5}{9} = \frac{5 \times 5}{9 \times 5} = +\frac{25}{45}$$

$$\frac{91}{45} = 2\frac{1}{45}$$

b. Add $1\frac{5}{6}$ and $2\frac{5}{9}$.

A common denominator is $6 \times 9 = 54$.

$$1\frac{5}{6} = 1\frac{5 \times 9}{6 \times 9} = 1\frac{45}{54}$$

$$+2\frac{5}{9} = +2\frac{6 \times 5}{6 \times 9} = +2\frac{30}{54}$$

$$3\frac{75}{54} = 4\frac{21}{54} = 4\frac{7}{18}$$

Subtracting Fractions and Mixed Numbers

Learning Objective 4

Subtract fractions and mixed numbers.

The procedure for subtracting one fraction from another is almost the same as the procedure for adding one fraction to another. When you calculate $3\frac{1}{4} - \frac{3}{4}$, $3\frac{1}{4}$ is called the *minuend* and $\frac{3}{4}$ is called the *subtrahend*, as in the subtraction of whole numbers.

BORROWING 1

Sometimes, as with $3\frac{1}{4} - \frac{3}{4}$, the fraction part of the minuend is smaller than the fraction part of the subtrahend. To make the fraction part of the minuend larger than the fraction part of the subtrahend, you have to "borrow 1" from the whole-number part of the minuend. Actually, you're just rewriting the minuend. Remember that $3\frac{1}{4}$ means $3 + \frac{1}{4}$, or the same as $2 + 1 + \frac{1}{4}$, $2 + \frac{4}{4} + \frac{1}{4}$, or $2\frac{5}{4}$. These are simply four different ways to express the same quantity. Figure 1-3 is useful in understanding borrowing.

Figure 1-3

Adding and Subtracting
Fractions and Mixed
Numbers

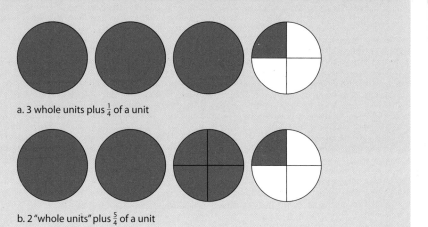

a. 3 whole units plus $\frac{1}{4}$ of a unit

b. 2 "whole units" plus $\frac{5}{4}$ of a unit

STEPS **to Subtract One Fraction or Mixed Number from Another**

1. If necessary, change the fractions so that all fractions have a common denominator. The common denominator is the denominator in the fraction part of the answer.
2. If necessary, "borrow 1" from the whole-number part of the minuend so that the fraction part of the minuend is at least as large as the fraction part of the subtrahend.
3. Subtract the numerators in the fractions to make the numerator in the fraction part of the answer.
4. If there are any whole-number parts, subtract them to make the whole-number part of the answer.
5. Reduce the fraction part of the answer to lowest terms.

EXAMPLE H

STEP 3   STEP 5

$$\frac{7}{8} - \frac{3}{8} = \frac{7-3}{8} = \frac{4}{8} = \frac{1}{2}$$

EXAMPLE I

STEP 1   STEP 3

$$\frac{3}{4} - \frac{1}{5} = \frac{3 \times 5}{4 \times 5} - \frac{1 \times 4}{5 \times 4} = \frac{15}{20} - \frac{4}{20} = \frac{11}{20}$$

EXAMPLE J

STEP 1

$$
\begin{array}{r}
5\dfrac{3}{4} = \quad 5\dfrac{9}{12} \\[2mm]
-2\dfrac{1}{3} = -2\dfrac{4}{12} \\[1mm]
\hline
\end{array}
$$

STEPS 3 & 4 $3\dfrac{5}{12}$

EXAMPLE K

STEP 1   STEP 2

$$
\begin{array}{r}
4\dfrac{4}{9} = \quad 4\dfrac{8}{18} = \quad 3\dfrac{18}{18} + \dfrac{8}{18} = \quad 3\dfrac{26}{18} \\[2mm]
-1\dfrac{5}{6} = -1\dfrac{15}{18} = -1\dfrac{15}{18} \qquad\quad = -1\dfrac{15}{18} \\[1mm]
\hline
\end{array}
$$

STEPS 3 & 4 $2\dfrac{11}{18}$

a. Subtract $\frac{5}{6}$ from $\frac{7}{8}$.

The least common denominator is 24.

$$\frac{7}{8} = \frac{21}{24}$$
$$-\frac{5}{6} = -\frac{20}{24}$$
$$\frac{1}{24}$$

b. Subtract $2\frac{9}{10}$ from $6\frac{5}{6}$.

The least common denominator is 30.

$$6\frac{5}{6} = 6\frac{25}{30} = 5\frac{55}{30}$$
$$-2\frac{9}{10} = -2\frac{27}{30} = -2\frac{27}{30}$$
$$3\frac{28}{30} = 3\frac{14}{15}$$

COMPLETE ASSIGNMENT 1.1.

Multiplying Fractions and Mixed Numbers

Learning Objective **5**

Multiply fractions and mixed numbers.

In fractions, multiplication and division do not require common denominators. This means that multiplication and division are simpler than addition and subtraction. Recall that any mixed number can be changed to an improper fraction. Also, a whole number can be written as an improper fraction by writing the whole number in the numerator with a denominator of 1. For example, the whole number 5 can be written as the improper fraction $\frac{5}{1}$.

▶ STREAMING VIDEO

Multiplication and Division of Mixed Numbers

STEPS **to Multiply Fractions and Mixed Numbers**

1. Change any mixed (or whole) numbers to improper fractions.
2. Multiply all the numerators to get the numerator of the product.
3. Multiply all the denominators to get the denominator of the product.
4. Change the product to a proper fraction or mixed number in lowest terms.

● **EXAMPLE L**

| | STEP 1 | STEPS 2 & 3 | STEP 4 | |

$$1\frac{2}{3} \times \frac{4}{5} = \frac{5}{3} \times \frac{4}{5} = \frac{5 \times 4}{3 \times 5} = \frac{20}{15} = 1\frac{5}{15} = 1\frac{1}{3}$$

● **EXAMPLE M**

| | STEPS 2 & 3 | STEP 4 |

$$\frac{2}{3} \times \frac{4}{5} \times \frac{5}{6} = \frac{2 \times 4 \times 5}{3 \times 5 \times 6} = \frac{40}{90} = \frac{4}{9}$$

Note: The word *of* often means *multiply* when it is used with fractions. For example, you know that "$\frac{1}{2}$ *of* 6 bottles" is 3 bottles. And $\frac{1}{2}$ *of* $6 = \frac{1}{2} \times \frac{6}{1} = \frac{6}{2} = 3$. For this reason, multiplication may even be the most important arithmetic operation with fractions. In verbal communication, we will often be saying expressions like "$\frac{1}{2}$ of 6."

Canceling Common Factors in Numerators and Denominators

As the last step in example M, we reduced the fraction $\frac{40}{90}$ to its lowest terms, $\frac{4}{9}$. Recall that reducing this fraction means that we divide both the numerator and the denominator by 10. As an option, we can do that division in advance, before doing any multiplication.

Examining the three numerators and three denominators, we discover that they have common factors of 2 and 5. Divide out, or **cancel**, both the 2 and the 5 in both the numerators and denominators as shown in example N. This division of the common factors is often called **cancellation.** Canceling common factors is an option; it is not required to calculate the correct product.

EXAMPLE N

Multiply the three fractions, using cancellation.

|STEP 1|STEPS 2 & 3|STEP 4|

$$\frac{2}{3} \times \frac{4}{5} \times \frac{5}{6} = \frac{2}{3} \times \frac{4}{5} \times \frac{\overset{1}{5}}{6} = \frac{2}{3} \times \frac{\overset{2}{4}}{5} \times \frac{\overset{1}{5}}{6} = \frac{2 \times 2 \times 1}{3 \times 1 \times 3} = \frac{4}{9}$$

EXAMPLE O

Multiply the fraction and the whole number, using cancellation.

|STEP 1|STEPS 2 & 3|STEP 4|

$$\frac{3}{4} \text{ of } 12 = \frac{3}{4} \times 12 = \frac{3}{4} \times \frac{12}{1} = \frac{3}{4} \times \frac{\overset{3}{12}}{1} = \frac{3 \times 3}{1 \times 1} = \frac{9}{1} = 9$$

EXAMPLE P

Multiply the fraction and the mixed number, using cancellation.

|STEP 1|STEPS 2 & 3|STEP 4|

$$\frac{2}{5} \text{ of } 2\frac{3}{4} = \frac{2}{5} \times 2\frac{3}{4} = \frac{2}{5} \times \frac{11}{4} = \frac{\overset{1}{2}}{5} \times \frac{11}{\underset{2}{4}} = \frac{1 \times 11}{5 \times 2} = \frac{11}{10} = 1\frac{1}{10}$$

✓ CONCEPT CHECK 1.3

Multiply the fraction, whole number, and mixed number, using cancellation.

$$\frac{1}{8} \times 4 \times 2\frac{1}{3} = \frac{1}{8} \times \frac{4}{1} \times \frac{7}{3} = \frac{1}{\underset{2}{8}} \times \frac{\overset{1}{4}}{1} \times \frac{7}{3} = \frac{1 \times 1 \times 7}{2 \times 1 \times 3} = \frac{7}{6} = 1\frac{1}{6}$$

Dividing Fractions and Mixed Numbers

Recall that with whole numbers, division is the *inverse* of multiplication. You can check a multiplication problem with division. With fractions, you actually perform a division problem by doing multiplication. That is, you *invert the divisor and multiply.*

Learning Objective **6**

Divide fractions and mixed numbers.

STREAMING VIDEO

Multiplication and Division of Mixed Numbers

© BRENT WALKER/SHUTTERSTOCK.COM

● EXAMPLE Q

STEPS 2 & 3   STEP 4

$$\frac{3}{10} \div \frac{2}{5} = \frac{3}{10} \times \frac{5}{2} = \frac{3}{\overset{}{\underset{2}{10}}} \times \frac{\overset{1}{5}}{2} = \frac{3 \times 1}{2 \times 2} = \frac{3}{4}$$

● EXAMPLE R

STEP 1   STEPS 2 & 3   STEP 4   STEP 5

$$6 \div 1\frac{3}{5} = \frac{6}{1} \div \frac{8}{5} = \frac{6}{1} \times \frac{5}{8} = \frac{\overset{3}{6}}{1} \times \frac{5}{\overset{8}{4}} = \frac{3 \times 5}{1 \times 4} = \frac{15}{4} = 3\frac{3}{4}$$

✔ CONCEPT CHECK 1.4

Divide $3\frac{3}{4}$ by $1\frac{1}{2}$.

Change both mixed numbers to improper fractions: $\frac{15}{4} \div \frac{3}{2}$.

Invert the divisor $\frac{3}{2}$ to $\frac{2}{3}$ and multiply:

$$\frac{15}{4} \times \frac{2}{3} = \frac{\overset{5}{15}}{\underset{2}{4}} \times \frac{\overset{1}{2}}{\underset{1}{3}} = \frac{5 \times 1}{2 \times 1} = \frac{5}{2} = 2\frac{1}{2}$$

COMPLETE ASSIGNMENT 1.2.

Chapter Terms for Review

cancel	higher terms	lowest terms
cancellation	improper fraction	mixed number
common denominator	least common denominator	numerator
denominator	lower terms	proper fraction
fractions		

Summary of chapter learning objectives:

Learning Objective	Example
1.1 Change improper fractions and mixed numbers.	1(a). Change $\frac{18}{5}$ to a mixed number. 1(b). Change $2\frac{5}{6}$ to an improper fraction.
1.2 Change fractions to lower and higher terms.	2(a). Reduce $\frac{12}{30}$ to lowest terms. 2(b). Raise $\frac{7}{12}$ to sixtieths; that is, $\frac{7}{12} = \frac{?}{60}$.
1.3 Add fractions and mixed numbers.	3. Add $\frac{7}{8}$, $\frac{5}{6}$, and $2\frac{3}{4}$.
1.4 Subtract fractions and mixed numbers.	4. Subtract $1\frac{3}{4}$ from $4\frac{2}{5}$.
1.5 Multiply fractions and mixed numbers.	5. Multiply: $\frac{2}{9} \times \frac{6}{7}$.
1.6 Divide fractions and mixed numbers.	6. Divide: $1\frac{4}{5} \div \frac{3}{4}$.

Answers: 1(a). $3\frac{3}{5}$ 1(b). $\frac{17}{6}$ 2(a). $\frac{2}{5}$ 2(b). $\frac{35}{60}$ 3. $4\frac{11}{24}$ 4. $2\frac{13}{20}$ 5. $\frac{4}{21}$ 6. $2\frac{2}{5}$

Review Problems for Chapter 1

Write all answers as proper fractions or mixed numbers in lowest terms.

1 Change $2\frac{5}{6}$ to an improper fraction _____

2 Change $\frac{90}{12}$ to a mixed number _____

3 Reduce $\frac{54}{63}$ to lowest terms _____

4 Raise $\frac{10}{14}$ to 56ths _____

5 Add $\frac{2}{3}$, $\frac{3}{5}$, and $\frac{3}{10}$ _____

6 Add $\frac{5}{8}$ and $1\frac{1}{6}$ _____

7 Add $\frac{3}{4}$, $2\frac{4}{5}$, and 4 _____

8 Subtract $\frac{1}{3}$ from $\frac{4}{5}$ _____

9 Subtract $\frac{8}{9}$ from $2\frac{5}{6}$ _____

10 Subtract $2\frac{4}{9}$ from $4\frac{1}{5}$ _____

11 Multiply $\frac{5}{6}$ by $\frac{12}{35}$ _____

12 Multiply $\frac{9}{16}$ by $1\frac{13}{15}$ _____

13 Multiply $2\frac{1}{10}$, $\frac{8}{15}$, and $2\frac{1}{12}$ _____

14 Divide $\frac{15}{16}$ by $\frac{5}{12}$ _____

15 Divide $1\frac{11}{25}$ by $\frac{24}{35}$ _____

16 Divide $1\frac{2}{7}$ by $1\frac{1}{14}$ _____

17 JoAnn Brandt decided to use an expensive, but effective, herbicide to kill weeds and brush on a client's land. For one part of the land, she needed $3\frac{2}{3}$ quarts of herbicide; for a second part, she needed $2\frac{3}{4}$ quarts; and for the third part, she needed $1\frac{5}{6}$ quarts. In total, how many quarts of herbicide did JoAnn need for this client? _____

18 An electrician had a piece of electrical conduit that was $12\frac{1}{2}$ feet long. She cut off two pieces that were $4\frac{3}{4}$ feet and $5\frac{2}{3}$ feet long, respectively. How many feet of conduit did she have left over? _____

19 The Central Hotel just hired a new chef. This chef makes a hot sauce that uses $1\frac{3}{4}$ tablespoons of chili powder, but he needs to increase the recipe by $3\frac{1}{2}$ times. How many tablespoons of chili powder should he use? _____

20 How many whole pieces of copper $2\frac{5}{8}$ inches long can be cut out of one piece that is $24\frac{1}{2}$ inches long? _____ How long is the shorter piece that is left over? _____

Answers to the Self-Check can be found in Appendix B at the back of the text.

_____

_____

_____

Assignment 1.1: Addition and Subtraction of Fractions

Name _____

Date _____ Score _____

Learning Objectives **1** **2** **3** **4**

A (12 points) Change the improper fractions to whole numbers or to mixed numbers. Change the mixed numbers to improper fractions. (1 point for each correct answer)

1. $\dfrac{13}{6}$ _____   2. $\dfrac{32}{10}$ _____   3. $\dfrac{18}{3}$ _____   4. $\dfrac{25}{15}$ _____

5. $\dfrac{23}{13}$ _____   6. $\dfrac{30}{7}$ _____   7. $3\dfrac{7}{10}$ _____   8. $2\dfrac{11}{12}$ _____

9. $2\dfrac{5}{8}$ _____   10. $3\dfrac{3}{4}$ _____   11. $6\dfrac{3}{5}$ _____   12. $4\dfrac{5}{6}$ _____

_____
Score for A (12)

B (15 points) In problems 13–20, reduce each fraction to lowest terms. In problems 21–27, raise each fraction to higher terms, as indicated. (1 point for each correct answer)

13. $\dfrac{10}{25} =$ _____   14. $\dfrac{9}{24} =$ _____   15. $\dfrac{18}{30} =$ _____   16. $\dfrac{12}{15} =$ _____

17. $\dfrac{32}{48} =$ _____   18. $\dfrac{24}{42} =$ _____   19. $\dfrac{42}{60} =$ _____   20. $\dfrac{16}{32} =$ _____

21. $\dfrac{5}{6} = \dfrac{}{18}$ 22. $\dfrac{3}{4} = \dfrac{}{20}$ 23. $\dfrac{5}{8} = \dfrac{}{24}$ 24. $\dfrac{7}{12} = \dfrac{}{36}$

25. $\dfrac{3}{7} = \dfrac{}{35}$ 26. $\dfrac{2}{3} = \dfrac{}{15}$ 27. $\dfrac{4}{5} = \dfrac{}{45}$

_____
Score for B (15)

C (24 points) Add the following fractions and mixed numbers. Write the answers as fractions or mixed numbers, with fractions in lowest terms. (3 points for each correct answer)

28. $\dfrac{3}{8}$ $+\dfrac{3}{8}$ _____

29. $\dfrac{7}{10}$ $+\dfrac{3}{10}$ _____

30. $\dfrac{9}{16}$ $+2\dfrac{11}{16}$ _____

31. $1\dfrac{2}{3} =$ $+2\dfrac{3}{4} =$ _____

32. $1\dfrac{1}{4} =$ $\dfrac{5}{8} =$ $+4\dfrac{11}{12} =$ _____

33. $4\dfrac{1}{2} =$ $3\dfrac{2}{3} =$ $+\dfrac{5}{6} =$ _____

34. $\dfrac{4}{5} =$ $3\dfrac{5}{6} =$ $+5\dfrac{2}{3} =$ _____

35. $2\dfrac{5}{9} =$ $3\dfrac{8}{15} =$ $+1\dfrac{1}{5} =$ _____

_____
Score for C (24)

D **(24 points) Subtract the following fractions and mixed numbers. Write the answers as proper fractions or mixed numbers, with fractions in lowest terms. (3 points for each correct answer)**

36. $\dfrac{5}{8}$

$-\dfrac{3}{8}$

_____

37. $2\dfrac{7}{12}$

$-1\dfrac{5}{12}$

_____

38. $\dfrac{1}{2}=$

$-\dfrac{7}{24}=$

_____

39. $2\dfrac{3}{4}=$

$-1\dfrac{1}{12}=$

_____

40. $3\dfrac{2}{3}=$ $=$

$-2\dfrac{5}{6}=$ $=$

_____

41. $3\dfrac{3}{5}=$ $=$

$-1\dfrac{3}{4}=$ $=$

_____

42. $6\dfrac{5}{8}=$

$-3\dfrac{1}{6}=$

_____

43. $4\dfrac{2}{5}=$ $=$

$-1\dfrac{5}{6}=$ $=$

_____

Score for D (24)

E **(25 points) Business Applications and Critical Thinking. Solve the following. Write your answers as fractions or mixed numbers in lowest terms. (5 points for each correct answer)**

44. A restaurant sells three different hamburgers, based on the amount of meat used: "The Mini" ($\frac{1}{4}$ lb); "The Regular" ($\frac{1}{3}$ lb); and "The Maxi" ($\frac{1}{2}$ lb). Students bought one of each to compare them. What was the total amount of meat used in the three hamburgers? _____

45. Ted Terry specializes in custom faux painting, but for the first coat he could combine leftover paints when the colors were relatively the same. He has three containers of different shades of white: $2\frac{2}{3}$ quarts, $3\frac{1}{4}$ quarts, and $2\frac{1}{2}$ quarts. If Ted combines the contents of all the containers, how many quarts of paint will he have? _____

46. Contractor Don Fleming has a top board that is $\frac{13}{16}$ inch thick. Don wants to use wood screws to attach it to a bottom board. If a wood screw is $1\frac{1}{2}$ inches long, how much of the screw will be left over to go into the bottom board? _____

47. Robert Landles is planning to attach a plywood panel to a wall using nails that are $1\frac{3}{4}$ inches long. The panel is $\frac{3}{8}$ inch thick. Beneath the panel is a layer of sheetrock that is $\frac{1}{2}$ inch thick. How many inches of the nail should go into the wood frame that is underneath the sheetrock? _____

48. Paris Fabric Center sold four pieces of wool fabric to a tailor. The pieces measured $3\frac{1}{4}$ yards, $2\frac{1}{3}$ yards, $1\frac{3}{4}$ yards, and $4\frac{1}{2}$ yards in length. How many yards of fabric did the tailor purchase? _____

Score for E (25)

Assignment 1.2: Multiplication and Division of Fractions

Learning Objectives **1** **2** **5** **6**

Name

Date   Score

A **(32 points) Change any whole or mixed numbers to improper fractions and multiply. Cancel if possible. Where the word *of* appears, replace it with the multiplication symbol. Write the answers as mixed numbers or proper fractions in lowest terms. (4 points for each correct answer)**

1. $\dfrac{4}{15} \times \dfrac{5}{8} =$ _____

2. $\dfrac{9}{10} \times \dfrac{2}{3} \times \dfrac{5}{8} =$ _____

3. $\dfrac{3}{4}$ of $\dfrac{5}{6} =$ _____

4. $\dfrac{5}{18} \times \dfrac{4}{9} \times \dfrac{3}{10} =$ _____

5. $4\dfrac{1}{2} \times 1\dfrac{5}{9} =$ _____

6. $\dfrac{5}{8}$ of $18 =$ _____

7. $1\dfrac{7}{8} \times 12 \times \dfrac{3}{10} =$ _____

8. $1\dfrac{1}{3} \times 1\dfrac{7}{8} \times 1\dfrac{1}{5} =$ _____

_____

Score for A (32)

B **(32 points) Change any whole or mixed numbers to improper fractions and divide. Cancel if possible. Write the quotients as mixed numbers or proper fractions in lowest terms. (4 points for each correct answer)**

9. $\dfrac{7}{8} \div \dfrac{3}{4} =$ _____

10. $\dfrac{4}{15} \div \dfrac{3}{10} =$ _____

11. $\dfrac{5}{6} \div \dfrac{4}{9} =$ _____

12. $\dfrac{7}{10} \div 2\dfrac{4}{5} =$ _____

13. $6\dfrac{1}{4} \div 4\dfrac{3}{8} =$ _____

14. $5\dfrac{1}{3} \div 4 =$ _____

15. $3\frac{1}{3} \div \frac{4}{5} = $ _____

16. $2\frac{1}{3} \div 1\frac{3}{4} = $ _____

Score for B (32)

C **(36 points) Business Applications and Critical Thinking. Use fractions and mixed numbers to solve each of the following. State the answers as whole numbers, proper fractions, or mixed numbers in lowest terms. (6 points for each correct answer)**

17. Last week, Eastside Concrete Co. built a small driveway that required $5\frac{1}{3}$ cubic yards of concrete. This week, Eastside must build another driveway that is $2\frac{1}{2}$ times larger. How many yards of concrete will be required? _____

18. John Nielsen bought ten pieces of copper tubing that were each $7\frac{2}{5}$ inches long. What was the total length of tubing that John bought? (Give the answer in inches.) _____

19. Linda Johanssen had $2\frac{1}{4}$ quarts of liquid fertilizer in a container. Her supervisor asked her to mix $\frac{2}{3}$ of the fertilizer with water and save the remainder. How many quarts of fertilizer did Linda mix with water? _____

20. Landscaper Roger Hillman needs several pieces of PVC irrigation pipe, each 3 feet 4 inches long. PVC pipe comes in 20-foot lengths. How many pieces can Roger cut out of one length of pipe? (*Hint:* 4 inches equal $\frac{1}{3}$ foot.) _____

21. Robert Burke has a diesel-powered generator on his ranch. The generator has a tank that holds $3\frac{3}{4}$ gallons of diesel fuel. He stores the diesel fuel in 55-gallon drums (barrels). How many times can Robert refill his generator from one drum of fuel? _____

22. Home builders Bill and John Walter are planning a narrow stairway to an attic. The stairs will each be 2 feet 8 inches long. They will cut the stairs from boards that are 8 feet long. How many whole stairs can they cut from one 8-foot board? (*Hint:* 8 inches is $\frac{2}{3}$ foot.) _____

Score for C (36)

Decimals

2

Learning Objectives

By studying this chapter and completing all assignments, you will be able to:

Learning Objective 1 Read decimal numbers.

Learning Objective 2 Round decimal numbers.

Learning Objective 3 Add two or more decimal numbers.

Learning Objective 4 Subtract one decimal number from another.

Learning Objective 5 Multiply two decimal numbers.

Learning Objective 6 Divide one decimal number by another decimal number.

Learning Objective 7 Multiply and divide by decimal numbers that end with zeros.

Learning Objective 8 Approximate products and quotients.

Fractions Versus Decimal Numbers

McDonald's restaurant sells a hamburger sandwich called the Quarter Pounder. The sandwich is named for the amount of meat: one-quarter pound of ground beef. McDonald's—or anyone—can describe the same amount of meat in four different ways: 4 ounces, $\frac{1}{4}$ pound, 0.25 pound, or 25% of a pound. To express less than 1 pound, McDonald's could use smaller units, fractions, decimals, or percents.

All four expressions are useful, but which one is best? It may depend on what you're doing: whether you're buying or selling, whether you're speaking or writing, whether you're just estimating or making accurate financial records, or whether you're working with large volumes of something cheap or small quantities of something very expensive. For McDonald's, a Four Ouncer might not sell as well as a Quarter Pounder, but Bloomingdale's sells perfume by the (fluid) ounce rather than by the gallon, quart, pint, or even cup.

Verbal expressions such as "half of a candy bar" or "a third of the pizza" are so common that children use them before they can even read. Because they are usually interested in money, most children begin to learn decimals as soon as they learn to read cash register receipts. We studied fractions in Chapter 1. Because of calculators, most calculations are now performed using decimal numbers. We will study decimals here in Chapter 2. Percents are a combination of decimal numbers and a few common fractions. Percents are as easy to use as decimals and also allow simple verbal expressions. We will study percents in Chapter 5.

Chapter 2 has three main concepts: vocabulary, calculating, and estimating. Calculating with decimals is the same as with whole numbers except that there is a decimal point. Thus, calculating with decimals is actually "managing the decimal point," which your calculator does automatically. Estimating, which is important in checking your calculations, still requires that you "manage the decimal point."

Decimal Numbers and Electronic Displays

A customer in a delicatessen might ask for "a quarter of a pound of salami, please" or perhaps "four ounces of salami." However, the food scale in the delicatessen probably has an electronic display that is calibrated only in pounds. It will likely display "0.25" or "0.250." As a fraction, a quarter of a pound is written as $\frac{1}{4}$ pound; three quarters of a pound is $\frac{3}{4}$ pound. In the U.S. monetary system, a quarter is the name of the coin whose value is twenty-five cents. And three quarters are worth seventy-five cents. When we write these monetary amounts, we write either whole numbers or decimals: 25¢ and 75¢, or $0.25 and $0.75. It is highly unlikely that anyone would ever write $\frac{1}{4}$ or $\frac{3}{4}$.

Almost all business transactions and record keeping are best done using decimals rather than fractions. The calculations are usually more straightforward and more accurate. Today, specialized calculators, computers, and measurement instruments have electronic displays that are calibrated in decimals, not fractions.

Modern gasoline pumps used in the United States are calibrated in gallons and typically measure the volume of gasoline sold accurate to three decimal places. Suppose that an automobile owner buys gasoline and the display shows 12.762 gallons. 12.762 is a number; it is called a **mixed decimal.** The 12 is the whole number part of the number;

the 762 is the **pure decimal** part. The period (or dot) that separates the 12 from the 762 is the **decimal point.** We say that the number 12.762 has three **decimal places** because there are three digits to the right of the decimal point.

Many calculators and all computer spreadsheets permit you to change the number of decimal places that are displayed. A new calculator may be preset to display exactly two decimal places because that is how the monetary system is designed. Divide 1 by 3 with your calculator. The correct answer is 0.333333333 . . . , a repeating number that never stops. Count the number of 3s that appear in the calculator. That is the number of decimal places your calculator is set to display. Read the instruction manual. Perhaps you can change the display to show more or fewer decimal places. *Note:* Your calculator also displays a zero (0) to the left of the decimal point. We follow that same convention in this book. Every pure decimal number is preceded by a zero (0).

Reading Decimal Numbers

Reading decimal numbers, both mixed and pure, is like reading whole numbers: Each "place," or column, represents a different value. Starting at the decimal point and reading to the *left*, the places represent ones, tens, hundreds, thousands, and so on. Starting at the decimal point and reading to the *right*, the vocabulary is different: The places represent *tenths, hundredths, thousandths,* and so on.

Learning Objective **1**

Read decimal numbers.

Recall words such as *tenths, hundredths,* and *thousandths* from our review of fractions in Chapter 1. As money, the decimal $0.10 represents 10¢, but also $\frac{10}{100}$. $\frac{10}{100}$ is pronounced as "ten *hundredths.*" But $\frac{10}{100}$ can be reduced to $\frac{1}{10}$ which is "one *tenth.*" Like fractions, the decimal 0.10 is read as "ten *hundredths*"; the decimal 0.1 is "one *tenth.*" At the gasoline pump, the display showed 12.762. As a fraction, it is written $12\frac{762}{1000}$. Both numbers are pronounced "twelve *and* seven hundred sixty-two *thousandths.* The decimal point is read as the word "*and.*"

Figure 2-1 illustrates the place values of the number system on both sides of the decimal point for the number 607,194.35824. The pure decimal part of the number in Figure 2-1 is 0.35824, which is pronounced "thirty-five thousand eight hundred twenty-four *hundred-thousandths.*"

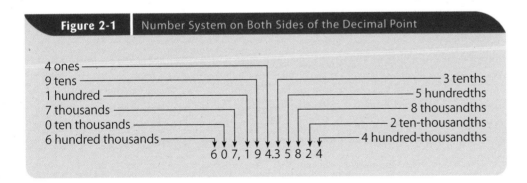

| Figure 2-1 | Number System on Both Sides of the Decimal Point |

4 ones
9 tens
1 hundred
7 thousands
0 ten thousands
6 hundred thousands

3 tenths
5 hundredths
8 thousandths
2 ten-thousandths
4 hundred-thousandths

6 0 7, 1 9 4.3 5 8 2 4

READING LONG DECIMAL NUMBERS

The entire number in Figure 2-1—607,194.35824—is read as "six hundred seven thousand, one hundred ninety-four and thirty-five thousand eight hundred twenty-four hundred-thousandths." For a long number, reciting it orally is inefficient and can be confusing to the listener. For such a number, it may be better simply to read the digits and commas, from left to right. The word *point* is used for the decimal point.

Recite orally the number 607,194.35824.

Number	Oral Recitation
607,194.35824	"six zero seven comma one nine four point three five eight two four"

✔ **CONCEPT CHECK 2.1**

a. Write 37.045 using words: Thirty-seven and forty-five thousandths
b. Write fifteen and seven hundredths using digits: 15.07

Rounding Decimal Numbers

Learning Objective 2

Round decimal numbers.

In the preceding section, you reviewed how to read and write decimal numbers such as 148.65392. However, in many business applications, if the whole-number part is as large as 148, the digits on the extreme right may not be very important. Maybe only the digit in the tenths or hundredths column is significant. **Rounding off** such a number to make it simpler is common. Rounding off a decimal is similar to rounding off a whole number.

STEPS **to Round Decimal Numbers**

1. Find the last place, or digit, to be retained.
2. Examine the digit to the right of the last digit to be retained.
3. a. If it is equal to or greater than 5, increase the digit to be retained by 1. Drop all digits to the right of the ones retained.
   b. If it is less than 5, leave the digit to be retained unchanged. Drop all digits to the right of the ones retained.

● **EXAMPLE B**

Round 7.3951 and 148.65392 to one decimal place, to two decimal places, and to three decimal places.

Round to the nearest tenth	7.3951 ⟶ 7.4	148.65392 ⟶ 148.7
Round to the nearest hundredth	7.3951 ⟶ 7.40	148.65392 ⟶ 148.65
Round to the nearest thousandth	7.3951 ⟶ 7.395	148.65392 ⟶ 148.654

ROUNDING UP

Retail businesses, such as grocery stores, often use a different method of rounding to a whole number of cents. Suppose that a grocery store has lemons priced at 3 for $1.00. Usually the store will charge $0.34 for one lemon, even though $1.00 divided by 3 is $0.3333 (to four places). The store has rounded up to the next larger whole cent. To round up monetary amounts, always increase any partial cent to the next whole cent. For example, $27.842 would round up to $27.85.

a. Round 3.4681 to the nearest hundredth (that is, to two decimal places).

Find the hundredths digit.	3.4681	(The 6)
Examine the digit to the right of the 6.	3.4681	(It is greater than 5.)
Increase the 6 to a 7 and drop the digits 81 at the right.	3.47	(The answer)

b. Round up 8.5014 to the *next* tenth (that is, to one decimal place).

Find the tenths digit.	8.5014	(The 5)
Increase the 5 to a 6 and drop the digits 014 at the right.	8.6	(The answer)

Whole Numbers, Decimal Numbers, and Arithmetic

The arithmetic of decimal numbers is almost identical to the arithmetic of whole numbers. The only difference is that you must "manage the decimal point." There are simple decimal point rules for each operation: addition, subtraction, multiplication, and division. Calculators have these rules built into them. Remember that a whole number is simply a mixed decimal where the pure decimal part is zero. In the examples that follow, when you see a whole number, you may need to place a decimal point at the right end. You may even need to write one or more zeros after the decimal point.

Adding Decimal Numbers

To add two or more decimal numbers, follow these steps.

Learning Objective **3**

Add two or more decimal numbers.

> **STEPS** **to Add Decimal Numbers**
>
> 1. Arrange the numbers in columns, with the decimal points in a vertical line.
> 2. Add each column, from right to left, as with whole numbers. Insert the decimal point.
>
> *Option:* You may want to write zeros in some of the right-hand columns of decimal numbers so that each number has the same number of decimal places.

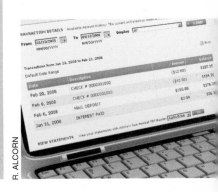

R. ALCORN

Add 4.326, 218.6004, 7.09, 15, and 0.87782.

STEP 1	STEP 2		STEP 2 WITH OPTION
4.326	4.326		4.32600
218.6004	218.6004		218.60040
7.09	7.09	or	7.09000
15.	15.		15.00000
0.87782	+ 0.87782		+ 0.87782
	245.89422		245.89422

✔ CONCEPT CHECK 2.3

Add these decimal numbers: 8.95, 13.791, and 0.6.

First align:	Then add:	Or, write zeros and add:
8.95	8.95	8.950
13.791	13.791	13.791
0.6	+ 0.6	+ 0.600
	23.341	23.341

Subtracting Decimal Numbers

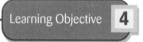

Learning Objective **4**

Subtract one decimal number from another.

Subtracting one decimal number from another is similar to subtracting whole numbers. When you aren't using a calculator, it may be helpful to write enough zeros so that both numbers have the same number of places. To subtract one decimal number from another, follow these steps.

STEPS **to Subtract Decimal Numbers**

1. Arrange the numbers in columns, with the decimal points in a vertical line.
2. If necessary, write enough extra zeros so that both numbers have the same number of decimal places.
3. Subtract each column, from right to left, as with whole numbers. Insert the decimal point.

Subtract 4.935 from 12.8.

STEP 1	STEPS 2 & 3
12.8	12.800
− 4.935	− 4.935
	7.865

Subtract 9.4 from 82.113.

STEP 1	STEPS 2 & 3
82.113	82.113
− 9.4	− 9.400
	72.713

Subtract 53.784 from 207.6.

Align: Write zeros and subtract:

207.6   207.600
  53.784   − 53.784
                    153.816

COMPLETE ASSIGNMENT 2.1.

Multiplying Decimal Numbers

To multiply one decimal number by another, follow these steps.

Learning Objective **5**

Multiply two decimal numbers.

STEPS **to Multiply Decimal Numbers**

1. Multiply the two numbers as if they were whole numbers.
2. Count the *total* number of decimal places in the two original numbers.
3. **a.** In the product, place the decimal point so that the number of decimal places is the same as the number in Step 2. (Count from right to left.)
   b. If necessary, insert zeros in front of the left-hand digit to provide enough decimal places. (See example G.)

EXAMPLE F

3.764 × 2.1

	3.764	(3 places)
	× 2.1	(1 place)
STEP 1	3764	
	+7528	STEP 2
STEP 3	7.9044	(3 + 1 = 4 places)

EXAMPLE G

3.764 × 0.0021

	3.764	(3 places)
	× 0.0021	(4 places)
STEP 1	3764	
	+7528	STEP 2
STEP 3	0.0079044	(3 + 4 = 7 places; insert 2 zeros)

In business applications, zeros that come at the right end of the decimal part of the product are often omitted (example H). Do not omit zeros that come at the end of the whole-number part (example I). When the product is written in dollars and cents, exactly two decimal places are written, including zeros at the right end (example J). Please be aware that some calculators may not display any zeros at the right end of a decimal.

EXAMPLE H

$0.76 \times 0.5 = 0.380$ (3 places)

May be written as 0.38

EXAMPLE I

$12.5 \times 1.6 = 20.00$ (2 places)

May be written as 20

EXAMPLE J

$\$8.40 \times 6.5 = \$54.600$ (3 places)

Should be written as $54.60

✔ CONCEPT CHECK 2.5

a. Multiply 2.36×3.4

$$
\begin{array}{r}
2.36 \quad \text{(2 places)} \\
\times\ 3.4 \quad \text{(1 place)} \\
\hline
944 \\
+708 \\
\hline
8.024 \quad \text{(3 places)}
\end{array}
$$

b. Multiply 0.236×0.34

$$
\begin{array}{r}
0.236 \quad \text{(3 places)} \\
\times\ 0.34 \quad \text{(2 places)} \\
\hline
944 \\
+708 \\
\hline
0.08024 \quad \text{(5 places; insert 1 zero)}
\end{array}
$$

Dividing Decimal Numbers

Learning Objective **6**

Divide one decimal number by another decimal number.

When dividing decimal numbers, remember that a whole number will have its decimal point immediately to the right of the units digit.

To divide one decimal number by another, follow these steps.

STEPS **to Divide one Decimal Number by Another**

1. Arrange the divisor, dividend, and division bracket (⟍) as in whole-number long division.

2. Move the decimal point in the divisor to the right until the divisor is a whole number. (You won't have to move it if the divisor is already a whole number.)

3. Move the decimal point in the dividend to the right exactly the same number of decimal places as you did in Step 2. If necessary, attach more zeros to the right end of the dividend. (See example K.)

4. Write the decimal point in the quotient directly above the new decimal point in the dividend (in Step 3).

5. Write zeros, if necessary, in the quotient between the decimal point and the first nonzero digit. (See example L.)

6. Divide as you would for whole numbers.

● **EXAMPLE K**

| | STEP 1 | STEP 2 | STEP 3 | STEP 4 | STEP 6 |

$$2.7 \div 0.15 \quad is \quad 0.15\overline{)2.7} \;=\; 0.15\overline{)2.70} \;=\; 15\overline{)270} \;=\; 15\overline{)270.}$$

$$
\begin{array}{r}
18. \\
15\overline{)270.} \\
-15 \\
\hline
120 \\
-120 \\
\hline
0
\end{array}
$$

● **EXAMPLE L**

| | STEP 1 | STEP 4 | STEPS 5 & 6 |

$$0.096 \div 4 \quad is \quad 4\overline{)0.096} \;=\; 4\overline{)0.096} \;=\; 4\overline{)0.096}$$

$$
\begin{array}{r}
0.024 \\
4\overline{)0.096} \\
-8 \\
\hline
16 \\
-16 \\
\hline
0
\end{array}
$$

Recall from Chapter 1, example A, that the fraction $\frac{11}{8}$ was changed to $1\frac{3}{8}$ using division. Recall also that in long division with two whole numbers, you get a remainder when the division does not work out evenly. For example, $11 \div 8$ equals 1 with a remainder of 3. In division with decimals, we do not write remainders. We simply keep dividing until either the division ends evenly (examples K and L), or you reach some desired number of decimal places. You may have to keep attaching zeros to the right end of the dividend. *Note:* When the division does not work out evenly, you must calculate one additional decimal place and then round off the quotient to the desired number of places (example M).

● **EXAMPLE M**

Calculate $19 \div 7$ to two decimal places.

| | STEP 1 | STEP 4 | STEP 6 |

$$19 \div 7 \quad is \quad 7\overline{)19} \;=\; 7\overline{)19.} = 7\overline{)19.} =$$

$$
\begin{array}{r}
2.714 \\
7\overline{)19.000} \\
-14 \\
\hline
50 \\
-49 \\
\hline
10 \\
-7 \\
\hline
30 \\
-28 \\
\hline
2
\end{array}
$$

The quotient, 2.714, rounds off to 2.71. $19 \div 7 = 2.71$ to two decimal places.

a. Divide 1.026 by 15.

$$15\overline{)1.026} \quad = \quad 15\overline{)1.0260}$$

$$
\begin{array}{r}
0.0684 \\
15\overline{)1.0260} \\
\underline{-90} \\
126 \\
\underline{-120} \\
60 \\
\underline{-60} \\
0
\end{array}
$$

b. Divide 0.009 by 0.4.

$$0.4\overline{)0.0.09} \quad = \quad 4\overline{)0.0900}$$

$$
\begin{array}{r}
0.0225 \\
4\overline{)0.0900} \\
\underline{-8} \\
10 \\
\underline{-8} \\
20 \\
\underline{-20} \\
0
\end{array}
$$

Using division, you can verify that $17 \div 4 = 4.25$. But $17 \div 4$ can be written as the improper fraction $\frac{17}{4}$. The decimal 4.25 is called the **decimal equivalent** of the fraction $\frac{17}{4}$ and of the mixed number $4\frac{1}{4}$. Decimal equivalents can be useful when you are working with fractions and have a calculator available. Even with simple fractions, and no calculator, it is often simpler to use decimal equivalents because you don't need a common denominator.

● EXAMPLE N

Compute $\frac{1}{2} + \frac{3}{4} - \frac{2}{5}$. This requires that all fractions have a common denominator of 20. But $\frac{1}{2} = 0.5, \frac{3}{4} = 0.75,$ and $\frac{2}{5} = 0.4$. Therefore, we have $\frac{1}{2} + \frac{3}{4} - \frac{2}{5} = 0.5 + 0.75 - 0.4 = 0.85$.

For difficult fractions, use a calculator to convert the fractions to their decimal equivalents. Then use the calculator to perform the required operation. (If possible, you should use the memory of your calculator to store the intermediate answers.)

● EXAMPLE O

Compute $\dfrac{8}{15} + \dfrac{7}{12} + \dfrac{3}{7}$.

[8] [÷] [15] [=] gives   0.53333333
[7] [÷] [12] [=] gives   0.58333333
[3] [÷] [7] [=] gives   + 0.42857143
                    1.54523809

The preceeding example assumes that the calculator is displaying eight decimal places. Also, if you use the memory to store the intermediate answers, your calculator may round off the intermediate answers and give you a final answer of 1.54523810 or 1.5452381.

Using Multipliers and Divisors that End with Zeros

With whole-number arithmetic, there are some simple shortcuts to use when the *multiplier* or the *divisor* is a whole number ending in zeros (e.g., 30, 200, or 1,000). We can use the same shortcuts with decimal numbers. We must remember only to "manage the decimal point."

If the multiplier is 10, 100, 1,000, etc., there is just one step.

Step 1   Move the decimal point in the *multiplicand* to the *right* the same number of places as the number of zeros in the multiplier. (See example P.) If necessary, attach zeros to the *right* end of the multiplicand before multiplying. (See example Q.)

Learning Objective **7**

Multiply and divide by decimal numbers that end with zeros.

EXAMPLE P

$0.56 \times 10 = 0.5\underset{\frown}{.}6 = 5.6$

(1 place)

EXAMPLE Q

$4.73 \times 1,000 = 4.730. = 4,730$

(3 places)

If the multiplier ends in zeros but has a first digit that is not 1 (for example, 300 or 2,000), there are two steps.

Step 1   Multiply the multiplicand by the nonzero part of the multiplier.

Step 2   Move the decimal point in the product from Step 1 to the *right* the same number of places as the number of zeros in the multiplier.

EXAMPLE R

Multiply 3.431 by 2,000

Multiply by 2: $3.431 \times 2 = 6.862$

Move the decimal point three places to the right: $6.862. \longrightarrow 6,862.$

If the divisor is 10, 100, 1,000, etc., there is just one step.

Step 1   Move the decimal point in the dividend to the *left* the same number of places as the number of zeros in the divisor. (See example S.) If necessary, attach zeros to the *left* end of the dividend. (See example T.)

EXAMPLE S

$735.1 \div 100$

$735.1 \div 100 = 7.35.1 = 7.351$

(2 places)

EXAMPLE T

$9.64 \div 1,000$

$9.64 \div 1,000 = .009.64 = 0.00964$

(3 places)

If the divisor ends in zeros but has a first digit that is not 1 (for example, 300 or 2,000), there are two steps.

Step 1   Divide the dividend by the nonzero part of the divisor.

Step 2   Move the decimal point in the quotient from Step 1 to the *left* the same number of places as the number of zeros in the divisor.

Divide 615.24 by 300

Divide by 3:   615.24 ÷ 3 = 205.08

Move the decimal point two places to the left: 2.05.08 ⟶ 2.0508

✔ **CONCEPT CHECK 2.7**

a. Multiply 0.413 by 300

0.413 × 3 = 1.239

Move the decimal point
two places to the right:

1.23.9 ⟶ 123.9

b. Divide 4.375 by 10

Move the decimal point
one place to the left:

4.375 ÷ 10 = .4.375 ⟶ 0.4375

Approximating Products and Quotients

Learning Objective **8**

Approximate products and quotients.

Business people today almost always use calculators or computers to do important computations. But calculators are perfect only if every single key is pressed correctly. Often, you can discover a calculator error by doing some simple mental approximations. The objective is to determine whether the answer is approximately the right size—that is, whether the decimal point is in the correct position. To do so, we round each decimal number to only one nonzero digit and all the rest to zeros. Follow these steps.

STEPS **to Approximate a Multiplication Problem**

1. Round the first nonzero digit from the left end in each factor. (How does the digit to its right compare to 5?)
2. Change all the digits to the right of the first nonzero digit to zero.
3. Multiply the two new factors.
4. Place the decimal point in the product.

● **EXAMPLE V**

Approximate 3.764 × 7.4

	STEP 1	STEPS 2 & 3
3.764	⟶ 4.000	4
× 7.4	⟶ × 7.0	× 7
		28

● **EXAMPLE W**

Approximate 0.089 × 61.18

	STEP 1	STEPS 2 & 3
0.089	⟶ 0.090	0.09
× 61.18	⟶ × 60.00	× 60
		5.40

The actual answers are 27.8536 and 5.44502.

In division, the mental approximation will be easier if you change the decimal numbers so that the division will end evenly after one step. To do this, first round the divisor to one nonzero digit and then round the dividend to two nonzero digits, evenly divisible by the new divisor.

EXAMPLE X

Approximate 4.764 ÷ 8.1

| STEP 1 | STEP 2 | STEPS 3 & 4 |

$$8.1\overline{)4.764} \longrightarrow 8.0\overline{)4.764} \longrightarrow 8.\overline{)4.800} \longrightarrow \begin{array}{r} 0.6 \\ 8.\overline{)4.8} \\ -4.8 \\ \hline 0 \end{array}$$

EXAMPLE Y

Approximate 61.18 ÷ 0.089

| STEP 1 | STEP 2 | STEPS 3 & 4 |

$$0.089\overline{)61.18} \longrightarrow 0.090\overline{)61.18} \longrightarrow 0.09\overline{)63.00} \longrightarrow \begin{array}{r} 700. \\ 9.\overline{)6300.} \\ -63 \\ \hline 0 \end{array}$$

The actual answers are 0.5881 and 687.4157 (to four decimal places).

✔ CONCEPT CHECK 2.8

a. Approximate 6.891 × 0.614

6.891 ⟶ 7.000
0.614 ⟶ 0.600

$$\begin{array}{r} 0.6 \quad \text{(1 place)} \\ \times 7 \quad \text{(0 places)} \\ \hline 4.2 \quad \text{(1 place)} \end{array}$$

Compare with 6.891 × 0.614 = 4.231074

b. Approximate 0.0738 ÷ 92.65
Remember to round off the divisor first.

92.65 ⟶ 90.00
0.0738 ⟶ 0.0720

$$90\overline{)0.072} \longrightarrow \begin{array}{r} 0.0008 \\ 90\overline{)0.0720} \\ 720 \\ \hline 0 \end{array}$$

Compare with 0.0738 ÷ 92.65 = 0.000796546

COMPLETE ASSIGNMENTS 2.2 and 2.3.

decimal equivalent   mixed decimal

decimal places   pure decimal

decimal point   rounding off

Try working the problems using the Microsoft Excel templates found on the companion website. Solutions for the problems are also shown on the companion website.

1. Set up and complete the following tables using the appropriate Excel formulas.

Date	Auto Sales	Part Sales	Total Sales
6/4/12	$ 36,628.14	$ 1,782.28	
6/5/12	$ 42,789.40	$ 2,047.33	
6/6/12	$ 58,334.98	$ 1,132.48	
6/7/12	$ 96,782.04	$ 3,006.04	
6/8/12	$ 29,765.55	$ 2,333.33	
Total			

Date	Total Receipts	Total Cash	Cash Short
7/15/12	$ 974.58	$ 969.30	
7/16/12	$ 888.07	$ 888.02	
7/17/12	$ 1,384.17	$ 1,350.23	
Total			

Date	Units Sold	Price Per Unit	Total Sales
5/24/12	47	$ 107.16	
5/25/12	63	$ 107.16	
5/26/12	72	$ 107.16	
5/27/12	39	$ 107.16	
Total			

Date	Total Sale	Price Per Unit	Units Sold
5/24/12	$ 5,036.52	$ 107.16	
5/25/12	$ 6,751.08	$ 107.16	
5/26/12	$ 7,715.52	$ 107.16	
5/27/12	$ 4,179.24	$ 107.16	
Total			

THE BOTTOM LINE

Summary of chapter learning objectives:

Learning Objective	Example
2.1 Read decimal numbers.	1. Write 8.427 using words. 2. Write forty-one and eleven ten-thousandths using digits.
2.2 Round decimal numbers.	3. Round 0.506489 to the nearest thousandth (that is, to three decimal places). 4. Round up 13.26012 to the *next* hundredth (that is, to two decimal places).
2.3 Add two or more decimal numbers.	5. Add 82.9, 14.872, and 2.09.
2.4 Subtract one decimal number from another.	6. Subtract 14.5977 from 19.34.
2.5 Multiply two decimal numbers.	7. Multiply: 4.68×3.5 _____
2.6 Divide one decimal number by another decimal number.	8. Divide: $0.084 \div 4$ _____ 9. Divide: $0.064 \div 2.5$ _____
2.7 Multiply and divide by decimals that end with zeros.	10. Multiply: 0.069782×1000 _____ 11. Divide: 9.462 by 100 _____ 12. Multiply: 0.0623×20 _____ 13. Divide: 84.6 by 300 _____
2.8 Approximate products and quotients.	14. Approximate 48.79×0.47 _____ 15. Approximate $0.2688 \div 0.713$ _____

Answers: **1.** eight and four hundred twenty-seven thousandths **2.** 41.0011 **3.** 0.506 **4.** 13.27 **5.** 99.862 **6.** 4.7423 **7.** 16.38 **8.** 0.021 **9.** 0.0256 **10.** 69.782 **11.** 0.09462 **12.** 1.246 **13.** 0.282 **14.** 25 **15.** 0.4

Review Problems for Chapter 2

1. Write "one hundred sixteen and fourteen ten-thousandths" as a number _____

2. Write 6,431.719, using words _____

3. Round 3.475 feet to the nearest tenth _____

4. Round $12.667 to the nearest cent _____

5. Add 3.79475 and 739.85 _____

6. Add 12.42, 0.087, and 8.3 _____

7. Subtract 8.693 from 11.41 _____

8. Subtract 287.963 from 410.4511 _____

9. Multiply 3.722 by 0.483 (do not round off) _____

10. Multiply $19.75 by 22.45 (round off to the nearest cent) _____

In problems 11 and 12, divide to three places and round to the nearest hundredth.

11. Divide 45.88 by 14.2 _____

12. Divide $6.25 by 8.41 _____

In problems 13 and 14, use shortcuts to solve each problem and round to the nearest hundredth.

13. Multiply 86.493 by 100 _8649.3_

14. Divide $2,762.35 by 1,000 _2.76_
    2.7627

In problems 15 and 16, pick the best approximate answers from the possible answers.

15. Multiply 48.98 by 11.2 _____   **(a)** 0.5   **(b)** 5   **(c)** 50   **(d)** 500   **(e)** 5,000

16. Divide $6.65 by 8.21 _____   **(a)** $0.008   **(b)** $0.08   **(c)** $0.80   **(d)** $8.00   **(e)** $80.0

17. Lois McBryde owns a chain of very large, upscale bookstores. She decides to start selling coffee drinks such as espresso and cappuccino at one of her stores. During the first day, the store has total sales of $4,188.25. Of the total, $362.50 was from coffee drinks. How much of the total was from books and other items? _____

18. Gary Gehlert operates tennis and golf shops at a mountain resort. Last year, he started selling on the Internet as well. He had the following profits last year: Tennis (shop), $52,418.12; Golf (shop), $168,078.51; Tennis (Internet), $28,570.12; and Golf (Internet), $32,904.82. What were the total profits from these sources? _____

19. Dean Treggas, a landscape contractor, needed to plant 226 one-gallon plants and 164 five-gallon plants. Dean uses about 0.8 cubic foot of planting soil for each one-gallon plant and 2.5 cubic feet of planting soil for each five-gallon plant. How many cubic feet of planting soil will Dean need for all these plants? _____

20. Planting soil is sold by the cubic yard. To two decimals, how many cubic yards of planting soil will Dean Treggas need to do his planting in question 19? (*Hint:* 1 cubic yard equals 27 cubic feet.) _____

Answers to the Self-Check can be found in Appendix B at the back of the text.

Assignment 2.1: Addition and Subtraction of Decimal Numbers

Name _____

Date _____ Score _____

Learning Objectives **1** **2** **3** **4**

A (13 points) Use digits to write each number that is expressed in words. Use words to write each number that is expressed in digits. (1 point for each correct answer)

1. Six hundred thirteen ten-thousandths _____ *613,000* _____ *.0613*
2. Sixteen thousandths _____ *.016*
3. Sixty-four hundredths _____ *.64*
4. Seventy-six and ninety-two ten-thousandths _____ *76,0092*
5. Eight hundred sixty and ninety-eight hundred-thousandths _____ *860.00098*
6. Eighteen and six thousandths _____ *18.006*
7. 308.97 _____ *Three Hundred Eight and ninety Seven Hundredths*
8. 0.0014 _____ *fourteen Ten Thousands*
9. 592.3 _____ *Five Hundred Ninety Two and Three tenths*
10. 0.081 _____ *Eighty one Thousandths*
11. 42.0481 _____ *Forty Two and Four Hundred Eighty one Ten thousands*
12. 6.018 _____ *Six and 18 thousands*
13. 1,007.4 _____ *One Thousands Seven and Four Tenths*

Score for A (13)

B (24 points) Round as indicated. (1 point for each correct answer)

Nearest Tenth		Nearest Cent	Hundredths
14. 6.3517 qt	*6.4 = 64*	20. $17.375	*17.38*
15. 48.97 mi	*49.0*	21. $0.098	_____
16. 3.824 gal	*X 3.8*	22. $942.3449	_____
17. 374.29 lb	*374.3*	23. $8.1047	_____
18. 5.75 ft	*5.8*	24. $0.0549	_____
19. 6.375 oz	*6.4*	25. $52.996	_____

Nearest Thousandth		UP to the *Next* Cent	
26. 5.37575 pt	_____	32. $9.681	*9.69*
27. 0.00549 gal	_____	33. $0.159	*.16*
28. 12.5435 oz	_____	34. $72.535	*.54*
29. 8.1855 in.	_____	35. $2.0917	_____
30. 8.9989 mi	_____	36. $13.6106	_____
31. 0.200499 lb	_____	37. $0.6545	_____

Score for B (24)

C (27 points) Write the following numbers in columns, and then add. (3 points for each correct answer)

38. 3.84, 42.81, 747.114

39. 0.7323, 4.084, 17.42

40. 15.4, 32.574, 9.51, 74.0822

41. 24.78, 71.402, 8.3176

42. 7.911, 56.4398, 288.69

43. 6.4, 3.211, 12.6, 7.07

44. 337.51, 6.1761, 16.078

45. 36.7, 208.51, 3.992

46. 0.592, 1.82, 0.774, 6.5

———————————

Score for C (27)

D (36 points) Subtract the following. (3 points for each correct answer)

47. 0.734
   -0.37

48. 0.05155
   -0.00497

49. 26.04
   $-\ 8.625$

50. 0.7212
   -0.034

51. 6.1
   -2.418

52. 804.07
   -167.1

53. 3.2525
   -2.843

54. 708.932
   -339.999

55. 0.365
   -0.189

56. 4.37
   -1.9055

57. 7.624
   -5.947

58. 5.6976
   -4.6913

———————————

Score for D (36)

Assignment 2.2: Multiplication and Division of Decimal Numbers

Name

Date   Score

A **(32 points) Multiply the following. Round monetary products to the nearest cent. Do not round nonmonetary products. (4 points for each correct answer)**

| 1. | $15.67 $\times$ 83.7 | 2. | $24.60 $\times$ 4.5 | 3. | $420.00 $\times$ 0.806 | 4. | $48.40 $\times$ 0.65 |

_____   _____   _____   _____

| 5. | 107.21 $\times$ 0.74 | 6. | 52.93 $\times$ 0.45 | 7. | 285.70326 $\times$ 0.28 | 8. | 816.04 $\times$ 0.403 |

_____   _____   _____   _____

_____
Score for A (32)

B **(24 points) Divide the following. Round monetary quotients to the nearest cent. Round nonmonetary quotients to two decimal places. (4 points for each correct answer)**

9. $7\overline{)\$12.95}$ **10.** $0.24\overline{)\$3.90}$ **11.** $1.2\overline{)\$54.30}$

_____   _____   _____

12. $1.5\overline{)2.5\,9}$ **13.** $0.11\overline{)0.6735}$ **14.** $0.09\overline{)0.7888}$

_____   _____   _____

_____

Score for B (24)

C (12 points) Multiply and/or divide by just moving the decimal point or by doing some simple multiplication/division and moving the decimal point. Round monetary answers to the nearest cent. Do not round nonmonetary answers. (1 point for each correct answer)

15. $0.0625 \times 1,000 =$ _____

16. $36.519 \times 100 =$ _____

17. $0.047 \times 10,000 =$ _____

18. $763 \div 100 =$ _____

19. $6.32 \div 10 =$ _____

20. $27.469 \div 1,000 =$ _____

21. $\$72.41 \times 300 =$ _____

22. $\$32.25 \times 20 =$ _____

23. $\$0.12 \times 6,000 =$ _____

24. $\$40.00 \times 80 =$ _____

25. $\$86.50 \div 200 =$ _____

26. $\$9,612 \div 40 =$ _____

Score for C (12)

D (32 points) For each of the following problems, underline the estimate that is most nearly correct. (2 points for each correct answer)

#	Problem	(a)	(b)	(c)	(d)
27.	0.077×0.52	(a) 4.0	(b) 0.4	(c) 0.04	(d) 0.004
28.	5.78×0.9345	(a) 5.4	(b) 0.54	(c) 0.054	(d) 0.0054
29.	0.38×71.918	(a) 0.28	(b) 2.8	(c) 28	(d) 280
30.	8.191×0.88	(a) 0.0072	(b) 0.072	(c) 0.72	(d) 7.2
31.	0.0782×0.5503	(a) 0.0048	(b) 0.048	(c) 0.48	(d) 4.8
32.	0.0417×0.0957	(a) 0.04	(b) 0.004	(c) 0.0004	(d) 0.00004
33.	268.25×0.9175	(a) 27,000	(b) 2,700	(c) 270	(d) 27
34.	0.0487×0.0059	(a) 0.000003	(b) 0.00003	(c) 0.0003	(d) 0.003
35.	19.1×6104	(a) 120	(b) 1,200	(c) 12,000	(d) 120,000
36.	$7.958 \div 0.514$	(a) 16	(b) 160	(c) 1,600	(d) 16,000
37.	$3.575 \div 893.12$	(a) 0.004	(b) 0.04	(c) 0.4	(d) 4
38.	$0.0064 \div 0.897$	(a) 7.1	(b) 0.71	(c) 0.071	(d) 0.0071
39.	$8.397 \div 7.12$	(a) 0.12	(b) 1.2	(c) 12	(d) 120
40.	$0.5379 \div 0.591$	(a) 900	(b) 90	(c) 9	(d) 0.9
41.	$5.112 \div 0.0692$	(a) 70	(b) 7	(c) 0.7	(d) 0.07
42.	$2.671 \div 0.0926$	(a) 300	(b) 30	(c) 3	(d) 0.3

Score for D (32)

Assignment 2.3: Decimal Numbers in Business

Name

Date   Score

A **(36 points) Business Applications and Critical Thinking. Solve the following. Do not round your final answers. (6 points for each correct answer)**

1. Bob Jones had 24.75 feet of rope. He cut off a piece 16.5 feet long. How much did he have left?

   _____

2. Cho Jewelers had only 12.7 ounces of gold on hand, so Mr. Cho bought 22.5 ounces more to make Christmas items. He used 18.7 ounces for gold rings. How much gold did he have left?

   _____

3. Judy Taylor reads meters for the gas and electric company. She walked 3.6 miles on Monday; 3.7 miles on Tuesday, 2.9 miles on Wednesday, 3.25 miles on Thursday, and 3.4 miles on Friday. What was her total distance for the week?

   _____

4. Four drivers for Secure Document Delivery need gasoline for their cars. Individually, they buy 9.8, 10.4, 11.7, and 13.9 gallons. How much do they purchase all together?

   _____

5. Rosemary Wardlaw owes a total of $226.54 on her department store account. She visits the store to return an item that cost $47.79. While there, she buys two items that cost $55.88 and $67.50. What is Rosemary's new account balance at the store?

   _____

6. Parker Paving Co. delivered 6.7 tons of asphalt. It used 4.8 tons for a driveway and 1.4 tons for a walkway. How much asphalt was left?

   _____

Score for A (36)

B (64 points) Business Applications and Critical Thinking. Solve the following business problems. Use short-cuts where possible. If necessary, round answers to two decimal places. (8 points for each correct answer)

7. Bill Wells Hardware sells $\frac{5}{8}$-inch plastic tubing for $1.59 per foot and copper tubing for $3.99 per foot. How much will Kathy Fogg save by using plastic tubing if she needs 300 feet of tubing? _____

1.59

8. Benoit Landscaping sent three truckloads of topsoil to a job. The soil cost $37.95 per cubic yard. Two trucks carried 7.25 cubic yards each; the third carried 6.75 cubic yards. What was the total cost of all the topsoil? _____

9. Wholesale, 1,000 2-ounce plastic bottles cost 3.5 cents each, and 2,000 4-ounce bottles cost 4.5 cents each. What is the total cost of all 3,000 bottles? _____

10. Evelyn Haynes often used her motorcycle as a delivery vehicle. One Monday, when gasoline was priced at $4.499 per gallon, Evelyn bought 2.62 gallons. The following Thursday, gasoline prices rose to $4.799 per gallon and she bought 2.87 gallons. What was the total amount that Evelyn spent for gasoline those two days? _____

11. Electrician Tom Stewart paid $134.50 for 200 feet of three-strand electrical cable. What was the cost per foot for this particular cable?

_____

12. A pizza chef has 24 pounds of flour on hand. He needs 3.75 pounds of flour for one large recipe of pizza dough. How many recipes can he make with the flour on hand? (Round to the nearest tenth.) _____

13. Paint thinner costs $8.47 per gallon. How many gallons can a painting contractor buy for $200? (Round to the nearest tenth.) _____

14. Jackie Barner earns $22.60 per hour. How many hours did she work during a partial day for which her pay was $152.55? _____

_____

Score for B (64)

Phoebe split her profit evenly with her partner. How much did her partner receive from last week's cakes?

STEP 1   Read the problem completely and carefully.

STEP 2   Determine what is requested: How much money did Phoebe's partner receive?

STEP3   Determine the processes to use.
Add the cakes baked: $6 + 9 + 11 + 8 + 6 = 40$.
Subtract the cost from the sales price: $\$9 - \$5 = \$4$ profit per cake.
Multiply the number of cakes sold by the \$4 profit per cake: $40 \times \$4 = \$160$.
Divide the total profit by 2: $\$160 \div 2 = \$80$ received by the partner.

✔ CONCEPT CHECK 3.1

Summary of steps for solving word problems:
1. Read the problem completely and carefully.
2. Determine what is requested.
3. Determine the processes to use.

> Problem: Maria wants to upholster three chairs. Two chairs will require 4 yards of material each; the third will require 3 yards. One material costs \$32 per yard; the other costs \$15 per yard. What is the difference between the costs of the two materials for upholstering the chairs?
>
> Read the problem completely and carefully.
>
> Determine what is requested: Difference in cost between the two materials.
>
> Determine the processes to use.
> *Add* amount of material needed: $4 \text{ yd} + 4 \text{ yd} + 3 \text{ yd} = 11 \text{ yd}$.
> *Multiply* amount of material needed by cost per yard—first material: $11 \text{ yd} \times \$32$ per yd = \$352.
> *Multiply* amount of material needed by cost per yard—second material: $11 \text{ yd} \times \$15$ per yd = \$165.
> *Subtract* cost between the two materials: $\$352 - \$165 = \$187$ difference in cost.

Solving Rate, Time, and Distance Problems

In some business word problems, you must compute how much is done (or distance traveled) in a given amount of time at a specific speed. These rate, time, and distance problems are solved with a simple formula: Rate (speed) × Time = Distance (amount done). If you are given any two factors, it is easy, by formula, to find the third.

Rate × Time = Distance
Distance ÷ Time = Rate
Distance ÷ Rate = Time

Learning Objective 2

Apply formulas to solve rate, time, and distance problems.

● EXAMPLE C

Jan traveled at 35 miles per hour for 5 hours. How far did Jan travel?

35 mph × 5 hr = 175 mi

(Rate × Time = Distance)

● EXAMPLE D

Jan traveled 175 miles in 5 hours. How fast was Jan traveling?

175 mi ÷ 5 hr = 35 mph

(Distance ÷ Time = Rate)

● EXAMPLE E

At 35 miles per hour, how long would it take Jan to travel a total of 175 miles?

175 mi ÷ 35 mph = 5 hr

(Distance ÷ Rate = Time)

● EXAMPLE F

Jan and Ahmed start traveling toward each other from 300 miles apart. Jan is traveling at 35 miles per hour; Ahmed is traveling at 40 miles per hour. How much time will elapse before they meet?

Distance = 300 mi

Total rate = 35 mph (Jan) + 40 mph (Ahmed) = 75 mph

300 mi ÷ 75 mph = 4 hr

(Distance ÷ Rate = Time)

● EXAMPLE G

Jan and Ahmed start traveling toward each other from 300 miles apart. Jan is traveling at 35 miles per hour; Ahmed is traveling at 40 miles per hour. How much distance will Jan travel before they meet?

Total rate = 35 mph (Jan) + 40 mph (Ahmed) = 75 mph

Time = 300 mi ÷ 75 mph = 4 hr

Jan's distance = 35 mph (Jan's Rate) × 4 hr (Time) = 140 mi

● EXAMPLE H

Mary needs to type a term paper that will be 30 pages long. Each page contains about 200 words. If Mary can type 40 words per minute, how many minutes will it take her to complete the paper?

Choose a formula: We know distance (amount to be done) and speed (rate). Therefore, we choose the formula for time.

Distance (amount done) ÷ Rate (speed) = Time

30 pages × 200 words = 6,000 words ÷ 40 wpm = 150 min

EXAMPLE I

Flora also had a paper to type, but hers was 9,000 words in length. She was able to type it in 150 minutes. How fast did she type?

Choose a formula: We know distance (amount done) and time. Therefore, we choose the formula for rate.

Distance (amount done) ÷ Time = Rate (speed) $P \div T = R$

9,000 words ÷ 150 min = 60 wpm

It is approximately 400 miles from San Francisco to Los Angeles. Roy's friends tell him that he can make the trip in 6 hours if he averages 60 miles per hour. Is this true?

Choose a formula: We know the rate and the time, so we choose the formula for distance.

Rate (speed) × Time = Distance (amount done)

60 mph × 6 hr = 360 mi

Can he get there in 6 hours? *No.*

✔ CONCEPT CHECK 3.2

The basic formulas:

a. Rate (speed) × Time = Distance (amount done)
   If you know any *two* factors, you can find the *third*.
b. Distance (amount done) ÷ Time = Rate (speed)
c. Distance (amount done) ÷ Rate (speed) = Time

> Apply the appropriate formula to answer the following question: A machine that produces tortillas at the Baja Restaurant can produce 200 tortillas per hour, or 1,600 tortillas in an 8-hour day. A new machine can produce 3,000 tortillas in 6 hours. How many more tortillas per hour can the new machine produce than the old one?
>
> Distance (amount done) ÷ Time = Rate
> 1,600 tortillas ÷ 8 hr   = 200 per hr
> 3,000 tortillas ÷ 6 hr   = 500 per hr
> Difference: 500 − 200 = 300 more tortillas per hr

Solving Simple Numerical Equations

A **numerical sentence** in which both sides of an equal sign contain calculations is called an **equation**. For example, five plus five equals twelve minus two (5 + 5 = 12 − 2) is an equation, as is seven minus one equals thirty divided by five (7 − 1 = 30 ÷ 5).

For an equation to be true, the numbers on the left of the equal sign must always compute to the same answer as the numbers on the right of the equal sign. Moving a number from one side of the equation to the other changes its sign. A plus sign will change to minus; a minus sign will change to plus. A multiplication sign will change to division; a division sign will change to multiplication.

Learning Objective **3**

Solve simple numerical equations.

Rule: When you change sides, you change signs.

▶ EXAMPLE K   Addition—Subtraction

$6 + 4 + 5 = 17 - 2$ (Move the negative 2 to the other side of the equation.)

Change the $- 2$:

$6 + 4 + 5 + 2 = 17$

Now change the $+ 5$:   (Move the positive 5 to the other side of the equation.)

$6 + 4 + 2 = 17 - 5$

▶ EXAMPLE L   Multiplication—Division

$3 \times 8 = 48 \div 2$

Change the $\div 2$:

$3 \times 8 \times 2 = 48$

Now change the $\times 8$:

$3 \times 2 = 48 \div 8$

A numerical equation may have one value that is *unknown* but still provide enough information to complete the sentence. To solve for the unknown value, you can *move* any or all of the known values to the other side of the equation by *reversing* their signs.

Move one or more numbers from one side of the equation to the other to leave the unknown alone on one side. Solve for the unknown by doing the calculations on the other side of the equation.

▶ EXAMPLE M

$6 + 2 = 5 + ?$

Change a number

$6 + 2 - 5 = ?$

Therefore, $? = 3$

▶ EXAMPLE N

$15 - 3 = 2 + ?$

Change a number

$15 - 3 - 2 = ?$

Therefore, $? = 10$

▶ EXAMPLE O

$7 + 3 + 6 = 4 + 4 + ?$

Change a number

$7 + 3 + 6 - 4 - 4 = ?$

Therefore, $? = 8$

▶ EXAMPLE P

$20 \div 5 = 2 \times ?$

Change a number

$20 \div 5 \div 2 = ?$

Therefore, $? = 2$

In business, numerical sentences with equations compare items. Note the following example.

▶ EXAMPLE Q

Last year a company had sales of $25,000 in Dept. A and $20,000 in Dept. B. If sales this year were $30,000 in Dept. A, what is the amount needed for Dept. B to equal last year's sales?

Last year: Dept. A $25,000 + Dept. B $20,000 = $45,000

This year: Dept. A $30,000 + Dept. B ?   = $45,000

Dept. B = $45,000 − Dept. A $30,000

Therefore, $? = \$15,000$

Both sides of a true equation are equal. Each side may contain calculations.

$7 + 5 = 14 - 2$

$2 \times 9 = 36 \div 2$

A number may be moved from one side of an equation to the other by reversing its sign.

$8 = 6 + 2$ $8 - 2 = 6$ $7 + 3 = 10$ $7 = 10 - 3$

$12 = 4 \times 3$ $12 \div 3 = 4$ $24 \div 12 = 2$ $24 = 2 \times 12$

Numerical Relationships in a Series

Relationships in a series of numbers may be found by comparing the first three or four terms in a series and then extrapolating the numbers that would most logically come next. For example, examining the series 320, 160, 80, 40 indicates that each term is found by dividing the preceding number by 2. The next two numbers in the series would logically be 20 and 10—that is, $40 \div 2 = 20$ and $20 \div 2 = 10$.

Examining the series 7, 14, 21, 28 suggests the addition of 7 to each preceding number. The next two numbers in this series would logically be 35 and 42 ($28 + 7 = 35$ and $35 + 7 = 42$).

In the series 5, 15, 35, 75, 155, seeing a relationship is difficult; however, a relationship does exist. Each number results from multiplying the preceding number by 2 and then adding 5. In this series, the next number would logically be 315 ($155 \times 2 + 5 = 315$).

Recognizing numerical and series relationships can be important in analyzing, communicating, and computing numbers. These relationship series are also used frequently in initial employment tests.

> Learning Objective **4**
>
> Recognize numerical relationships in a series

In studying relationships in a numerical series, look for patterns. Patterns most commonly fall into categories:

Addition	2, 7, 12, 17, 22, 27	(+5, or 32)
Alternating addition/subtraction	12, 24, 18, 30, 24, 36, 30	(+12, −6, or 42, 36)
Subtraction	39, 32, 25, 18, 11, 4	(−7, or −3)
Alternating subtraction/addition	64, 59, 61, 56, 58, 53, 55	(−5, +2, or 50, 52)
Multiplication	4, 12, 36, 108, 324, 972	(×3, or 2,916)
Division	384, 192, 96, 48, 24	(÷2, or 12)

You can also devise patterns such as multiplication with addition or subtraction, division with addition or subtraction, and many other combinations.

Making Quick Calculations by Rounding Numbers

Learning Objective **5**

Do quick mental calculations through a process of rounding numbers.

Quick calculations are beneficial when working in business situations. *Rounding* odd and difficult-to-compute amounts to even whole numbers that are easier to compute is a technique often used in business. By rounding, you will be able to get quick and accurate answers without having to write out the computations.

EXAMPLE R

How much would 5 items at $2.99 each cost?

To make this computation easily, think "$2.99 is $0.01 less than $3.00." Then think "5 times $3 equals $15." Finally, think "$15.00 less $0.05 (5 × $0.01) is $14.95," which is the correct answer.

EXAMPLE S

The total cost of three equally priced dresses is $119.85. How much does each dress cost?

To figure out this problem easily, think "$119.85 is $0.15 less than $120.00." Then think "$120 divided by 3 = $40, and $40.00 less $0.05 ($0.15 ÷ 3) is $39.95," the correct answer.

EXAMPLE T

At 19 miles per gallon, how many miles would a car go on 9 gallons of gas?

To figure out this problem easily, think "19 is just 1 mile less than 20." Then think "9 times 20 = 180, and 180 minus 9 (9 × 1) is 171," the correct answer.

© SHUTTERSTOCK.COM/ELENA ELISSEEVA

✔ CONCEPT CHECK 3.5

You may have noticed that making quick calculations is quite similar to making estimations, which you did in Chapter 1. In fact, quick calculation is only an additional step. After estimating an answer, you determine the degree to which the estimated, or rounded, answer differs from the actual answer by mentally correcting for the amount of the estimation or rounding.

COMPLETE ASSIGNMENTS 3.1 AND 3.2.

Chapter Terms for Review

equation   numerical sentence

Summary of chapter learning objectives:

Learning Objective	Example
3.1 Use a systematic approach to solve word problems involving basic math processes.	Use the three-step process to solve the word problem. 1. Martha is preparing to make two dresses. One will require 3 yards of material; the other will require 4 yards of material. The material for the first dress costs $12.00 per yard; the material for the second costs $15.00 per yard. Buttons and trimming will cost $8.00 for each dress. What will be the total cost? Read the problem completely and carefully. Determine what is being requested. Determine the processes to be used to solve the problem. Answer:_____
3.2 Apply formulas to solve rate, time, and distance problems.	2. At an average rate of 50 miles per hour, how long would it take to drive 650 miles? _____ 3. At an average rate of 60 miles per hour, how far could you drive in 6 hours? _____ 4. If you drove 70 miles per hour and covered 280 miles, how much time did it take? _____
3.3 Solve simple numerical equations.	5. $5 \times 12 = 120 \div 2$ Move the 2 to the opposite side of the equation. 6. $7 + 8 - 3 = 5 + 2 + ?$ Solve for ? amount.

Answers: 1. $112 2. 13 hr 3. 360 mi 4. 4 hr 5. $5 \times 12 = 120$ 6. 5

THE BOTTOM LINE

Summary of chapter learning objectives:

Learning Objective	Example
3.4 Recognize numeric relationships in a series.	Insert the next two numbers. 7. 4, 7, 6, 9, 8, 11, _____ , _____ Pattern: _____ 8. 12, 48, 24, 96, 48, _____ , _____ Pattern: _____
3.5 Do quick mental calculations through a process of rounding numbers.	9. What is the cost of eight items at $3.99 each? 10. At 59 miles per hour, how far would a car go in 20 hours?

Review Problems for Chapter 3

1. 6 items at $5.99 each = _____

2. 3 items at $2.48 each = _____

3. 24 items at $1.99 each = _____

4. 40 items at $2.02 each = _____

5. In the first four months of the year, a corporation had monthly earnings of $12,493, $6,007, $3,028, and $9,728. What were its total earnings in the four months? _____

6. If the corporation in question 5 had earnings of $74,500 at the end of the year, how much did it earn in the last eight months of the year? _____

7. If a tour bus gets 7 miles per gallon of gas and used 61 gallons in a week, how many miles did it travel in the week? _____

8. An employer earned $4,000. Half the earnings went into an employee bonus pool. The pool was split among five employees. How much did each employee receive? _____

9. A delivery firm bought 21 gallons of gas on Monday, 15 on Tuesday, 24 on Wednesday, 34 on Thursday, and 11 on Friday. If gas cost $3.85 per gallon, how much did the delivery firm pay for the week's gas?
_____

10. A store owner planned to give away $1,200 at Christmas. The owner gave $150 to each of five full-time employees and $50 to each of four part-time employees. The remainder was given to a local charity. How much did the charity receive? _____

11. How long would it take to travel 1,265 miles at 55 miles per hour? _____

12. Bob and Mary start traveling toward each other from 1,330 miles apart. Bob is traveling at 30 miles per hour, Mary at 40 miles per hour. How many hours elapse before they meet? _____

13. Bob and Mary start traveling toward each other from 960 miles apart. Bob is traveling at 25 miles per hour, Mary at 55 miles per hour. How far had Bob traveled when they met? _____

14. $41 - 6 = 27 +$ _____

15. $72 + 72 = 300 -$ _____

16. $10 \times 3 = 90 \div$ _____

17. Four items at $9 each = _____ items at $12 each

18. What is the next number in the series 3, 7, 8, 12, ? _____

19. What is the next number in the series 5, 20, 10, 40, ? _____

20. To find the price of seven items at $1.99 you would think: 7 times $_____ less 7 times $_____ = $13.93

Answers to the Self-Check can be found in Appendix B at the back of the text.

Assignment 3.1: Word Problems, Equations, and Series

Name _____

Date _____ Score _____

Learning Objectives **1** **2** **4**

A (20 points) Use the three-step process to solve the following word problems. (5 points for each correct answer)

1. Budget Lamps and Lighting, Inc., conducted a direct-mail program. The manager determined that $64,000 in new business came from the program. If the profit was 40% of sales, how much profit did the program produce? _____

2. Martha's Beauty Salon charges $40 for a haircut, $48 for a facial, and $28 for hair coloring. If it had 20 haircut, 22 facial, and 18 coloring customers, what were its total sales? _____

3. Juan Lopez sold 11 life insurance policies with premiums totaling $24,200. He sold 14 auto policies with premiums totaling $31,920. Which type of policy had the greater premium per sale? _____

4. The Tulsa Taxi Service had four taxi vehicles. Two got 25 miles per gallon of gas; two got 20 miles per gallon of gas. The vehicles were each driven 8,000 miles per month. The gas cost $3.80 per gallon. What was the amount of the gas bill for the month? _____

Score for A (20) _____

B (10 points) Do these problems without using scratch paper or an electronic calculator. (2 points for each correct answer)

5. How much would you pay for 12 gallons of gasoline selling at $3.95 per gallon? _____

6. How many items would you have if you had 98 books, 98 cards, and 98 pencils? _____

7. What is the price of 15 items at $2.99 each? _____

8. How much would you have if you received $3.99 from one person, $7.99 from a second, $11.99 from a third, and $1.99 from a fourth? _____

9. If 24 people were divided into three equal groups and each group added 2 additional members, how many members would be in each group? _____

Score for B (10) _____

C (10 points) Do the steps in the order in which they occur. Do these problems without using scratch paper or an electronic calculator. (1 point for each correct answer)

10. 12 items at $3 each plus $2 tax = _____

11. 15 watches at $30 each less a $50 discount = _____

12. 3 lamps at $22 each plus 7 bulbs at $2 each = _____

13. 100 belts at $4 each less discounts of $60 and $30 = _____

14. 3 dozen scissors at $11.20 per dozen plus a $4 shipping charge = _____

15. 6 pounds of pears at $3 per pound plus 50¢ per pound for packaging = _____

16. $38 sale price plus $3 tax less an $11 discount plus a $5 delivery charge = _____

17. 6 bath towels at $8 each and 4 hand towels at $3 each plus $2.50 tax = _____

18. 4 dozen brushes at $25 per dozen plus $5 tax plus $7 shipping charge = _____

19. 2 shirts at $30 each, 4 ties at $10 each, and 7 pairs of socks at $2 each = _____

_____
Score for C (10)

D **(40 points) Complete the following equations by supplying the missing items. (4 points for each correct answer)**

20. $42 + 8 =$ _____ $+ 12$

21. $13 +$ _____ $= 7 + 28$

22. _____ $+ 4 = 4 + 16$

23. $400 = 17 - 2 +$ _____

24. $9 + 17 - 3 = 4 \times$ _____ $- 5$

25. $160 \div 4 + 2 = 7 \times 7 -$ _____

26. $13 - 11 \times$ _____ $= 8 \times 8 + 16$

27. _____ $\times 3 \times 3 = 9 \div 3 \times 9$

28. $64 \div 32 = 900 \div$ _____

29. $32 - 12 + 7 = 30 -$ _____

_____
Score for D (40)

E **(20 points) In each of the following problems, a definite relationship exists among the numbers in each series. Extend each series two items by following the correct process. (1 point for each correct line)**

30. Extend each series below through addition.

a. $4, 8, 12, 16,$ _____

c. $5, 8, 10, 13, 15,$ _____

b. $1, 4, 5, 8,$ _____

31. Extend each series below through subtraction.

a. $50, 45, 40, 35,$ _____

c. $100, 90, 81, 73,$ _____

b. $60, 55, 53, 48,$ _____

32. Extend each series below through multiplication.

a. $4, 8, 16, 32,$ _____

c. $2, 4, 20, 40,$ _____

b. $5, 25, 125,$ _____

33. Extend each series below through division.

a. $15,625, 3,125, 625, 125,$ _____

c. $10,000, 2,000, 1,000, 200,$ _____

b. $729, 243, 81, 27,$ _____

34. Extend each series below through combinations of the four processes above.

a. $72, 75, 69, 72,$ _____

e. $7, 4, 8, 5, 9,$ _____

b. $200, 100, 300, 150,$ _____

f. $30, 10, 60, 20,$ _____

c. $5, 7, 14, 16, 32,$ _____

g. $10, 40, 20, 80,$ _____

d. $240, 120, 600, 300, 1,500,$ _____

h. $100, 50, 40, 20,$ _____

_____
Score for E (20)

Assignment 3.2: Word Problems, Formulas, and Equations

Name _____

Date _____ Score _____

A   **(40 points) Solve the following word problems. (5 points for each correct answer)**

1. A store regularly sold 2 cans of soup for $1.28. It advertised a special sale of 6 cans for $3.12. A customer bought 12 cans at the sale. How much did the customer save over the regular price? _____

2. A sales representative's car gets 18 miles to a gallon of gas. It was driven 120 miles each day for 30 days. Gas cost an average of $3.68 per gallon. What was the sales representative's total 30-day cost for gas? _____

3. A store clerk sold a customer a ruler for $1.67, three pencils for $0.29 each, notebook paper for $0.99, and an eraser for $0.35 and was given $10.00 in payment. How much change did the clerk give the customer from the $10.00? (All prices include tax.) _____

4. A college student worked at a local store for $9.00 per hour, as his class schedule permitted. The student worked 3 hours each Monday, Tuesday, Wednesday, and Thursday. He also worked 2 hours each Friday and 8 hours each Saturday. How many weeks did the student have to work to earn $792 for a new bicycle?

   _____

5. A box, a crate, and a trunk weigh a total of 370 pounds. The crate weighs 160 pounds. The trunk weighs 4 pounds more than the box. What does the box weigh? _____

6. A hotel has 15 floors. Each floor has 26 *single-person* rooms and 38 *two-person* rooms. What is the total *guest* capacity of the hotel? _____

7. A department store offers its customers socks for $1.50 per pair or $15.00 per dozen. If two customers buy 1 dozen together and each pays half the cost, how much will each customer save by paying the quantity price? _____

8. Supply Clerk A ordered five staplers at $9 each and two large boxes of staples for $3 each. Supply Clerk B ordered a box of computer disks for $8.50 and a box of computer paper for $39.95. How much less did Clerk B spend than Clerk A? (All prices include tax.) _____

_____

Score for A (40)

B **(10 points) Solve the following time, rate, distance problems. (5 points for each correct answer)**

 9. Linda leaves Boise to travel the 2,160 miles to Austin, driving at a speed of 55 miles per hour. Mark leaves Austin to travel the same 2,160-mile route to Boise, driving at a speed of 65 miles per hour. How many miles will Mark have traveled when they meet? _____

10. Car A traveled to a destination 845 miles away at 65 miles per hour. Car B traveled to a destination 495 miles away at 55 miles per hour. How much longer did Car A travel than Car B? _____

Score for B (10)

C **(40 points) Solve each of the problems without writing any computations on paper and without using a calculator or a computer. (2 points for each correct answer)**

11. 12 items at $1.99 = _____   12. 2 items at $5.95 = _____

13. 4 items at $19.98 = _____   14. 2 items at $49.96 = _____

15. 15 items at $0.99 = _____   16. 10 items at $9.99 = _____

17. 6 items at $3.95 = _____   18. 5 items at $1.02 = _____

19. 19 items at $40 = _____   20. 3 items at $19.99 = _____

21. 20 items at $40.05 = _____   22. 30 items at $1.99 = _____

23. 20 items at $39.98 = _____   24. 2 items at $5.99 = _____

25. 48 items at $5 = _____   26. 5 items at $1.97 = _____

27. 7 items at $7.97 = _____   28. 2 items at $99.98 = _____

29. 30 items at $2.98 = _____   30. 99 items at $1.90 = _____

Score for C (40)

D **(10 points) In each of the following equations, rewrite the equation by moving the last number on each side of the equal sign to the other side and making appropriate sign changes so that the equation is still true. (Example: Given 13 + 7 + 2 = 10 + 12; Answer 13 + 7 − 12 = 10 − 2) (1 point for each correct equation)**

31. $6 + 4 + 5 = 17 - 2$ 32. $6 \times 2 \div 3 = 8 \div 4 \times 2$

33. $9 - 3 - 3 = 2 + 1$ 34. $8 \div 2 \times 4 = 24 \div 3 \times 2$

35. $20 + 1 - 7 = 16 - 2$ 36. $3 \times 3 \times 3 = 18 \div 2 \times 3$

37. $12 + 3 - 5 = 7 + 3$ 38. $7 \times 4 \div 2 = 28 \times 2 \div 4$

39. $64 - 32 - 16 = 8 + 8$ 40. $63 \div 7 \times 2 = 3 \times 2 \times 3$

Score for D (10)

International System of Units (SI):
The Metric System

4

Learning Objectives

By studying this chapter and completing all assignments you will be able to:

Learning Objective 1 Recognize and apply the basic elements of the International System of Units (SI) commonly known as "the metric system."

Learning Objective 2 Understand the SI measurements for length and be able to convert between the US and SI systems.

Learning Objective 3 Understand the SI measurements for volume and be able to convert between the US and SI systems.

Learning Objective 4 Understand the SI measurements for weight and be able to convert between the US and SI systems.

Basic Elements of the International System of Units (SI)

Learning Objective **1**

Recognize and apply the basic elements of the International System of Units (SI) commonly known as "the metric system."

In the United States, we measure distances by "inches," "feet," "yards," and "miles." In other parts of the world they use *meters*.

In the United States, we measure weight by "ounces," "pounds," and "tons." In other parts of the world they use *grams*.

In the United States, we measure volume (liquid) by "pints," "quarts," and "gallons." In other parts of the world, they use *liters*.

The measuring system used in the United States is commonly referred to as the "traditional," or the "US Traditional," system. The measuring system used in other parts of the world is called the *International System of Units* (abbreviated SI) and commonly referred to as the *metric system*.

The first metric system of measurement was developed in the late 1700s by the French Academy of Sciences. During the 1800s and early 1900s, the system spread rapidly and was adopted by most of the world's countries, including Spain, Mexico, Germany, and Russia.

The United States has tried but failed to adopt the metric system. An act of Congress passed in 1866 declared the metric system legal for use in the United States, but use of the system did not progress significantly. In 1975, Congress passed the Metric Conversion Act, which officially adopted the policy of changing our system to the metric system. However, once again, it never happened. Today the United States is the only industrialized country in the world that has not adopted the metric system.

Although not officially adopted by the United States today, the metric system is used in many areas of personal and business activities. Companies that export their products outside the United States use the metric system for their export items. Internationally oriented corporations like GM, IBM, and Microsoft have adopted the metric system for use in many of their manufacturing processes for global products.

Many high schools and universities have running tracks and engage in competitive events measured in meters. United States athletes who compete in the Olympic Games and other international contests compete in meters.

Many foreign-made automobiles sold in the United States have speedometers that indicate speed in both miles and kilometers. Virtually all pharmaceutical products manufactured in the United States and imported by pharmaceutical companies are dispensed with their quantities indicated in "grams." Our commonly used music CDs and video DVDs comply with an international metric standard established as 12 centimeters in diameter.

Because our economy is now global and world travel is so popular, it is important that a person is able to understand and use the metric system. To participate in the world economy, one needs to use, calculate, and convert measurements between the US traditional and the International System of Units (SI).

DECIMAL SYSTEM

The metric system is a decimal system. Prefixes and/or symbols are added to the metric base unit to indicate powers of 10, that is, 10, 100, 1,000. Likewise, prefixes or symbols are added to the base unit to indicate 1/10, 1/100, or 1/1, 000 part of the unit.

Some of the prefixes and symbols used with the metric system are as follows:

Number	US Term	Metric Prefix	Symbol
1,000,000,000	Billion	giga	G
1,000,000	Million	mega	M
1,000	Thousand	kilo	k
100	Hundred	hector	h
10	Ten	deka	da
1	One	(no prefix)	
1/10	One tenth	deci	d
1/100	One hundredth	centi	c
1/1000	One thousandth	milli	m
1/1,000,000	One millionth	micro	u
1/1,000,000,000	One billionth	nano	n

When writing numbers with prefixes in the metric system, we should note that the prefixes are usually written in lowercase and not capitalized. When writing numbers in the metric system, there are spaces but no commas, so 1,000 is 1 000 and 1,000,000 is 1 000 000. Also, when writing numbers with prefixes, there is a "0" before a decimal point such as 0.3 and 0.0007.

METRIC UNITS

The three metric units most widely used are

meter (m) — a measure of length
liter (L) — a measure of liquid capacity (volume)
gram (g) — a measure of weight (mass)

EXAMPLE A

"kilo" means 1 000, so five kilometers = 5 000 meters = (5 km).
"deci" means 1/10, so three decimeters = 0.3 meter = (0.3 m).
"mega" means 1 000 000, so two megameters = 2 000 000 meters = (2 Mm).

✔ CONCEPT CHECK 4.1

Use SI prefixes and symbols to express 3 000 grams.
    3 kilogram = 3 kg

Use SI prefixes and symbols to express 6/100 gram.
    6 centigram = 6 cg

Use SI prefixes and symbols to express 1/100 liter.
    1 centiliter = 1cL

The Measurement of Length

Learning Objective **2**

Understand the SI measurements for length and be able to convert between the US and SI systems.

The *meter (m)* is the base unit of the metric measure of length. Some of the multiples of the *meter* are shown below. Of these, the ones most frequently used are the millimeter, centimeter, and kilometer.

kilometer	(km)	=	1 000 meters
hectometer	(hm)	=	100 meters
dekameter	(dam)	=	10 meters
meter	(m)	=	1 meter
decimeter	(dm)	=	0.1 meter
centimeter	(cm)	=	0.01 meter
millimeter	(mm)	=	0.001 meter

CHANGING TO LARGER OR SMALLER UNITS

It is very easy to change from one unit to another in the metric systems, with the exception of numbers one million and above. To change a value to the next higher value, simply divide by 10. To change a value to the next lower value, simply multiply by 10.

EXAMPLE B

To change from meters to kilometers (smaller to larger) the steps are:

6 000 meters (m)	÷ 10 =	600 dekameters (dam)
600 dekameters (dam)	÷ 10 =	60 hectometers (hm)
60 hectometers (hm)	÷ 10 =	6 kilometers (km)

To change from meters to millimeters (larger to smaller) the steps are:

6 meters (m)	× 10 =	60 decimeters (dm)
60 decimeters (dm)	× 10 =	600 centimeters (cm)
600 centimeters (cm)	× 10 =	6 000 millimeters (mm)

COMPARISON OF US AND SI SYSTEMS MEASUREMENT OF LENGTH

It will undoubtedly take some time for those using the "traditional" US system of measurement to learn the metric system. The conversion table below is designed to facilitate calculations to convert values between the US Traditional and the SI systems.

Conversion Tables for Measurement of Length (Approximate)

Metric SI to Traditional US

1 kilometer	(km)	=	0.621 mile
1 kilometer	(km)	=	3,280.840 feet
1 hecktometer	(hm)	=	328.084 feet
1 dekameter	(dam)	=	32.808 feet
1 meter	(m)	=	39.370 inches
1 meter	(m)	=	3.281 feet
1 meter	(m)	=	1.094 yards
1 decimeter	(dm)	=	3.937 inches
1 centimeter	(cm)	=	0.393 inches
1 millimeter	(mm)	=	0.039 inches

US Traditional to Metric SI

1 inch = 2.540 centimeters (cm)
1 foot = 0.305 meter (m)
1 yard = 0.914 meter (m)
1 mile = 1.609 kilometers (km)

Some of the values in metric/US and US/metric conversion tables can be carried out to many decimal places. For practical use, the values in these conversion tables have been rounded to three decimal places.

For instance, a more accurate conversion between foot and meter would be seven decimal places, or 0.3047997; however, in most personal and business conversions, this is rounded to 0.305 meters per foot. Other examples are one kilometer equals 0.6214 mile and one mile equals 1.6093 kilometers; these have been rounded to 0.621 and 1.609, respectively.

Note: When traveling to almost any country outside the United States, highway signs will show distances and speed by kilometers. For quicker mental conversion, people commonly use a conversion of 6/10 of a mile per kilometer. So for a distance sign that reads "70 kilometers" one would quickly multiply by 0.6 and say 42 miles knowing that it approximates the actual distance computed using the three-decimal number of 0.621 miles per kilometer for an actual distance of 43.47 miles.

A measure of length used in the US system is the yard. The conversion table above shows that one meter is equal to 1.094 yards. To calculate the conversion of 5 meters to yards, one would multiply 1.094 by 5 to calculate that 5 meters equals 5.47 yards.

EXAMPLE C

Convert 20 meters to yards.

Using the conversion table, note that 1 meter equals 1.094 yards.

Multiply: 20 × 1.094 = 21.88 (yards)

EXAMPLE D

What is the speed limit in miles per hour on a highway where there is a sign that reads "80 kilometers"?

From the conversion table: 1 kilometer equals 0.621 miles.
Multiply: 80 × 0.621 = 49.68 mph

(*Note:* The 49.68 mph calculation is routinely rounded to 50 mph.)

If the distance between San Francisco and San Jose is 48 miles, what is the distance measured in kilometers?

One mile = 1.609 kilometers
48 × 1.609 = 77.232 kilometers

Convert 30 meters to yards.
One meter = 1.094 yards
30 × 1.094 = 32.82 yards

Change 2 000 meters to kilometers.

2 000 meters (m)	÷ 10 =	200 dekameters (dam)
200 dekameters (dam)	÷ 10 =	20 hectometers (hm)
20 hectometers (hm)	÷ 10 =	2 kilometers (km)

Learning Objective **3**

Understand the SI measurements for volume and be able to convert between the US and SI systems.

Volume and *capacity* simply mean "how much something holds." The terms *volume* and *capacity* are commonly used interchangeably. Basically, the terms refer to cubic units such as the number of cubic inches in a box or cylinder or to liquid capacity such as pints and quarts. This chapter will be limited to and focused on liquid capacity. The basic metric unit for liquid capacity is the *liter*.

Although metric symbols are usually lowercase, the symbol for liter is the capital letter "L" in order to avoid confusion with the number 1. Some multiples of the liter are

kiloliter	(kL)	=	1 000 liters
hectoliter	(hL)	=	100 liters
dekaliter	(daL)	=	10 liters
liter	(L)	=	1 liter
deciliter	(dL)	=	0.1 liter
centiliter	(cL)	=	0.01 liter
milliliter	(mL)	=	0.001 liter

The liter, milliliter, and kiloliter are the most frequently used of these measures. One liter is about equal to one quart (1.057 quarts). The milliliter is used in the measurement of small quantities such as eye drops while the kiloliter is used in the measurement of large quantities such as swimming pools.

CHANGING TO LARGER OR SMALLER UNITS

As shown in the table above, the liter, like all other metric measurements, is based on the decimal system. To change the value of a unit to the next higher one, divide by 10. To change the value of a unit to the next lower one, multiply by 10.

● EXAMPLE E

To change from liters to kiloliters (smaller to larger) or from liters to milliliters (larger to smaller) the steps are as follows:

7 000 L	÷ 10 =	700 daL	(dekaliters)
700 daL	÷ 10 =	70 hL	(hectoliters)
70 hL	÷ 10 =	7 kL	(kiloliters)
7 L	× 10 =	70 dL	(deciliters)
70 dL	× 10 =	700 cL	(centiliters)
700 cL	× 10 =	7 000 mL	(milliliters)

COMPARISON OF US AND SI SYSTEMS
MEASUREMENT OF CAPACITY

The approximate equivalents of the metric liter and the US unit of measurement are shown in the conversion tables below. All items are rounded to three decimal places.

Conversion Tables for Measurement of Capacity (Approximate)

Metric SI to Traditional US

1 kiloliter	kL	=	264,178	gallons
1 hectoliter	hL	=	26,418	gallons
1 dekaliter	daL	=	2,642	gallons
1 liter	L	=	2.113	pints
	L	=	1.057	quarts
	L	=	0.264	gallon
1 deciliter	dL	=	0.211	pint
1 centiliter	cL	=	0.338	ounce
1 milliliter	mL	=	0.034	ounce

US Traditional to Metric SI

1 cup	=	0.237 liter	(L)
1 pint	=	0.473 liter	(L)
1 quart	=	0.946 liter	(L)
1 gallon	=	3.785 liter	(L)
1 ounce	=	29.573 milliliters	(mL)

Every year more and more liquid products sold in the United States are measured by liters. Many soft drinks, wines, dairy products, hard liquors, and specialty products are sold by the liter. One of the factors that brought this about is that the amount of liquid in a quart and a liter are close to the same.

EIRIK SOLHEIM/SHUTTERSTOCK.COM

● **EXAMPLE F**

Five liters equal how many quarts?
1 liter equals 1.057 quarts. $5 \times 1.057 = 5.285$ quarts

Seven quarts equal how many liters?
1 quart equals 0.946 liter. $7 \times 0.946 = 6.622$ liters

How many liters are there in four gallons?
1 gallon equals 3.785 liters. $4 \times 3.785 = 15.14$ liters

How many gallons are there in 12 liters?
1 liter = 0.264 gallons. $12 \times 0.264 = 3.168$ gallons

Change 15 kiloliters to liters.

$$15 \text{ kiloliters} \times 10 = 150 \text{ hectoliters}$$
$$150 \text{ hectoliters} \times 10 = 1\,500 \text{ dekaliters}$$
$$1\,500 \text{ dekaliters} \times 10 = 15\,000 \text{ liters}$$

How many liters would it take to fill a 20-gallon gas tank?

$$20 \times 3.785 = 75.7 \text{ liters}$$

The metric unit of weight is the *gram,* but because of its small size (0.035 ounce) the kilogram, which is equivalent to 2.205 pounds, is commonly considered as the base unit. The kilogram, the gram, the milligram, and the metric ton are the most frequently used metric units in measuring weight. The following are some of the metric system multiples of weight:

metric ton t   = 1 000 kilogram
kilogram   kg = 1 000 gram
hectogram hg = 100 gram
dekagram   dag =   10 gram
gram   g =   1 gram
decigram   dg = 0.1 gram
centigram cg = 0.01 gram
milligram mg = 0.001 gram

CHANGING TO LARGER OR SMALLER UNITS

To change the value of a unit to the next higher one, divide by 10. To change the value of a unit to the next lower one, multiply by 10.

EXAMPLE G
Smaller to Larger
$$4\,000 \text{ g} \div 10 = 400 \text{ dag (dekagram)}$$
$$400 \text{ dag} \div 10 = 40 \text{ hg (hectogram)}$$
$$40 \text{ hg} \div 10 = 4 \text{ kg (kilogram)}$$

Larger to Smaller
$$4 \text{ g} \times 10 = 40 \text{ dg (decigram)}$$
$$40 \text{ dg} \times 10 = 400 \text{ cg (centigram)}$$
$$400 \text{ cg} \times 10 = 4\,000 \text{ mg (milligram)}$$

COMPARISON OF US AND SI SYSTEMS
MEASUREMENT OF WEIGHT

The table below provides a comparison of the US Traditional and SI systems of weight.

Conversion Tables for Measurement of Weight (Approximate)

Metric SI to Traditional US

1 metric ton	t	=	1.102	short tons
1 metric ton	t	=	2,204.623	pounds
1 kilogram	kg	=	2.205	pounds
1 kilogram	kg	=	35.274	ounces
1 hectogram	hg	=	3.527	ounces
1 dekagram	dag	=	0.353	ounces
1 gram	g	=	0.035	ounce
1 decigram	dg	=	1.543	grains
1 centigram	cg	=	0.154	grain
1 milligram	mg	=	0.015	grain

Traditional US to Metric SI

1 grain	=	0.065 gram	g
1 ounce	=	28.349 gram	g
1 pound	=	453.592 gram	g
1 pound	=	0.453 kilogram	kg
1 short ton	=	0.907 metric ton	t

EXAMPLE H

How many pounds are there in 4 metric tons?

4 × 2,204.623 pounds per metric ton = 8,818.492 pounds

EXAMPLE I

What would be the cost of a bag of chips that weighed 0.213 kilogram and sold for $0.40 per ounce?

0.213 × 35.274 = 7.513 ounces × $0.40 = $3.01

Change 1500 milligrams to grams.

$$1500 \text{ milligrams} \div 10 = 150 \text{ centigrams}$$
$$150 \text{ centigrams} \div 10 = 15 \text{ decigrams}$$
$$15 \text{ decigrams} \div 10 = 1.5 \text{ grams}$$

Three European dogs weigh 12, 20, and 40 kilograms. What is their average weight in pounds?

$$12 + 20 + 40 = 72 \div 3 = 24 \text{ kilogram average}$$
$$24 \times 2.205 = 52.92 \text{ pound average}$$

If Judy weighs 98 pounds and Mary weighs 112 pounds, what is their average weight in kilograms?

$$98 + 112 = 210 \div 2 = 105 \text{ pound average}$$
$$105 \times 0.453 = 47.565 \text{ kilogram average}$$

In the metric system, food and related products will generally be quoted in milligrams, grams, and kilograms. Milligrams are used for very small items such as aspirin and medical prescriptions; in fact, for many years drugs and prescription medications have been dispensed in the United States in grams and milligrams with no reference to US Traditional weight.

Grams are used to indicate weight for regular cans of food, packages of frozen foods, and other items of this size. The label on a can of green beans will likely state the net weight as 16 ounces (1 pound) or 454 grams.

Kilograms are used to measure larger items such as an animal's weight, a person's weight, or the weight of a piece of household furniture.

THE BOTTOM LINE

Summary of chapter learning objectives:

Learning Objective	Example
4.1 Recognize and apply the basic elements of the International System of Units (SI), commonly known as "the metric system."	1. Indicate the most common units of measurement in the SI system to measure: (a) Length _____ (b) Volume _____ (c) Weight _____ 2. Determine the unit of measurement as indicated for each item. (a) 5 meters = _____ decimeters (b) 700 centimeters = _____ decimeters
4.2 Understand the SI measurements for length and be able to convert between the US and SI systems.	3. Convert the following measurements from US Traditional to SI or from SI to US Traditional as indicated. (a) 6 yard = _____ meters (b) 20 kilometers = _____ miles
4.3 Understand the SI measurement for volumn and be able to convert between the US and SI systems.	4. Convert the following measurements from US Traditional to SI or from SI to US Traditional as indicated. (a) 3 quarts = _____ liters (b) 15 liters = _____ gallons
4.4 Understand the SI measurements for weight and be able to convert between the US and SI systems.	5. Convert the following measurements from US Traditional to SI or from IS to US Traditional as indicated. (a) 6 ounces = _____ grams (b) 30 kilograms = _____ pounds

Answers: 1(a). meter 1(b). liter 1(c). gram 2(a). 50 2(b). 70 3(a). 5.484 3(b). 12.42 4(a). 2.838 4(b). 3.96 5(a). 170.094 5(b). 66.15

Review Problems for Chapter 4

Write all answers as proper fractions or mixed numbers in lowest terms.

1. The metric system is a _____ system that uses powers of _____ for all measurements.

2. Indicate the metric symbol and US term or value for the following:

	Symbol	**Value**
(a) giga	_____	_____
(b) deci	_____	_____
(c) kilo	_____	_____

3. 12,000 meters = _____ kilometers

4. 7.2 grams = _____ centigrams

5. 16 miles = _____ kilometers

6. 5 inches = _____ centimeters

7. 42 meters = _____ yards

8. 5L = _____ dL

9. 17 liters = _____ gallons

10. 35 pounds = _____ kilograms

11. A two-pound box of salt sells for $3.00. What is the cost per kilogram? _____

12. Mark Goings used 22 gallons of gas to drive 1028 kilometers. How many miles per liter did he get? _____

13. How many liters are there in 2 quarts of apple juice? _____

14. 3 pounds 12 ounces of cat food = _____ grams

15. Three boards measured 2 m, 3 m, and 4 m. What were their lengths in inches? _____

    _____

    _____

Answers to the Self-Check can be found in Appendix B at the back of the text.

Assignment 4.1: International System of Units (SI) and Capacity

Name _____

Date _____   Score _____

Learning Objectives 1 2 3 4

A (30 points)

1. Fill in the missing information: (*10 points, 1 point each answer*)

Prefix	Symbol	Value
_____	_____	_____
_____	_____	_____
_____	_____	_____
_____	_____	_____
_____	_____	_____

2. The meter is the base unit of the measure of length. Provide the missing information: (*5 points, 1 point each*)

a. 1 kilometer   = _____ meters

b. 0.001 meter   = _____ millimeter

c. 1 dekameter   = _____ meters

d. 4 meters   = _____ decimeters

e. 240 millimeters = _____ centimeters

3. Convert 40 meters to: (*5 points, 1 point each*)

a. centimeters _____

b. kilometers _____

c. millimeters _____

Convert 5 kilometers to:

d. meters _____

e. millimeters _____

4. Convert the following lengths to the metric or traditional equivalent units. (*10 points, 2 points each*)

a. 25 miles per hour to kilometers per hour: _____

b. 5 meters to feet: _____

c. 100-meter track event to yards: _____

d. 12-inch ruler to centimeters: _____

e. 60-yard roll of tape to meters: _____

_____

Score for A (30)

B (40 points) (4 points for each correct answer)

5. A building is 180 feet high.

a. What metric unit would most likely be used to express its height? _____

b. How high is it in metric units? _____

6. Iona Valdez plans to build a house on a lot 80 feet wide and 120 feet deep.

a. How many meters wide is the lot? _____

b. How many meters deep is the lot? _____

7. If you were to change the highway speed limit signs from miles to kilometers, how would the following read? (Round to nearest km/h)

   a. 55 miles per hour: _____

   b. 35 miles per hour: _____

8. The height of a basketball player is 183 cm. How tall is this in feet? _____

9. Rick Blanc, a cabinet maker, needs screws 20 mm, 30 mm, and 40 mm, in length. What is the length of the screws in inches? (Round final answer to two decimal places)

   a. 20 mm: _____

   b. 30 mm: _____

   c. 40 mm: _____

Score for B (40)

C   (30 points) (2 points for each correct answer)

10. The liter is the basic unit of the measure of capacity and volume. Provide the missing information:

    a. 0.01 liter   = _____ cL

    b. 10 kiloliters   = _____ daL

    c. 12 liters   = _____ mL

    d. 750 milliliters = _____ L

    e. 42 hectoliters = _____ kL

11. Which measure probably would be used to express the capacity of the following:

	Metric Name and Symbol
a. Large water tank	_____
b. Quart of orange juice	_____
c. Teaspoon of medicine	_____
d. Gallon of gasoline	_____
e. Swimming pool	_____

12. Convert the following capacities to the equivalents of metric or traditional units:

    a. 5 gallons   = _____

    b. 2 liters = _____

    c. 32 ounces = _____

    d. $2\frac{1}{2}$ cups = _____

    e. 8 liters = _____

Score for C (30)

Assignment 4.2: International System of Units (SI) Measurement of Capacity and Weight

Name _____

Date _____ Score _____

A **(35 points) Round final answer to two decimal places. (5 points for each correct answer)**

1. What will be the price of 3 784 mL of milk that sells for 59¢ per quart? _____

2. Mike Mackie used 105 liters of gasoline when he drove from Chicago to New York, a distance of 1 210 kilometers.

   a. What was the average number of kilometers per liter? _____

   b. What was the average number of miles per gallon? _____

3. If an automatic dishwasher used 16 gallons of water, what is the equivalent number of liters?

   _____

4. The labels on many food products state the volume in both ounces and liters.

   a. How many milliliters are in a 12-ounce can of tomato juice? _____

   b. What is the volume in liters of 1 quart, 14 ounces of grapefruit juice? _____

5. A carton containing 1 liter of milk sells for 62¢, while a carton containing 5 deciliters is priced at 37¢. How much is saved by buying a carton containing 1 liter rather than two cartons containing 5 deciliters each?

   _____

   _____
   Score for A (35)

B **(25 points)**

6. The kilogram is considered the basic unit of the measurement of weight (mass). Provide the missing information: (*1 point each*)

   a. 1 gram   = _____ kg

   b. 150 kilograms = _____ dag

   c. 300 milligrams = _____ dg

   d. 26 hectograms = _____ g

   e. 280 centigrams = _____ g

7. Which measure probably would be used to express the weight of the following: (*2 points each*)
   Metric Name and Symbol

   a. A student's weight   _____

   b. A can of pepper   _____

   c. A truckload of iron   _____

   d. A turkey   _____

   e. One aspirin tablet   _____

8. Convert the following weights to the equivalent metric or traditional units: (*2 points each*)

    a. 482 grams of beans = _____ ounces

    b. 12,125 pounds of coal = _____ metric tons

    c. 5 kilograms of meat = _____ pounds

    d. 5 ounces of soap = _____ grams

    e. 0.500 milligrams of medicine = _____ grain

_____

Score for B (25)

C   **(40 points) (5 points for each correct answer to Problems 9–12; 1 point each for Problem 13)**

9. A five-pound bag of sugar sells for $1.66. A 16-ounce box sells for 53¢. What is the cost per kilogram for the large bag and the small box?

Large bag: _____

Small box: _____

10. It costs 45¢ for the first ounce (or fraction thereof) and 40¢ for each additional ounce (or fraction thereof) to mail a letter in the United States. How much will the postage be on a letter weighing 80 grams? _____

11. A canning factory packs corn in a small size can weighing $8\frac{3}{4}$ ounces. The cans are packed 48 cans to a carton. What is the metric weight of the carton? _____

12. What would be the weight in grams of the following items:

    a. $2\frac{1}{2}$ pounds of coffee = _____ grams _____

    b. 5 pounds, 8 ounces of dog biscuits = _____ grams

    c. $5\frac{1}{4}$ ounces of cookies = _____ grams _____

13. What metric measure would you use to express the following:

    a. The amount of water necessary to fill a 2-gallon bucket _____

    b. The weight of a football player _____

    c. A can of corn _____

    d. A 2-ounce bottle of cologne _____

    e. A small candy bar _____

_____

Score for C (40)

Percents

5

Learning Objectives

By studying this chapter and completing all assignments, you will be able to:

Learning Objective **1**   Change percents to decimals.

Learning Objective **2**   Change fractions and decimals to percents.

Learning Objective **3**   Find Base, Rate, and Percentage.

Learning Objective **4**   Use percents to measure increase and decrease.

Learning Objective **5**   Use percents to allocate overhead expenses.

Percents and percentages are used extensively in various business and nonbusiness applications. Airlines are required to publish the "on-time percentage" for each of their flights. Every bank publishes its loan rates as percents. The Food and Drug Administration (FDA) says that packaged foods must contain labels with nutritional information, much of which is written in percents. Colleges and universities often describe the ethnic diversity of their student bodies and faculty using percents. Various taxes are calculated using a percent of value or a percent of usage.

Changing Percents to Decimals

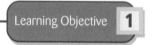
Learning Objective 1

Change percents to decimals.

We use percents because the word **percent** often makes verbal and written communication easier and more clear. Consider a state that has a 5% sales tax. Which of these phrases sounds better: (a) "five percent," (b) "five-hundredths," (c) "one-twentieth," or even (d) "point zero five"? Imagine how the latter three phrases would change if the sales tax rate were 5.25%. But by using the word *percent*, we can just say "five point two five percent."

When you use percents in arithmetic, before you can do any calculations, you must first change the percent to a decimal. If you use a calculator with a percent key [%], the calculator will convert the percent to a decimal. Using a calculator with a percent key, observe the display closely. To enter 75%, press the three keys [7] [5] [%]. After pressing the [%] key, the display shows **0.75**. There is no percent symbol and the decimal point has moved two places to the left. The calculator will use 0.75 in its calculations.

Sometimes a percent has a fractional part. For example, assume that the state tax rate is $5\frac{1}{2}$%. Even using a calculator, first we must change the fraction to a decimal, writing it as 5.5%. Using the calculator, press these keys: [5] [.] [5] [%]. After pressing [%], the display shows **0.055**. Notice that to move the decimal point two places to the left, the calculator had to insert an extra zero at the left.

> **STEPS** **to Change a Percent to a Decimal**
>
> 1. If the percent has a fractional part, convert the fraction to its decimal equivalent.
> 2. Remove the percent symbol.
> 3. Move the decimal point two places to the *left* (insert zeros if needed).

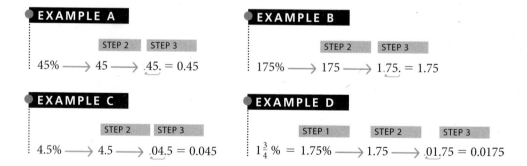

EXAMPLE A

STEP 2	STEP 3

45% $\longrightarrow$ 45 $\longrightarrow$ .45. = 0.45

EXAMPLE B

STEP 2	STEP 3

175% $\longrightarrow$ 175 $\longrightarrow$ 1.75. = 1.75

EXAMPLE C

STEP 2	STEP 3

4.5% $\longrightarrow$ 4.5 $\longrightarrow$ .04.5 = 0.045

EXAMPLE D

STEP 1	STEP 2	STEP 3

$1\frac{3}{4}$% = 1.75% $\longrightarrow$ 1.75 $\longrightarrow$ .01.75 = 0.0175

(*Note:* Check the answers to these examples with the percent key on your calculator.)

a. Change 250% to a decimal.

$250\% \longrightarrow 250 \longrightarrow 2.50. = 2.50$ or 2.5

b. Change $\frac{1}{4}\%$ to a decimal.

$\frac{1}{4}\% = 0.25\% \longrightarrow 0.25 \longrightarrow .00.25$

$= 0.0025$

Changing Fractions and Decimals to Percents

To change a fraction or decimal number to a percent requires that you move the decimal point two places to the *right*. However, if the number is a fraction or mixed number, you must first change it to a decimal as we reviewed in Chapter 2—examples E and F below. Then change the decimal to a percent by moving the decimal point. (A decimal point at the extreme right is omitted—examples E, G, and J below.)

Learning Objective **2**

Change fractions and decimals to percents.

STEPS to Change a Fraction or a Decimal to a Percent

1. If the number is a fraction, or a mixed number, convert it to its decimal equivalent.
2. Move the decimal point two places to the *right* (insert zeros if needed).
3. Write a percent symbol at the *right* end of the new number.

EXAMPLE E

| STEP 1 | STEP 2 | STEP 3 |

$\frac{4}{5} = 0.8 \longrightarrow 0.80. \longrightarrow 80\%$

EXAMPLE F

| STEP 1 | STEP 2 | STEP 3 |

$1\frac{3}{8} = 1.375 \longrightarrow 1.37.5 \longrightarrow 137.5\%$

EXAMPLE G

| STEP 2 | STEP 3 |

$0.4 \longrightarrow 0.40. \longrightarrow 40\%$

$0.14 = 0.14;$

EXAMPLE H

| STEP 2 | STEP 3 |

$1.1875 \longrightarrow 1.18.75 \longrightarrow 118.75\%$

EXAMPLE I

| STEP 2 | STEP 3 |

$2.5 \longrightarrow 2.50. \longrightarrow 250\%$

EXAMPLE J

| STEP 2 | STEP 3 |

$1 = 1. \longrightarrow 1.00. \longrightarrow 100\%$

(*Note:* To check these examples with your calculator, you can multiply the decimal number by 100 and write the percent symbol at the right end of the answer.)

a. Change $2\frac{7}{10}$ to a percent.

b. Change 0.075 to a percent.

$2\frac{7}{10} = 2.7 \longrightarrow 2.\underline{70}. \longrightarrow 270\%$

$0.075 \longrightarrow 0.0\underline{7}.5 \longrightarrow 7.5\%$

Finding Base, Rate, and ~~Percentage~~ *Portion*

Learning Objective 3

Find Base, Rate, and Percentage.

Suppose that you have $5 and spend $4 for coffee and a muffin. Example E showed that the fraction $\frac{4}{5}$ equals 80%. You can say that "you spent 80% of your money ($5) for your food ($4)." Without the context of the food, you have simply "80% of $5 = $4." In this text we call 80% the **Rate (R),** $5 the **Base (B)** amount, and $4 the **Percentage (P)** amount. The Base and the Percentage amounts will always have the same units (e.g., dollars, feet, or pounds). The Rate is the percent. (The word *rate* comes from the word *ratio*—in this case, $\frac{4}{5}$.) It may make sense for you to think of the Base amount as the denominator in the rate (that is, ratio = $\frac{4}{5}$) because the denominator is the "base" (i.e., bottom) of the fraction.

Note: In practice, the terms *percent* and *percentage* are often used interchangeably. Sometimes, you will see the word *percentage* used to mean a rate and the word *percent* used to mean an amount. You will even see the two words *percentage rate* to mean the rate. In this text, however, we use only one meaning for each word.

EXAMPLE K

80% of $5 = $4
80% is the Rate
$5 is the Base
$4 is the Percentage

EXAMPLE L

25% of 20 ft = 5 ft
25% is the Rate
20 ft is the Base
5 ft is the Percentage

EXAMPLE M

50% of 60 gal = 30 gal
50% is the Rate
60 gal is the Base
30 gal is the Percentage

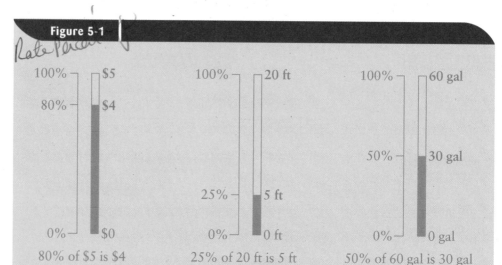

Figure 5-1

80% of $5 is $4

25% of 20 ft is 5 ft

50% of 60 gal is 30 gal

Figure 5-1 shows three diagrams, one each for examples K, L, and M. In each diagram, the Rate (or percent) is shown in the left-hand column. Each Percentage is represented by the shaded portion of the right-hand column. Each Base is represented by the entire height of the right-hand column.

The word *of* often appears in problems that involve percents. Recall from Chapter 1 that with fractions, *of* often means *multiply*. We just showed that 80% = $\frac{\$4}{\$5}$. Also recall that you can "check" a division problem by multiplication. We will get 80% × $5 = $4. In words, we say that "80% *of* $5 is $4."

Rule: The number that follows the word *of* is the Base (and is the denominator in the fraction); the number that follows the word *is* is the Percentage amount.

The preceding examples illustrate the basic relationship among the Rate, Base, and Percentage: Rate × Base = Percentage. As a formula, it is written as $R \times B = P$, or as $P = R \times B$.

When you know any two of these three numbers, you can calculate the third by changing the formula:

If you want to find B, the formula becomes $B = P \div R$, or $P \div R = B$.
If you want to find R, the formula becomes $R = P \div B$, or $P \div B = R$.

EXAMPLE N

Find *P* when
$R = 50\%$ and $B = 300$ yd

EXAMPLE O

Find *R* when
$B = 30$ lb and $P = 6$ lb

EXAMPLE P

Find *B* when
$P = \$45$ and $R = 75\%$

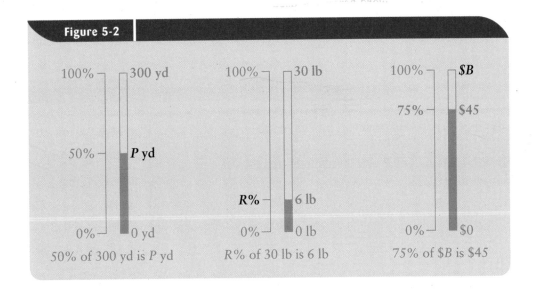

Figure 5-2

50% of 300 yd is *P* yd   R% of 30 lb is 6 lb   75% of $B is $45

Figure 5-2 illustrates these relationships, which are calculated as follows:

$P = R \times B$
$P = 50\% \times 300$ yd
$P = 0.50 \times 300$ yd
$P = 150$ yd
[5][0][%][×][3][0][0][=]

$R = P \div B$
$R = 6$ lb $\div 30$ lb
$R = 0.20$
$R = 20\%$
[6][÷][3][0][=]

$B = P \div R$
$B = \$45 \div 75\%$
$B = \$45 \div 0.75$
$B = \$60$
[4][5][÷][7][5][%][=]

Note that in example O, a calculator does not automatically "move" the decimal point two places to the right. If you want a calculator to do that, you must multiply 0.20 by 100. It is faster to just move the decimal point two places without using a calculator.

USING PERCENTS IN BUSINESS

Percent problems occur very frequently in business. Examples Q and R are typical applications in which we solve for the Base (B) amount and the Rate (R), respectively.

● EXAMPLE Q

Lena Hoover is a financial analyst. In December, she received a $600 bonus, which equaled 15% of her monthly salary. What was her monthly salary?

P = amount of bonus = $600

R = rate of bonus = 15%

B = monthly salary = ?

As $P \div R = B$,

$P \div R = \$600 \div 15\% = \$600 \div 0.15 = \$4,000$ monthly salary

● EXAMPLE R

KENISHIROTIE/SHUTTERSTOCK.COM

Last year Empire Bakery had total expenses of $300,000. Of that total, $210,000 was the expense for employee salaries. Last year at Empire, the employee salary expense was what percent of total expenses?

P = employee salaries = $210,000

R = ?

B = total expenses = $300,000

Since $P \div B = R$,

$P \div B = \$210,000 \div \$300,000 = 0.70 = 70\%$

✔ CONCEPT CHECK 5.3

a. Find the Base when the Rate is 40% and the Percentage amount is 50 ft.

$B = P \div R = 50 \text{ ft} \div 40\% = 50 \text{ ft} \div 0.40 = 125 \text{ ft}$

b. Find the Rate when the Base is 12 oz and the Percentage amount is 3 oz.

$R = P \div B = 3 \text{ oz} \div 12 \text{ oz} = 0.25 = 25\%$

COMPLETE ASSIGNMENT 5.1.

Using Percents to Measure Increase and Decrease

Learning Objective **4**

Use percents to measure increase and decrease.

In business, percents are used to measure change from one month to the next or from one year to the next. Real estate firms use percents to compare the number of homes sold this year with the number of homes sold last year. Read, and carefully compare, the following four statements about home sales last year and this year:

Joslin Realty sold 40% more homes this year than it did last year, when it sold 135 homes.

Rossi & Shanley Real Estate sold 25 more homes this year than last year, which represents 20% more homes sold this year than last year.

Real estate agent Silvia Jiminez sold 5 fewer homes this year than she did last year, when she sold 40 homes.

Charles Peterson, a real estate broker, sold 30 homes last year; this year he sold 36 homes.

The number of homes sold last year is the Base (B) amount (last year is called the *base year*). The change in homes sold can be reported as a number, which would be the Percentage amount (P), or as a percent, which would be the Rate (R). If any two of the three values are given, the third can be determined using one of the three formulas in this chapter.

EXAMPLE S

Find the number of additional homes (P) that Joslin Realty sold this year.

$B = 135$ and $R = 40\%$. Since $P = R \times B$,
$P = 40\% \times 135 = 0.40 \times 135 = 54$ more homes this year

EXAMPLE T

Find the number of homes that Rossi & Shanley Real Estate sold last year (B).

$P = 25$ and $R = 20\%$. Since $B = P \div R$,
$B = 25 \div 20\% = 25 \div 0.20 = 125$ homes sold last year

EXAMPLE U

Find Silvia Jiminez' rate of decrease (R) from last year's sales.

$P = 5$ and $B = 40$. Since $R = P \div B$,
$R = 5 \div 40 = 0.125 = 12.5\%$ decrease

To find the percent change when the only numbers reported are the amounts (B) for last year and this year, the first step is to find the **amount of increase** or the **amount of decrease.** P is the difference between the amounts for the two years. Then use $R = P \div B$ to find the **rate of increase** or the **rate of decrease.**

EXAMPLE V

Find Charles Peterson's rate of change (R).

Charles sold 30 homes last year (B) and 36 this year. The amount of change is

$P = 36 - 30 = 6$ more homes this year.

The rate of change is

$R = P \div B = 6 \div 30 = 0.20 = 20\%$ increase

COMPUTING AMOUNTS OF INCREASE AND DECREASE WITH A CALCULATOR

Review example S. Now consider a variation of example S that says, "Find the total number of homes that Joslin Realty sold this year." Last year it sold 135 homes. There was a 40% increase, which means 54 more homes were sold this year. The total number of homes sold this year was 135 + 54 = 189 homes. Many calculators allow you to calculate 189 with the following keystrokes: [1][3][5][+][4][0][%][=]. The display will show the answer, 189.

If you need to know the actual amount of the increase, it will usually show in the calculator display immediately after you press the [%] key, but just before you press the [=] key.

Similarly, suppose the original example had said, "The real estate agency sold 40% *fewer* homes this year than it did last year, when it sold 135 homes. Find the total number of homes that it sold this year." The amount of the *decrease* is 54 homes. Therefore, the total number sold this year is 135 − 54 = 81 homes. On the calculator, you would use the following keystrokes: [1][3][5][−][4][0][%][=]. The display will show the answer, 81.

✔ CONCEPT CHECK 5.4

Weil Warehousing Co. had sales of $200,000 this month and $160,000 last month (*B*). Find both the amount of increase (*P*) and the rate of increase (*R*).

The amount of increase is
$P = \$200{,}000 - \$160{,}000 = \$40{,}000$

The rate of increase is
$R = P \div B = \$40{,}000 \div \$160{,}000 = 0.25 = 25\%$

COMPLETE ASSIGNMENTS 5.2 AND 5.3.

Using Percents to Allocate Overhead Expenses

Learning Objective 5

Use percents to allocate overhead expenses.

Many businesses are organized into divisions or departments. Suppose Cotton's Clothing is a retailer of sportswear. It has three departments: women's clothes, men's clothes, and children's clothes. Management and owners of Cotton's need to measure the profitability of each department. Cotton's also knows the amounts it paid for the merchandise sold and the salaries of employees in each department. Cotton's can subtract these departmental costs from the departmental revenues.

But what about rent and other general costs such as electricity? These costs that are not directly related to the types of merchandise sold are called **overhead costs.** For example, Cotton's monthly rental expense might be $15,000 for the entire building. How should that single amount be divided among the three departments? Should each department be assigned $\frac{1}{3}$, or $5,000, of the total rent?

Businesses can **allocate,** or distribute, the total rent based on a measurement related to the total cost. Rent is a cost of using the building; it could be allocated on the basis of floor space, since each department occupies some of that space.

EXAMPLE W

The total rent is $15,000. Using the floor space of each department as shown below, determine the amount of rent to allocate to each department of Cotton's.

Department	STEP 1 Floor Space	STEP 2 Percent of Total	STEP 3 Distribution of Rent
Women's	100 ft × 50 ft = 5,000 sq ft	5,000 ÷ 10,000 = 50%	0.5 × $15,000 = $ 7,500
Children's	50 ft × 60 ft = 3,000 sq ft	3,000 ÷ 10,000 = 30%	0.3 × $15,000 = $ 4,500
Men's	40 ft × 50 ft = 2,000 sq ft	2,000 ÷ 10,000 = 20%	0.2 × $15,000 = $ 3,000
	10,000 sq ft		$15,000

This same method can be used for many other business expenses, such as utilities, fire insurance, and salaries of office personnel. Examples of other bases that might be used for allocation are number of employees, hours worked, and units produced.

✓ **CONCEPT CHECK 5.5**

Curtis Landscape Maintenance Company has two different divisions: commercial and residential. Employees spend 1,125 hours working on commercial landscapes and 375 hours working on residential landscapes. Curtis has office expenses of $8,000 that it wants to allocate between the two divisions, based on the percent of employee hours used by each division.

Total hours worked: 1,125 + 375 = 1,500

Commercial: 1,125 ÷ 1,500 = 0.75, or 75% of employee hours
75% of $8,000 = 0.75 × $8,000 = $6,000 of office expenses

Residential: 375 ÷ 1,500 = 0.25 or 25% of employee hours
25% of $8,000 = 0.25 × $8,000 = $2,000 of office expenses

COMPLETE ASSIGNMENT 5.4.

Try Microsoft® Excel

Try working the problems using the Microsoft Excel templates found on the companion website. Solutions for the problems are also shown on the companion website.

THE BOTTOM LINE

Summary of chapter learning objectives:

Learning Objective	Example
5.1 Change percents to decimals.	1. Change 4.25% to a decimal.
5.2 Change fractions and decimals to percents.	2. Change 0.45 to a percent. 3. Change $\frac{7}{8}$ to a percent.
5.3 Find Base, Rate, and Percentage.	4. Find the Percentage: 35% of 40 $= P$ 5. Find the Rate: R% of 140 $= 28$ 6. Find the Base: 80% of $B = 220$
5.4 Use percents to measure increase and decrease.	7. Increase a $5,000 salary by 25%. 8. From 300 to 240 is a decrease of what percent?
5.5 Use percents to allocate overhead expenses.	9. A company has three stores, A, B, and C, with 4, 6, and 10 employees, respectively. Based on the number of employees, allocate a $4,000 expense among the stores.

Answers: 1. 0.0425 2. 45% 3. 87.5% 4. 14 5. 20% 6. 275 7. The increase is $1,250. The new salary is $6,250. 8. 20% 9. Store A, $800, Store B, $1,200, Store C, $2,000

Review Problems for Chapter 5

1 Change 14.75% to a decimal _____

2 Change 0.625 to a percent _____

3 Change 150% to a decimal _____

4 Change 0.0075 to a percent _____

5 Change 0.06% to a decimal _____

6 Change $\frac{2}{5}$ to a percent _____

7 16% of 70 = _____

8 250% of 60 = _____

9 25% of _____ = 45

10 100% of _____ = 70

11 _____ % of 40 = 35

12 _____ % of 90 = 144

13 Sales were $100,000 two months ago and increased by 20% last month. How much were sales last month? _____

14 Sales were $120,000 last month and decreased by 20% this month. How much were sales this month? _____

15 Expenses were $200,000 two years ago and $400,000 last year. What was the percent increase last year? _____

16 Expenses were $400,000 last year and $200,000 this year. What was the percent decrease this year? _____

17 Peggy Covey owns a nursery. This year she sold 195 more rose bushes than she did last year. This represents a 12% increase over the previous year. How many rose bushes did Peggy's nursery sell last year? _____

18 Jim Dukes manages Internet sales for a company that started selling its product over the Internet two years ago. Last year, company sales over the Internet were only about $500,000. This year, sales were $1,625,000. Calculate the company's percent increase in Internet sales this year. _____

19 Ken Chard is a bank teller. When he started this morning, his cash drawer had coins worth $86. The coins represented only 2.5% of all the money that Ken had in his cash drawer. What was the total value of all this money? _____

20 Nancy McGraw is an orthopedic surgeon. Last winter, Dr. McGraw performed 50 emergency surgeries. Thirty-two of those surgeries were the result of ski injuries. What percent of Dr. McGraw's emergency surgeries were the result of ski injuries? _____

Answers to the Self-Check can be found in Appendix B at the back of the text.

Assignment 5.1: Base, Rate, and Percentage

Name _____

Date _____ Score _____

A (20 points) Change the percents to decimals. Change the nonpercents to percents. Write all answers without using fractions, rounding if necessary. (1 point for each correct answer)

1. $31\% =$ _____

2. $100\% =$ _____

3. $3\frac{1}{3}\% =$ _____

4. $0.59 =$ _____

5. $3 =$ _____

6. $33\frac{2}{3}\% =$ _____

7. $0.15 =$ _____

8. $0.3 =$ _____

9. $1\frac{3}{4} =$ _____

10. $0.7\% =$ _____

11. $224.5\% =$ _____

12. $0.0003\% =$ _____

13. $0.52 =$ _____

14. $2\frac{1}{4}\% =$ _____

15. $0.08\frac{1}{4} =$ _____

16. $\dfrac{5}{8} =$ _____

17. $4.0 =$ _____

18. $0.000025 =$ _____

19. $0.01\% =$ _____

20. $1,000\% =$ _____

_____

Score for A (20)

B (30 points) In the following problems, find each Percentage amount. (2 points for each correct answer)

21. 0.375% of $56 =$ _21_

22. 7.5% of $1,200 =$ _90_

23. 100% of $11.17 =$ _11.17_

24. 87.5% of $48 =$ _42_

25. 40% of $0.85 =$ _0.34_

26. $\frac{1}{2}\%$ of $8,000 =$ _40.00_

27. 25% of $\$1.16 =$ _29¢_

28. 120% of $\$45 =$ _54._

29. 2.5% of $\$66 =$ _1.65_

30. 12.5% of $\$160 =$ _$20_

31. 8% of $200 =$ _16.00_

32. 50% of $0.36 =$ _0.09 0.18¢_

33. 187.5% of $40 =$ _75.00_

34. $2\frac{1}{2}\%$ of $\$500 =$ _12.50_

35. 0.2% of $480 =$ _0.96¢_

0.25

_____

Score for B (30)

C **(50 points)** In each of the following problems, find the Percentage amount, the Rate, or the Base amount. Write rates as percents. Round dollars to the nearest cent. (2 points for each correct answer)

36. 25% of ___240___ = $60

60 ÷ .25
p

37. ___20%___ of $35 = $7

38. _____ of 1.12 = 1.4   .014
.0112

39. _____ of 14.2 = 28.4

40. _____ of 400 = 14

41. 80% of _____ = $0.96

42. 3.75% of ___720___ = 27

P ÷ R = B

43. ___1.50%___ of 80 = 120

120 ÷ 80

44. _____ of 0.056 = 0.014

45. 175% of ___48___ = $84

1.75 × = 84

46. 2.5% of $2,820 = _____

47. 0.25% of ___8000.___ = $20

48. _____ of $364.80 = $127.68

49. 62.5% of ___56___ = 35

.625
35 ÷

50. 0.025% of $16,400 = _____

51. 140% of _____ = 672

52. 300% of _____ = $82.50

53. _____ of 5.4 = 2.16

54. ___11544.1___ of $1,480 = $10,064

55. 15% of $140 = ___21___

.15 × 140

56. 180% of $90 = ___162.00___

1.8 × 90

57. _____ of 85 = 136

58. 1¼% of _____ = $8.25

59. 12% of ___25___ = 3

.12 ÷ 3

60. _____ of 3.2 = 0.704

_____
Score for C (50)

Assignment 5.2: Rate of Increase and Rate of Decrease

Name _____

Date _____   Score _____

A **(40 points) Calculate the missing values. ($2\frac{1}{2}$ points for each correct answer)**

1. Decreasing the base value of 280 by 25% gives the new value _____ .

2. Increasing the base value of 240 by 40% gives the new value _____ .

3. Start with 75, decrease it by 60%, and end up with _____ .

4. Start with 80, increase it by 14%, and end up with _____ .

5. Sales were $8,000 last month and increased by 4% this month. Sales were _____ this month.

6. Profits were $72,600 last month, but decreased by 5% this month. Profits were _____ this month.

7. Base value = 272; increase = 100%; new (final) value = _____

8. Base value = 250; decrease = 100%; new (final) value = _____

9. A $17 increase is 10% of the base value of _____ .

10. A decrease of 60 units is 25% of the base value of _____ units.

11. The price decreased from $450 to $378; the percent decrease was _____ .

12. Production increased from 8,000 units to 10,000 units; the percent increase was _____ .

13. $300 is what percent less than $400? _____

14. 480 is what percent greater than 160? _____

15. Sales were $500,000 in June but only $400,000 in July. The rate of decrease was _____ .

16. Profits were $12,600 last month and $12,000 the previous month. The rate of increase was _____ .

Score for A (40) _____

B (30 points) The following table shows the volumes of various items sold by Clyde's Auto Parts during the past two years. Compute the amount of change and the rate of change between this year and last year. Compute the rates to the nearest tenth of a percent. If the amount and rate are increases, write a + in front of them; if they are decreases, enclose them in parentheses (). (1 point for each correct amount; 2 points for each correct rate)

Clyde's Auto Parts
Volume Sold (number of units)

Description of Item	This Year	Last Year	Amount of Change	Rate of Change
17. Batteries	516	541	_____	_____
18. Brake fluid (pints)	1,781	1,602	_____	_____
19. Coolant (gallons)	2,045	1,815	_____	_____
20. Headlight lamps	5,829	5,294	_____	_____
21. Oil (quarts)	13,428	14,746	_____	_____
22. Mufflers	639	585	_____	_____
23. Shock absorbers	1,224	1,068	_____	_____
24. Tires, auto	6,742	5,866	_____	_____
25. Tires, truck	2,115	1,805	_____	_____
26. Wiper blades	1,927	2,342	_____	_____

Score for B (30)

C (30 points) During May and June, Kalman's Paint Store had sales in the amounts shown in the following table. Compute the amount of change and the rate of change between May and June. Compute the rates of change to the nearest tenth of a percent. If the amount and rate are increases, write a + in front of them; if they are decreases, enclose them in parentheses (). (1 point for each correct amount; 2 points for each correct rate)

Kalman's Paint Store
Volume Sold (in dollars)

Description of Item	June	May	Amount of Change	Rate of Change
27. Brush, 2″ wide	$ 611.14	$ 674.67	_____	_____
28. Brush, 3″ wide	564.20	512.51	_____	_____
29. Brush, 4″ wide	429.87	374.27	_____	_____
30. Drop cloth, 9 × 12	143.50	175.66	_____	_____
31. Drop cloth, 12 × 15	174.29	151.55	_____	_____
32. Paint, latex (gal)	56,320.94	52,245.77	_____	_____
33. Paint, latex (qt)	5,072.35	4,878.96	_____	_____
34. Paint, oil (gal)	7,308.44	7,564.27	_____	_____
35. Paint, oil (qt)	4,724.68	4,465.67	_____	_____
36. Paint scraper	274.10	238.82	_____	_____

Score for C (30)

Assignment 5.3: Business Applications

Name _____

Date _____ Score _____

A **(50 points) Solve the following problems. Round dollar amounts to the nearest cent. Round other amounts to the nearest tenth. Write rates as percents to the nearest tenth of a percent. (5 points for each correct answer)**

1. Horton Mfg. shipped 5,500 portable generators in May. Clients eventually returned 4% of the generators. How many of the generators shipped in May were eventually returned? _____

2. Julie Horton, CEO of Horton Mfg., wants the company to reduce the percent of generators that customers return. In June, the company shipped 6,000 generators, and 150 were eventually returned. What percent of the June shipment was eventually returned? _____

3. By July of the following year, Horton Mfg. had reduced the percent of generators returned to 2% of the number shipped. If 130 generators were returned from that month's shipment, how many had been shipped? _____

4. A European food importer, Mateski Products, imports 25% of its vinegars from France, 40% from Italy, and the rest from Spain. The total value of all the vinegars that it imports is $1,118,000. What is the value of the vinegars that are imported from Spain? _____

5. Next year, Mateski is planning to import $462,000 worth of vinegars from France, $532,000 worth of vinegars from Italy, and $406,000 worth of vinegars from Spain. If next year's imports occur as currently being planned, what percent of the total imports will be from Italy? _____

6. Rigik Parka Products, Inc., manufactures only parkas for adults and children. Last year, Rigik manufactured all its children's parkas in Asia. Those children's parkas represented 35% of all the Rigik production. If the company made a total of 240,000 parkas, how many children's parkas did it produce? _____

7. This year, Rigik again plans to manufacture all its children's parkas in Asia, and Rigik will expand the children's product line to 40% of the total number of parkas produced. If Rigik plans to produce 112,000 children's parkas, how many parkas does the company plan to produce in total? _____

8. Next year, Rigik plans to keep the percent of children's parkas at 40% but increase the number of children's parkas produced to 125,000. How many parkas does the company plan to produce for adults? (*Hint:* First you need to calculate the total number of all parkas to be produced next year.) _____

9. Ricardo Castíllo is a single father. He tries to save 15% of his monthly salary for his son's education. In August, Ricardo's salary was $4,800. How much should he save to meet his objective? _____

10. In September, Ricardo Castíllo got a promotion and a raise. Because his monthly expenses did not increase very much, Ricardo was able to save more dollars. He saved $1,120, which was 20% of his new salary. How much was Ricardo's new salary? _____

Score for A (50)

B (50 points) Solve the following problems. Round dollar amounts to the nearest cent. Round other amounts to the nearest tenth. Write rates as percents to the nearest tenth of a percent. (5 points for each correct answer)

11. Norman Brewer, a paralegal, will receive a 4% salary increase this month. Hence he will receive $130 more salary this month than he received last month. What was Norman's salary last month? _____

12. Roberta Coke works in the marketing research department of a soft-drink company. Yesterday Roberta received a raise of $375 per month. Roberta now earns 6% more than she did before the raise. How much does she earn now? _____

13. A farmers' market is held downtown every Saturday. The volume has been increasing by about 3% every week. If the volume was $51,400 this week, what should the volume be next week? _____

14. Marcia Almeida works as a sales analyst for a toy manufacturer. She predicts that toy sales will decrease by 5% from May to June. If the amount of the sales decrease is $175,000, what level of sales is she predicting for June? _____

15. Last month, Fred Gerhardt started working as an apprentice machinist. One of his first projects was to reduce the diameter of a metal shaft from 0.180 inch to 0.162 inch. By what percent did he reduce the diameter of the shaft? _____

16. Judy Gregory, a production engineer, was able to increase the efficiency of a manufacturing facility. By doing so, she decreased the cost to manufacture of a commercial quality lawn mower by $18, which was 15% of the former cost. What will be the new reduced cost to manufacture the lawn mower? _____

17. Richard Phipps is the purchasing manager for a janitorial service. He orders all the supplies used by his company. Because of new contracts to clean three new office buildings, Richard ordered an additional $5,000 worth of supplies this month. This was an 8% increase from last month. What was the value of the supplies that Richard ordered last month? _____

18. Grace Yasui owns a gift shop that had sales of $210,000 in October. Because of the Thanksgiving and Christmas holiday seasons, Grace predicts that the shop will have a 125% increase in sales in November. What total sales is Grace predicting for November? _____

19. Suppose that Yasui's Gift Shop had sales of $225,000 in October and then doubled its sales in November to $450,000. What would be the percent increase for November over October? _____

20. Because of Father's Day, Martin's Men's Wear had sales of $450,000 in June. Sales decreased by $225,000 in July. What was the percent decrease in Martin's sales in July? _____

Score for B (50)

Assignment 5.4: Allocation of Overhead

Name

Date   Score

A (20 points) Complete the square feet, percent, and allocation columns below. Round percents to the nearest whole number. (1 point for each correct answer in column 1; 2 points for each correct answer in columns 2 and 3)

1. Gerry Sher owns small restaurants in four different towns: (a) Alleghany, (b) Delwood, (c) Bangor, and (d) Lakeside. She manages all four restaurants from a central office that she maintains at the Alleghany restaurant. Monthly office expenses are allocated among the four restaurants based on the floor space of each. In the following table, complete the allocation table for monthly expenses of $15,000.

Store	Space Occupied	Square Feet	Percent of Total	Allocation of Expense
(a) Alleghany	40 ft × 30 ft	_____	_____	_____
(b) Delwood	40 ft × 45 ft	_____	_____	_____
(c) Bangor	70 ft × 30 ft	_____	_____	_____
(d) Lakeside	60 ft × 40 ft	_____	_____	_____
Total		7,500	100%	$15,000

Score for A (20)

B (16 points) Complete the percent and allocation columns in the following table. Before computing the allocation, round each percent to the nearest whole number. (2 points for each correct answer)

2. Diane Thrift owns a personnel services company that provides temporary employees in four employment categories: (a) office/clerical; (b) hotel/motel; (c) restaurant/dining; and (d) hospital/medical. Ms. Thrift has organized her company into four departments, one for each category. The lease expense for her company office space is $9,600 per month. She allocates the monthly lease expense among the four departments based on the number of temporary employees in each business category. Calculate the percents and the resulting allocations.

Department	Number of Employees	Percent of Total	Allocation of Rent
(a) Office/clerical	110	_____	_____
(b) Hotel/motel	130	_____	_____
(c) Restaurant/dining	170	_____	_____
(d) Hospital/medical	90	_____	_____
Total	500	100%	$9,600

Score for B (16)

C (64 points) The following situations provide practice in allocating monthly overhead expenses at a central office. From the information given in the following table, complete the allocations indicated in problems 3 through 6. Remember: Answers for each problem should sum to the total monthly overhead expense. (4 points for each correct answer)

Monthly Overhead Expense		Basis of Allocation	Location				
			East	West	North	South	TOTAL
Insurance	$20,000	Square feet	19,200	9,600	14,400	16,800	60,000
Utilities	18,000	Machine hours worked	32,000	12,000	20,000	16,000	80,000
Rent	26,000	Units produced	10,200	7,800	5,700	6,300	30,000
Maintenance	22,000	Number of employees	105	75	30	90	300

3. Allocate insurance expense based on the number of square feet at each location.

East _____ ; West _____ ; North _____ ; South _____ Check.

4. Allocate utilities expense based on the number of machine hours worked in each location.

East _____ ; West _____ ; North _____ ; South _____ Check.

5. Allocate rent expense based on the units produced at each location.

East _____ ; West _____ ; North _____ ; South _____ Check.

6. Allocate maintenance expense based on the number of employees at each location.

East _____ ; West _____ ; North _____ ; South _____ Check.

Score for C (64)

Commissions

6

Learning Objectives

By studying this chapter and completing all assignments, you will be able to:

Learning Objective **1**   Compute sales commissions and gross pay.

Learning Objective **2**   Compute graduated sales commissions.

Learning Objective **3**   Compute sales and purchases for principals.

A **commission** is a payment to an employee or to an agent for performing a business transaction or service. The most familiar type of commission is that received by a salesperson. Many companies have employees who are paid either totally or partially on a commission basis. People who sell insurance, real estate, and automobiles are typically in this category.

For a business owner, one advantage of using the commission method to pay employees is that the commission is an incentive. Employees are paid on the basis of the volume of business they produce for the company. They can earn more by being more productive.

Besides typical salespersons, other businesspeople provide selling and buying services. These include brokers, agents, and commission merchants, all of whom are paid a commission for their services. The person for whom the services are provided is called the **principal.** A commission merchant will normally take actual possession of the merchandise and make the sales transaction in his or her name. A **broker,** however, will usually make the transaction in the principal's name and will not take possession of the merchandise.

Computing Sales Commissions and Gross Pay

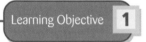

Learning Objective **1**

Compute sales commissions and gross pay.

A sales commission paid to a salesperson is usually a stated percent of the dollar value of the goods or services sold. Whether the commission is based on the wholesale or retail value of the goods will depend on the type of business and merchandise sold. The rate used to calculate the commission also will vary among different businesses. In some companies, the salesperson receives both some salary and a commission.

STEPS to Compute Commission and Total Pay

1. Multiply the commission rate by the amount sold to get the commission amount.
2. If there is a salary, add it to the commission amount to get the total gross pay.

EXAMPLE A

Judy Ahlquist sells yachts and marine equipment for Bay Area Marine Sales. She receives a base salary of $5,000 per month and earns a commission that is 2% of the value of all boating equipment that she sells during the month. Find her commission and total pay during September, a month in which she sold $132,000 worth of equipment.

STEP 1 2% × $132,000 = 0.02 × $132,000 = $2,640 commission

STEP 2 $2,640 commission + $5,000 base salary = $7,640 total pay

Total sales are often called **gross sales.** Commissions are normally paid on **net sales,** which are calculated by subtracting the amount of any returned goods, canceled orders, or other sales expenses. The reason for using net sales is to protect the company from loss or possible fraud. Suppose in example A, that Bay Area Marine Sales pays a 2% commission whether or not any goods are ever returned. Judy Ahlquist's commission on $132,000 worth of merchandise is $2,640. But if all of the merchandise is eventually returned, or if the orders are all canceled, the company would lose $2,640 by paying the commission.

> **STEPS** **to Compute Commission When a Sale Involves Returned Goods**
>
> 1. Subtract the value of the returned goods (or canceled orders) from the total sales to determine net sales.
> 2. Multiply the commission rate by net sales to get the commission amount.

● **EXAMPLE B**

Carl Gowey is a salesperson for Englewood Office Supply. He works on a commission-only basis—he receives a commission of 3.5% on his weekly sales, but no base salary. What are Carl's commission and total pay during a week when he sells $44,000 worth of office products, but one of his customers cancels an order for $5,000?

JEFF GREENBERG/ALAMY

STEP 1 $44,000 − $5,000 = $39,000 net sales

STEP 2   3.5% × $39,000 = 0.035 × $39,000 = $1,365 commission

                 Total Pay = $1,365, because he is paid on a commission-only basis

---

☑ **CONCEPT CHECK 6.1**

Compute the commission and gross pay for Pattie Burrows, who is paid a $1,800 salary and earns a 4% commission. Total sales were $88,000, but there were returns of $6,000.

$88,000 − $6,000 = $82,000 net sales

$$4\% \times \$82,000 = 0.04 \times \$82,000 = \$3,280 \quad \text{commission}$$

$$\underline{+\ 1,800} \quad \text{salary}$$

$$\$5,080 \quad \text{gross pay}$$

 # Computing Graduated Sales Commissions

Commission plans provide incentives for employees because employees can earn more money by selling more products. A company can provide additional incentives for even greater productivity by using **graduated commission rates.** As the level of sales increases, so does the commission rate.

> Learning Objective **2**
>
> Compute graduated sales commissions.

> **STEPS** **to Compute Commission Under a Graduated Rate Plan**
>
> 1. Compute the dollar amount at each rate level by using subtraction.
> 2. Multiply each level's sales dollars by that level's commission rate.
> 3. Add the products computed in Step 2 to determine the total commission.

EXAMPLE C

In addition to a salary, Donna Wu has a monthly commission plan under which she receives 2% on the first $40,000 of sales during the month and 3% on sales above $40,000. If Donna has sales of $75,000 during May, compute her commission for May.

STEP 1
$75,000 total sales
− 40,000 at 2%
$35,000 at 3%

STEP 2
STEP 3

→ $40,000 × 0.02 = $ 800
35,000 × 0.03 = + 1,050
Total commission = $1,850

EXAMPLE D

Assume that Donna has a monthly commission plan under which she receives 2% on the first $40,000 of sales during the month, 3% on sales from $40,000 to $80,000, and 4% on all sales over $80,000. If Donna has sales of $126,000 during April compute her commission for April.

STEP 1
$126,000 total sales
− 40,000 at 2%
$ 86,000
− 40,000 at 3%
$ 46,000 at 4%

STEP 2
STEP 3

→ $40,000 × 0.02 = $ 800
→ 40,000 × 0.03 = 1,200
→ 46,000 × 0.04 = + 1,840

Total commission = $3,840

The same graduated incentive plan can be defined in terms of bonus rates. The calculations are similar.

EXAMPLE E

Les Flake has a monthly commission plan under which he receives 2% on all sales during the month. If Les has sales above $40,000, he receives a bonus of 1% of everything over $40,000. If he sells more than $80,000, he receives a "super bonus" of an additional 1% of everything over $80,000. What was Les's commission for a month during which he sold $126,000?

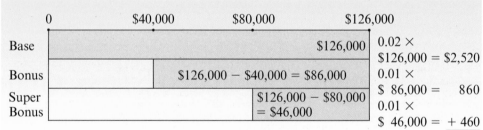

	0	$40,000	$80,000	$126,000	
Base	$126,000				$0.02 \times$ $126,000 = \$2,520$
Bonus		$126,000 − $40,000 = $86,000			$0.01 \times$ $\$ 86,000 = 860$
Super Bonus			$126,000 − $80,000 = $46,000		$0.01 \times$ $\$ 46,000 = + 460$

Total commission (add the three commission amounts) = $3,840

Observe that both example D and example E had a total commission of $3,840 on sales of $126,000. The two graduated incentive plans are identical except for the manner in which they are defined and calculated.

AP IMAGES

Compute the total commission on sales of $184,000. The commission is graduated: 2% on sales to $50,000, 3% on sales from $50,000 to $100,000, and 4% on sales above $100,000.

$184,000 - $50,000 - $50,000 = $84,000

2% × $50,000 = 0.02 × $50,000	=	$1,000	
3% × $50,000 = 0.03 × $50,000	=	1,500	
4% × $84,000 = 0.04 × $84,000	=	3,360	
Total commission	=	$5,860	

Computing Sales and Purchases for Principals

A producer may send goods to an agent, often called a **commission merchant,** for sale at the best possible price. Such a shipment is a **consignment.** The party who sends the shipment is the **consignor;** the party to whom it is sent—that is, the commission merchant—is the **consignee.**

Compute sales and purchases for principals.

Whatever amount the commission merchant gets for the consignment is the **gross proceeds.** The commission amount is generally a certain percentage of the gross proceeds. Sometimes it is a certain amount per unit of weight or measure of the goods sold. The commission and any other sales expenses (e.g., transportation, advertising, storage, and insurance) are the **charges.** The charges are deducted from the gross proceeds. The resulting amount, which is sent to the consignor, is the **net proceeds.**

● **EXAMPLE F**

Kathy Palmer, owner of Willowbrook Farms, has been trying to sell a used livestock truck and a used tractor. Unsuccessful after 3 months, Ms. Palmer consigns the items to Acme Equipment Brokers. They agree on commission rates of 6% of the gross proceeds from the truck and 9% of the gross proceeds from the tractor. Acme sells the truck for $42,500 and the tractor for $78,600. Acme also pays $610 to deliver the truck and $835 to deliver the tractor. What are the net proceeds due Willowbrook Farms from the sale of the equipment?

Truck:	Commission: 0.06 × $42,500 = $2,550		Gross proceeds:	$42,500
	Freight:	+ 610	less charges	− 3,160
	Total charges	$3,160	Net Proceeds:	$39,340
Tractor:	Commission: 0.09 × $78,600 = $7,074		Gross proceeds:	$78,600
	Freight:	+ 835	less charges	− 7,909
	Total charges	$7,909	Net proceeds:	$70,691

$39,340 + $70,691 = $110,031 Total Net Proceeds

Along with a check for the net proceeds, the commission merchant sends the consignor a form known as an **account sales.** It is a detailed statement of the amount of the sales and the various deductions. Figure 6-1 shows a typical account sales form. Notice that the left side and the right side of the form balance at $121,100. The two sides should always balance.

Figure 6-1 | Account Sales

ACME EQUIPMENT BROKERS

August 16, 20--   NO. 67324

309 Sule Road, Wilbraham, MA 01095-2073

BELOW ARE ACCOUNT SALES OF Consignment No. 876

RECEIVED August 1, 20--

and sold for account of Same

NAME Willowbrook Farms
ADDRESS 127 N. Kaye
Albany, GA   31704-5606

DATE	CHARGES	AMOUNT	DATE	SALES	AMOUNT
Aug. 16	Freight (truck)	$ 610	Aug. 10	Truck	$42,500
	6% Commission (truck)	2,550			
	Net proceeds (truck)	39,340	13	Tractor	78,600
				Gross proceeds	$121,100
16	Freight (tractor)	835			
	9% Commission (tractor)	7,074			
	Net proceeds (tractor)	70,691			
	Total	$121,100			

When commission merchants purchase goods for their principals, the price they pay for the merchandise is the **prime cost.** The prime cost and all charges are the **gross cost,** which is the cost the principal pays.

● **EXAMPLE G**

Asia-Pacific Tours commissioned Specialty Marketing Group to purchase 10,000 vinyl travel bags that will be labeled with Asia-Pacific's logo and used as promotional items. For this size order, Specialty Marketing purchased the bags for $4.29 each. Charges included the commission, which was 6% of the prime cost; storage, $125; and freight, $168. What is the gross cost that Asia-Pacific should pay to Specialty Marketing?

$$\begin{array}{ll} \$\quad 4.29 \\ \underline{\times\ 10,000} \quad \text{units} \\ \$\ 42,900 \quad \text{prime cost} \end{array} \qquad \begin{array}{ll} \$42,900 \quad \text{prime cost} \\ \underline{\times\ 0.06} \\ \$\ 2,574 \quad \text{commission} \end{array}$$

$2,574 commission + $125 storage + $168 freight = $2,867 charges

$42,900 prime cost + $2,867 charges = $45,767 gross cost

An **account purchase** is a detailed statement from the commission merchant to the principal. It shows the cost of goods purchased, including charges. Figure 6-2 shows a typical account purchase, for the transaction in example G.

Figure 6-2 | **Account Purchase**

SPECIALTY MARKETING GROUP

4445 Mission Street
San Francisco, CA 94112

ACCOUNT PURCHASE

NO. 1311

Bought on Consignment for

October 26   20 --
Asia-Pacific Tours
7300 Harbor Place
San Francisco, CA 94104

DATE	DESCRIPTION	CHARGES	AMOUNT
Oct. 23	10,000 units stock #T805 @ $4.29		$42,900.00
23	6% commission	$2,574.00	
	Storage	125.00	
	Freight	168.00	2,867.00
	Gross Cost		$45,767.00

✔ CONCEPT CHECK 6.3

a. Compute the commission and the net proceeds on a consignment sale of $7,500. The commission rate is 6%, local delivery charges are $427.72, and storage charges are $145.
$6\% \times \$7,500 = 0.06 \times \$7,500 = \$450$ commission
$\$7,500 - \$450 - \$427.72 - \$145 = \$6,477.28$ net proceeds

b. Compute the commission and gross cost on a $12,500 purchase for a principal. The commission rate is 7%, air freight is $138.70, and local delivery charges are $64.60.
$7\% \times \$12,500 = 0.07 \times \$12,500 = \$875$ commission
$\$12,500 + \$875 + \$138.70 + \$64.60 = \$13,578.30$ gross cost

COMPLETE ASSIGNMENTS 6.1 AND 6.2.

Chapter Terms for Review

account purchase	consignee	gross proceeds
account sales	consignment	gross sales
broker	consignor	net proceeds
charges	graduated	net sales
commission	commission rates	prime cost
commission merchant	gross cost	principal

Try Microsoft® Excel

Try working the problems using the Microsoft Excel templates found on the companion website. Solutions for the problems are also shown on the companion website.

THE BOTTOM LINE

Summary of chapter learning objectives:

Learning Objective	Example
6.1 Compute sales commissions and gross pay.	1. Sharon Hilliard, a salesperson, earns a $3,750 salary and a 1.75% commission. Find her commission and gross pay when sales are $164,000 and returns are $5,600.
6.2 Compute graduated sales commissions.	2. Melvin Maugh has a graduated commission rate: 1% on sales up to $100,000; 2% on sales from $100,000 to $200,000; and 2.5% on sales above $200,000. Find his commission when his sales are $318,000.
6.3 Compute sales and purchases for principals.	3. A broker sells a principal's merchandise at a gross sales price of $15,600 at a commission rate of 3.5%. There are sales costs of $300 for storage and $119 for delivery. Find the commission and net proceeds.
	4. A commission merchant purchases merchandise for a principal at a prime cost of $8,400. The commission rate is 8%, air freight is $139, and local delivery is $75. Find the commission and gross cost.

Answers: 1. Commission: $2,772; Gross pay: $6,522 2. $5,950 3. Commission: $546; Net proceeds: $14,635 4. Commission: $672; Gross cost: $9,286

Review Problems for Chapter 6

In problems 1–4, compute both the commission and the total pay based on the information given.

1 Salary, $3,000; commission rate, 6%; total sales, $58,000; returns, $0

    a. Commission _____   **b.** Total pay _____

2 Salary, $2,500; commission rate, 5%; total sales, $91,000; returns, $5,000

    a. Commission _____   **b.** Total pay _____

3 Salary, $3,600; commission rate, 4.5%; total sales, $76,000; returns, $6,800

    a. Commission _____   **b.** Total pay _____

4 Salary, $0; commission rate, 8%; total sales, $98,000; returns, $11,425

    a. Commission _____   **b.** Total pay _____

5 Compute the total commission on sales of $160,000 if the commission rates are 3% on the first $100,000 and 5% on everything above $100,000. _____

6 Compute the total commission on sales of $85,000 if the commission rates are 3% on the first $100,000 and 5% on everything above $100,000. _____

7 Compute the total commission on sales of $250,000 if the commission rates are 2% on the first $75,000; then 3% on the next $75,000; and 4% on everything above $150,000. _____

8 Compute the total commission on sales of $135,000 if the commission rates are 2% on the first $75,000; then 3% on the next $75,000; and 4% on everything above $150,000. _____

9 Compute the total commission on sales of $70,000 if the commission rates are 2% on the first $75,000; then 3% on the next $75,000; and 4% on everything above $150,000. _____

10 Compute the total commission on sales of $115,000 if the commission rates are 4% on the first $35,000; then 6% on the next $45,000; and 8% on everything above $80,000. _____

11 Larry Leong is paid 2.5% on all sales. He is also paid a bonus of an additional 1.5% on any sales above $70,000. Calculate Larry's total commission on sales of $120,000. _____

12 Nadia Curto is paid 4% on all sales. She is also paid a bonus of an additional 2% on any sales above $40,000. Calculate Nadia's total commission on sales of $105,000. _____

13 Don Davenport sells used logging equipment on consignment. He charges 20% commission plus expenses. Calculate Don's commission on a log truck he sold for $42,750. _____

14 For the sale in problem 13, Don also paid an additional $290 to deliver the truck to the new owner. Calculate the net proceeds that Don's principal should receive. _____

15 Sue Lyon is a designer who purchases furniture for clients. She charges 15% of the price, plus expenses. Calculate Sue's commission on furniture priced at $21,400. _____

16 For the sale in problem 15, calculate the gross cost to the client if Sue also had expenses of $646.

_____

Answers to the Self-Check can be found in Appendix B at the back of the text.

Assignment 6.1: Commission

Name _____

Date _____   Score _____

Learning Objectives 1 2 3

A **(24 points) Find the commission and the total gross pay. (2 points for each correct answer)**

Employee	Monthly Salary	Commission Rate	Monthly Sales	Commission	Gross Pay
1. Cornelius, Jane	$ 0	8%	$84,500	_____	_____
2. Conway, Sue	3,000	4%	$108,600	_____	_____
3. Aguire, Luis	3,750	5%	$42,000	_____	_____
4. Brandon, Carol	3,275	3.5%	$94,600	_____	_____
5. Rogerro, George	1,800	6%	$64,000	_____	_____
6. Tang, Jonathan	2,800	5%	$68,000	_____	_____

Score for A (24)

B **(36 points) Compute the total commission for the following commission payment plans. (6 points for each correct answer)**

Graduated Commission Rates	Sales	Commission
7. 3% on sales to $60,000 6% on sales above $60,000	$137,000	_____
8. 1% on sales to $200,000 2% on sales above $200,000	$394,000	_____
9. 3% on sales to $80,000 5% on sales above $80,000	$174,000	_____
10. 1% on sales to $75,000 2% on sales from $75,000 to $150,000 3% on sales above $150,000	$240,000	_____
11. 3% on sales to $50,000 4% on sales from $50,000 to $100,000 5% on sales above $100,000	$128,000	_____

12. 2% on sales to $80,000 $156,400 _____
    3% on sales from $80,000 to $160,000
    4% on sales above $160,000

Score for B (36)

C **(20 points) Diane Hoffman is a commission merchant. She charges different commission rates to sell different types of merchandise. During May, she completed the following consignment sales for consignors. Find Diane's commission on each sale and the net proceeds sent to each consignor. (2 points for each correct answer)**

Gross Sales	Comm. Rate	Commission	Local Delivery	Storage	Air Freight	Net Proceeds
13. $38,400	3%	_____	$ 68	$ 0	$183	_____
14. $1,600	4.5%	_____	88	65	0	_____
15. $8,400	6%	_____	284	0	0	_____
16. $14,625	4%	_____	0	0	137	_____
17. $14,100	7%	_____	75	85	112	_____

Score for C (20)

D **(20 points) Angel Guiterez, a commission merchant in Dallas, buys merchandise exclusively for principals. Listed below are five recent transactions. Compute Angel's commission on each purchase and the gross cost. (2 points for each correct answer)**

Prime Cost	Comm. Rate	Commission	Local Delivery	Storage	Air Freight	Gross Cost
18. $16,600	5%	_____	$89	$ 88	$ 0	_____
19. $4,900	11%	_____	0	0	195	_____
20. $7,280	7.5%	_____	43	75	94	_____
21. $4,850	8%	_____	0	110	108	_____
22. $26,450	10%	_____	50	0	246	_____

Score for D (20)

Assignment 6.2: Applications with Commission

Name _____

Date _____ Score _____

A **(56 points) Solve each of the following business application problems involving salespeople who are paid partly or entirely on a commission basis. Solve the problems in order, because some of the questions are sequential. (8 points for each correct answer)**

1. Sa-Lei Loi sells memberships to an athletic club. She receives a monthly salary of $2,150 plus a commission of 15% on new membership fees. What was Sa-Lei's monthly pay for May, when she sold new memberships valued at $27,500? _____

2. Maria Rios sells commercial restaurant supplies and equipment. She is paid on a commission-only basis. She receives 2% for her sales up to $60,000. For the next $90,000 of sales, she is paid 3%, and for any sales above $150,000 she is paid 4%. How much commission would Maria earn in a month when her sales were $195,000? _____

3. Maria Rios (problem 2) is not paid commission on any restaurant supplies or equipment that are later returned. If an item is returned, its price is deducted from Maria's total sales to get her net sales. The commission-only rate is applied to her net sales. Suppose that Maria sold merchandise worth $195,000 but that $40,000 of that was later returned. What would be Maria's commission on net sales? _____

4. Luisa Gomes works for Southeast Appliance Mart. She receives a biweekly salary of $1,500 for which she must sell $20,000 worth of appliances. She also receives a commission of 4% on net sales above $20,000. What will be Luisa's pay for two weeks when her net appliance sales were $42,000? _____

5. Southeast Appliance Mart (problem 4) offers service contracts with all appliance sales. To encourage sales-people such as Luisa to sell more service contracts, the company pays a commission of 20% on all service contracts. What will be her total pay for two weeks when she sells $42,000 worth of appliances and $1,200 worth of service contracts? _____

6. Amin Pesah is a stockbroker for an investment firm that pays Amin a 0.5% commission on all the stocks that he buys and sells for his clients. What will be Amin's commission on 800 shares of Apple stock that is selling for $331.25 per share? _____

7. Michelle Navarra works in telemarketing. Her job is to make telephone calls from a computerized list of names and try to convince people to make an appointment with a life insurance salesperson. Michelle receives 40¢ for each completed telephone call, $7.00 for each appointment made and kept, and 1% of any initial revenue that results from the appointment. How much would Michelle earn if she completed 968 calls, 153 persons made and kept appointments, and $37,600 in revenue resulted from the appointments? _____

Score for A (56)

B **(24 points) Solve each of the following business applications about consignment sales and commission merchants. (8 points for each correct answer)**

8. Kathleen Donaldson is a commission merchant who charges a 15% commission to sell antique furniture from her showroom. Gary Floyd owns antique furniture, which he transports to her showroom where Kathleen sells it for $9,800. Gary agrees to pay Kathleen $265 to have the furniture delivered to the buyer from the showroom. What will be Gary's net proceeds from the sale? _____

9. Suppose, in problem 8, that payment of the $265 delivery expense was Kathleen's responsibility instead of Gary's. Then what would be Kathleen's net earnings from the sale? _____

10. Sandy Kalina makes artistic weavings that are used as wall hangings. She sells her weavings primarily at open-air art shows and street fairs through her agent, Ruth Nielsen. Ruth charges 25% on all sales, plus the fees to operate the sales booths and transportation expenses. After selling at four art shows, Ruth had total sales of $32,800. Each art show charged a booth fee of $500, and Ruth's total transportation expenses were $625. What were Sandy's net proceeds? _____

Score for B (24)

C **(20 points) The following problems involve the purchase of a home. (10 points for each correct answer)**

11. JoAnn Andrews has a condominium that she would like to sell and she asks real estate broker Jerry Weekly to sell it. Jerry, co-owner of Counts/Weekly Real Estate, advises JoAnn that she should be able to sell her condominium for $180,000 and the commission rate for selling it will be 6%. If the condominium sells for the expected price, what will be the total commission amount that JoAnn pays? _____

12. See problem 11. To sell her condominium, JoAnn Andrews must also pay some additional fees for inspections, title insurance, and to record the sale. These fees total $3,500 and are added to the 6% commission. What will JoAnn's net proceeds be from the sale of her $180,000 condominium? _____

Score for C (20)

Discounts

7

Learning Objectives

By studying this chapter and completing all assignments, you will be able to:

| Learning Objective | **1** | Compute trade discounts. |

| Learning Objective | **2** | Compute a series of trade discounts. |

| Learning Objective | **3** | Compute the equivalent single discount rate for a series of trade discounts. |

| Learning Objective | **4** | Compute cash discounts and remittance amounts for fully paid invoices. |

| Learning Objective | **5** | Compute cash discounts and remittance amounts for partially paid invoices. |

When one business sells merchandise to another business, the seller, also called a vendor, often offers two types of discounts: trade discounts and cash discounts. Trade discounts affect the agreed-upon selling price *before* the sale happens. Cash discounts affect the amount actually paid *after* the transaction.

Computing Trade Discounts

Learning Objective **1**

Compute trade discounts.

Manufacturers, distributors, and wholesalers are all **vendors** who want to attract and keep good customers who make repeated, large-volume, more expensive purchases. To do this, vendors frequently offer **trade discounts** to these customers who are "in the trade." Trade discounts are usually based on the volume purchased.

For example, Northeast Restaurant Supply gives a 40% discount to The Dancing Dog, a regional chain of 68 sidewalk sandwich carts that primarily sell hot dogs, sausage sandwiches, and giant pretzels. Another Northeast customer is Sarah Watterman, founder and proprietor of Gideon's Bagels & Bialys. Sarah's business is still small. She bakes her products between 10 p.m. and 3 a.m. in oven space that she leases from another bakery. Northeast gives Sarah only a 25% discount because she doesn't do as much business with Northeast as The Dancing Dog does. Northeast also sells to people who are "not in the trade." These retail customers pay the regular **list price,** or full price without any trade discount.

Large restaurant chains such as McDonald's and Burger King can go directly to the manufacturer for most items or even do their own manufacturing. They can have items manufactured to their exact specifications for a contracted price. They reduce their costs by eliminating the distributors (the "middle men").

The two traditional methods for computing trade discounts are the discount method and the complement method. You can use both methods to find the **net price** that a distributor will charge the customer after the discount. The **discount method** is useful when you want to know both the net price and the actual amount of the trade discount. The **complement method** is used to find only the net price. It gets its name because you use the **complement rate,** which is 100% minus the discount rate. Each method has only two steps.

STEPS **to Compute Net Price with the Discount Method**

1. Multiply the discount rate by the list price to get the discount amount:
Discount = Trade discount rate × List price

2. Subtract the discount from the list price to get the net price:
Net price = List price − Discount

▶ EXAMPLE A

Northeast Restaurant Supply sells a set of stainless steel trays to Gideon's Bagels. The list price is $120, and Gideon qualifies for a 25% trade discount. Compute the net price using the discount method.

STEP 1   Discount = 0.25 × $120 = $30

STEP 2   Net price = $120 − $30 = $90

EXAMPLE B

Using the data in example A, compute the net price, using the complement method.

STEP 1 Complement rate = 100% − 25% = 75%

STEP 2 Net price = 0.75 × $120 = $90

✔ CONCEPT CHECK 7.1

a. Compute the trade discount amount and the net price, using the discount method.

List price = $240   Trade discount = 30%
Discount amount = 0.30 × $240 = $72
Net price = $240 − $72 = $168

b. Compute the complement rate and the net price, using the complement method.

List price = $240   Trade discount = 30%
Complement rate = 100% − 30% = 70%
Net price = 0.70 × $240 = $168

Computing a Series of Trade Discounts

Learning Objective **2**

Compute a series of trade discounts.

A distributor or manufacturer may give additional discounts to customers who actually buy larger volumes. Suppose that Northeast Restaurant Supply gives all food preparation businesses a 25% discount for being in the trade. However, if one business buys twice as much from Northeast, it may be rewarded with additional discounts. For example, Gideon's Bagels may receive its first discount of 25% automatically. Then, Gideon's gets an additional 20% discount if its accumulated purchases were between $10,000 and $25,000 during the previous year and another 10% if accumulated purchases were more than $25,000 during the previous year. Therefore, Gideon's Bagels could have discounts of 25%, 20%, and 10%, called a **series of discounts.**

Both the discount method and the complement method can be used to compute the net price for a series of discounts. *The two methods are the same as shown previously, except that the steps are repeated for each discount in the series.* For example, if there are three discounts, repeat the steps three times. Apply the first **discount rate** to the list price. For the second and third discounts, compute intermediate prices and then apply the discount rates to them.

EXAMPLE C

Northeast Restaurant Supply sells a set of mixing bowls with a list price of $200. Gideon's Bagels qualifies for the series of discounts: 25%, 20%, 10%. Compute the net price using the discount method.

	First Discount	**Second Discount**	**Third Discount**
STEP 1	$0.25 \times \$200 = \$50$	$0.20 \times \$150 = \$30$	$0.10 \times \$120 = \$12$
STEP 2	$\$200 - \$50 = \$150$	$\$150 - \$30 = \$120$	$\$120 - \$12 = \$108$

EXAMPLE D

Using the data in example C, calculate the net price using the complement method.

	First Discount	**Second Discount**	**Third Discount**
STEP 1	$100\% - 25\% = 75\%$	$100\% - 20\% = 80\%$	$100\% - 10\% = 90\%$
STEP 2	$0.75 \times \$200 = \$150$	$0.80 \times \$150 = \$120$	$0.90 \times \$120 = \$108$

COMPLEMENT METHOD SHORTCUT

When using complement rates, the buyer may not need to know all of the intermediate prices. If not, an efficient shortcut is to multiply the list price by all of the complement rates successively.

EXAMPLE E

Repeat example D, using the shortcut. The list price is $200, and the discounts are 25%, 20%, and 10%. The complement rates are 75%, 80%, and 90%.

Net price = $\$200 \times 0.75 \times 0.80 \times 0.90 = \$108$

Note: Remember that there should be *no rounding* until you reach the final net price. Then round it to the nearest cent.

✔ CONCEPT CHECK 7.2

a. A wholesaler offers a series of trade discounts: 30%, 25%, and 10%. Find each of the discount amounts and the final net price on a $1,500 purchase.

First discount amount:	$\$1,500 \times 0.30 = \$450$
Second discount amount:	$\$1,500 - \$450 = \$1,050; \$1,050 \times 0.25 = \$262.50$
Third discount amount:	$\$1,050 - \$262.50 = \$787.50; \$787.50 \times 0.10 = \$78.75$
Net price:	$\$787.50 - \$78.75 = \$708.75$

b. A series of trade discounts is 30%, 25%, and 10%. Find each of the complement rates, and use the shortcut to calculate the final net price on a purchase of $1,500.

First complement rate:	$100\% - 30\% = 70\%$
Second complement rate:	$100\% - 25\% = 75\%$
Third complement rate:	$100\% - 10\% = 90\%$
Net price:	$\$1,500 \times 0.70 \times 0.75 \times 0.90 = \$708.75$

Computing the Equivalent Single Discount Rate

Suppose that a Northeast competitor, New England Food Service, offers a single discount of 45% to Gideon's Bagels. How does that rate compare to the series of discounts from Northeast, 25%, 20%, and 10%? Sarah, or Gideon's accountant, could check by calculating the **equivalent single discount rate,** which is the single discount rate that can be used in place of two or more trade discount rates to determine the same discount amount.

The most efficient way to find the single discount rate that is equivalent to a series of discounts is similar to the shortcut used in example E.

Learning Objective **3**

Compute the equivalent single discount rate for a series of trade discounts.

STEPS **to Compute the Equivalent Single Discount Rate**

1. Compute the complement of each rate.
2. Multiply all the complement rates (as decimals), and then write the product as a percent.
3. Subtract the product (Step 2) from 100% to get the equivalent single discount rate.

EXAMPLE F

Find the equivalent single discount rate for Northeast's series of discounts: 25%, 20%, and 10%.

STEP 1
First complement rate	$= 100\% - 25\% = 75\%$
Second complement rate	$= 100\% - 20\% = 80\%$
Third complement rate	$= 100\% - 10\% = 90\%$

STEP 2 Product of complements $= 0.75 \times 0.80 \times 0.90 = 54\%$

STEP 3 Equivalent single discount $= 100\% - 54\% = 46\%$

✔ CONCEPT CHECK 7.3

A series of trade discounts is 50%, 30%, and 10%. Find the three complement rates and then find the equivalent single trade discount rate.

Complement rates: $100\% - 50\% = 50\%$, $100\% - 30\% = 70\%$, $100\% - 10\% = 90\%$

Product of the complement rates: $0.50 \times 0.70 \times 0.90 = 0.315$, or 31.5%

Equivalent single discount rate: $100\% - 31.5\% = 68.5\%$

COMPLETE ASSIGNMENT 7.1.

Computing Cash Discounts for Fully Paid Invoices

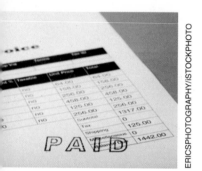

ERICSPHOTOGRAPHY/iSTOCKPHOTO

Learning Objective **4**

Compute cash discounts and remittance amounts for fully paid invoices.

When a vendor sells merchandise to a buyer, the vendor usually wants to receive its payment quickly. However, some buyers often try to delay making the payment as long as possible. Vendors can encourage early payment by offering a **cash discount;** they can discourage late payment by assessing an extra interest payment; or they can do both. These stipulations are called the **terms of payment,** or simply the *terms.* The terms describe details about cash discounts and/or penalty periods.

After shipping merchandise to a buyer, the vendor usually sends a document called an invoice, requesting payment. An **invoice** lists each item, its cost, and the total cost (including packaging and freight). The invoice also states the terms of payment. The amount the buyer pays is called the **remittance.** The **net purchase amount** is the price of the merchandise actually purchased, including allowances for returns and excluding handling and freight costs.

STEPS **to Compute the Remittance**

1. Multiply the discount rate by the net purchase amount to get the cash discount:

   Cash discount = Discount rate × Net purchase amount

2. Subtract the cash discount from the net purchase amount to get the remittance:

   Remittance = Net purchase amount − Cash discount

Figure 7-1 shows an invoice from National Automotive Supply, which sold car wax to Broadway Motors for $528. The wax will be shipped via UPS, and National will pay for the shipping. The invoice lists terms of 2/10, n/30. The **invoice date,** or the beginning of the discount period, is May 23.

VIDEO

Cash Discounts

Figure 7-1	Sales Invoice

NATIONAL AUTOMOTIVE SUPPLY

INVOICE NO. 782535

SOLD TO Broadway Motors
730 W. Columbia Dr.
Peoria, IL 62170-1184

DATE May 23, 20--
TERMS 2/10, n/30
SHIP VIA UPS

QUANTITY	DESCRIPTION	UNIT PRICE	GROSS AMOUNT	NET AMOUNT
24 gals.	Car wax	$22.00	$528.00	$528.00

The expression *2/10, n/30* means that Broadway Motors can get a 2% discount if it pays the full invoice within 10 days of the invoice date. Ten days after May 23 is June 2, which is called the **discount date.** The 10-day period between May 23 and June 2 is called the **discount period.** The n/30 is short for net 30, which means that if Broadway Motors does not pay within 30 days, National will charge an interest penalty. Thirty days after May 23 is June 22, which is called the **due date.** (See Figure 7-2.)

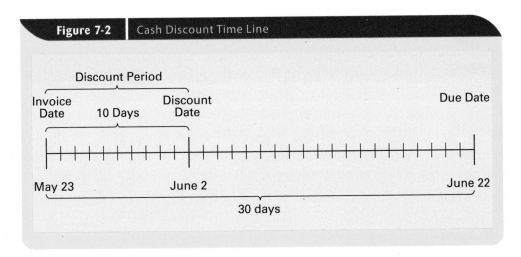

Figure 7-2 | Cash Discount Time Line

● **EXAMPLE G**

Compute the remittance due if Broadway Motors pays National for the $528 invoice amount within the 10-day discount period under the terms 2/10, n/30.

STEP 1   Cash discount = 2% of $528 = 0.02 × $528 = $10.56

STEP 2   Remittance   = $528 − $10.56 = $517.44

All companies do not use exactly the same notation for stating their terms; 2/10, n/30 is also written as 2/10, net 30 or as 2-10, n-30. Likewise, there can be more than one discount rate and discount period. For example 2/5, 1/15, n/30 means that the buyer gets a 2% discount by paying within 5 days, gets a 1% discount by paying between 6 and 15 days, and must pay a penalty after 30 days. To illustrate several different notations, this book will write cash discounts in various ways.

RETURNED MERCHANDISE AND FREIGHT CHARGES

The vendor gives a discount only on merchandise that is actually purchased—the net purchases. For example, there is no discount on returned items. Likewise, there is no discount on charges from a third party, such as freight.

STEPS to Compute the Remittance When There Are Merchandise Returns and/or Freight Charges

1. Net purchase = Invoice amount − Merchandise returns − Freight
2. Cash discount = Discount rate × Net purchase
3. Cost of merchandise = Net purchase − Cash discount
4. Remittance = Cost of merchandise + Freight, if any

● **EXAMPLE H**

National Automotive Supply, a major distributor, sells merchandise to Broadway Motors. The invoice amount is $510, which includes $30 in freight charges. The invoice date is August 13, and the terms are 2/10, n/30. Broadway Motors returns $200 worth of merchandise and pays the balance of the invoice prior to the discount date. Compute the cash discount and the remittance. Also, determine the discount date and due date.

STEP 1	Net purchase = $510 − $200 − $30 = $280
STEP 2	Cash discount = 0.02 × $280 = $5.60
STEP 3	Cost of merchandise = $280 − $5.60 = $274.40
STEP 4	Remittance = $274.40 + $30 = $304.40

Discount date = August 13 + 10 days = August 23
Due date = August 13 + 30 days = September 12

If you do not need to know the actual cost of only the merchandise, you can eliminate Step 3 and calculate the remittance directly:

Remittance = $280.00 − $5.60 + $30.00 = $304.40

There is also a complement method for cash discounts. However, it is not used universally because many businesses prefer to know the amount of the cash discount before deciding whether to pay the invoice early. In the complement method for cash discounts, only Steps 2 and 3 change.

STEPS **to Compute the Remittance with the Complement Method**

1. Net purchase = Invoice amount − Merchandise returns − Freight
2. Complement rate = 100% − Cash discount rate
3. Cost of merchandise = Net purchase × Complement rate
4. Remittance = Cost of merchandise + Freight, if any

● **EXAMPLE I**

Solve example H by using the complement method for cash discounts. The invoice amount is $510, merchandise returns are $200, and freight is $30.

STEP 1	Net purchase = $510 − $200 − $30 = $280
STEP 2	Complement rate = 100% − 2% = 98%
STEP 3	Cost of merchandise = 0.98 × $280 = $274.40
STEP 4	Remittance = $274.40 + $30 = $304.40

a. Use the given information to calculate the discount date, due date, cash discount, and remittance.

Terms:	1/10, n/60	Discount date = August 24 + 10 days = September 3
Invoice date:	August 24	Due date = August 24 + 60 days = October 23
Invoice amount:	$852.43	Net purchases = $852.43 − $187.23 − $47.20 = $618.00
Returned goods:	$187.23	Cash discount = 0.01 × $618 = $6.18
Freight:	$47.20	Remittance = $618 − $6.18 + $47.20 = $659.02

b. Calculate the remittance for the problem in part (a), using the complement method.

Net purchases = $852.43 − $187.23 − $47.20 = $618.00
Complement rate = 100% − 1% = 99%
Cost of merchandise = 0.99 × $618 = $611.82
Remittance = $611.82 + $47.20 = $659.02

Computing Cash Discounts for Partially Paid Invoices

Sometimes a buyer would like to take advantage of a cash discount but wants to pay only part of the invoice within the discount period. If the vendor allows discounts for partial payment, the invoice will be reduced by the amount paid (remittance) plus the amount of the discount. The total of the amount paid plus the amount of cash discount is called the **amount credited** to the buyer's account. To compute the amount credited, you need to know the complement rate: 100% − Discount rate.

Learning Objective **5**

Compute cash discounts and remittance amounts for partially paid invoices.

STEPS to Compute the Unpaid Balance

1. Compute the complement of the discount rate (100% − Discount rate).
2. Compute the amount credited by dividing the dollar amount paid (remittance) by the complement rate.
3. Compute the unpaid balance by subtracting the amount credited (Step 2) from the invoice amount.

EXAMPLE J

Ike's Storage Center is a do-it-yourself center for closet and storage materials. The owner, Larry Eickworth, buys shelving supplies with an invoice price of $484 and terms of 2/10, net 60. Within the 10-day discount period, he sends in a check for $300. With a discount for the partial payment, how much credit should Larry receive, and what will be his new unpaid balance?

STEP 1	Complement rate = 100% − 2% = 98%
STEP 2	Amount credited = $300 ÷ 0.98 = $306.1224, or $306.12
STEP 3	Unpaid balance = $484.00 − $306.12 = $177.88

Note that, in example J, Larry receives $1.00 credit for every $0.98 paid. In other words, the $300 actually remitted is 98% of the total amount credited. We can check this result with multiplication:

Cash discount = 0.02 × $306.12 = $6.1224, or $6.12
Remittance = $306.12 − $6.12 = $300.00

A slightly different situation, which arises less frequently, is when a buyer decides in advance the total amount that he or she wants to have credited to the account. This problem is exactly like the original cash discount problems.

● **EXAMPLE K**

Suppose that Ike's Storage Center buys $484 worth of shelving materials. The terms are 2/10, net 60. It wants to pay enough within the 10-day discount period to reduce the unpaid balance by exactly $300. What amount should Ike's remit to the seller? What will be the new unpaid balance?

STEP 1	Cash discount = 2% × $300 = $6
STEP 2	Remittance = $300 − $6 = $294
STEP 3	Unpaid balance = $484 − $300 = $184

✔ CONCEPT CHECK 7.5

a. An invoice for $476 has terms of 1/15, net 25. How much is the unpaid balance after a $350 remittance is made within the discount period?
Complement rate = 100% − 1% = 99%
Amount credited = $350 ÷ 0.99 = $353.54
Unpaid balance = $476.00 − $353.54 = $122.46

b. An invoice for $476 has terms of 1/15, net 25. What size remittance should be made in order to have a total of $350 credited to the account?
Cash discount = $350 × 0.01 = $3.50
Remittance = $350.00 − $3.50 = $346.50

COMPLETE ASSIGNMENT 7.2.

amount credited

cash discount

complement method

complement rate

discount date

discount method

discount period

discount rate

due date

equivalent single discount rate

invoice

invoice date

list price

net price

net purchase amount

remittance

series of discounts

terms of payment

trade discounts

vendor

Try Microsoft® Excel

Try working the problems using the Microsoft Excel templates found on the companion website. Solutions for the problems are also shown on the companion website.

1. Find the required remittance for goods with a list price of $240, a trade discount of 25%, and a cash discount of 5%.

   The formula is List Price × (1 − Trade Discount %) × (1 − Cash Discount %) = Remittance. Enter the values in the columns as labeled, and enter the formula in the Remittance cell. Format the Remittance cell for Currency with two digits after the decimal point.

List Price	Trade Discount	Cash Discount	Remittance

2. What is the net price for goods with a list price of $2,200, a trade discount of 40%, and another trade discount of 25%?

List Price	Trade Discount	Trade Discount	Net Price

3. What is the net price for goods with a list price of $1,650, a trade discount of 30%, and another trade discount of 20%?

List Price	Trade Discount	Trade Discount	Net Price

THE BOTTOM LINE

Summary of chapter learning objectives:

Learning Objective	Example
7.1 Compute trade discounts.	1. Find the net price on a list price of $280 with a 25% trade discount, using the discount and the complement methods.
7.2 Compute a series of trade discounts.	2. Find the net price on a list price of $800 with a series of trade discounts of 25% and 10%. Use both the discount method and the complement method.
7.3 Compute the equivalent single discount rate for a series of trade discounts.	3. A series of trade discounts is 25%, 20%, 15%. Use complement rates to find the equivalent single discount rate.
7.4 Compute cash discounts and remittance amounts for fully paid invoices.	An invoice is dated May 26 and has terms of 2/10, n/25. The total invoice is $826.44, with $108.12 of returned goods and $67.37 freight. 4. Compute the discount date, due date, cash discount, and remittance. 5. Compute the remittance using the complement rate.
7.5 Compute cash discounts and remittance amounts for partially paid invoices.	An invoice for $500 has terms of 3/5, net 45. 6. Compute the unpaid balance after a $400 payment within the discount period. 7. Compute the remittance required within the discount period in order to have $400 credited to the account.

Review Problems for Chapter 7

In problems 1 and 2, use the discount method to compute the missing terms.

1 List price, $760; trade discount, 25%

    a. Discount amount _____

    b. Net price _____

2 List price, $1,200; trade discounts, 30% and 20%

    a. First discount amount _____

    b. Second discount amount _____

    c. Net price _____

In problems 3 and 4, use the complement method to compute the missing terms.

3 List price, $875; trade discount, 40%

    a. Complement rate _____

    b. Net price _____

4 List price, $1,800; trade discounts, 30% and 15%

    a. First complement rate _____

    b. Second complement rate _____

    c. Net price _____

5 Patty Duncan is a broker of hotel rooms in Europe. To tour directors, she offers a standard trade discount of 40% off the list price. She has additional discounts of 20% and 10%, which are based on the number of tours in a season and the total number of tourists. Compute the equivalent single discount rate for a major tour organizer, Kristi Atchison, who qualifies for all three discounts.

    a. First complement rate _____

    b. Second complement rate _____

    c. Third complement rate _____

    d. Equivalent single discount rate _____

Use the invoice information given in problems 6 and 7 to compute the missing terms.

6 Terms: 2/10, n/30
Invoice Date: July 25
Invoice Amount: $874.55
Freight: 0
Returned Goods: 0

    a. Discount date _____

    b. Due date _____

    c. Discount amount _____

    d. Remittance _____

7 Terms: 3/5, net 45
Invoice Date: December 28
Invoice Amount: $2,480
Freight: $143
Returned Goods: $642

    a. Discount date _____

    b. Due date _____

    c. Complement rate _____

    d. Remittance _____

8 Joyce Thompson purchased some new pieces of office furniture for her Internet consulting firm. The invoice amount was $16,540 with terms of 2/10, net 60 and the discount would apply to any partial payment made within the discount period. Joyce sent in a check for $10,000 by the discount date. Find: (a) the amount credited to Joyce's account _____; and (b) the unpaid balance _____.

Answers to the Self-Check can be found in Appendix B at the back of the text.

Assignment 7.1: Trade Discounts

Name

Date   Score

Learning Objectives **1** **2** **3**

A **(24 points) Problems 1–3: Find the dollar amount of the trade discount and the net price, using the discount method. Problems 4–6: Find the complement rate and the net price, using the complement method. (2 points for each correct answer)**

Trade Discount	List Price	Discount Amount	Net Price
1. 35%	$1,260	_____	_____
2. 20%	$5,328	_____	_____
3. 25%	$8,480	_____	_____

Trade Discount	List Price	Complement Rate	Net Price
4. 30%	$1,670	_____	_____
5. 20%	$6,990	_____	_____
6. 35%	$4,720	_____	_____

_____

Score for A (24)

B **(16 points) Find the amount of each discount in the given series of trade discounts. Then find the net price. Where a discount amount doesn't exist write a dash. (2 points for each correct answer)**

List Price	Trade Discounts	Trade Discount Amounts			Net Price
		First	Second	Third	
7. $2,400	30%, 25%	_____	_____	_____	_____
8. $1,800	40%, 30%, 25%	_____	_____	_____	_____

_____

Score for B (16)

C **(20 points) Find the complement rate for each discount in the given series of trade discounts. Then find the net price, using the complement method. Where a complement rate doesn't exist write a dash. (2.5 points for each correct answer)**

List Price	Trade Discounts	Complement Rates			Net Price
		First	Second	Third	
9. $1,800	40%, 20%	_____	_____	_____	_____
10. $4,000	30%, 25%, 15%	_____	_____	_____	_____

_____

Score for C (20)

D **(20 points) Find the complement rate for each discount in the given series of trade discounts. Then find the equivalent single discount rate, to the nearest $\frac{1}{10}$ of a percent. (2.5 points for each correct answer)**

Trade Discounts	Complement Rates			Equivalent Single Discount Rates
	First	Second	Third	
11. 30%, 20%, 5%	_____	_____	_____	_____
12. 20%, 10%, 5%	_____	_____	_____	_____

_____

Score for D (20)

E **(20 points) Solve each of the following business applications about trade discounts. Use either the discount method or the complement method. (10 points for each correct answer)**

13. Gifford Landscaping, Inc., purchased $425 worth of plants and $180 worth of soil and fertilizer from a garden supply wholesaler. The wholesaler gives Gifford a 20% trade discount on the plants and a 30% trade discount on the other items. Compute the net price that Gifford Landscaping will be required to pay. _____

14. Chet Hackett Roofing is purchasing cedar shingles to reroof a house. The shingles have a list price of $10,400. The Cranhill Roofing Supply Company gives Chet the normal trade discount of 30%. In addition, Cranhill gives Chet two further trade discounts of 20% and 10% because of the large volume of business that the company has done with Cranhill so far this year. What is Chet's net price on the order of cedar shingles? _____

_____

Score for E (20)

Assignment 7.2: Cash Discounts

Name _____

Date _____ Score _____

A **(64 points) For the following problems, find the discount date, the due date, the amount of the cash discount, and the amount of the remittance. (2 points for each correct date and 6 points for each correct amount)**

1. Terms: 3/5, n/25 Discount date: _____
   Invoice date: May 27 Due date: _____
   Invoice amount: $2,875.12 Discount amount: _____
   Remittance: _____

2. Terms: 2-10, n-30 Discount date: _____
   Invoice date: Oct. 25 Due date: _____
   Invoice amount: $636.21 Discount amount: _____
   Freight: $65.00 Remittance: _____

3. Terms: 1.5/15, net 45 Discount date: _____
   Invoice date: Aug. 20 Due date: _____
   Invoice amount: $692.00 Discount amount: _____
   Returned goods: $242.00 Remittance: _____

4. Terms: 2.5/20, n/60 Discount date: _____
   Invoice date: July 29 Due date: _____
   Invoice amount: $1,645.55 Discount amount: _____
   Returned goods: $498.75 Remittance: _____
   Freight: $90.00

Score for A (64)

B **(16 points) For the following problems, find the discount date, the complement rate, and the amount of the remittance. (2 points for each date and rate; 4 points for each correct remittance)**

5. Terms: 2/10, n/35   Discount date: _____

    Invoice date: March 29   Complement rate: _____

    Invoice amount: $582.50   Remittance: _____

6. Terms: 1-15, net 30   Discount date: _____

    Invoice date: Jan. 18   Complement rate: _____

    Invoice amount: $2,457.88   Remittance: _____

    Returned goods: $456.71

    Freight: $62.85

Score for B (16)

C **(20 points) The following problems involve partial payments made within the discount period. Solve for the items indicated. (5 points for each correct answer)**

7. Terms: 4/5, n/20   Amount credited: _____

    Invoice date: Feb. 28   Remittance: $600

    Invoice amount: $981.94   Unpaid balance: _____

8. Terms: 2/15, net 40   Amount credited: _____

    Invoice date: Feb. 15   Remittance: $500

    Invoice amount: $832.90   Unpaid balance: _____

    Returned goods: $186.00

Score for C (20)

Markup

8

Learning Objectives

By studying this chapter and completing all assignments, you will be able to:

| Learning Objective | 1 | Compute the variables in the basic markup formula. |

| Learning Objective | 2 | Compute the markup variables when the markup percent is based on cost. |

| Learning Objective | 3 | Compute markup percent based on cost. |

| Learning Objective | 4 | Compute the markup variables when the markup percent is based on selling price. |

| Learning Objective | 5 | Compute markup percent based on selling price. |

Computing Markup Variables

Some businesses manufacture products and sell them. Other businesses buy products from someone else and then resell them. Both types of businesses must sell their products for more than it costs to produce or purchase them. This price increase is called the **markup.**

Athletes' World is a chain of discount stores that sells sporting equipment and clothing. The store buys running shoes directly from a manufacturer. Suppose that the manufacturer charges $43.00 per pair for one particular type of running shoe. The prorated amount to deliver one pair to the store is $0.50. The total cost of the shoes, with delivery, is $43.50. $43.50 is called the **cost of goods sold,** or just the cost.

If Athletes' World sells the shoes for exactly the cost, $43.50, it will actually lose money on the sale. The store has many other expenses—such as rent, utilities, and salaries—that are not part of the cost of acquiring the shoes. Athletes' World must mark up the selling price far enough above the cost of the shoes to cover all these additional costs—and also leave some profit for the owners.

The total amount that Athletes' World marks up the selling price is called the **dollar markup.** (*Note:* Markup is expressed both in dollars and in percents. To eliminate confusion, in this book we use two separate terms: *dollar markup* and *markup percent.*)

Suppose that the accountants for Athletes' World estimate that $18.80 of additional expenses should be allocated to each pair of athletic shoes. Also, suppose that the store would like a profit of $16.00 on each pair of shoes. Then the total dollar markup that it should give the shoes is $18.80 + $16.00 = $34.80.

To determine the selling price of the shoes, Athletes' World adds the dollar markup to the cost of goods sold (cost), using the basic markup formula:

> Selling price = Cost + Dollar markup = $43.50 + $34.80 = $78.30

Because the dollar markup is the difference between the selling price and the cost of goods sold, it is sometimes useful to rewrite the formula as

> Dollar markup = Selling price − Cost = $78.30 − $43.50 = $34.80

Likewise, cost is the difference between selling price and dollar markup. Thus,

> Cost = Selling price − Dollar markup = $78.30 − $34.80 = $43.50

✔ CONCEPT CHECK 8.1

Compute the missing terms in the three markup formulas:

a. Cost = $384.39; Dollar markup = $195.50

b. Cost = $154.40; Selling price = $392.12

c. Dollar markup = $41.26; Selling price = $93.20

Selling price = Cost + Dollar markup
  = $384.39 + $195.50 = $579.89

Dollar markup = Selling price − Cost
  = $392.12 − $154.40 = $237.72

Cost = Selling price − Dollar markup
  = $93.20 − $41.26 = $51.94

Computing Markup Based on Cost

In the example, Athletes' World computed its markup directly by determining its expenses and the desired profit. However, this method isn't practical when a business has hundreds or thousands of items. Allocating expenses and profit to each item would be too tedious. A more practical method is for the owner, an analyst, or an accountant to analyze prior sales of the company or a similar company. The analyst can look at the costs of goods, additional expenses, and desired profit to determine a percent to use to mark up various items, called the **markup percent.**

One company may use different markup percents for different types of items. For example, an appliance store often performs repair services and sells replacement parts for the appliances it sells. The store may have one markup percent for the actual appliance, a second markup percent for repair services, and a third markup percent for replacement parts.

In Chapter 5 on percents, we introduced three terms: rate, base, and percentage. In this chapter, rate is the *markup percent,* or **markup rate.** Percentage is the *dollar markup.* Determining the base is different because sometimes *cost* is the base and sometimes *selling price* is the base. For some businesses, cost is the more logical base for calculating dollar markup. However, calculating dollar markup based on selling price can be advantageous method for many retail stores.

The accountant for Athletes' World says that, in order to pay all expenses and have a reasonable profit, and based upon a cost of $43.50, the company's markup should be 80% of the cost. When the cost and the markup percent are known, the dollar markup and the selling price can be computed.

Learning Objective **2**

Compute the markup variables when the markup percent is based on cost.

STEPS **to Compute the Selling Price Based on Cost**

1. Multiply the cost by the markup percent to get the dollar markup.
2. Add the dollar markup to the cost to get the selling price.

VIDEO

Markup Based on Cost/Selling Price

For Athletes' World's running shoes:

STEP 1   Dollar markup = Markup percent × Cost = 0.80 × $43.50 = $34.80

STEP 2   Selling price = Cost + Dollar markup = $43.50 + $34.80 = $78.30

● EXAMPLE A

Using markup based on cost, what are the dollar markup and the selling price for merchandise that costs $60 and has a 35% markup?

STEP 1   Dollar markup = Markup percent × Cost = 0.35 × $60 = $21

STEP 2   Selling price = Cost + Dollar markup = $60 + $21 = $81

COMPUTING SELLING PRICE DIRECTLY FROM COST

When you know the cost and markup percent (based on cost), you can compute the selling price directly, without computing the dollar markup.

● **EXAMPLE B**

What is the selling price of a large camping tent that has a cost of $250 and a markup percent of 40% based on cost?

STEP 1   100% + Markup percent = 100% + 40% = 140%

STEP 2   Selling price = (100% + Markup percent) × Cost = 1.40 × $250 = $350

COMPUTING COST DIRECTLY FROM SELLING PRICE

Likewise, you can use the reverse procedure to compute the cost directly from the selling price and the markup percent (based on cost), without computing the dollar markup.

● **EXAMPLE C**

The selling price of a hiking vest is $65. The markup percent based on cost is 30%. Find the cost.

STEP 1   100% + Markup percent = 100% + 30% = 130%

STEP 2   Cost = Selling price ÷ (100% + Markup percent) = $65 ÷ 1.30 = $50

You can always check your work in markup problems.

Cost is $50, and markup percent is 30%.

Dollar markup = Cost × Markup percent = $50 × 0.30 = $15

Selling Price = Cost + Dollar markup = $50 + $15 = $65

It checks!

✔ CONCEPT CHECK 8.2

Compute the required values when the markup percent is based on cost.

a. Cost = $1,240; Markup percent = 40%
   Find dollar markup, and then find selling price.

b. Cost = $330; Markup percent = 50%
   Find 100% + Markup percent, and then find selling price directly.

c. Selling price = $780; Markup percent = 25%
   Find 100% + Markup percent, and then find cost directly.

Dollar markup = 0.40 × $1,240 = $496
Selling price = $1,240 + $496 = $1,736
100% + Markup percent = 100% + 50% = 150%
Selling price = 1.50 × $330 = $495
100% + Markup percent = 100% + 25% = 125%
Cost = $780 ÷ 1.25 = $624

Computing Markup Percent Based on Cost

In the illustration for Athletes' World, the accountant determined that the markup percent needed to be 80% of cost, which meant that the selling price needed to be $78.30. However, management may simply decide to price the running shoes at $79.95. Now, the markup is no longer 80% of cost. The **markup percent based on cost** can be computed in two steps.

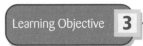

Learning Objective **3**

Compute markup percent based on cost.

STEPS to Compute the Markup Percent Based on Cost

1. Subtract the cost from the selling price to get the dollar markup.
2. Divide the dollar markup by the cost to get the markup percent.

For the running shoes from Athletes' World, now priced at $79.95:

STEP 1   Dollar markup = Selling price − Cost = $79.95 − $43.50 = $36.45

STEP 2   Markup percent = Dollar markup ÷ Cost = $36.45 ÷ $43.50 = 0.838, or 83.8% (as a percent, rounded to one decimal place)

AP IMAGES

EXAMPLE D

What is the markup percent based on cost when the selling price of an exercise machine is $480 and the cost is $320?

STEP 1   Dollar markup = Selling price − Cost = $480 − $320 = $160

STEP 2   Markup percent = Dollar markup ÷ Cost = $160 ÷ $320 = 0.50, or 50%

EXAMPLE E

What is the markup percent based on cost when the dollar markup is already known to be $30 and the cost is $75? (Step 1 is not necessary.)

STEP 2   Markup percent = Dollar markup ÷ Cost = $30 ÷ $75 = 0.40, or 40%

✔ CONCEPT CHECK 8.3

Cost = $1,600; Selling price = $2,560   Dollar markup = $2,560 − $1,600 = $960
Find the markup percent based on cost.   Markup percent = $960 ÷ $1,600 = 0.60, or 60%

COMPLETE ASSIGNMENT 8.1.

Computing Markup Based on Selling Price

Learning Objective **4**

Compute the markup variables when the markup percent is based on selling price.

Although many businesses base their markup on cost, many others, often retailers, commonly use a percent of selling price—that is, they use **markup based on selling price.** That doesn't mean that selling price is determined without considering cost or even before considering cost. It merely means that the dollar markup is computed by multiplying the markup percent by the selling price.

Many individuals start their own business when they observe another successful business selling a product. New owners believe that they can acquire the product, pay all expenses, and still sell it for less than the existing business is selling its product. Instead of basing the selling price on costs, expenses, and satisfactory profit, the new owners could price their product just under the competition's price. They base their selling price on the competition's selling price rather than marking up from their own costs.

Basing markup calculations on selling price can be an advantage in a retail store where the salesperson or sales manager has the authority to lower the sales price immediately in order to make a sale. In a larger business, these persons may not even know the exact cost.

STEPS **to Compute the Cost Based on Selling Price**

1. Multiply the selling price by the markup percent to get the dollar markup.
2. Subtract the dollar markup from the selling price to get the cost.

EXAMPLE F

Rosa Buckles enters Mel's Appliance Store to buy a washing machine. She finds one with a selling price of $400. She knows that she can buy it for $375 at another store, but she prefers this store because of its reputation for good service. She tells the sales manager, "I would buy it for $375." The manager, Mike Haynes, knows that the markup percent is 40% based on selling price. Based on $400, what was Mike's cost for the washing machine?

STEP 1   Dollar markup = Markup percent $\times$ Selling price = 0.40 $\times$ $400 = $160

STEP 2   Cost = Selling price − Dollar markup = $400 − $160 = $240

Mike can then decide whether he prefers a sale for which he gets a $135 markup or no sale at all for which he was hoping to have a $160 markup. Although it would be helpful if Mike knew how much markup he would need to pay for expenses, at least he would know the cost.

EXAMPLE G

Find the dollar markup and the cost of microwave oven that sells for $140 and has a markup percent that is 35% based on selling price.

STEP 1   Dollar markup = Markup percent $\times$ Selling price = 0.35 $\times$ $140 = $49

STEP 2   Cost = Selling price − Dollar markup = $140 − $49 = $91

COMPUTING COST DIRECTLY FROM SELLING PRICE

When you know the selling price and the markup percent (based on selling price), you can compute the cost directly, wihout computing the dollar markup.

STEPS to Compute the Cost Directly from the Selling Price

1. Subtract the markup percent from 100%.
2. Multiply this difference by the selling price to get the cost.

EXAMPLE H

What is the cost of a clothes dryer that has a selling price of $340 and a markup percent of 60% based on selling price?

STEP 1 $\qquad$ 100% − Markup percent = 100% − 60% = 40%

STEP 2 $\qquad$ Cost = (100% − Markup percent) × Selling price = 0.40 × $340 = $136

COMPUTING SELLING PRICE DIRECTLY FROM COST

Likewise, you can use the reverse procedure to compute the selling price directly from the cost and the markup percent (based on selling price), without computing the dollar markup.

STEPS to Compute the Selling Price Directly from the Cost

1. Subtract the markup percent from 100%.
2. Divide the cost by this difference to get the selling price.

EXAMPLE I

The cost of a new mountain bike is $210. The markup percent based on selling price is 40%. Find the selling price.

STEP 1 $\qquad$ 100% − Markup percent = 100% − 40% = 60%

STEP 2 $\qquad$ Selling price = Cost ÷ (100% − Markup percent) = $210 ÷ 0.60 = $350

You can always check your work in markup problems:
Selling price is $350, and markup percent is 40% based on selling price.
Dollar markup = Markup percent × Selling price = 0.40 × $350 = $140
Cost = Selling price − Dollar markup = $350 − $140 = $210
It checks!

DAVID CHADWICK/ISTOCKPHOTO.COM

CONCEPT CHECK 8.4

Compute the required values when the markup percent is based on selling price.

a. Selling price = $750; Markup percent = 50%
   Find dollar markup, and then find cost.

   Dollar markup = 0.50 × $750 = $375
   Cost = $750 − $375 = $375

b. Selling price = $40; Markup percent = 30%
   Find 100% − Markup percent, and then find cost directly.

   100% − Markup percent = 100% − 30% = 70%
   Cost = 0.70 × $40 = $28

c. Cost = $150; Markup percent = 40%
   Find 100% − Markup percent, and then find selling price directly.

   100% − Markup percent = 100% − 40% = 60%
   Selling price = $150 ÷ 0.60 = $250

Computing Markup Percent Based on Selling Price

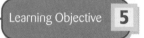

Learning Objective **5**

Compute markup percent based on selling price.

In the illustration for Athletes' World, the pair of running shoes had a cost of $43.50. Management had decided that the selling price of the running shoes should be $79.95. The markup percent based on selling price can be calculated in two steps.

> **STEPS** **to Compute the Markup Percent from the Selling Price**
>
> 1. Subtract the cost from the selling price to get the dollar markup.
> 2. Divide the dollar markup by the selling price to get the markup percent.

For Athletes' World's running shoes,

STEP 1   Dollar markup = Selling price − Cost = $79.95 − $43.50 = $36.45

STEP 2   Markup percent = Dollar markup ÷ Selling price = $36.45 ÷ $79.95 = 0.456, or 45.6% (as a percent, rounded to one decimal place)

● EXAMPLE J

What is the markup percent based on selling price when the selling price is $80 and the cost is $50?

STEP 1   Dollar markup = Selling price − Cost = $80 − $50 = $30

STEP 2   Markup percent = Dollar markup ÷ Selling price = $30 ÷ $80 = 0.375, or 37.5%

● EXAMPLE K

What is the markup percent based on selling price when the dollar markup is already known to be $150 and the selling price is $375? (Step 1 is not necessary.)

STEP 2   Markup percent = Dollar markup ÷ Selling price = $150 ÷ $375 = 0.40, or 40%

✔ CONCEPT CHECK 8.5

Cost = $1,600; Selling price = $2,560
Find the markup percent based on selling price.

Dollar markup = $2,560 − $1,600 = $960
Markup percent = $960 ÷ $2,560 = 0.375, or 37.5%

COMPLETE ASSIGNMENT 8.2.

Chapter Terms for Review

cost of goods sold

dollar markup

markup

markup based on selling price

markup percent

markup percent based on cost

markup rate

Try Microsoft® Excel

Try working the problems using the Microsoft Excel templates found on the companion website. Solutions for the problems are also shown on the companion website.

Summary of chapter learning objectives:

Learning Objective	Example
8.1 Compute the variables in the basic markup formula.	Find the missing variables in the basic markup formula: 1. Cost = \$231.50; Dollar markup = \$109.12 2. Cost = \$34.20; Selling price = \$59.95 3. Dollar markup = \$475; Selling price = \$900
8.2 Compute the markup variables when the markup percent is based on cost.	4. Cost = \$800; Markup percent = 35% a. Find the dollar markup and then find the selling price. b. Find 100% + Markup percent, and then find the selling price. 5. Selling price = \$2,100; Markup percent = 40% Find 100% + Markup percent, and then find the cost.
8.3 Compute the markup percent based on cost.	6. Cost = \$80; Selling price = \$108 Find the markup percent based on cost.
8.4 Compute the markup variables when the markup percent is based on selling price.	7. Selling price = \$820; Markup percent = 25% a. Find the dollar markup and then find the cost. b. Find 100% − Markup percent and then find the cost. 8. Cost = \$1,350; Markup percent = 40% Find 100% − Markup percent, and then find the selling price.
8.5 Compute the markup percent based on selling price.	9. Cost = \$825; Selling price = \$1,100 Find the markup percent based on the selling price.

Answers: 1. Selling price = \$340.62 2. Dollar markup = \$25.75 3. Cost = \$425 4. a. \$280; \$1,080 b. 135%; \$1,080 5. 140%; \$1,500 6. 35% 7. a. \$205; \$615 b. 75%; \$615 8. 60%; \$2,250 9. 25%

Review Problems for Chapter 8

1 Find the missing terms.

	Cost of Goods Sold	Dollar Markup	Selling Price		Cost of Goods Sold	Dollar Markup	Selling Price
a.	$28.90	$14.45	_____	**c.**	_____	$1,405	$2,975
b.	$188.12	_____	$399.95	**d.**	$426.25	_____	$998.88

In problems 2–9, the markup percent is based on cost. Find the missing terms. Round all percents to the nearest one tenth of a percent.

	Cost	Markup Percent	Dollar Markup	Selling Price			Cost	Markup Percent	100% + Markup Percent	Selling Price
2	$500	50%	**a.** _____	**b.** _____		**4**	$225	60%	**a.** _____	**b.** _____
3	$36	65%	**a.** _____	**b.** _____		**5**	$240	75%	**a.** _____	**b.** _____

	Selling Price	Markup Percent	100% + Markup Percent	Cost			Selling Price	Cost	Dollar Markup	Markup Percent
6	$1,012	100%	**a.** _____	**b.** _____		**8**	$540	$240	**a.** _____	**b.** _____
7	$98	40%	**a.** _____	**b.** _____		**9**	$2,000	$1,600	**a.** _____	**b.** _____

In problems 10–17 the markup percent is based on selling price. Find the missing terms. Round all percents to the nearest one tenth of a percent.

	Selling Price	Markup Percent	Dollar Markup	Cost			Selling Price	Markup Percent	100% − Markup Percent	Cost
10	$240	30%	**a.** _____	**b.** _____		**12**	$1,240	40%	**a.** _____	**b.** _____
11	$144	25%	**a.** _____	**b.** _____		**13**	$528	75%	**a.** _____	**b.** _____

	Cost	Markup Percent	100% − Markup Percent	Selling Price			Selling Price	Cost	Dollar Markup	Markup Percent
14	$960	60%	**a.** _____	**b.** _____		**16**	$800	$480	**a.** _____	**b.** _____
15	$36	25%	**a.** _____	**b.** _____		**17**	$3,750	$1,500	**a.** _____	**b.** _____

18 Carol Wilson sells high-end toys, specializing in all wooden toys for preschool children. She pays $40 for a toy truck. Carol sells the toy truck for $50. a. Find the dollar markup. _____ b. Find the markup percent based on cost. _____ c. Find the markup percent based on selling price. _____

Answers to the Self-Check can be found in Appendix B at the back of the text.

Assignment 8.1: Markup Based on Cost

Name _____

Date _____ Score _____

Learning Objectives **1** **2** **3**

A **(12 points) Calculate the missing terms. (2 points for each correct answer)**

	Cost	Dollar Markup	Selling Price		Cost	Dollar Markup	Selling Price
1.	$480.70	$175.25	_____	**2.**	$51.37	_____	$74.95
3.	_____	$374.50	$829.98	**4.**	$175.50	$57.50	_____
5.	$629.00	_____	$909.99	**6.**	_____	$415.50	$799.49

Score for A (12)

B **(32 points) In the following problems, the markup percent is based on *cost*. Find the missing terms.**
(2 points for each correct answer)

	Cost	Markup Percent	Dollar Markup	Selling Price		Cost	Markup Percent	100% + Markup Percent	Selling Price
7.	$850	40%	_____	_____	**8.**	$160	125%	_____	_____
9.	$1,500	70%	_____	_____	**10.**	$240	100%	_____	_____
11.	$640	75%	_____	_____	**12.**	$900	40%	_____	_____
13.	$2,500	90%	_____	_____	**14.**	$150	210%	_____	_____

Score for B (32)

C (32 points) In the following problems, the markup percent is based on cost. Find the missing terms. Round all percents to the nearest tenth of a percent. (2 points for each correct answer)

Selling Price	Markup Percent	100% + Markup Percent	Cost		Selling Price	Cost	Dollar Markup	Markup Percent
15. $1,240	60%	_____	_____		**16.** $48	$30	_____	_____
17. $110	120%	_____	_____		**18.** $1,683	$1,100	_____	_____
19. $594	35%	_____	_____		**20.** $679	$388	_____	_____
21. $2,250	50%	_____	_____		**22.** $216	$96	_____	_____

Score for C (32)

D (24 points) Business Applications. In the following problems, the markup percent is based on cost. Round all percents to the nearest tenth of a percent. (3 points for each correct answer)

23. Patty Wales owns a firm that sells office furniture to regional businesses. One set of six matched pieces costs Patty $2,100. To cover her own business expenses and allow a reasonable profit, Patty marks up this set by 75% of the cost. Find the dollar markup and the selling price.

Dollar markup _____

Selling price _____

24. Lew Devlin manufactures a handheld heart monitoring device. He sells it for $960, which represents a markup of 275% on his production cost. Lew marks it up this much to cover additional business expenses and profit as well as his product development. Find Lew's production cost and the dollar markup.

Cost _____

Dollar markup _____

25. Digital Alarm Company sells burglar and fire alarm systems for homes and small businesses. One new system costs Digital $720. Digital marks up the alarm system by $396. Find the selling price, and find the markup percent based on cost.

Selling price _____

Markup percent _____

26. After Buzz Landles drove his pickup in a desert race, the truck needed a new motor. A local mechanic charged Buzz $3,300 for a rebuilt motor that had cost the mechanic $2,500. All labor was additional. Compute the dollar markup and the markup percent based on the cost of the rebuilt motor.

Dollar markup _____

Markup percent _____

Score for D (24)

Assignment 8.2: Markup Based on Selling Price

Name _____

Date _____ Score _____

A (12 points) Calculate the missing terms. (2 points for each correct answer)

	Cost	Dollar Markup	Selling Price		Cost	Dollar Markup	Selling Price
1.	$67.34	$82.15	_____	**2.**	$193.19	_____	$458.88
3.	_____	$840	$2,659	**4.**	$632.75	$325.40	_____
5.	$62.50	_____	$99.99	**6.**	_____	$307.15	$978.95

Score for A (12)

B (32 points) In the following problems, the markup percent is based on selling price. Find the missing terms. (2 points for each correct answer)

	Selling Price	Markup Percent	Dollar Markup	Cost		Selling Price	Markup Percent	100% − Markup Percent	Cost
7.	$120	55%	_____	_____	**8.**	$150	25%	_____	_____
9.	$360	40%	_____	_____	**10.**	$1,040	45%	_____	_____
11.	$1,998	50%	_____	_____	**12.**	$75	70%	_____	_____
13.	$824	60%	_____	_____	**14.**	$2,150	30%	_____	_____

Score for B (32)

C (32 points) In the following problems, the markup percent is based on selling price. Find the missing terms. (2 points for each correct answer)

	Cost	Markup Percent	100% − Markup Percent	Selling Price		Selling Price	Cost	Dollar Markup	Markup Percent
15.	$855	40%	_____	_____	**16.**	$1,040	$676	_____	_____
17.	$143	45%	_____	_____	**18.**	$56	$28	_____	_____
19.	$2,520	30%	_____	_____	**20.**	$1,400	$924	_____	_____
21.	$533	35%	_____	_____	**22.**	$840	$462	_____	_____

_____

Score for C (32)

D (24 points) Business Applications. In the following problems, the markup percent is based on selling price. Round all percents to the nearest tenth of a percent. (3 points for each correct answer)

23. At the start of spring, Portola Hardware features garden equipment specials. One rototiller has a selling price of $348. The markup to cover expenses and profit is 50% based on the selling price. Calculate the dollar markup and the cost.

Dollar markup _____

Cost _____

24. Oceanside Biking is a retail bicycle store. For last year's *summer racing* season, Oceanside purchased one new model of racing bike to use in a special promotion. The bicycles cost $287 each. For the promotion, Oceanside's markup was 30% of the selling price. Find the selling price and the dollar markup.

Selling price _____

Dollar markup _____

25. Blenz TV & Stereo sells telephones, along with televisions and stereos. A two-line cordless telephone set with a speaker phone base, four extra remote handsets, and an answering machine is priced at $182.40. This price includes a markup of $109.44. If this set actually sells for $182.40, what are the cost and the markup percent based on selling price?

Cost _____

Markup percent _____

26. Patio World, a volume discount store, purchased a large quantity of cedar picnic chairs for $66 each. Seating pads were included in the price. To sell the chairs and pads quickly, the store priced the chairs at $110 each. Compute the dollar markup and the markup percent based on selling price.

Dollar markup _____

Markup percent _____

_____

Score for D (24)

Banking

9

Learning Objectives

By studying this chapter and completing all assignments, you will be able to:

Learning Objective | **1** | Maintain a checking account.

Learning Objective | **2** | Reconcile a bank statement with a checkbook balance.

Using Deposit Slips and Bank Checks

Bank customers usually make deposits to their checking accounts by using **deposit slips.** Figure 9-1 shows a typical deposit slip, with spaces to list cash and checks being deposited.

In most businesses, each deposit will include a number of checks. Each check is individually listed on each deposit slip. Deposits are also made electronically. Many employees have their pay electronically transmitted directly from their employer's bank accounts to their individual bank accounts.

A bank **check** is a written order directing the bank to pay a certain sum to a designated party, called the **payee.** Banks normally provide checkbooks to their customers. Figure 9-2 shows a typical business check. These usually come in a binder with three checks on each page. Figure 9-3 shows a typical bank check, with the stub on the top used for individual personal checks.

Figure 9-1 | Deposit Slip

WELLS FARGO BANK
VAN NESS-CALIFORNIA OFFICE   1560 VAN NESS AVENUE   SAN FRANCISCO, CA   94109

35-6686
3130

DATE _____ 20 _____

DEPOSITS MAY NOT BE AVAILABLE FOR IMMEDIATE WITHDRAWAL

SIGN HERE FOR LESS CASH IN TELLER'S PRESENCE

HART FURNITURE CO.
1039 BROADWAY
SAN FRANCISCO, CA 94103

USE OTHER SIDE FOR ADDITIONAL LISTING. BE SURE EACH ITEM IS PROPERLY ENDORSED.

CASH	CURRENCY	300	00
	COIN	60	49
LIST CHECKS SINGLY	16–30	250	00
	18–21	125	00
	17–17	216	00
TOTAL FROM OTHER SIDE		209	00
TOTAL		1,160	49
LESS CASH RECEIVED		—	
NET DEPOSIT		1,160	49

Back of Deposit Slip:

PLEASE LIST EACH CHECK SEPARATELY BY BANK NUMBER

CHECKS		DOLLARS			CENTS
1	14–36		7	6	75
2	13–22		1	3	25
3	13–22	1	1	9	00
4					
5					
6					
7					
8					
9					
10					
11					
12					
PLEASE FORWARD TOTAL TO REVERSE SIDE		2	0	9	00

© CENGAGE LEARNING 2013

Figure 9-2   Check with Check Stub on Left

No. _2506_	$ _124.35_		
September 24	20 --		

To _Ace Auto Repair_

For _Delivery truck_

	$	¢
Balance Bro't Fwd.	1,332	80
Amount Deposited	1,160	49
Total	2,493	29
Amount This Check	124	35
Balance Car'd Fwd.	2,368	94

HART FURNITURE CO.
1039 Broadway
San Francisco, CA 94103

No. 2506

September 24   20 --

35-6686
3130

Pay to the order of _Ace Auto Repair_ $ | 124.35 |

One hundred twenty – four and 35/100 _____ DOLLARS

WELLS FARGO BANK
VAN NESS-CALIFORNIA OFFICE   1560 VAN NESS AVENUE   SAN FRANCISCO, CA   94109

For _Delivery truck repair_   _Robert S. Hart_

⑆313066⑆86⑆   2506⑈   117⑈020⑈8

© CENGAGE LEARNING 2013

Today, many bank transactions are completed electronically. Funds that are transmitted electronically, primarily via computers, are called **electronic fund transfers (EFTs)**. They include **automatic teller machine (ATM)** and computer-generated transactions by which customers can check their balances, make deposits, transfer funds between accounts, make payments and withdraw funds from their accounts using the ATM machine or their personal computer. Computer programs also initiate many electronic fund transfers. These transactions are processed through the Automated Clearing House Association and include direct deposits of payroll, government, and other payments specified for direct deposit.

INTI ST. CLAIR/JUPITERIMAGES

Figure 9-3   Check with Check Stub on Top

BAL. FWD.	997 03	DATE	_10/1/20--_	3500	
DEPOSITS	451 04	TO:	_Men's Wearhouse_	NEW BAL.	1,555 08
	707 01	FOR:	_Suit-Slacks_	THIS CHECK	300 00
NEW BAL.	1,555 08			BAL. FWD.	1,255 08

VALUED CUSTOMER SINCE 1976

WELLS FARGO BANK   🔒   3500

91-119
1221(1)

October 1,   20 --

Pay to the order of _Men's Wearhouse_ $ | 300.00 |

Three hundred no/100——————— DOLLARS

MARY MAHEW
40 ACELA DR.
TIBURON, CA 94920

For _Suit-Slacks_   _Mary Mayhew_

⑆122101191⑆3500 0255 355521⑈

© CENGAGE LEARNING 2013

Fill in the total (as necessary) and balance on each check stub. Carry each balance forward to the next stub.

No. 1	$ 65.00
May 1	20--
To Citizens News	
For Advertising	

	$	¢
Balance Bro't Fwd.	890	00
Amount Deposited		
Total		
Amount This Check	65	00
Balance Car'd Fwd.	825	00

No. 2	$ 79.00
May 4	20--
To District Utilities	
For Gas & electric	

	$	¢
Balance Bro't Fwd.	825	00
Amount Deposited		
Total		
Amount This Check	79	00
Balance Car'd Fwd.	746	00

No. 3	$ 25.00
May 5	20--
To U.S. Postal Service	
For Stamps	

	$	¢
Balance Bro't Fwd.	746	00
Amount Deposited	100	00
Total	846	00
Amount This Check	25	00
Balance Car'd Fwd.	821	00

Using Checkbooks and Check Registers

A bank **checkbook** provides check stubs or a special page on which to record deposits, withdrawals, check numbers, dates, check amounts, other additions and subtractions, and account balances.

Figure 9-2 shows that check number 2506 was written against the account of Hart Furniture Co. on September 24 to Ace Auto Repair. The check was for $124.35 for repairs

Figure 9-4	Check Register

CHECK REGISTER			DEDUCT ALL PER CHECK OR SERVICE CHARGES THAT APPLY			BALANCE
DATE		CHECK NUMBER	CHECKS ISSUED TO OR DEPOSITS RECEIVED FROM	AMOUNT OF CHECK	AMOUNT OF DEPOSIT	$1,332.80
Sept	24		Deposit cash receipts		1,160.49	2,493.29
	24	2506	Ace Auto Repair	124.35		2,368.94
	24	2507	Morton Window Decorators	450.00		1,918.94
	24	2508	Donation to Guide Dogs	100.00		1,818.94
	25	2509	Secure Alarm Systems	150.00		1,668.94
Oct	19	2514	Best Janitorial Service	325.00		855.94
	20		Deposit cash receipts		980.00	1,835.94

to the delivery truck. The stub shows a balance brought forward of $1,332.80, a deposit on September 24 of $1,160.49, the amount of this check ($124.35), and the available balance carried forward of $2,368.94.

Today, most small businesses and many individuals use a **check register.** Like a check stub, a check register provides a place to record information about each bank transaction. Figure 9-4 shows a typical check register. Note that a continuous balance is maintained.

✔ CONCEPT CHECK 9.2

In this check register, fill in the cash balance resulting from each transaction.

CHECK REGISTER			DEDUCT ALL PER CHECK OR SERVICE CHARGES THAT APPLY			BALANCE
DATE		CHECK NUMBER	CHECKS ISSUED TO OR DEPOSITS RECEIVED FROM	AMOUNT OF CHECK	AMOUNT OF DEPOSIT	$520.42
Mar	27	123	Replenish petty cash	$ 65.20		455.22
	31	124	Jiffy Janitorial Service	150.00		305.22
Apr	01	125	Sun County Water District	96.72		208.50
	03	–	Deposit weekly receipts		$2,470.80	2,679.30
	03	126	Midtown Mortgage Co.	835.20		1,844.10
	03	127	Sun Gas and Electric Co.	72.18		1,771.92
	04	128	Midtown Weekly Advertiser	32.80		1,739.12
	04	129	Trash Disposal, Inc.	60.00		1,679.12
	04	130	Pacific Plumbing Supplies	906.97		772.15
	10	–	Deposit weekly receipts		2,942.50	3,714.65

Reconciling Bank Statements

Checking account customers receive an electronic or a printed **bank statement** every month. The bank statement shows an opening balance; deposits and credits, including EFTs; checks paid; withdrawals, including EFTs; service charges; general information about the account; and the balance at the end of the period. In addition, most banks now provide electronic banking that allows you to view your current account activity and bank statement at any time. Figure 9-5 shows a typical bank statement.

The balance shown in your checkbook or check register is usually different from the balance shown on the bank statement. Some of the items that cause this difference are as follows:

An **outstanding check** is one that has been written but hasn't yet cleared the bank. Almost always you will have written and recorded some checks that haven't yet been presented to or processed by the bank for payment and charged to the customer's account.

A **bank charge** is a fee for services performed by the bank. At the time the bank statement is made up, your account may have been charged for bank service fees, printing checks, extra copies of statements, wired funds, traveler's checks, cashier's checks, safe-deposit box rentals, bad checks returned, or EFTs that you haven't yet recorded. These charges would therefore not yet be deducted from your checkbook or check register balance.

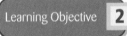

Learning Objective **2**

Reconcile a bank statement with a checkbook balance.

© ISTOCKPHOTO/MARTIN MCCARTHY

Figure 9-5 | Bank Statement

WELLS FARGO BANK

VAN NESS-CALIFORNIA OFFICE   #307
1560 VAN NESS AVE.
SAN FRANCISCO CA   94109

HART FURNITURE CO.
1039 BROADWAY
SAN FRANCISCO, CA 94103

CALL (415) 456-9081
24 HOURS/DAY, 7 DAYS/WEEK
FOR ASSISTANCE WITH
YOUR ACCOUNT.

PAGE 1 OF 1   THIS STATEMENT COVERS: 09/21/– – THROUGH 10/20/– –

WELLS FARGO NEWSLINE   NEW! GET STAMPS AT EXPRESS ATMS WHEN YOU STOP BY FOR CASH. AND, PLEASE NOTE THAT THE COMBINED TOTAL OF CASH WITHDRAWN AND STAMP PURCHASES CANNOT EXCEED YOUR DAILY CASH LIMIT.

REWARD ACCOUNT
31306686

SUMMARY

PREVIOUS BALANCE	$1,332.80
DEPOSITS	1,560.49
WITHDRAWALS	1,081.23
INTEREST	6.30
MONTHLY CHECKING FEE AND OTHER CHARGES	13.00
▶ **NEW BALANCE**	**$1,805.36**

MINIMUM BALANCE	$980.17
AVERAGE BALANCE	$1,336.91

CHECKS AND WITHDRAWALS	CHECK	DATE PAID	AMOUNT
	2506	9/26	124.35
	2507	9/26	450.00
	2508	9/26	100.00
	2509	9/27	150.00
ATM WITHDRAWAL		10/08	50.00
POS PURCHASE	SAFEWAY	10/09	132.50
POS PURCHASE	CHEVRON	10/10	74.38

DEPOSITS	CUSTOMER DEPOSIT	DATE POSTED	AMOUNT
	CUSTOMER DEPOSIT	9/25	1,160.49
	EFT CREDIT	9/26	400.00

A **debit card** (sometimes referred to as a "check card") is a plastic card that is used much like a bank check or cash where the amount of a purchase, ATM withdrawal, or other debit use is instantly deducted from the bank account. These **POS (Point of Sale)** transactions are posted to the bank account immediately and must be considered for daily and monthly reconciliations.

A **credit** is a deposit or addition to a bank account. In many cases, the bank will have credited your account for an item such as an EFT deposited into the account or interest earned on the account. You, the customer, don't know the amount of these credits until the bank statement arrives, so the credits haven't yet been entered in your checkbook or check register.

An **outstanding deposit** is a credit that hasn't yet been recorded by the bank. A deposit that you made near the end of the statement period may have been recorded in your checkbook or check register but not recorded by the bank in time to appear on the statement.

Because these items cause a difference between the bank statement balance and your checkbook or check register balance, you should always reconcile the two balances immediately upon receipt of the statement.

To start the reconciliation, compare the check stubs or check register, all deposit slips, and any company records of ATM transactions with the bank statement. Such a comparison is called a **reconciliation of the bank balance.**

When Hart Furniture Company received its monthly bank statement, the bookkeeper noted that the ending balance was $1,805.36 but that the balance in the company checkbook was $2092.82. To determine the correct balance, the bookkeeper noted the following differences:

1. An EFT credit for $400 had been made to the account but not recorded by Hart.
2. A bank service charge of $13 had been subtracted from Hart's account by the bank. Three ATM debit card charges ($50; $132.50; $74.38) with a total of $256.88 had been subtracted from the account by the bank.
3. Interest earnings of $6.30 had been added to Hart's account.
4. A deposit on October 20 of $980 had not yet been recorded by the bank.
5. Checks for $27.92, $10, $48.95, $144.25, and $325 had not yet been processed and deducted by the bank.

Most bank statements have printed on the back of the statement a form that can be used to quickly and easily reconcile the customer's checkbook or check register balance with the statement balance. Figure 9-6 shows this form as completed by the Hart Furniture bookkeeper using the information just noted. Note that the adjusted checkbook balance and the adjusted bank balance now agree, showing the correct cash balance of $2,229.24.

DIGITAL VISION/GETTY IMAGES

Figure 9-6 | Reconciliation Form

Balance Your Account

DATE ___10 / 20 / -- ___

Checks Outstanding

1 Check off (✓) checks appearing on your statement. Those checks not checked off (✓) should be recorded in the checks outstanding column.

Check No.	Amount	
2510	27	92
2511	10	00
2512	48	95
2513	144	25
2514	325	00
TOTAL	556	12

2

Enter your checkbook balance	$ 2,092	82
Add any credits made to your account through interest, etc. as shown on this statement. (Be sure to enter these in your checkbook).	6	30
	400	00
SUBTOTAL	2,499	12
Subtract any debits made to your account through debit card and bank charges, account fees, etc. as shown on this statement. (Be sure to enter these in your …checkbook.)	− 13	00
	− 256	88
Adjusted checkbook balance.	$ 2,229	24 **A**

3

Bank balance shown on this statement.	$ 1,805	36
Add deposits shown in your checkbook but not shown on this statement, because they were made and received after date on this statement.	980	00
Subtotal	2,785	36
Subtract checks outstanding	556	12
Adjusted bank balance.	$ 2,229	24 **B**

Your checkbook is in balance if line **A** agrees with line **B**.

STEPS **to Reconcile Bank Balances**

1. Reconcile the checkbook (check register) balance. Start with the last balance as recorded in the checkbook.
   a. Add any bank statement credits, such as interest earned or EFT deposits not yet recorded in the checkbook.
   b. Subtract any charges or debits made by the bank, such as debit card charges including ATM withdrawals service charges, check printing charges, returned check charges, or EFT charges not yet recorded in the checkbook.
   This gives you your **adjusted checkbook balance.**
2. Reconcile the bank balance. Start with the balance as presented on the statement.
   a. Add any deposits or other credits not yet recorded by the bank.
   b. Subtract all outstanding checks.
   This gives you your **adjusted bank balance.**
3. Be sure that the two adjusted balances agree.

At month end, Johnson Hardware received the following bank statement. Use the forms that follow the statement to reconcile the check register shown in Concept Check 9.2 and the bank statement.

MIDTOWN BANK

JOHNSON HARDWARE COMPANY
346 POPLAR STREET
MIDTOWN, CA 94872

THIS STATEMENT COVERS: 3/27/-- THROUGH 4/24/--

SUMMARY	
PREVIOUS BALANCE	$ 520.42
DEPOSITS	2,470.80+
WITHDRAWALS	2,062.35
INTEREST	5.60+
SERVICE CHARGES	7.00-
NEW BALANCE	$ 927.47

CHECKS AND WITHDRAWALS	CHECK	DATE PAID	AMOUNT	CHECK	DATE PAID	AMOUNT
	123	3/29	65.20	130*	4/06	906.97
	124	4/02	150.00			
	126*	4/03	835.20			
	127	4/05	72.18			
	128	4/05	32.80			

DEPOSITS	CUSTOMER DEPOSIT	DATE POSTED	AMOUNT
	CUSTOMER DEPOSIT	4/05	2,470.80

* Indicates checks out of sequence

Enter your checkbook balance	$ 3,714	65
Add any credits made to your account through interest, etc. as shown on this statement. (Be sure to enter these in your checkbook).	5	60
SUBTOTAL	3,720	25
Subtract any debits made to your account through bank charges, account fees, etc. as shown on this statement. (Be sure to enter these in your checkbook).	7	00
Adjusted checkbook balance.	$ 3,713	25

Bank balance shown on this statement.	$ 927	47
Add deposits shown in your checkbook but not shown on this statement, because they were made and received after date on this statement.	2,942	50
Subtotal	3,869	97
Subtract checks outstanding	156	72
Adjusted bank balance.	$ 3,713	25

Your checkbook is in balance if line **A** agrees with line **B**.

Checks Outstanding

Check No.	Amount	
125	$ 96	72
129	60	00
TOTAL	$ 156	72

COMPLETE ASSIGNMENTS 9.1, 9.2, AND 9.3.

Chapter Terms for Review

adjusted bank balance	debit card
adjusted checkbook balance	deposit slip
automatic teller machine (ATM)	electronic fund transfer (EFT)
bank charge	outstanding check
bank statement	outstanding deposit
check	payee
checkbook	POS—Point of Sale
check register	reconciliation of the bank balance
credit	

Try working the following problems using the Microsoft Excel templates found on the companion website. Solutions for the problems are also shown on the companion website.

1. Complete the following worksheet by adding formulas in shaded cells to calculate the balance after each transaction in the check register. Formulas should work for either the addition of a deposit or subtraction of a check and be able to be copied down the **Balance** column.

	A	B	C	D	E	F
1	Check Register					Balance
2	Date	Check Number	Checks issued to or deposits received from	Amount of Check	Amount of Deposit	895.42
3	May 4	237	Echo Computer Repair Service	235.00		
4	5		Deposit cash sales		1,569.12	
5	6	238	Glendale Gas Co.	127.90		
6	6	239	Yellow Pages - ad	212.33		
7	8	240	City Stationers - supplies	582.91		
8	10		Deposit cash sales		1,243.32	
9	12	241	Acme Cleaning Service	450.00		
10	13	242	General Telephone	82.57		
11	15		Deposit tax refund		750.00	

2. Jessica Flint's monthly bank statement balance was $1,753.04. Her checkbook balance was $2,590.24. She noted that the following checks were outstanding: #134 for $17.35, #137 for $128.45, and #138 for $52.00. She also noted that a deposit of $974.50 was not yet recorded by the bank. The bank statement lists a service charge of $15 and a bad check of $45.50 returned to Jessica by the bank from a recent deposit.

Enter the data given above in the appropriate cells and complete the worksheet to reconcile the bank statement and checkbook balances by adding formulas in shaded cells.

	A	B	C
1	Checkbook balance		
2	Less bank charges:		
3	Service charge		
4	Bad check		
5	Total subtractions		
6	Adjusted checkbook balance		
7			
8	Bank statement balance		
9	Add unrecorded deposit		
10	Subtotal		
11	Less outstanding checks: #134		
12	#137		
13	#138		
14	Total outstanding check		
15	Adjusted bank balance		

THE BOTTOM LINE

Summary of chapter learning objectives:

Learning Objective	Example
9.1 Maintain a checking account.	1. Fill in the New Bal. and Bal. Fwd. on each check stub. Carry Bal. Fwd. to the next stub. **#1** **#2** Bal. Fwd. $100.00 Date 01/17 | Bal. Fwd. _____ Date 01/22 Deposit 350.50 To AAA | Deposit 375.00 To Longs New Bal. _____ | New Bal. _____ This Ck 175.09 For Ins. | This Ck 78.88 For Misc Bal. Fwd. _____ | Bal. Fwd. _____
9.2 Reconcile a bank statement with a checkbook balance.	2. Fill in the cash balance for each date.

CHECK REGISTER

DATE	CHECK NUMBER	CHECK TO—DEPOSIT INFORMATION	DEPOSIT AMOUNT	CHECK AMOUNT	BALANCE
					$453.90
12/11	100	Albertsons		$85.92	
12/12		Monthly Salary Check	$1,580.65		
12/13	101	C.Dobbs-Rent		$850.00	
12/14	102	TJ Max		$ 99.97	
12/15	103	Ace Hardware		$ 107.16	
12/17		Income from Stocks	$212.37		

9.2

Reconcile a bank statement with a checkbook balance.

3. Mike Kent's monthly bank statement balance was $1,418. His checkbook balance was $1,620. He noted the following checks outstanding: #119 for $350 and #125 for $197. He noted a deposit of $1,600 as not recorded by the bank. The bank had charged him $17 for checks and $32 for a bad check he had deposited. The bank had credited his account with an electronic transfer for $900. Reconcile the bank and checkbook balances.

Checkbook balance:	$1,620
Add electronic transfer:	_____
Subtotal	_____
Less bank charges: _____	
_____	_____
Adjusted checkbook balance:	_____
Bank balance on statement:	$1,418
Add unrecorded deposit:	_____
Subtotal	_____
Less outstanding checks: #119 _____	
#125 _____	_____
Adjusted bank balance	_____

Review Problems for Chapter 9

1. Each of the following items requires an adjustment to either the bank statement balance or the check register balance. Indicate the correct handling of each item by writing the appropriate letter in the blank.

> A = add to bank statement balance
> B = subtract from bank statement balance
> C = add to checkbook balance
> D = subtract from checkbook balance

_____ (a) Outstanding check written to the landlord for rent

_____ (b) Bank charge for printing checks

_____ (c) A deposit made at the end of the period that was not included on the bank statement

_____ (d) A customer's check that was returned by the bank for insufficient funds (a bounced check)

_____ (e) An error in recording a check in the check register. A check written to Acme Services for $92.20 was recorded in the check register as $95.50

_____ (f) Interest on the checking account

_____ (g) A bank fee of $20 for the bounced check

_____ (h) Bank fees for ATM withdrawals

_____ (i) A debit card purchase shown on the monthly bank statement

2. The balance in Ferndale Construction Company's check register May 31 was $12,583.40. The bank statement for Ferndale Construction Company listed the following information:

Previous balance (May 1)	$12,620.10
Deposits	16,265.00
Checks and withdrawals	17,805.95
Interest	52.50
Service charges	20.00
Check returned for insufficient funds	150.00
New balance (May 31)	$10,961.65

By comparing the bank statement and the check register, the company's bookkeeper determined that a deposit of $1,850.15 was not included on the statement and that the following checks were outstanding:

No. 602	$ 35.80
No. 610	212.00
No. 612	95.10

While preparing the reconciliation, the company's bookkeeper noted that check number 585, which had been written for $82.50, had been recorded in the check register as $85.50.

Prepare a bank reconciliation statement for Ferndale Construction Company.

Answers to the Self-Check can be found in Appendix B at the back of the text.

Assignment 9.1: Check Register and Check Stubs

Name _____

Date _____ Score _____

A (20 points) In the following check register, fill in the cash balance resulting from each transaction. (2 points for each correct answer)

1.

CHECK REGISTER			DEDUCT ALL PER CHECK OR SERVICE CHARGES THAT APPLY			BALANCE
DATE		CHECK NUMBER	CHECKS ISSUED TO OR DEPOSITS RECEIVED FROM	AMOUNT OF CHECK	AMOUNT OF DEPOSIT	$1,450.00
Apr	04	842	Alliance Mortgage Company	865.00		
	04	–	Deposit weekly cash receipts		4,197.50	
	05	843	U.S. Treasury	1,520.00		
	06	844	State Income Tax	990.00		
	07	845	General Telephone	65.30		
	08	846	Maxwell Office Supply	289.70		
	12	–	Deposit weekly cash receipts		3,845.25	
	12	847	Eastwood Water Co.	126.42		
	12	848	Central Advertising, Inc.	965.00		
	12	849	Johnson Tax Services	650.00		

Score for A (20)

B (15 points) Fill in the new balance (New. Bal.) and balance forward (Bal. Fwd.) on each check stub, carrying each balance forward to the next stub. (1$\frac{1}{2}$ points for each correct New Bal. answer)

2.
```
#101
Bal. Fwd. 920.15   Date 6-1    New Bal. _____
Deposit  300.00  To  ACE     This Ck  29.30
New Bal. _____  For REPAIR  Bal. Fwd. _____
```

3.
```
#102
Bal. Fwd. _____  Date 6-5    New Bal. _____
Deposit _____   To  DON     This Ck  312.80
New Bal. _____  For NOTE    Bal. Fwd. _____
```

4.
```
#103
Bal. Fwd. _____  Date 6-8    New Bal. _____
Deposit  862.13  To  NEC     This Ck  862.42
New Bal. _____  For COMPUTER Bal. Fwd. _____
```

5.
```
#104
Bal. Fwd. _____  Date 6-10   New Bal. _____
Deposit 2,160.00 To  CHRON   This Ck  1,200.27
New Bal. _____  For AD      Bal. Fwd. _____
```

6.
```
#105
Bal. Fwd. _____  Date 6-15   New Bal. _____
Deposit  907.16  To  B/A     This Ck  317.77
New Bal. _____  For CAR PAYMENT Bal. Fwd. _____
```

Score for B (15)

C (20 points) According to the check register of Kyber Electronics, the cash balance on July 1 was $1,335.60. During the month, deposits of $281.75, $681.10, and $385.60 were made. Checks for $98.99, $307.53, $19.56, $212.40, $287.60, and $88.62 were recorded. (15 points for a correct answer in 7; 5 points for a correct answer in 8)

7. What was the cash balance shown in the check register on July 31? _____

8. After entering all the items in the check register, the bookkeeper found that the check recorded as $212.40 was actually written as $224.20. What is the correct cash balance? _____

_____
Score for C (20)

D (45 points) The following problems show the deposits and checks that were recorded on a series of check stubs. In each problem, find the bank balance after each deposit or check. (3 points for each correct answer)

9.

Balance	$2,420	80
Check #1	279	10
Balance		
Check #2	148	20
Balance		
Deposit	976	80
Balance		
Check #3	814	00
Balance		
Check #4	285	17
Balance		

10.

Balance	$205	55
Check #21	25	00
Balance		
Deposit	721	45
Balance		
Check #22	188	14
Balance		
Check #23	415	92
Balance		
Check #24	72	38
Balance		

11.

Balance	$2,670	10
Deposit	350	00
Balance		
Check #31	265	72
Balance		
Check #32	85	70
Balance		
Deposit	935	62
Balance		
Check #33	1,230	14
Balance		

_____
Score for D (45)

Assignment 9.2: Check Register and Bank Statements

Name

Date   Score

A (40 points) Solve the following problems. (10 points for a correct final balance in 1; 30 points for a correct final answer in 2)

1. On October 31, the balance of the account of Hobbies Unlimited at the Citizens Bank was $922.10. This amount was also the balance on the check register at that time. Company checks written and deposits made during November are shown on the check register. Fill in the cash balance for each transaction.

CHECK REGISTER			DEDUCT ALL PER CHECK OR SERVICE CHARGES THAT APPLY			BALANCE
DATE		CHECK NUMBER	CHECKS ISSUED TO OR DEPOSITS RECEIVED FROM	AMOUNT OF CHECK	AMOUNT OF DEPOSIT	$922.10
Nov 01		551	Muni. Water, Inc. (2 mos)	119.60		
06		552	Fenton Gas Co.	49.60		
07		553	Olympia Telephone	74.19		
07		–	Deposit cash receipts		225.50	
21		554	City Trash Disposal (3 mos)	112.32		
21		555	Jack's Janitorial Service	33.33		
24		556	United Fund	12.00		
24		557	Guide Dogs for the Blind	67.77		
26		558	Wilson Insurance	212.00		
28		559	Security Systems, Inc.	138.00		
28		–	Deposit cash receipts		94.00	

2. On December 3, Hobbies Unlimited, whose check register you completed in problem 1, received the following bank statement. Reconcile the balance on the check register at the end of the month with the final balance on the bank statement. In reconciling the bank statement, you can find which of the checks are outstanding by comparing the list of checks on the statement with the register. Interest and a service charge were recorded on the statement.

C_B CITIZEN'S BANK

STATEMENT OF ACCOUNT

HOBBIES UNLIMITED
4617 GILMORE ROAD
WHEATLAND, WI 54828-6075

ACCOUNT NUMBER
072 4736

11/30/--

DATE OF STATEMENT

Balance From Previous Statement	Number of Debits	Amount of Checks and Debits	No. of Credits	Amount of Deposits and Credits	Service Charge	Statement Balance
922.10	8	594.81	2	229.70	9.00	547.99

DATE	CHECKS - DEBITS	CHECKS - DEBITS	DEPOSITS - CREDITS	BALANCE
11/03	119.60			802.50
11/05	49.60			752.90
11/09	9.00 SC			743.90
11/09	74.19			669.71
11/09			225.50 ATM	895.21
11/23	112.32	33.33		749.56
11/26	67.77			681.79
11/30	138.00			543.79
11/30			4.20 INT	547.99

PLEASE EXAMINE AND REPORT ANY DISCREPANCIES WITHIN 10 DAYS   DM-Debit Memo OD-Overdraft   ATM-Automated Teller Machine INT-Interest Paid   CM-Credit Memo SC-Service Charge

HOBBIES UNLIMITED
Reconciliation of Bank Statement
November 30

Bank balance on statement
Plus deposit not recorded by bank

Minus outstanding checks:

Checkbook balance
Plus bank interest

Minus service charge

Score for A (40)

B **(60 points) Solve the following problems. (12 points for each correct answer)**

3. Compute the reconciled balance for each of the problems from the information given.

	Bank Statement Balance	Checkbook Balance	Other Information	Reconciled Balance
a.	$ 769.12	$ 794.47	Outstanding checks: $9.50, $31.15 Automatic transfer to savings: $50.00 Automatic charge, safe-deposit box: $16.00	_____
b.	$1,559.39	$1,672.00	Outstanding checks: $84.62, $14.20, $55.00 Outstanding deposit: $224.70 Automatic transfer to savings: $50.00 Bank interest credited: $8.27	_____
c.	$ 893.17	$ 944.73	Outstanding checks: $7.50, $4.18, $62.40 Outstanding deposits: $12.32, $120.00 Bank interest credited: $24.18 Charge for printing new checks: $17.50	_____
d.	$ 824.90	$ 739.47	Outstanding checks: $87.50 Deposit of $76.89 shown in check register as $78.96	_____
e.	$ 412.50	$1,274.18	Outstanding checks: $150.00, $37.82 Outstanding deposit: $440.00 Deposit of $312.00 shown twice in check register Debit card charges deducted by bank: $224.00 ATM withdrawal: $73.50	_____

Score for B (60)

Assignment 9.3: Bank Balance Reconciliation Statements

Name _____

Date _____ Score _____

A **(50 points) Using the data provided, prepare a bank reconciliation statement in each of the following problems. Space is provided for your solutions. (25 points for each correct reconciliation)**

1. The balance shown in the bank statement of Cogswell Cooling, Inc., on November 30 was $1,050.82. The balance shown on the check register was $480.77. The following checks were outstanding:

No. 148	$13.90	No. 161	$ 96.35
No. 156	235.10	No. 165	222.20

   There was a bank interest credit of $12.00 and a service charge of $9.50 that had not been entered on Cogswell Cooling's check register.

2. The June 30 bank statement for Furgison Electric Company shows that a customer's bad check in the amount of $960 was returned and charged against Furgison Electric Company's account by the bank. This is the first knowledge the company had that one of the checks deposited was not good.

   The balance shown on Furgison Electric Company's bank statement was $22,367.14. The balance shown on the check register was $24,696.83. The following checks were outstanding:

No. 363	$1,066.20	No. 396	$1,544.14
No. 387	1,972.81	No. 397	772.86

   The following items required adjustment on the bank reconciliation statement:

Outstanding deposit:	$3,001.87
Automatic transfer to note payment:	$4,000.00
Bad check returned and charged to Furgison Electric Company's account by the bank:	$ 960.00
Bank interest credit:	$ 276.17

Score for A (50)

B **(50 points) Using the data provided, prepare a bank reconciliation statement in each of the following problems. Space is provided for your solutions. (25 points for each correct reconciliation)**

3. The balance shown on the May 31 bank statement of Judy Linberg was $17,595.26. The balance shown in the checkbook was $19,512.54. A deposit of $2,004.35 had not been credited by the bank, and the following checks were outstanding:

No. 730	$85.17	No. 753	$462.95	No. 761	$19.75
No. 749	1,216.20	No. 757	512.80	No. 768	982.90

The following items required adjustment on the bank reconciliation statement:

An ATM withdrawal on May 20	$ 80.00
Charge for printing checks	$ 18.00
Automatic insurance payment charged to depositor's account by the bank	$1,765.00
Check deposited by Linberg Floors, returned by bank as bad check	$ 920.00
Interest on bank account credited by the bank	$ 35.20
Debit card charges: $38.50; $29.30; $365.00; $12.10	$ 444.90

4. The balance shown on the June 30 bank statement of Greenwood Stables was $9,527.72. The balance shown on the check register was $7,124.13. The following checks were outstanding:

No. 516	$621.50	No. 521	$93.21	No. 523	$144.80
No. 526	935.11	No. 527	250.00	No. 528	416.35

The following items were listed on the bank statement:

Charge made by the bank for safe-deposit box	$ 20.00
Bank error: AA Realty's check was charged in error to Greenwood Stables' account	$ 82.50
Interest on bank account credited by the bank	$ 72.12
Bank charge for printing checks	$ 27.00

Score for B (50)

Payroll Records

10

Learning Objectives

By studying this chapter and completing all assignments, you will be able to:

Learning Objective	1	Prepare a payroll register.
Learning Objective	2	Compute federal income tax withholding amounts.
Learning Objective	3	Compute Social Security, Medicare, and other withholdings.
Learning Objective	4	Complete an employee's earnings record.
Learning Objective	5	Compute an employer's quarterly federal tax return.
Learning Objective	6	Compute an employer's federal and state unemployment tax liability.

Employers must keep payroll records, withhold and pay payroll taxes, and file quarterly and annual reports with state and federal government offices. The payroll records and processes described in this chapter are common to all employers.

Federal taxes paid by all employees include the federal income tax and the two contributions (commonly referred to as taxes) required by the Federal Insurance Contributions Act (FICA): Old-Age, Survivors, and Disability Insurance, commonly called Social Security; and Hospital Insurance, commonly called Medicare.

When hiring new employees, employers must verify each employee's eligibility to work in the United States, get the employee's Social Security number, and have the employee complete a **Form W-4.** The W-4 form shown in Figure 10-1 indicates that Kyle Abrum is married and claims four exemptions, which constitutes his **withholding allowance.**

Preparing a Payroll Register

Learning Objective 1

Prepare a payroll register.

A **payroll register** is a summary of employee status information, wages earned, payroll deductions, and take-home pay. Whether they do it manually or by computer, all employers maintain some form of payroll register.

A payroll register is prepared for each payroll period. Payroll periods are weekly, biweekly, semimonthly, or monthly. Figure 10-2 shows a payroll register for one weekly period. The line for Kyle Abrum shows that he is married, claims four withholding allowances, and is paid on an hourly basis at the rate of $17 per hour ($25.50 for overtime hours). For the current week, he worked 40 regular hours and 3 overtime hours, for gross earnings of $756.50. From his gross pay he had deductions for Social Security ($46.90), Medicare ($10.97), Federal Income Tax ($31.99), Group Medical Insurance ($39), Group Dental Insurance ($12), and Other ($42), totaling $182.86. His net pay was $573.64.

The Fair Labor Standards Act (FLSA), commonly called the federal wage and hour law, requires that nonexempt employees be paid 1½ times their regular hourly rate for all hours worked in excess of 40 per week. Following the FLSA requirements, the calculations for gross pay are as follows:

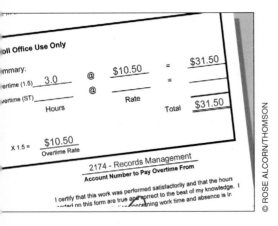

© ROSE ALCORN/THOMSON

STEP 1	Multiply hours worked (up to 40) times the regular rate.
STEP 2	Multiply the regular rate times 1.5 to calculate the overtime rate.
STEP 3	Multiply the hours in excess of 40 times the overtime rate.
STEP 4	Add the results of Steps 1 and 3 to determine gross pay.

Gross pay calculations for Kyle Abrum:

STEP 1	40 hours × $17 = $680 regular pay
STEP 2	$17 × 1.5 = $25.50 overtime rate
STEP 3	3 hours × $25.50 = $76.50 overtime pay
STEP 4	$680 + $76.50 = $756.50

Figure 10-1 | Form W-4 (2011)

Form W-4 (2011)

Purpose. Complete Form W-4 so that your employer can withhold the correct federal income tax from your pay. Consider completing a new Form W-4 each year and when your personal or financial situation changes.

Exemption from withholding. If you are exempt, complete **only** lines 1, 2, 3, 4, and 7 and sign the form to validate it. Your exemption for 2011 expires February 16, 2012. See Pub. 505, Tax Withholding and Estimated Tax.

Note. If another person can claim you as a dependent on his or her tax return, you cannot claim exemption from withholding if your income exceeds $950 and includes more than $300 of unearned income (for example, interest and dividends).

Basic instructions. If you are not exempt, complete the **Personal Allowances Worksheet** below. The worksheets on page 2 further adjust your withholding allowances based on itemized deductions, certain credits, adjustments to income, or two-earners/multiple jobs situations.

Complete all worksheets that apply. However, you may claim fewer (or zero) allowances. For regular wages, withholding must be based on allowances you claimed and may not be a flat amount or percentage of wages.

Head of household. Generally, you may claim head of household filing status on your tax return only if you are unmarried and pay more than 50% of the costs of keeping up a home for yourself and your dependent(s) or other qualifying individuals. See Pub. 501, Exemptions, Standard Deduction, and Filing Information, for information.

Tax credits. You can take projected tax credits into account in figuring your allowable number of withholding allowances. Credits for child or dependent care expenses and the child tax credit may be claimed using the **Personal Allowances Worksheet** below. See Pub. 919, How Do I Adjust My Tax Withholding, for information on converting your other credits into withholding allowances.

Nonwage income. If you have a large amount of nonwage income, such as interest or dividends, consider making estimated tax payments using

Form 1040-ES, Estimated Tax for Individuals. Otherwise, you may owe additional tax. If you have pension or annuity income, see Pub. 919 to find out if you should adjust your withholding on Form W-4 or W-4P.

Two earners or multiple jobs. If you have a working spouse or more than one job, figure the total number of allowances you are entitled to claim on all jobs using worksheets from only one Form W-4. Your withholding usually will be most accurate when all allowances are claimed on the Form W-4 for the highest paying job and zero allowances are claimed on the others. See Pub. 919 for details.

Nonresident alien. If you are a nonresident alien, see Notice 1392, Supplemental Form W-4 Instructions for Nonresident Aliens, before completing this form.

Check your withholding. After your Form W-4 takes effect, use Pub. 919 to see how the amount you are having withheld compares to your projected total tax for 2011. See Pub. 919, especially if your earnings exceed $130,000 (Single) or $180,000 (Married).

Personal Allowances Worksheet (Keep for your records.)

A	Enter "1" for **yourself** if no one else can claim you as a dependent	A _____
B	Enter "1" if: { • You are single and have only one job; or • You are married, have only one job, and your spouse does not work; or • Your wages from a second job or your spouse's wages (or the total of both) are $1,500 or less. } . . .	B _____
C	Enter "1" for your **spouse.** But, you may choose to enter "-0-" if you are married and have either a working spouse or more than one job. (Entering "-0-" may help you avoid having too little tax withheld.)	C _____
D	Enter number of **dependents** (other than your spouse or yourself) you will claim on your tax return . . .	D _____
E	Enter "1" if you will file as **head of household** on your tax return (see conditions under **Head of household** above) . .	E _____
F	Enter "1" if you have at least $1,900 of **child or dependent care expenses** for which you plan to claim a credit . .	F _____
	(**Note.** Do **not** include child support payments. See Pub. 503, Child and Dependent Care Expenses, for details.)	
G	**Child Tax Credit** (including additional child tax credit). See Pub. 972, Child Tax Credit, for more information. • If your total income will be less than $61,000 ($90,000 if married), enter "2" for each eligible child; then **less** "1" if you have three or more eligible children. • If your total income will be between $61,000 and $84,000 ($90,000 and $119,000 if married), enter "1" for each eligible child plus "1" **additional** if you have six or more eligible children	G _____
H	Add lines A through G and enter total here. (**Note.** This may be different from the number of exemptions you claim on your tax return.) ▶ H _____	

For accuracy, complete all worksheets that apply.	{ • If you plan to **itemize** or **claim adjustments to income** and want to reduce your withholding, see the **Deductions and Adjustments Worksheet** on page 2. • If you have **more than one job** or are **married and you and your spouse both work** and the combined earnings from all jobs exceed $40,000 ($10,000 if married), see the **Two-Earners/Multiple Jobs Worksheet** on page 2 to avoid having too little tax withheld. • If **neither** of the above situations applies, **stop here** and enter the number from line H on line 5 of Form W-4 below. }

Cut here and give Form W-4 to your employer. Keep the top part for your records.

Form **W-4** Department of the Treasury Internal Revenue Service	**Employee's Withholding Allowance Certificate** ▶ Whether you are entitled to claim a certain number of allowances or exemption from withholding is subject to review by the IRS. Your employer may be required to send a copy of this form to the IRS.	OMB No. 1545-0074 20**11**

1	Type or print your first name and middle initial. *Kyle B.*	Last name *Abrum*	2	Your social security number *123-45-6789*

Home address (number and street or rural route) *4052 Oak Avenue*	3 ☐ Single ☒ Married ☐ Married, but withhold at higher Single rate.
City or town, state, and ZIP code *Lawton, OK 12345*	**Note.** If married, but legally separated, or spouse is a nonresident alien, check the "Single" box.
	4 If your last name differs from that shown on your social security card, check here. You must call 1-800-772-1213 for a replacement card. ▶ ☐

5	Total number of allowances you are claiming (from line H above **or** from the applicable worksheet on page 2)	5	*4*
6	Additional amount, if any, you want withheld from each paycheck	6	$
7	I claim exemption from withholding for 2011, and I certify that I meet **both** of the following conditions for exemption. • Last year I had a right to a refund of **all** federal income tax withheld because I had **no** tax liability **and** • This year I expect a refund of **all** federal income tax withheld because I expect to have **no** tax liability. If you meet both conditions, write "Exempt" here . . . . ▶	7	

Under penalties of perjury, I declare that I have examined this certificate and to the best of my knowledge and belief, it is true, correct, and complete.

Employee's signature (This form is not valid unless you sign it.) ▶ *Kyle B. Abram*　　　　Date ▶ *2/16/20--*

8	Employer's name and address (Employer: Complete lines 8 and 10 only if sending to the IRS.)	9 Office code (optional)	10 Employer identification number (EIN)

For Privacy Act and Paperwork Reduction Act Notice, see page 2.　　　　Cat. No. 10220Q　　　　Form **W-4** (2011)

Figure 10-2 | Weekly Payroll Register

Name	Marital Status	Withholding Allowances	W = Weekly H = Hourly	Rate	Hours Reg.	Hours O/T	Gross Earnings	Social Security	Medi-care	Fed. Inc. Tax	Group Med. Ins.	Group Dental Ins.	Other	Total Deduc-tions	Net Earnings
Abrum, Kyle	M	4	H	17.00	40	3	756.50	46.90	10.97	31.99	39.00	12.00	42.00	182.86	573.64
Garcia, Fran	S	2	W	680.00	40		680.00	42.16	9.86	67.06	18.00	9.00	—	146.08	533.92
Parker, Marie	S	1	H	12.10	32		387.20	24.01	5.61	33.21	18.00	—	—	80.83	306.37
Thomas, Robert	M	5	H	15.70	40	4	722.20	44.78	10.47	21.45	39.00	12.00	13.10	140.80	581.40
Weber, James	S	1	H	16.80	40		672.00	41.66	9.74	75.93	18.00	9.00	—	154.33	517.67
TOTALS							3,217.90	199.51	46.65	229.64	132.00	42.00	55.10	704.90	2,513.00

✔ **CONCEPT CHECK 10.1**

After completion of the payroll register entries, one way to check on the accuracy of computations is to subtract the Total Deductions column from the Gross Earnings total; the difference should equal the total of the Net Earnings column. From the payroll register shown in Figure 10-2, check the accuracy of the column totals:

Total of Gross Earnings column	$3,217.90
Less Total Deductions column	− 704.90
Total of Net Earnings column	$2,513.00

Computing Federal Income Tax Withholding Amounts

The federal income tax is a payroll tax that the employer must withhold from the employee's pay and turn over to the Internal Revenue Service (IRS). The amount of the deduction varies with the amount of earnings, the employee's marital status, and the number of withholding allowances claimed.

The *Employer's Tax Guide,* published annually by the Internal Revenue Service, gives employers two primary methods to figure how much income tax to withhold from their employees. These two methods are the **percentage method** and the **wage-bracket method.**

Figure 10-2 shows that Kyle Abrum's federal income tax withholding amount was $31.99, computed by the percentage method. With the percentage method, a deduction is granted for each withholding allowance claimed, based on a chart in the *Employer's Tax Guide.* The amount for each withholding allowance is provided in a table labeled Income Tax Withholding Percentage Method Table. Figure 10-3 illustrates a recent table. It shows that, for weekly pay, a deduction of $71.15 is allowed for each withholding allowance. (For monthly pay, a deduction of $308.33 is allowed for each withholding allowance.)

| Figure 10-3 | Percentage Method Amount for One Withholding Allowance |

Payroll Period	One Withholding Allowance
Weekly	$ 71.15
Biweekly	$142.31
Semimonthly	$154.17
Monthly	$308.33

After the total withholding allowance is subtracted from an employee's gross earnings, the amount to be withheld is computed by taking a percentage of the difference. The percentage to be used is given by the IRS in the Tables for Percentage Method of Withholding. Figure 10-4 illustrates a recent table for weekly, biweekly, semimonthly, and monthly payroll periods.

STEPS **to Figure the Amount of Federal Income Tax Withholding, Using the Percentage Method**

1. Determine the employee's gross earnings.
2. Multiply the appropriate (weekly/monthly) "one withholding allowance" amount (from the withholding table in Figure 10-3) by the number of allowances the employee claims.
3. Subtract that amount from the employee's gross earnings.
4. From the appropriate (weekly/monthly and single/married) percentage method table, subtract the "of excess over" figure to get the amount subject to the tax.
5. Multiply the amount from Step 4 by the appropriate percentage from the percentage method table.
6. If required, add the base tax amount (if any) shown next to the percentage from the percentage method table. (For example, see Table 1, WEEKLY Payroll Period, Married, the second line of the table: $32.70 plus 15% of excess over $479.)

Figure 10-4 | Tables for Percentage Method of Withholding

Percentage Method Tables for Income Tax Withholding
(For Wages Paid in 2011)

TABLE 1—WEEKLY Payroll Period

(a) SINGLE person (including head of household)—

If the amount of wages (after subtracting withholding allowances) is:

Not over $40 . . . . $0

Over—	But not over—		of excess over—
$40	—$204	. . . $0.00 plus 10%	—$40
$204	—$704	. . . $16.40 plus 15%	—$204
$704	—$1,648	. . . $91.40 plus 25%	—$704
$1,648	—$3,394	. . . $327.40 plus 28%	—$1,648
$3,394	—$7,332	. . . $816.28 plus 33%	—$3,394
$7,332	. . . .	. . . $2,115.82 plus 35%	—$7,332

(b) MARRIED person—

If the amount of wages (after subtracting withholding allowances) is:

Not over $152 . . . . $0

Over—	But not over—		of excess over—
$152	—$479	. . . $0.00 plus 10%	—$152
$479	—$1,479	. . . $32.70 plus 15%	—$479
$1,479	—$2,832	. . . $182.70 plus 25%	—$1,479
$2,832	—$4,235	. . . $520.95 plus 28%	—$2,832
$4,235	—$7,443	. . . $913.79 plus 33%	—$4,235
$7,443	. . . .	. . . $1,972.43 plus 35%	—$7,443

TABLE 2—BIWEEKLY Payroll Period

(a) SINGLE person (including head of household)—

If the amount of wages (after subtracting withholding allowances) is:

Not over $81 . . . . $0

Over—	But not over—		of excess over—
$81	—$408	. . . $0.00 plus 10%	—$81
$408	—$1,408	. . . $32.70 plus 15%	—$408
$1,408	—$3,296	. . . $182.70 plus 25%	—$1,408
$3,296	—$6,788	. . . $654.70 plus 28%	—$3,296
$6,788	—$14,663	. . . $1,632.46 plus 33%	—$6,788
$14,663	. . . .	. . . $4,231.21 plus 35%	—$14,663

(b) MARRIED person—

If the amount of wages (after subtracting withholding allowances) is:

Not over $304 . . . . $0

Over—	But not over—		of excess over—
$304	—$958	. . . $0.00 plus 10%	—$304
$958	—$2,958	. . . $65.40 plus 15%	—$958
$2,958	—$5,663	. . . $365.40 plus 25%	—$2,958
$5,663	—$8,469	. . . $1,041.65 plus 28%	—$5,663
$8,469	—$14,887	. . . $1,827.33 plus 33%	—$8,469
$14,887	. . . .	. . . $3,945.27 plus 35%	—$14,887

TABLE 3—SEMIMONTHLY Payroll Period

(a) SINGLE person (including head of household)—

If the amount of wages (after subtracting withholding allowances) is:

Not over $88 . . . . $0

Over—	But not over—		of excess over—
$88	—$442	. . . $0.00 plus 10%	—$88
$442	—$1,525	. . . $35.40 plus 15%	—$442
$1,525	—$3,571	. . . $197.85 plus 25%	—$1,525
$3,571	—$7,354	. . . $709.35 plus 28%	—$3,571
$7,354	—$15,885	. . . $1,768.59 plus 33%	—$7,354
$15,885	. . . .	. . . $4,583.82 plus 35%	—$15,885

(b) MARRIED person—

If the amount of wages (after subtracting withholding allowances) is:

Not over $329 . . . . $0

Over—	But not over—		of excess over—
$329	—$1,038	. . . $0.00 plus 10%	—$329
$1,038	—$3,204	. . . $70.90 plus 15%	—$1,038
$3,204	—$6,135	. . . $395.80 plus 25%	—$3,204
$6,135	—$9,175	. . . $1,128.55 plus 28%	—$6,135
$9,175	—$16,127	. . . $1,979.75 plus 33%	—$9,175
$16,127	. . . .	. . . $4,273.91 plus 35%	—$16,127

TABLE 4—MONTHLY Payroll Period

(a) SINGLE person (including head of household)—

If the amount of wages (after subtracting withholding allowances) is:

Not over $175 . . . . $0

Over—	But not over—		of excess over—
$175	—$883	. . . $0.00 plus 10%	—$175
$883	—$3,050	. . . $70.80 plus 15%	—$883
$3,050	—$7,142	. . . $395.85 plus 25%	—$3,050
$7,142	—$14,708	. . . $1,418.85 plus 28%	—$7,142
$14,708	—$31,771	. . . $3,537.33 plus 33%	—$14,708
$31,771	. . . .	. . . $9,168.12 plus 35%	—$31,771

(b) MARRIED person—

If the amount of wages (after subtracting withholding allowances) is:

Not over $658 . . . . $0

Over—	But not over—		of excess over—
$658	—$2,075	. . . $0.00 plus 10%	—$658
$2,075	—$6,408	. . . $141.70 plus 15%	—$2,075
$6,408	—$12,271	. . . $791.65 plus 25%	—$6,408
$12,271	—$18,350	. . . $2,257.40 plus 28%	—$12,271
$18,350	—$32,254	. . . $3,959.52 plus 33%	—$18,350
$32,254	. . . .	. . . $8,547.84 plus 35%	—$32,254

EXAMPLE A

Using the six steps given, we compute Kyle Abrum's withholding as follows:

STEP 1
    $756.50   (gross earnings from payroll register)

STEP 2
    $ 71.15   (one withholding allowance)
    × 4   (number of withholding allowances)
    $284.60   (total withholding allowance amount)

STEP 3
    $756.50   (gross earnings)
    284.60   (total withholding allowance amount)
    $471.90   (amount subject to withholding)

STEP 4
    $471.90   (amount subject to withholding)
    152.00   (less "excess over" amount in Figure 10-4)
    $319.90   (amount subject to percentage computation)

STEP 5
    $319.90   (amount subject to percentage computation)
    × 0.1   (10% computation)
    $ 31.99   (amount of tax withheld)

STEP 6
    The wage range $152–$479 doesn't have a base tax amount and therefore doesn't apply in the case of Kyle Abrum.

The second method of figuring the amount of tax to be withheld from an employee's pay, the wage-bracket method, involves use of a series of wage-bracket tables published in the IRS *Employer's Tax Guide*. Figures 10-5 and 10-6 illustrate the tables for single and married persons, respectively, who are paid on a weekly basis.

Using the tables from Figure 10-6, we see that a married employee earning a weekly wage of between $530 and $540 and claiming four withholding allowances will have $10 withheld. Note that the amount of federal income tax withheld from Kyle Abrum's pay, using the wage-bracket method, is approximately the same as the amount withheld using the percentage method: $32 versus $31.99. Small differences will frequently result because the wage-bracket method uses tables based on $10 divisions and rounded amounts. Over a period of a year, these differences tend to be relatively insignificant and are accepted by the IRS.

Figure 10-5 | Single Persons—Weekly Payroll Period

SINGLE Persons—WEEKLY Payroll Period
(For Wages Paid through December 2011)

And the wages are—		And the number of withholding allowances claimed is—										
At least	But less than	0	1	2	3	4	5	6	7	8	9	10
		The amount of income tax to be withheld is—										
$ 0	$55	$0	$0	$0	$0	$0	$0	$0	$0	$0	$0	$0
55	60	2	0	0	0	0	0	0	0	0	0	0
60	65	2	0	0	0	0	0	0	0	0	0	0
65	70	3	0	0	0	0	0	0	0	0	0	0
70	75	3	0	0	0	0	0	0	0	0	0	0
75	80	4	0	0	0	0	0	0	0	0	0	0
80	85	4	0	0	0	0	0	0	0	0	0	0
85	90	5	0	0	0	0	0	0	0	0	0	0
90	95	5	0	0	0	0	0	0	0	0	0	0
95	100	6	0	0	0	0	0	0	0	0	0	0
100	105	6	0	0	0	0	0	0	0	0	0	0
105	110	7	0	0	0	0	0	0	0	0	0	0
110	115	7	0	0	0	0	0	0	0	0	0	0
115	120	8	1	0	0	0	0	0	0	0	0	0
120	125	8	1	0	0	0	0	0	0	0	0	0
125	130	9	2	0	0	0	0	0	0	0	0	0
130	135	9	2	0	0	0	0	0	0	0	0	0
135	140	10	3	0	0	0	0	0	0	0	0	0
140	145	10	3	0	0	0	0	0	0	0	0	0
145	150	11	4	0	0	0	0	0	0	0	0	0
150	155	11	4	0	0	0	0	0	0	0	0	0
155	160	12	5	0	0	0	0	0	0	0	0	0
160	165	12	5	0	0	0	0	0	0	0	0	0
165	170	13	6	0	0	0	0	0	0	0	0	0
170	175	13	6	0	0	0	0	0	0	0	0	0
175	180	14	7	0	0	0	0	0	0	0	0	0
180	185	14	7	0	0	0	0	0	0	0	0	0
185	190	15	8	0	0	0	0	0	0	0	0	0
190	195	15	8	1	0	0	0	0	0	0	0	0
195	200	16	9	1	0	0	0	0	0	0	0	0
200	210	17	9	2	0	0	0	0	0	0	0	0
210	220	18	10	3	0	0	0	0	0	0	0	0
220	230	20	11	4	0	0	0	0	0	0	0	0
230	240	21	12	5	0	0	0	0	0	0	0	0
240	250	23	13	6	0	0	0	0	0	0	0	0
250	260	24	14	7	0	0	0	0	0	0	0	0
260	270	26	15	8	1	0	0	0	0	0	0	0
270	280	27	16	9	2	0	0	0	0	0	0	0
280	290	29	18	10	3	0	0	0	0	0	0	0
290	300	30	19	11	4	0	0	0	0	0	0	0
300	310	32	21	12	5	0	0	0	0	0	0	0
310	320	33	22	13	6	0	0	0	0	0	0	0
320	330	35	24	14	7	0	0	0	0	0	0	0
330	340	36	25	15	8	1	0	0	0	0	0	0
340	350	38	27	16	9	2	0	0	0	0	0	0
350	360	39	28	18	10	3	0	0	0	0	0	0
360	370	41	30	19	11	4	0	0	0	0	0	0
370	380	42	31	21	12	5	0	0	0	0	0	0
380	390	44	33	22	13	6	0	0	0	0	0	0
390	400	45	34	24	14	7	0	0	0	0	0	0
400	410	47	36	25	15	8	1	0	0	0	0	0
410	420	48	37	27	16	9	2	0	0	0	0	0
420	430	50	39	28	18	10	3	0	0	0	0	0
430	440	51	40	30	19	11	4	0	0	0	0	0
440	450	53	42	31	21	12	5	0	0	0	0	0
450	460	54	43	33	22	13	6	0	0	0	0	0
460	470	56	45	34	24	14	7	0	0	0	0	0
470	480	57	46	36	25	15	8	1	0	0	0	0
480	490	59	48	37	27	16	9	2	0	0	0	0
490	500	60	49	39	28	17	10	3	0	0	0	0
500	510	62	51	40	30	19	11	4	0	0	0	0
510	520	63	52	42	31	20	12	5	0	0	0	0
520	530	65	54	43	33	22	13	6	0	0	0	0
530	540	66	55	45	34	23	14	7	0	0	0	0
540	550	68	57	46	36	25	15	8	1	0	0	0
550	560	69	58	48	37	26	16	9	2	0	0	0
560	570	71	60	49	39	28	17	10	3	0	0	0
570	580	72	61	51	40	29	19	11	4	0	0	0
580	590	74	63	52	42	31	20	12	5	0	0	0
590	600	75	64	54	43	32	22	13	6	0	0	0

Figure 10-5 | (Continued)

SINGLE Persons—WEEKLY Payroll Period
(For Wages Paid through December 2011)

And the wages are—		And the number of withholding allowances claimed is—										
At least	But less than	0	1	2	3	4	5	6	7	8	9	10
		The amount of income tax to be withheld is—										
$600	$610	$77	$66	$55	$45	$34	$23	$14	$7	$0	$0	$0
610	620	78	67	57	46	35	25	15	8	1	0	0
620	630	80	69	58	48	37	26	16	9	2	0	0
630	640	81	70	60	49	38	28	17	10	3	0	0
640	650	83	72	61	51	40	29	18	11	4	0	0
650	660	84	73	63	52	41	31	20	12	5	0	0
660	670	86	75	64	54	43	32	21	13	6	0	0
670	680	87	76	66	55	44	34	23	14	7	0	0
680	690	89	78	67	57	46	35	24	15	8	0	0
690	700	90	79	69	58	47	37	26	16	9	1	0
700	710	92	81	70	60	49	38	27	17	10	2	0
710	720	94	82	72	61	50	40	29	18	11	3	0
720	730	97	84	73	63	52	41	30	20	12	4	0
730	740	99	85	75	64	53	43	32	21	13	5	0
740	750	102	87	76	66	55	44	33	23	14	6	0
750	760	104	88	78	67	56	46	35	24	15	7	0
760	770	107	90	79	69	58	47	36	26	16	8	1
770	780	109	91	81	70	59	49	38	27	17	9	2
780	790	112	94	82	72	61	50	39	29	18	10	3
790	800	114	96	84	73	62	52	41	30	20	11	4
800	810	117	99	85	75	64	53	42	32	21	12	5
810	820	119	101	87	76	65	55	44	33	23	13	6
820	830	122	104	88	78	67	56	45	35	24	14	7
830	840	124	106	90	79	68	58	47	36	26	15	8
840	850	127	109	91	81	70	59	48	38	27	16	9
850	860	129	111	94	82	71	61	50	39	29	18	10
860	870	132	114	96	84	73	62	51	41	30	19	11
870	880	134	116	99	85	74	64	53	42	32	21	12
880	890	137	119	101	87	76	65	54	44	33	22	13
890	900	139	121	104	88	77	67	56	45	35	24	14
900	910	142	124	106	90	79	68	57	47	36	25	15
910	920	144	126	109	91	80	70	59	48	38	27	16
920	930	147	129	111	93	82	71	60	50	39	28	18
930	940	149	131	114	96	83	73	62	51	41	30	19
940	950	152	134	116	98	85	74	63	53	42	31	21
950	960	154	136	119	101	86	76	65	54	44	33	22
960	970	157	139	121	103	88	77	66	56	45	34	24
970	980	159	141	124	106	89	79	68	57	47	36	25
980	990	162	144	126	108	91	80	69	59	48	37	27
990	1,000	164	146	129	111	93	82	71	60	50	39	28
1,000	1,010	167	149	131	113	95	83	72	62	51	40	30
1,010	1,020	169	151	134	116	98	85	74	63	53	42	31
1,020	1,030	172	154	136	118	100	86	75	65	54	43	33
1,030	1,040	174	156	139	121	103	88	77	66	56	45	34
1,040	1,050	177	159	141	123	105	89	78	68	57	46	36
1,050	1,060	179	161	144	126	108	91	80	69	59	48	37
1,060	1,070	182	164	146	128	110	93	81	71	60	49	39
1,070	1,080	184	166	149	131	113	95	83	72	62	51	40
1,080	1,090	187	169	151	133	115	98	84	74	63	52	42
1,090	1,100	189	171	154	136	118	100	86	75	65	54	43
1,100	1,110	192	174	156	138	120	103	87	77	66	55	45
1,110	1,120	194	176	159	141	123	105	89	78	68	57	46
1,120	1,130	197	179	161	143	125	108	90	80	69	58	48
1,130	1,140	199	181	164	146	128	110	92	81	71	60	49
1,140	1,150	202	184	166	148	130	113	95	83	72	61	51
1,150	1,160	204	186	169	151	133	115	97	84	74	63	52
1,160	1,170	207	189	171	153	135	118	100	86	75	64	54
1,170	1,180	209	191	174	156	138	120	102	87	77	66	55
1,180	1,190	212	194	176	158	140	123	105	89	78	67	57
1,190	1,200	214	196	179	161	143	125	107	90	80	69	58
1,200	1,210	217	199	181	163	145	128	110	92	81	70	60
1,210	1,220	219	201	184	166	148	130	112	95	83	72	61
1,220	1,230	222	204	186	168	150	133	115	97	84	73	63
1,230	1,240	224	206	189	171	153	135	117	100	86	75	64
1,240	1,250	227	209	191	173	155	138	120	102	87	76	66

| $1,250 and over | Use Table 1(a) for a **SINGLE person** on page 36. Also see the instructions on page 35. |

Figure 10-6 | Married Persons—Weekly Payroll Period

MARRIED Persons—WEEKLY Payroll Period

(For Wages Paid through December 2011)

And the wages are—		And the number of withholding allowances claimed is—										
At least	But less than	0	1	2	3	4	5	6	7	8	9	10
		The amount of income tax to be withheld is—										
$ 0	$155	$0	$0	$0	$0	$0	$0	$0	$0	$0	$0	$0
155	160	1	0	0	0	0	0	0	0	0	0	0
160	165	1	0	0	0	0	0	0	0	0	0	0
165	170	2	0	0	0	0	0	0	0	0	0	0
170	175	2	0	0	0	0	0	0	0	0	0	0
175	180	3	0	0	0	0	0	0	0	0	0	0
180	185	3	0	0	0	0	0	0	0	0	0	0
185	190	4	0	0	0	0	0	0	0	0	0	0
190	195	4	0	0	0	0	0	0	0	0	0	0
195	200	5	0	0	0	0	0	0	0	0	0	0
200	210	5	0	0	0	0	0	0	0	0	0	0
210	220	6	0	0	0	0	0	0	0	0	0	0
220	230	7	0	0	0	0	0	0	0	0	0	0
230	240	8	1	0	0	0	0	0	0	0	0	0
240	250	9	2	0	0	0	0	0	0	0	0	0
250	260	10	3	0	0	0	0	0	0	0	0	0
260	270	11	4	0	0	0	0	0	0	0	0	0
270	280	12	5	0	0	0	0	0	0	0	0	0
280	290	13	6	0	0	0	0	0	0	0	0	0
290	300	14	7	0	0	0	0	0	0	0	0	0
300	310	15	8	1	0	0	0	0	0	0	0	0
310	320	16	9	2	0	0	0	0	0	0	0	0
320	330	17	10	3	0	0	0	0	0	0	0	0
330	340	18	11	4	0	0	0	0	0	0	0	0
340	350	19	12	5	0	0	0	0	0	0	0	0
350	360	20	13	6	0	0	0	0	0	0	0	0
360	370	21	14	7	0	0	0	0	0	0	0	0
370	380	22	15	8	1	0	0	0	0	0	0	0
380	390	23	16	9	2	0	0	0	0	0	0	0
390	400	24	17	10	3	0	0	0	0	0	0	0
400	410	25	18	11	4	0	0	0	0	0	0	0
410	420	26	19	12	5	0	0	0	0	0	0	0
420	430	27	20	13	6	0	0	0	0	0	0	0
430	440	28	21	14	7	0	0	0	0	0	0	0
440	450	29	22	15	8	1	0	0	0	0	0	0
450	460	30	23	16	9	2	0	0	0	0	0	0
460	470	31	24	17	10	3	0	0	0	0	0	0
470	480	32	25	18	11	4	0	0	0	0	0	0
480	490	34	26	19	12	5	0	0	0	0	0	0
490	500	35	27	20	13	6	0	0	0	0	0	0
500	510	37	28	21	14	7	0	0	0	0	0	0
510	520	38	29	22	15	8	1	0	0	0	0	0
520	530	40	30	23	16	9	2	0	0	0	0	0
530	540	41	31	24	17	10	3	0	0	0	0	0
540	550	43	32	25	18	11	4	0	0	0	0	0
550	560	44	33	26	19	12	5	0	0	0	0	0
560	570	46	35	27	20	13	6	0	0	0	0	0
570	580	47	36	28	21	14	7	0	0	0	0	0
580	590	49	38	29	22	15	8	1	0	0	0	0
590	600	50	39	30	23	16	9	2	0	0	0	0
600	610	52	41	31	24	17	10	3	0	0	0	0
610	620	53	42	32	25	18	11	4	0	0	0	0
620	630	55	44	33	26	19	12	5	0	0	0	0
630	640	56	45	35	27	20	13	6	0	0	0	0
640	650	58	47	36	28	21	14	7	0	0	0	0
650	660	59	48	38	29	22	15	8	1	0	0	0
660	670	61	50	39	30	23	16	9	2	0	0	0
670	680	62	51	41	31	24	17	10	3	0	0	0
680	690	64	53	42	32	25	18	11	4	0	0	0
690	700	65	54	44	33	26	19	12	5	0	0	0
700	710	67	56	45	35	27	20	13	6	0	0	0
710	720	68	57	47	36	28	21	14	7	0	0	0
720	730	70	59	48	38	29	22	15	8	0	0	0
730	740	71	60	50	39	30	23	16	9	1	0	0
740	750	73	62	51	41	31	24	17	10	2	0	0
750	760	74	63	53	42	32	25	18	11	3	0	0
760	770	76	65	54	44	33	26	19	12	4	0	0
770	780	77	66	56	45	34	27	20	13	5	0	0
780	790	79	68	57	47	36	28	21	14	6	0	0
790	800	80	69	59	48	37	29	22	15	7	0	0

Figure 10-6 | (Continued)

MARRIED Persons—WEEKLY Payroll Period
(For Wages Paid through December 2011)

And the wages are—		And the number of withholding allowances claimed is—										
At least	But less than	0	1	2	3	4	5	6	7	8	9	10
		The amount of income tax to be withheld is—										
$800	$810	$82	$71	$60	$50	$39	$30	$23	$16	$8	$1	$0
810	820	83	72	62	51	40	31	24	17	9	2	0
820	830	85	74	63	53	42	32	25	18	10	3	0
830	840	86	75	65	54	43	33	26	19	11	4	0
840	850	88	77	66	56	45	34	27	20	12	5	0
850	860	89	78	68	57	46	36	28	21	13	6	0
860	870	91	80	69	59	48	37	29	22	14	7	0
870	880	92	81	71	60	49	39	30	23	15	8	1
880	890	94	83	72	62	51	40	31	24	16	9	2
890	900	95	84	74	63	52	42	32	25	17	10	3
900	910	97	86	75	65	54	43	33	26	18	11	4
910	920	98	87	77	66	55	45	34	27	19	12	5
920	930	100	89	78	68	57	46	36	28	20	13	6
930	940	101	90	80	69	58	48	37	29	21	14	7
940	950	103	92	81	71	60	49	39	30	22	15	8
950	960	104	93	83	72	61	51	40	31	23	16	9
960	970	106	95	84	74	63	52	42	32	24	17	10
970	980	107	96	86	75	64	54	43	33	25	18	11
980	990	109	98	87	77	66	55	45	34	26	19	12
990	1,000	110	99	89	78	67	57	46	35	27	20	13
1,000	1,010	112	101	90	80	69	58	48	37	28	21	14
1,010	1,020	113	102	92	81	70	60	49	38	29	22	15
1,020	1,030	115	104	93	83	72	61	51	40	30	23	16
1,030	1,040	116	105	95	84	73	63	52	41	31	24	17
1,040	1,050	118	107	96	86	75	64	54	43	32	25	18
1,050	1,060	119	108	98	87	76	66	55	44	34	26	19
1,060	1,070	121	110	99	89	78	67	57	46	35	27	20
1,070	1,080	122	111	101	90	79	69	58	47	37	28	21
1,080	1,090	124	113	102	92	81	70	60	49	38	29	22
1,090	1,100	125	114	104	93	82	72	61	50	40	30	23
1,100	1,110	127	116	105	95	84	73	63	52	41	31	24
1,110	1,120	128	117	107	96	85	75	64	53	43	32	25
1,120	1,130	130	119	108	98	87	76	66	55	44	34	26
1,130	1,140	131	120	110	99	88	78	67	56	46	35	27
1,140	1,150	133	122	111	101	90	79	69	58	47	37	28
1,150	1,160	134	123	113	102	91	81	70	59	49	38	29
1,160	1,170	136	125	114	104	93	82	72	61	50	40	30
1,170	1,180	137	126	116	105	94	84	73	62	52	41	31
1,180	1,190	139	128	117	107	96	85	75	64	53	43	32
1,190	1,200	140	129	119	108	97	87	76	65	55	44	33
1,200	1,210	142	131	120	110	99	88	78	67	56	46	35
1,210	1,220	143	132	122	111	100	90	79	68	58	47	36
1,220	1,230	145	134	123	113	102	91	81	70	59	49	38
1,230	1,240	146	135	125	114	103	93	82	71	61	50	39
1,240	1,250	148	137	126	116	105	94	84	73	62	52	41
1,250	1,260	149	138	128	117	106	96	85	74	64	53	42
1,260	1,270	151	140	129	119	108	97	87	76	65	55	44
1,270	1,280	152	141	131	120	109	99	88	77	67	56	45
1,280	1,290	154	143	132	122	111	100	90	79	68	58	47
1,290	1,300	155	144	134	123	112	102	91	80	70	59	48
1,300	1,310	157	146	135	125	114	103	93	82	71	61	50
1,310	1,320	158	147	137	126	115	105	94	83	73	62	51
1,320	1,330	160	149	138	128	117	106	96	85	74	64	53
1,330	1,340	161	150	140	129	118	108	97	86	76	65	54
1,340	1,350	163	152	141	131	120	109	99	88	77	67	56
1,350	1,360	164	153	143	132	121	111	100	89	79	68	57
1,360	1,370	166	155	144	134	123	112	102	91	80	70	59
1,370	1,380	167	156	146	135	124	114	103	92	82	71	60
1,380	1,390	169	158	147	137	126	115	105	94	83	73	62
1,390	1,400	170	159	149	138	127	117	106	95	85	74	63

$1,400 and over   Use Table 1(b) for a **MARRIED person** on page 36. Also see the instructions on page 35.

INTERNAL REVENUE SERVICE; HTTP://WWW.IRS.GOV

Using the percentage method steps given, verify the federal income tax withholding for Fran Garcia as recorded in the payroll register.

| STEP 1 | $680.00 | (gross earnings from payroll register) |

STEP 2	$ 71.15	(one withholding allowance)
	× 2	(number of withholding allowances)
	$142.30	(total withholding allowance amount)

STEP 3	$680.00	(gross earnings)
	142.30	(total withholding allowance amount)
	$537.70	(amount subject to withholding)

STEP 4	$537.70	(amount subject to withholding)
	−204.00	(less "excess over" amount in Figure 10-4)
	$337.70	(amount subject to percentage computation)

STEP 5	$337.70	(amount subject to percentage computation)
	× 0.15	(15% computation)
	$ 50.66	(amount of tax withheld on percentage computation)

STEP 6	$ 50.66	(amount of tax withhold on percentage computation)
	+16.40	(base tax amount)
	$ 67.06	(total amount of tax withheld)

Use the wage-bracket method to find the federal income tax withholding for Fran Garcia. Then compute the difference between the percentage method and the wage-bracket method.

Percentage method (Step 6)	$67.06
Wage-bracket method (Figure 10-5 because she is single)	−67.00
Difference	$ 0.06

Computing Social Security, Medicare, and Other Withholdings

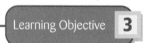

Learning Objective 3

Compute Social Security, Medicare, and other withholdings.

The **Federal Insurance Contributions Act (FICA)** provides for a federal system of old-age, survivors, disability, and hospital insurance. The old-age, survivors, and disability insurance part of FICA is financed by the *Social Security tax*. The hospital insurance part of FICA is financed by the *Medicare tax*. These taxes are reported separately and are levied on both the employer and the employee. These taxes have different rates, but only the Social Security tax has a wage base, which is the *maximum* wage that is subject to the tax for the year.

The Social Security tax rate of 6.2% (reduced to 4.2% for 2011) is levied on both the employer and the employee. For 2010 and 2011, the wage base was $106,800.

The Medicare tax rate of 1.45% is levied on both the employer and the employee. There is no wage-base limit for Medicare; all covered wages are subject to the Medicare tax.

Although both rates are subject to change by legislation, they were current when we compiled the payroll register illustrated in this chapter. All amounts are rounded to the nearest cent. The amounts for Kyle Abrum were $46.90 for Social Security and $10.97 for Medicare.

EXAMPLE B

Social Security deduction:

$756.50	(gross earnings)
× 0.062	(Social Security rate)
$ 46.90	(Social Security amount)

EXAMPLE C

Medicare deduction:

$756.50	(gross earnings)
× .0145	(Medicare rate)
$ 10.97	(Medicare amount)

Many employers today provide some form of group medical insurance for their employees. Frequently, the employee is asked to pay a portion of the premium charged for such insurance, based on the number of dependents the employee has named to be insured. For the payroll register shown in Figure 10-2, we assumed the weekly rates for medical and dental plans shown in Figure 10-7.

Figure 10-7	Weekly Medical and Dental Plan Rates	
	Weekly Medical Plan Premium Paid by Employee	**Weekly Dental Plan Premium Paid by Employee**
Employee only	$18.00	$9.00
Employee plus one dependent	$22.00	$10.00
Employee plus 2 or more dependents	$39.00	$12.00

The payroll register presented in Figure 10-2 showed that Kyle Abrum subscribed to both the medical and the dental programs. Because of his three dependents, the amounts of his deductions were $39 and $12, respectively.

Frequently, employees will arrange to have special payroll deductions made by the employer to pay union dues, put money into special retirement or savings plans, or make contributions to charitable organizations.

In addition, 42 of the 50 states have some form of state income tax, which normally requires withholding in the same manner as the federal income tax. In such states, state income tax withholding columns are added to the payroll register and withholdings are made according to wage-bracket or percentage charts established by the state, in the same manner as federal income tax withholdings.

The payroll register illustrated in Figure 10-2 reflects a $42 weekly deduction that Kyle Abrum requested be made for payment of his union dues (other).

Using the format in examples B and C, compute Social Security and Medicare amounts for Fran Garcia, based on her gross weekly earnings of $680.

Social Security deduction:

$ 680	(gross earnings)
× 0.062	(Social Security rate)
$42.16	(Social Security amount)

Medicare deduction:

$ 680	(gross earnings)
× 0.0145	(Medicare rate)
$9.86	(Medicare amount)

Completing an Employee's Earnings Record

Learning Objective 4

Complete an employee's earnings record.

An employer must submit quarterly and annual reports to the federal government and appropriate state government and pay the amount of taxes withheld from employees' earnings for the period. To obtain the necessary information, most employers keep an **employee's earnings record** for each employee. The employee's earnings record summarizes by quarter the employee's gross earnings, deductions, and net pay.

EXAMPLE D

Figure 10-8 Employee's Earnings Record

Name **Kyle Abrum**   Social Security No. **123-45-6789**
Address **3721 Kiber Road**   No. of Allowances **4**   Marital Status **Married**

Period Ending	Total Wages	Cumulative Wages	Deductions					Net Pay
			Social Security	Medicare	Federal Inc. Tax	Other Deductions	Total	
1/4	$ 680.00	$ 680.00	$ 42.16	$ 9.86	$ 24.34	$ 93.00	$ 169.36	$ 510.64
1/11	680.00	1,360.00	42.16	9.86	24.34	93.00	169.36	510.64
3/29	756.50	7,250.00	46.90	10.97	31.99	93.00	182.86	573.64
Quarter Totals	$8,950.00		$554.90	$129.78	$334.24	$ 1,209	$2,227.92	$6,722.09

The employee's earnings record presented in Figure 10-8 shows that Kyle Abrum is married, claims four allowances, and for the first quarter of the year earned total wages of $8,950. His net pay was $6,722.09 after first-quarter withholdings as follows:

Federal income tax withholding	$ 334.24
Social Security withholding	554.90
Medicare withholding	129.78
Other deductions	+1,209.00
Total deductions	$2,227.92

Assuming that Fran Garcia's weekly earnings and deductions have remained constant for each of the 13 weeks in the first quarter of the year, compute the following totals, which would appear on her employee's earnings record for the first quarter:

Total wages	$8,840.00	($680.00 × 13)
Federal income tax withholding	871.78	($67.06 × 13)
Social Security withholding	548.08	($42.16 × 13)
Medicare withholding	128.18	($9.86 × 13)
Group medical insurance deductions	234.00	($18.00 × 13)
Group dental insurance deductions	117.00	($9.00 × 13)
Total deductions	$1,899.04	
Net pay	$6,940.96	

Computing an Employer's Quarterly Federal Tax Return

Every employer who withholds federal income tax and FICA taxes (Social Security and Medicare) must file a quarterly return, Form 941—**Employer's Quarterly Federal Tax Return.** Figure 10-9 shows the data that the employer must include on Form 941 (the completed form is slightly abbreviated here). The return must be filed with the IRS within one month after the end of the quarter.

The employer obtains Social Security and Medicare amounts by multiplying the taxable wages paid by 12.4% for the first $106,800 for Social Security and by 2.9% for all wages for Medicare. These amounts represent the employees' deductions and matching amounts required to be paid by the employer.

Learning Objective **5**

Compute an employer's quarterly federal tax return.

● **EXAMPLE E**

For the first quarter of 2010, Yeager Manufacturing paid total wages of $2,132,684.27. The company withheld $372,486.20 for federal income tax. Since no employee earned more than $106,800 in taxable wages, all wages paid were subject to Social Security and Medicare taxes. If during the quarter Yeager had deposited $680,000 toward its taxes due, how much would it be required to send in with its first-quarter Form 941?

Gross wages $2,132,684.27 × 12.4% (Social Security)	$264,452.85
Gross wages $2,132,684.27 × 2.9% (Medicare)	+ 61,847.84
Subtotal	326,300.69
Income taxes withheld	+372,486.20
Total	698,786.89
Less deposit	−680,000.00
Balance due	$ 18,786.89

Figure 10-9 | Form 941 Employer's Quarterly Federal Tax Return (extract)

1 Number of employees who received wages, tips, or other compensation for the pay period
    including: *Mar. 12* (Quarter 1), *June 12* (Quarter 2), *Sept. 12* (Quarter 3), *Dec. 12* (Quarter 4)   **1** | 5

2 Wages, tips, and other compensation . . . .   **2** | 60,138 . 12

3 Total income tax withheld from wages, tips, and other compensation . . . .   **3** | 4,997 . 45

4 If no wages, tips, and other compensation are subject to social security or Medicare tax . . ☐ Check and go to line 6.

5 Taxable social security and Medicare wages and tips:

	Column 1		Column 2
5a Taxable social security wages	60,138 . 12	× .124 =	7,457 . 13
5b Taxable social security tips	.	× .124 =	.
5c Taxable Medicare wages & tips	60,138 . 12	× .029 =	1,744 . 01

5d Total social security and Medicare taxes (*Column 2*, lines 5a + 5b + 5c = line 5d) . . **5d** | 9,201 . 14

6 Total taxes before adjustments (lines 3 + 5d = line 6) . . . .   **6** | 14,198 . 59

7 TAX ADJUSTMENTS (read the instructions for line 7 before completing lines 7a through 7g):

7a Current quarter's fractions of cents . . . .

7b Current quarter's sick pay . . . .

7c Current quarter's adjustments for tips and group-term life insurance   .

7d Current year's income tax withholding (attach Form 941c) . .   .

7e Prior quarters' social security and Medicare taxes (attach Form 941c)   .

7f Special additions to federal income tax (attach Form 941c) . .   .

7g Special additions to social security and Medicare (attach Form 941c)   .

7h TOTAL ADJUSTMENTS (combine all amounts: lines 7a through 7g) . . . . .   **7h** | 0 . 00

8 Total taxes after adjustments (combine lines 6 and 7h) . . . .   **8** | 14,198 . 59

9 Advance earned income credit (EIC) payments made to employees . . . . . .   **9** | .

10 Total taxes after adjustment for advance EIC (line 8 – line 9 = line 10) . . . . . .   **10** | 14,198 . 59

11 Total deposits for this quarter, including overpayment applied from a prior quarter . .   **11** | 14,107 . 58

12 Balance due (If line 10 is more than line 11, write the difference here.) . . . .   **12** | 91 . 01
    For information on how to pay, see the instructions.

13 Overpayment (If line 11 is more than line 10, write the difference here.)   .   Check one ☐ Apply to next return.
                                                                                            ☐ Send a refund.

▶ You **MUST** fill out both pages of this form and **SIGN** it.   [Next ▶]

✔ CONCEPT CHECK 10.5

As displayed in Figure 10-9, the total taxes due the IRS consist of the $4,997.45 in federal income taxes withheld from employees, plus $7,457.13 and $1,744.01 for Social Security and Medicare taxes, respectively, half of which is withheld from the employees' paychecks and half of which is paid by the employer. Although the employer files Form 941 quarterly, the amount of taxes due is usually deposited in a qualified depository (bank) monthly or more often, and it is only the difference between the monthly deposits and the total taxes due that is sent with the Form 941 report.

Computing an Employer's Federal and State Unemployment Tax Liability

In the preceding section, you learned that the employer must match the employee's contributions to Social Security and Medicare taxes. In addition, employers must pay two payroll taxes for federal and state unemployment programs.

Learning Objective **6**

The **Federal Unemployment Tax Act (FUTA)** annually requires the employer to pay a 6.2% tax on the first $7,000 paid to each employee to fund the federal unemployment compensation program for those who have lost their jobs. Most states have also passed a **State Unemployment Tax Act (SUTA),** requiring the employer to pay at least 5.4% tax on the first $7,000 paid to each employee to fund state programs for the unemployed. This 5.4% state tax is *deductible* from the federal tax payment. Thus, in most cases, employers pay the federal government just 0.8% FUTA tax: 6.2% FUTA − 5.4% SUTA = 0.8% requirement.

Compute an employer's federal and state unemployment tax liability.

● EXAMPLE F

During the first quarter, Johnson and Johnson paid wages of $976,550.80. Of this amount, $172,400.60 was paid to employees who had been paid $7,000 earlier in the quarter. What was the employer's liability for FUTA and SUTA taxes, assuming that the state rate was 5.4%?

$976,550.80 − $172,400.60 = $804,150.20 subject to FUTA and SUTA taxes

$804,150.20 × 0.008 = $6,433.20 FUTA tax payment

$804,150.20 × 0.054 = $43,424.11 SUTA tax payment

$6,433.20 + $43,424.11 = $49,857.31

✔ CONCEPT CHECK 10.6

Warner-Lambert Company employed Rojas Perez for 13 weeks during the period January 1 through March 31, 2011. His salary was $1,350 per week. At the end of the quarter, how much in FUTA and SUTA taxes did the company have to pay to the federal and state governments based on Rojas's income?

$1,350 per week × 13 weeks = $17,550 total wage

$7,000 maximum × 0.008 = $56 FUTA tax

$7,000 maximum × 0.054 = $378 SUTA tax

$56 + $378 = $434 total federal and state unemployment taxes

COMPLETE ASSIGNMENTS 10.1 AND 10.2.

employee's earnings record

Employer's Quarterly Federal Tax Return

Federal Insurance Contributions Act (FICA)

Federal Unemployment Tax Act (FUTA)

Form W-4

payroll register

percentage method

State Unemployment Tax Act (SUTA)

wage-bracket method

withholding allowance

Try Microsoft® Excel

Try working the following problems using the Microsoft Excel templates found on the companion website. Solutions for the problems are also shown on the companion website.

1. Brighton Company pays its employees at the regular hourly rate for all hours worked up to 40 hours per week. Hours in excess of 40 are paid at $1\frac{1}{2}$ times the regular rate. Set up the following spreadsheet in Excel and add formulas to calculate **Overtime Hours, Regular Pay, Overtime Pay,** and **Total Gross Pay** for each employee in the shaded cells.

Hint: Use the IF function to determine overtime hours.

Employees	Total Hours Worked	Regular Hourly Rate	Overtime Hours	Regular Pay	Overtime Pay	Total Gross Pay
Baker, Jason	42	$12.80				
Castro, Jill	38	15.70				
Dobson, Jack	40	12.00				
Ellis, Jennifer	45	14.50				

2. Set up the following worksheet and add formulas in the shaded cells to calculate the **Social Security, Medicare, Total Deductions,** and **Net Pay** for each employee. Assume all wages are taxable and use the following rates: Social Security = 6.2%, Medicare = 1.45%.

Employees	Wages	Social Security	Medicare	Income Tax	Total Deductions	Net Pay
Carter, Janes	$460.35			$45.80		
Edison, Alice	289.50			25.00		
Garcia, Joseph	375.00			36.90		
Kilmer, Martha	450.70			52.00		

Summary of chapter learning objectives:

Learning Objective	Example
10.1 Prepare a payroll register.	Based on the data presented below, complete the following payroll register. Fill out the total wages section and then compute the federal income tax, Social Security, Medicare, and other withholdings. Total all columns and check. Use the percentage method for federal income tax.
10.2 Compute federal income tax withholding amounts.	1. G. Lee is paid $14.20 per hour. He worked 40 regular hours and 6 overtime hours during the week ending January 7. He is single and claims one withholding allowance. He takes a weekly medical deduction of $7. 2. E. Berg is paid $13 per hour. He worked 40 regular hours and 8 overtime hours during the week of January 7. He is married and claims four withholding allowances. He takes a weekly medical deduction of $15.
10.3 Compute Social Security, Medicare, and other withholdings.	

Name	Marital Status	W/H Allow	Total Hours	Regular Earnings		Overtime Earnings			Total Wages	Deductions					Net Pay
				Rate per Hour	Amt	Hours Worked	Rate per Hour	Amt		Social Security	Medi-care	Fed. Inc. Tax	Med. Insurance	Total	
Lee, G.															
Berg, E.															

10.4 Complete an employee's earnings record.	3. Complete the earnings record for D. Chan. Use 6.2% for Social Security and 1.45% for Medicare taxes. Use the percentage method for federal income tax withholding, on the monthly wages.

Name __D. Chan__   Social Security No. __125-11-3296__

Address __7821 Oak Ave.__   No. of Allowances __2__   Marital Status __Married__

Period Ending	Total Wages	Cumulative Total	Deductions					Net Pay
			Social Security	Medicare	Federal Inc. Tax	Other Deductions	Total	
1/31	$3,100	$3,100				$18.00		
2/28	3,000	6,100				18.00		
3/31	3,450	$9,550				18.00		
Quarter Total	$9,550					$54.00		

THE BOTTOM LINE

Summary of chapter learning objectives:

Learning Objective	Example

10.5
 	
Compute an employer's quarterly federal tax return.
	4. The Frazer Company had a total payroll of $279,440 for the first quarter of the year. It withheld $29,700 for federal income tax. It made monthly tax deposits of $24,100. Frazer is now filing its quarterly Form 941. Complete the following to determine the amount of the check that Frazer must send to the IRS for undeposited taxes due.
	  a. Social Security tax due for the quarter _____
	  b. Medicare tax due for the quarter _____
	  c. Total taxes due for the quarter _____
	  d. Total deposits for the quarter _____
	  e. Undeposited taxes due IRS _____

10.6
 	
Compute an employer's federal and state unemployment tax liability.
	5. Miller Outfitters employed R. Rehnquist for the period from January 1 through March 31, 13 weeks, at a salary of $1,230 per week. At the end of the quarter, how much in FUTA and SUTA taxes are owed to the federal and state governments if the state had a 0.8% FUTA rate and a 5.4% SUTA rate?
	  a. Total wages
	  b. FUTA tax
	  c. SUTA tax
	  d. Total federal and state unemployment taxes paid

Review Problems for Chapter 10

1   Alex Muñoz is paid $20 per hour for the first 40 hours and $1\frac{1}{2}$ times his regular rate for all hours worked over 40 per week.

   a. Determine Alex's gross pay for the week if he works 45 hours.
   b. Calculate the amount to be deducted for Social Security and Medicare taxes for the week.
   c. Determine the amount to be withheld for federal income tax, using the percentage method, if Alex is single and claims one withholding allowance.
   d. What is Alex's net pay for the week, assuming that his only payroll deductions are for Social Security, Medicare, and federal income tax?

2   Determine the amount to be withheld for federal income tax for each of the following, using both the percentage and the wage-bracket methods.

   a. A married employee, claiming two allowances, has weekly gross pay of $650.
   b. A single employee, with one allowance, has weekly gross pay of $525.

3   Calculate the employer's payroll taxes for each of the first three months of the year for three employees who are paid as follows:

Albertson, K.	$3,000 per month
Becket, W.	$4,000 per month
Jones, C.	$2,100 per month

   Include FUTA (0.8%), SUTA (5.4%), Social Security (6.2%), and Medicare (1.45%) taxes. Be sure to consider the maximum taxable amount for unemployment taxes ($7,000) per employee.

4   Determine the taxes to be reported on the quarterly 941 form for an employer who paid total gross wages of $62,000 and withheld $7,800 for federal income tax.

Social Security	_____
Medicare	_____
Federal income tax	_____
Total	_____

5   Determine the amount to be withheld from the current period's gross pay of $9,800 for Social Security and Medicare for an employee whose cumulative wages were $99,700, not including pay for the current period. Use the rates and taxable maximum given in the chapter.

6   Employees of Xper Co. are paid at their regular rate for the first 40 hours, at $1\frac{1}{2}$ times their regular rate for hours worked between 40 and 48, and double their regular rate for all hours worked over 48, per week. Calculate each employee's gross pay for the week.

   John Kowalski, regular rate $12.16, worked 47 hours
   Martha Madison, regular rate $15.50, worked 50 hours
   Joy Weston, regular rate $10.80, worked 42 hours

Answers to the Self-Check can be found in Appendix B at the back of the text.

Assignment 10.1: Payroll Problems

Name

Date _____ Score _____

A (52 points) Complete the payroll. (1 point for each correct answer)

1. In this company, employees are paid $1\frac{1}{2}$ times their regular rate for overtime hours between 40 and 48 and 2 times their regular rate for overtime hours over 48 per week.

Name	Total Hours	Regular Rate Per Hour	Regular Earnings		Time and a Half		Double Time		Total Earnings
			Hours	Amount	Hours	Amount	Hours	Amount	
Akerman, Gail	49	12.80	40		8		1		
Carson, James	40	15.60	40		—		—		
Kula, Mary	50	13.50	40		8		2		
Murphy, Tom	46	18.00	40		6		—		
Norton, Alice	40	17.40	40		—		—		
Payton, Alan	36	15.00	36		—		—		
Perry, Lance	47	12.80	40		7		—		
Ponce, Barbara	41	12.00	40		1		—		
Quinn, Carl	49	18.00	40		8		1		
Reston, Sally	40	13.50	40		—		—		
Sacco, Dom	43	12.80	40		3		—		
Wilson, Ken	50	17.40	40		8		2		
TOTALS									

Score for A (52)

B (28 points) Solve the following problems. (7 points for each correct answer)

2. Mark Johnston is employed at a monthly salary of $2,980. How much is deducted from his monthly salary for FICA taxes (Social Security and Medicare)? _____

3. Joleen Dole is employed by a company that pays her $3,600 a month. She is single and claims one withholding allowance. What is her net pay after Social Security, Medicare, and federal income tax withholding? Use the percentage method for federal income tax. _____

4. On April 1, the company in problem 3 changed its pay plan from monthly to weekly and began paying Joleen $830.77 per week. What is her net weekly pay after Social Security, Medicare, and income tax deductions? Use the percentage method. _____

5. William Diggs is married and claims four withholding allowances. His weekly wages are $725. Calculate his Social Security and Medicare deductions and, using the wage-bracket method, his federal income tax withholding. Find his weekly net pay. _____

_____

Score for B (28)

C **(20 points) Compute and compare the federal income tax withholding amounts for each of the following individuals using the percentage method and the wage-bracket method. (Follow the steps in Section 10.2 for the percentage method.) (5 points for each correct difference)**

6. Martha Gail: weekly wages, $412; single; 1 withholding allowance
   Percentage method: _____
   Wage-bracket method: _____
   Difference: _____

7. George Wilson: weekly wages, $445; married; 3 withholding allowances
   Percentage method: _____
   Wage-bracket method: _____
   Difference: _____

8. Fred Greys: weekly wages, $387; single; 2 withholding allowances
   Percentage method: _____
   Wage-bracket method: _____
   Difference: _____

9. Josephine Creighton: weekly wages, $732; married; 1 withholding allowance
   Percentage method: _____
   Wage-bracket method: _____
   Difference: _____

_____

Score for C (20)

Assignment 10.2: Payroll, Earnings Record, Payroll Tax Returns

A **(40 points) Solve the following problems. (1 point for each correct answer in the Total Wages column in 1; 2 points for each correct answer in the Net Pay column in 1 and 2)**

1. Complete the following weekly payroll register. Workers receive overtime pay for any time worked in excess of 40 hours per week at the rate of 1 1/2 their regular rate per hour. There is a 6.2% deduction for Social Security and a 1.45% deduction for Medicare taxes. Use the wage-bracket method for federal income tax withholding. Be sure to use the correct table based on the marital status of each employee.

Name	Marital Status	W/H Allow.	Total Hours	Regular Earnings Rate Per Hour	Regular Earnings Amount	Overtime Earnings Hours Worked	Overtime Earnings Rate Per Hour	Overtime Earnings Amount	Total Wages	Social Security	Medi-care	Fed. Inc. Tax	Med. Ins.	Total	Net Pay
Baker, C.	S	1	40	$14.90									$ 15.00		
Clark, T.	M	2	42	14.20									12.00		
Frank, B.	S	0	32	13.50									12.00		
Hawn, K.	M	3	40	15.00									18.00		
Jung, S.	M	2	45	15.50									18.00		
Kiber, J.	M	4	43	14.80									18.00		
Nelson, R.	S	1	40	14.50									12.00		
Oliver, B.	M	5	42	18.00									12.00		
Valdez, M.	M	1	40	16.80									15.00		
TOTALS													$132.00		

2. The total monthly wages of four employees are listed below. Determine the amount of the deductions and the net pay due to each employee. Use 6.2% for Social Security and 1.45% for Medicare tax deductions, and use the percentage method for federal income tax withholding. Determine the deductions and totals.

Name	Marital Status	W/H Allow.	Total Wages	Deductions Social Security	Deductions Medicare	Deductions Federal Income Tax	Deductions Total	Net Pay
Ali, Kyber	S	1	$2,650.00					
Dawson, William	M	3	3,480.00					
Rivers, Lydia	S	0	3,200.00					
Stevenson, Robert	M	2	3,195.00					
TOTALS								

Score for A (40)

B (20 points) Solve the following problems. (1 point for each correct answer in the Net Pay column and 2 points for the correct Net Pay quarter total in 3; 1 point for each correct answer in 4)

3. Complete the employee's earnings record for Michelle Lee. Use 6.2% for Social Security and 1.45% for Medicare taxes. Use the percentage method for federal income tax withholding.

Name __Michelle Lee__   Social Security No. __125-55-1254__

Address __645 Abby Lane__   No. of Allowances __2__   Marital Status __Single__

Period Ending	Total Wages	Cumulative Wages	Social Security	Medicare	Federal Inc. Tax	United Fund	Total	Net Pay
1/6	$ 595.65	$ 595.65				$ 5.00		
1/13	620.00	1,215.65				5.00		
1/20	550.00	1,765.65				5.00		
1/27	635.80	2,401.45				5.00		
2/3	550.00	2,951.45				5.00		
2/10	598.27	3,549.72				5.00		
2/17	620.00	4,169.72				5.00		
2/24	597.50	4,767.22				5.00		
3/3	678.00	5,445.22				5.00		
3/10	650.00	6,095.22				5.00		
3/17	582.90	6,678.12				5.00		
3/24	620.00	7,298.12				5.00		
3/31	550.00	7,848.12				5.00		
Quarter Totals	$7,848.12	$54,781.31				$65.00		

4. The following is a summary of quarterly earnings of a company's employees. Determine the information requested for the employer's quarterly federal tax return.

Name	Total Wages	Taxes Withheld		
		Social Security	Medi-care	Fed. Inc. Tax
Carter, M.	$ 6,084.85	$ 377.27	$ 88.22	$ 451.42
Davis, L.	5,368.00	332.82	77.84	437.50
Gordon, J.	4,266.35	264.51	61.86	398.65
McBride, C.	7,230.00	448.26	104.84	595.80
Taggert, L.	6,240.50	386.91	90.49	465.50
Walton, N.	5,285.92	327.73	76.65	566.00
TOTALS				

a. Total earnings paid _____   b. Federal income tax withheld _____

c. Total Social Security tax paid _____   d. Total Medicare tax paid _____

e. Total taxes withheld _____

Score for B (20)

C **(40 points) Solve the following problems. (4 points for each correct answer in 5 and 6; 1 point for each correct answer in 7)**

5. The quarterly earnings of the employees of the Alpha Company are listed in the following table. Determine the employee information needed for the employer's quarterly federal tax return (Form 941).

Name	Total Wages	Taxes Withheld		
		Social Security	Medicare	Fed. Inc. Tax
Caldwell, Janice	$ 3,420.00	$ 212.04	$ 49.59	$ 423.90
Dorman, J.A.	3,600.00	223.20	52.20	473.67
Eagie, T.W.	4,016.50	249.02	58.24	433.33
Fortune, Mark	3,774.90	234.04	54.74	410.05
Morris, Regina	3,605.40	223.53	52.28	399.83
Tracy, Joseph	4,111.60	254.92	59.62	360.17
TOTALS				

a. Total earnings paid   _____

b. Employee's contribution of Social Security tax   _____

c. Employee's contribution of Medicare tax   _____

d. Federal income tax withheld from wages   _____

e. Total taxes withheld   _____

6. The Primo Company had a total payroll of $148,600.34 for the first quarter of the current year. It withheld $28,531.27 from the employees for federal income tax during this quarter. The company made the following deposits in a qualified bank depository for the amount of the income and Social Security and Medicare taxes withheld from the employees and for the company's contribution to the FICA tax: $17,050 on February 6; $17,050 on March 4; and $17,050 on April 5. Primo Company's bookkeeper is now filling out Form 941 (quarterly return), which is due by the end of April. Complete the following to determine the amount of the check that the company must send to the IRS for the undeposited taxes due.

a. Total Social Security and Medicare taxes to be paid for quarter   _____

b. Total taxes   _____

c. Total deposits for quarter (sent to qualified bank depository)   _____

d. Undeposited taxes due IRS   _____

7. Jordan Mills employed Ruth Liebowitz for the period January 1 through March 31 (13 weeks) at a salary of $1,500 per week. At the end of the first quarter of the year, how much in FUTA and SUTA taxes did the company owe to the federal and state governments if the state had an 0.8% FUTA rate and a 5.4% SUTA rate?

a. Total wages and taxable wages   _____ _____

b. FUTA tax   _____

c. SUTA tax   _____

d. Total federal and state
unemployment taxes paid   _____

_____

Score for C (40)

Taxes

11

Learning Objectives

By studying this chapter and completing all assignments, you will be able to:

| Learning Objective | **1** | Compute sales taxes, using rate tables and percents. |

| Learning Objective | **2** | Compute assessed valuations and property taxes based on assessed valuation. |

| Learning Objective | **3** | Compute tax rates in percents. |

| Learning Objective | **4** | Compute property tax payments involving special assessments, prorations, and exemptions. |

| Learning Objective | **5** | Make basic computations to determine taxable income for taxpayers who use the standard federal income tax Form 1040. |

| Learning Objective | **6** | Make basic computations to determine the tax liability for taxpayers who use the standard federal income tax From 1040. |

Most retail businesses collect a sales tax from customers when a sale occurs. The tax money must be turned over to the government. People and companies owning property usually pay taxes on the property's value. In this chapter we explain calculations involving sales, property, and income taxes.

Computing Sales Taxes

Learning Objective 1

Compute sales taxes, using rate tables and percents.

A **sales tax** is a government **levy,** or charge, on retail sales of certain goods and services. Most states and many cities and other local government entities levy sales taxes. State **tax rates**—the percent used to compute the amount of sales tax—currently range from 1.4% to 7%, and city and county rates range from 0.925% to 7%.

Retail sales taxes, which usually are a combination of state and local taxes, are calculated as a single percent of taxable sales. For example, a sale is subject to a state sales tax of 5% and a local sales tax of 1%. The combined rate of 6% is applied to all taxable sales in that locality.

SALES TAX AS A PERCENT OF PRICE

Sales taxes generally are rounded to the nearest cent. For example, sales taxes of 4% and 5% on amounts of up to $1 are charged as shown in Figure 11-1.

Figure 11-1	Sales Taxes			
4% on Sales of	**Tax Due**	**5% on Sales of**	**Tax Due**
$0.01 to $0.12	none	$0.01 to $0.09	none
$0.13 to $0.37	$0.01	$0.10 to $0.29	$0.01
$0.38 to $0.62	$0.02	$0.30 to $0.49	$0.02
$0.63 to $0.87	$0.03	$0.50 to $0.69	$0.03
$0.88 to $1.00	$0.04	$0.70 to $0.89	$0.04
		$0.90 to $1.00	$0.05

STEPS to Compute Sales Tax and Total Sales Amount

1. Multiply the taxable sales amount by the tax rate.
2. Add the sales tax amount to the taxable sales amount to get the total sales amount.

EXAMPLE A

If taxable merchandise of $60.39 is sold in a state with a 5% sales tax, what are the amount of tax and the total amount to be paid?

Amount of tax: $60.39 \times 0.05 = \$3.0195$, which rounds to $3.02
Total amount to be paid: $60.39 + \$3.02 = \$63.41$

Most retail stores have cash registers that recognize a code such as the Uniform Product Code (UPC) to determine taxable sales and to calculate the sales tax automatically. The sales receipt usually shows the total taxable sales as a subtotal, the sales tax, and the total sales plus tax. Usually, discounts on a sale are subtracted from the sale price before the tax is figured. Shipping and installation labor charges are generally not taxed.

EXAMPLE B

A customer living in a city with a 6% state sales tax and a 1.5% city sales tax purchased a refrigerator regularly priced at $850. He was given a 10% discount. Delivery charges were $45. What were the amount of tax and the total cost to the buyer?

Discount amount: $850 × 10% = $850 × 0.10 = $85
Price after discount: $850 − $85 = $765, or $850 × 0.90 = $765
Sales tax: $765 × (0.06 + 0.015) = $57.38
Cost to buyer: $765 + $57.38 tax + $45 delivery = $867.38

State laws regarding the items subject to sales tax vary. Most states do not tax groceries; however, most do tax meals served in restaurants. Certain nonfood items also sold in grocery stores (such as laundry detergent) are generally taxed. When nontaxable and taxable items are purchased together, the register usually computes the total price of items purchased and automatically adds the correct amount of tax for each taxable item. The taxable items are clearly marked on the register tape along with the total amount of tax charged.

EXAMPLE C

A customer living in a state in which the tax rate is 7% went to a grocery store and purchased a quart of milk for $1.29, a loaf of bread for $2.79, potatoes for $3.85, and two taxable items—laundry detergent for $10.35 and fabric softener for $5.30. What was her total charge at the checkout counter?

Taxable items: $10.35 + $5.30 = $15.65
Tax: $15.65 × 0.07 = $1.0955 = $1.10
Total: $1.29 + $2.79 + $3.85 + $10.35 + $5.30 + $1.10 = $24.68

DIGITAL VISION/GETTY IMAGES

SALES TAX AS AN AMOUNT PER UNIT

All of the states and the District of Columbia levy special taxes on gasoline and cigarettes, usually stated in cents per unit (gallon or pack). State taxes on gasoline vary widely, from $0.075 in Georgia to $0.321 in Wisconsin; in addition, the federal tax is currently $0.184 per gallon. State taxes on cigarettes currently range from $0.30 (Virginia) to $4.35 (New York) per pack; the federal tax is currently $1.01 per pack.

EXCISE TAX AS AN AMOUNT PER UNIT

An **excise tax** is a tax assessed on each unit. In some states both the excise tax and the general sales tax apply to items such as gasoline, cigarettes, and alcoholic beverages. In such instances, the excise tax may be part of the taxable sales price for general sales tax purposes. For example, in a certain locality gasoline costs $3.40 per gallon, plus state and federal excise taxes of $0.48, and is subject to a general sales tax of 6%. The total price per gallon is $4.11 ($3.40 + $0.48 excise tax + $0.23 general sales tax). The general sales tax is calculated as 6% of $3.88.

In a state in which the combined state and city sales tax rate is 6%, a customer went to a convenience store and purchased the following items: bread, $2.50; ground meat, $6.79; cheese, $4.79; lightbulbs, $4.25; and motor oil, $5.80. Only the last two items are taxable. Rounding the tax to the nearest cent, compute the total cost of all items and tax.

Nontaxable items: $2.50 + $6.79 + $4.79 = $14.08
Taxable items: $4.25 + $5.80 = $10.05
Total tax: $10.05 × 0.06 tax rate = $0.60

$14.08	Nontaxable items
10.05	Taxable items
+ 0.60	Tax
$24.73	Total

Computing Assessed Valuations and Property Taxes

Learning Objective **2**

Compute assessed valuations and property taxes based on assessed valuation.

A **property tax** for a business is a tax on real estate or other property, such as machinery, owned by the business. Businesses usually pay property tax bills semiannually. Taxes are based on a value, known as the **assessed valuation,** determined by a representative of the local or state government.

Assessed valuation ordinarily is based on the current **market value** of the property (what the property could be sold for). In many states it is fixed by law at 100%, but it is a fraction of that value in other states. Thus a particular community may use 60% of property values as the basis for tax billing. In most instances, land and buildings are assessed separately.

● **EXAMPLE D**

The Kinsey family lives in a town in which assessed valuation is 60% of market value. The Bailey family lives in a town in which assessed valuation is 75% of market value. Each home has a market value of $260,000. What is the assessed valuation of each home?

Kinsey: $260,000 × 0.60 = $156,000
Bailey: $260,000 × 0.75 = $195,000

Assessed valuation often is increased by improvements to the property, such as the addition of an enclosed porch, a pool, or landscaping: Ordinary maintenance—a new coat of paint, for instance, or repairs to the roof—isn't justification for an increased assessment.

EXAMPLE E

The Lee family and the Kelly family live in a town in which assessed valuation is set by law at 80% of market value. They live in identical houses having a market value of $220,000. The Lee family added an enclosed deck costing $10,500 and a family room costing $32,000. The Kelly family made extensive repairs and repainted the house a new color at a total cost of $15,000. What was the assessed valuation on each home the following year?

INGER ANNE HULBÆKDAL/
SHUTTERSTOCK.COM

Lee: $220,000 + $10,500 + $32,000 = $262,500 × 0.8 = $210,000
Kelly: $220,000 × 0.8 = $176,000 (repairs and painting are not considered improvements)

✔ CONCEPT CHECK 11.2

a. The Coles family owns a home with a market value of $300,000 in a community that assesses property at 100% of market value. The Jensen family owns a home with a market value of $400,000 in a community that assesses property at 60% of market value. What is the difference between the actual assessments of the two homes?
Coles: $300,000 × 1 = $300,000
Jensen: $400,000 × 0.6 = $240,000
Difference = $60,000

b. The Bay family home has a present market value of $280,000 in a community that assesses property at 80% of market value. If they add a family room and an additional bathroom at a cost of $42,000, what will be the new assessed valuation?
Revised market value: $280,000 + $42,000 = $322,000
New assessed value: $322,000 × 0.80 = $257,600

Computing Tax Rates in Percents

PERCENTS

For a city, county, or special district, the tax rate is found by dividing the amount of money the government unit needs to raise by the total assessed valuation of the particular unit.

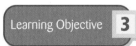

Learning Objective **3**

Compute tax rates in percents.

EXAMPLE F

The town of Lakeside has a total assessed valuation of $570,000,000. The amount to be raised by taxation is $9,975,000. What is the tax rate?
   The tax rate is

$9,975,000 ÷ $570,000,000 = 0.0175, or 1.75%.

This rate is usually written as 1.75% of value, or $1.75 on each $100 of value.

If a property in Lakeside is assessed for $160,000, what is the tax?

The tax can be found by multiplying the assessed amount by the rate:

$160,000 × 0.0175 = $2,800

✔ CONCEPT CHECK 11.3

a. A town has a total assessed valuation of $960,000,000. A total of $12,000,000 must be raised by taxation for the operating expenses of the town. What will be the tax rate?

$12,000,000 ÷ $960,000,000 = 0.0125, or 1.25%

b. If property in a town is assessed at the rate of $0.74 per $100 of assessed value, how much tax will be due on property assessed at $475,000?

$475,000 ÷ 100 = $4,750

$4,750 × $0.74 = $3,515 tax due or $475,000 × .0074

Computing Special Assessments, Prorations, and Exemptions

Learning Objective 4

Compute property tax payments involving special assessments, prorations, and exemptions.

Communities can levy special assessments for improvements such as sewers, roads, or sidewalks. Sometimes the cost is spread over a period of years and added to the annual property tax bill of each property owner.

◗ EXAMPLE H

The residents of Sonora voted to widen their roads and add sidewalks at a cost of $480 per residence, with the cost to be spread over a 12-year period. The Walker family had an annual tax bill of $1,230 before the improvements. If they pay their property taxes semiannually, what will be the amount of their next tax payment?

Annual cost for improvement: $480 ÷ 12 = $40
Annual property tax and improvement payment:
$1,230 + $40 = $1,270
Next semiannual tax payment: $1,270 ÷ 2 = $635

Whenever property is sold, it is customary to *prorate,* or distribute, the taxes between seller and buyer as of the date of the settlement.

◗ EXAMPLE I

A home having an annual tax bill of $1,440 was sold at the end of the seventh month of the taxable year. The seller had already paid the tax for the full year. How much tax was the seller reimbursed on proration of taxes at the time of the sale?

Months prepaid by seller: 12 − 7 = 5

Tax reimbursed by buyer: $1,440 × $\dfrac{5}{12}$ = $600

In almost all states, property used exclusively by nonprofit organizations, such as schools, churches, governments, and charities, is exempt from taxation. Some states also allow partial exemptions for veterans and the elderly.

EXAMPLE J

The town of Baxter assesses property at 75% of market value. The tax rate is 2.1%. A church has a total market value of $560,000. How much does the church save each year by being exempt from property taxes?

$560,000 × 0.75 = $420,000 $420,000 × 0.021 = $8,820 saved

EXAMPLE K

A veteran living in Conton receives a partial exemption of 15% of regular property taxes. The veteran owns property valued at $380,000. If the property is assessed at 80% of value and the current rate is 1.3%, how much tax is due each six months?

Assessed value: $380,000 × 0.80 = $304,000
Regular taxes: $304,000 × 0.013 = $3,952
Taxes due after exemption: $3,952 × 0.85 (100% − 15%) = $3,359.20
Taxes due each six months: $3,359.20 ÷ 2 = $1,679.60

✔ CONCEPT CHECK 11.4

a. The city of Belton voted to build a new library at a cost of $540 per residence, to be spread over a period of 15 years. If the Douglas family presently has a yearly tax bill of $2,600, paid semiannually, what will be the amount of their next tax payment?
$540 per residence ÷ 15 years = $36 per year
$2,600 present yearly tax amount + $36 = $2,636 new yearly tax amount
$2,636 ÷ 2 = $1,318 new semiannual tax amount

b. If a home with an annual tax bill of $780 is sold at the end of the third month of the tax year, after taxes have already been paid for the full year, how much will the buyer reimburse the seller when taxes are prorated?
12 − 3 = 9 months prepaid by seller

$780 × $\dfrac{9}{12}$ = $585 reimbursed by buyer

c. A 70-year-old man lives in a state that grants senior citizens a 10% exemption from property taxes. If his home has a market value of $250,000 and the tax rate is 1.3%, how much will his yearly taxes be? The county in which he resides assesses property at 70% of market value.
$250,000 market value × 0.7 = $175,000 assessed valuation
$175,000 assessed valuation × 0.013 = $2,275 regular taxes
$2,275 regular taxes × 0.10 = $227.50 reduction
$2,275 regular taxes − $227.50 reduction = $2,047.50 revised taxes

COMPLETE ASSIGNMENTS 11.1 AND 11.2.

Personal income taxes provide 26% of all income of the federal government. Social Security and Medicare taxes, which you studied in Chapter 10, provide another 25%. Together, these three taxes make up 51% of all federal government income.

Outlays for Social Security, Medicare, and retirement programs constitute 34% of all government expenditures. Payment of interest on government debt represents 5% of all government expenditures.

Figure 11-2 shows the breakdown of federal government income and the allocation of federal government spending.

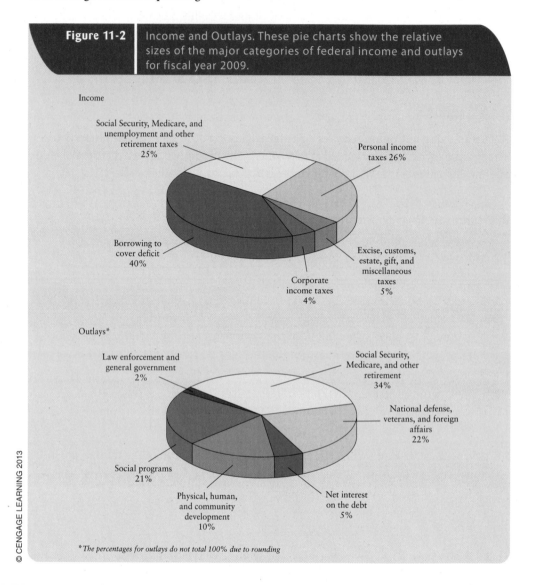

Figure 11-2   Income and Outlays. These pie charts show the relative sizes of the major categories of federal income and outlays for fiscal year 2009.

Income

Social Security, Medicare, and unemployment and other retirement taxes 25%

Personal income taxes 26%

Borrowing to cover deficit 40%

Excise, customs, estate, gift, and miscellaneous taxes 5%

Corporate income taxes 4%

Outlays*

Law enforcement and general government 2%

Social Security, Medicare, and other retirement 34%

National defense, veterans, and foreign affairs 22%

Social programs 21%

Physical, human, and community development 10%

Net interest on the debt 5%

*The percentages for outlays do not total 100% due to rounding

© CENGAGE LEARNING 2013

Determining Taxable Income, Using Standard Form 1040

Learning Objective **5**

Make basic computations to determine taxable income for taxpayers who use the standard federal income tax Form 1040.

Form 1040 is the basic form filed by the majority of taxpayers. There are two simplified variations of this form: Form 1040A and Form 1040EZ. The income tax calculation process is illustrated for Form 1040 in Figures 11-3 through 11-8. The label in Figure 11-3 contains spaces for names, address, and Social Security numbers, as well as boxes to check to designate $3 to finance presidential elections.

A taxpayer's current **filing status** is indicated in the second section of Form 1040, shown in Figure 11-4. Five choices are given. The one selected determines the tax rate the taxpayer uses, as well as many of the taxpayer's deductions.

Personal exemptions, shown in Figure 11-5, are reductions to taxable income for the primary taxpayer and a spouse. One **dependency exemption** is granted for each dependent. The amount deducted for each exemption was $3,650 for 2010. This amount is usually adjusted for inflation each year.

Taxable income, shown in Figure 11-6, includes wages, salaries, tips, dividends, interest, commissions, back pay, bonuses and awards, refunds of state and local taxes, alimony received, property received for services, severance pay, accrued leave payments, sick pay, unemployment compensation payments, capital gains, and any other income not specifically exempted by statute. Taxable income may include a portion of Social Security payments, IRA distributions, and pensions and annuities. It also includes income from businesses, professions, farming, partnerships, rents, royalties, estates, trusts, and other sources. It does not include income from gifts, inheritances, bequests, interest on tax-exempt state and local municipal bonds, life insurance proceeds at death, workers' compensation benefits, and certain income items for veterans.

Figure 11-3	Form 1040 Label Section

Figure 11-4	Form 1040 Filing Status Section

Figure 11-5	Form 1040 Exemptions Section

INTERNAL REVENUE SERVICE, HTTP://WWW.IRS.GOV

Figure 11-6 | Form 1040 Income Section

Income	7	Wages, salaries, tips, etc. Attach Form(s) W-2	7	65,000	00
	8a	**Taxable** interest. Attach Schedule B if required	8a	500	00
Attach Form(s) W-2 here. Also attach Forms W-2G and 1099-R if tax was withheld.	b	**Tax-exempt** interest. **Do not** include on line 8a 8b			
	9a	Ordinary dividends. Attach Schedule B if required	9a		
	b	Qualified dividends 9b			
	10	Taxable refunds, credits, or offsets of state and local income taxes	10		
	11	Alimony received	11		
	12	Business income or (loss). Attach Schedule C or C-EZ	12		
If you did not get a W-2, see page 20.	13	Capital gain or (loss). Attach Schedule D if required. If not required, check here ▶ ☐	13		
	14	Other gains or (losses). Attach Form 4797	14		
	15a	IRA distributions 15a b Taxable amount	15b		
	16a	Pensions and annuities 16a b Taxable amount	16b		
	17	Rental real estate, royalties, partnerships, S corporations, trusts, etc. Attach Schedule E	17		
Enclose, but do not attach, any payment. Also, please use Form 1040-V.	18	Farm income or (loss). Attach Schedule F	18		
	19	Unemployment compensation	19	1,300	00
	20a	Social security benefits 20a b Taxable amount	20b		
	21	Other income. List type and amount	21		
	22	Combine the amounts in the far right column for lines 7 through 21. This is your **total income** ▶	22	66,800	00

Adjusted Gross Income	23	Educator expenses	23		
	24	Certain business expenses of reservists, performing artists, and fee-basis government officials. Attach Form 2106 or 2106-EZ	24		
	25	Health savings account deduction. Attach Form 8889	25		
	26	Moving expenses. Attach Form 3903	26		
	27	One-half of self-employment tax. Attach Schedule SE	27		
	28	Self-employed SEP, SIMPLE, and qualified plans	28		
	29	Self-employed health insurance deduction	29		
	30	Penalty on early withdrawal of savings	30		
	31a	Alimony paid b Recipient's SSN ▶	31a		
	32	IRA deduction	32	5,000	00
	33	Student loan interest deduction	33		
	34	Tuition and fees. Attach Form 8917	34		
	35	Domestic production activities deduction. Attach Form 8903	35		
	36	Add lines 23 through 31a and 32 through 35	36	5,000	00
	37	Subtract line 36 from line 22. This is your **adjusted gross income** ▶	37	61,800	00

The Adjustments to Income section, shown in Figure 11-7, allows the taxpayer to list certain items that are allowed as reductions to the total income. These adjustments include payments by the taxpayer or spouse to an individual retirement account (IRA), student loan interest, payments into a health savings account, moving expenses, one half of self-employment tax paid, and payments to a retirement plan for the self-employed, penalty on early withdrawal of savings, and alimony paid. **Adjusted gross income (AGI)** is a taxpayer's income after subtraction of adjustments to income from total income. (See line 37 of Adjusted Gross Income in Figure 11-7.)

After the adjusted gross income figure is computed, *deductions*—either the standard deduction or itemized deductions—are subtracted in order to figure taxable income (see Figure 11-8). The standard deductions for most taxpayers are shown in Figure 11-9. There are higher standard deductions for individuals who are 65 or over and for individuals who are blind.

Some taxpayers choose to itemize deductions rather than use the IRS-approved standard deduction. **Itemized deductions** are deductions allowed for specific payments made by the taxpayer during the tax year. These deductions include charitable

Figure 11-8 | Form 1040 Taxable Income and Income Tax Section

Tax and Credits	38	Amount from line 37 (adjusted gross income)		38	61,800	00
	39a	Check if: ☐ **You** were born before January 2, 1946, ☐ Blind.	Total boxes checked ▶ 39a			
		☐ **Spouse** was born before January 2, 1946, ☐ Blind.				
	b	If your spouse itemizes on a separate return or you were a dual-status alien, check here ▶ 39b ☐				
	40	**Itemized deductions** (from Schedule A) **or** your **standard deduction** (see instructions) . .		40	11,400	00
	41	Subtract line 40 from line 38		41	50,400	00
	42	**Exemptions.** Multiply $3,650 by the number on line 6d		42	14,600	00
	43	**Taxable income.** Subtract line 42 from line 41. If line 42 is more than line 41, enter -0- . .		43	35,800	00
	44	**Tax** (see instructions). Check if any tax is from: **a** ☐ Form(s) 8814 **b** ☐ Form 4972 .		44	4,532	50

Form 1040 (2010) — Page **2**

Figure 11-9 | Standard Deduction Chart for Most People

Single or Married Filing Separately	$5,700
Married Filing Jointly or Qualifying Widow(er)	$11,400
Head of Househlod	$8,400

contributions, certain interest payments, state and local income (or sales) and property taxes, a portion of medical and dental expenses, casualty and theft losses, tax preparation fees, and other annually identified deductions. Illustrations, examples, and problems in this book are based on the assumption that all state and local taxes and all donations to charity are deductible.

COMPUTING TAXABLE INCOME

Line 43 of Form 1040 shows "taxable income." Taxable income is the amount of income on which the income tax is based. Taxable income for most taxpayers is computed as follows (amounts from the preceding figures):

Total income (income from all sources) (line 22)	$66,800
Less adjustments to income (reductions of Total Income) (line 36)	− 5,000
Adjusted gross income (line 37)	61,800
Less deductions (line 40)(from Figure 11-9)	−11,400
Less exemptions (line 6d × $3,650, per line 42)	−14,600
Taxable income (the amount on which taxes are computed) (line 43)	$35,800

✔ CONCEPT CHECK 11.5

Catherine, age 25, had an annual adjusted gross income of $34,000. She filed a return claiming a single exemption and standard deduction. What is her taxable income?

Adjusted gross income	$34,000
Less standard deduction: single	− 5,700
	28,300
Less 1 exemption	− 3,650
Taxable income	$24,650

Determining Taxes Due, Using Standard Form 1040

Make basic computations to determine the tax liability for taxpayers who use the standard federal income tax Form 1040.

Taxes are computed from taxable income (line 43). **Tax Rate Schedules** (Figure 11–10) show the tax rate for (1) single, (2) married filing joint return (even if only one had income), (3) married filing separate returns, (4) head of household, and (5) qualifying widow or widower. The Tax Rate Schedules shown are used for all illustrations, examples, and problems in this book.

The remaining sections of Form 1040 permit listing of special credits, other taxes, and payments to arrive at the final refund or amount owed, and have spaces for signatures of the taxpayers and of paid preparers.

● EXAMPLE L

For the Form 1040 illustrated in the text, the tax is computed as follows:

Line 43—Taxable income	$35,800.00
From Schedule Y-1: (married filing jointly):	
Tax on the first $16,750	1,675.00
Plus 15% of amount over $16,750	
$35,800 − $16,750 = $19,050 × 0.15	+ 2,857.50
Total tax	$4,532.50

● EXAMPLE M

Filing as head of household, Dave has an adjusted gross income of $110,000. He itemizes the following deductions: $700 to Goodwill, $900 to his church, $8,200 interest on his mortgage, and $3,300 state taxes. He claims two exemptions. Compute his federal tax.

Adjusted gross income	$110,000
Minus itemized deductions	− 13,100
	96,900
Minus 2 exemptions	− 7,300
Taxable income	$ 89,600
From Schedule Z Head of Household:	
Tax on the first $45,550	$ 6,235.00
Plus 25% (0.25) of excess over $45,550	
$89,600 − $45,550 = $44,050 × 0.25	+ 11,012.50
Total tax	$ 17,247.50

MOODBOARD RF/PHOTOLIBRARY

TAX CREDITS AND NET TAX

Credits allowed are subtracted from the tax to calculate the net tax. One of the most common credits is the **Child Tax Credit** (line 51). Taxpayers with dependent children under age 17 can receive a credit of $1,000 per qualifying child. The credit phases out at higher income levels.

Figure 11-10 | Tax Rate Schedules

Schedule X—If your filing status is Single

If your taxable income is:		The tax is:	of the amount over—
Over—	But not over—		
$0	$8,375	.... 10%	$0
8,375	34,000	$837.50 + 15%	8,375
34,000	82,400	4,681.25 + 25%	34,000
82,400	171,850	16,781.25 + 28%	82,400
171,850	373,650	41,827.25 + 33%	171,850
373,650	....	108,421.25 + 35%	373,650

Schedule Y-1—If your filing status is Married filing jointly or Qualifying widow(er)

If your taxable income is:		The tax is:	of the amount over—
Over—	But not over—		
$0	$16,750	.... 10%	$0
16,750	68,000	$1,675.00 + 15%	16,750
68,000	137,300	9,362.50 + 25%	68,000
137,300	209,250	26,687.50 + 28%	137,300
209,250	373,650	46,833.50 + 33%	209,250
373,650	....	101,085.50 + 35%	373,650

Schedule Y-2—If your filing status is Married filing separately

If your taxable income is:		The tax is:	of the amount over—
Over—	But not over—		
$0	$8,375	.... 10%	$0
8,375	34,000	$837.50 + 15%	8,375
34,000	68,650	4,681.25 + 25%	34,000
68,650	104,625	13,343.75 + 28%	68,650
104,625	186,825	23,416.75 + 33%	104,625
186,825	....	50,542.75 + 35%	186,825

Schedule Z—If your filing status is Head of household

If your taxable income is:		The tax is:	of the amount over—
Over—	But not over—		
$0	$11,950	.... 10%	$0
11,950	45,550	$1,195.00 + 15%	11,950
45,550	117,650	6,235.00 + 25%	45,550
117,650	190,550	24,260.00 + 28%	117,650
190,550	373,650	44,672.00 + 33%	190,550
373,650	....	105,095.00 + 35%	373,650

Figure 11-11 shows that John and Mary Sample received a Child Tax Credit of $1,000. Look back at Figure 11-5 and note a check mark in the "qualifying child" box for Johnny Sample but not for Maria Sample. This distinction means that the son qualified for the credit because he was under age 17. The daughter qualifies as a dependent for exemption purposes, but no Child Tax Credit is allowed because she is age 17 or older.

Figure 11-11 | Form 1040 Credits Section

46	Add lines 44 and 45 . . . . ▶	**46**	4,532 50
47	Foreign tax credit. Attach Form 1116 if required	**47**	
48	Credit for child and dependent care expenses. Attach Form 2441	**48**	
49	Education credits from Form 8863, line 23	**49**	
50	Retirement savings contributions credit. Attach Form 8880	**50**	
51	Child tax credit (see instructions)	**51**	1,000 00
52	Residential energy credits. Attach Form 5695	**52**	
53	Other credits from Form: **a** ☐ 3800 **b** ☐ 8801 **c** ☐ ___	**53**	
54	Add lines 47 through 53. These are your **total credits**	**54**	1,000 00
55	Subtract line 54 from line 46. If line 54 is more than line 46, enter -0- . . . . . . ▶	**55**	3,532 50

EXAMPLE N

Eric and Audrey Vaughn file a joint return. Their adjusted gross income is $52,900, and they take the standard deduction. They have three children, aged 12, 15, and 17, and claim five exemptions. Compute their net federal income tax after credits.

Adjusted gross income	$52,900
Standard deduction (joint)	−11,400
	41,500
Minus 5 exemptions × $3,650	−18,250
Taxable income	$23,250
From Schedule Y-1:	
Tax on the first $16,750	$ 1,675
Plus 15% on amount over $16,750	
($23,250 − $16,750) = $6,500 × 0.15	+ 975
Total	$ 2,650
Minus child tax credit ($1,000 × 2)	−2,000
Net tax after credit	$ 650

The final step is to determine whether there is a refund or a balance due. If more has been paid (usually through withholding by the employer) than the net tax, the difference is a refund. Conversely, if the net tax exceeds the amount already paid, the difference is the balance due with the return.

Brian and Margaret Lee had wages of $33,200 and interest income of $2,400. They put $3,000 into a deductible IRA. They filed a joint return—claiming three exemptions (Brian, Margaret, and their daughter, aged 5)—and used the standard deduction. During the year, $950 in federal income tax had been withheld from their wages. What was the refund or tax due with the return?

Total income	$35,600
Adjustments to income: IRA deduction	− 3,000
Adjusted gross income	32,600
Standard deduction: married, filing jointly	−11,400
	21,200
Minus 3 exemptions: 3 × $3,650	−10,950
Taxable income	$10,250
From Schedule Y-1:	
$10,250 × 0.10	$ 1,025
Minus child tax credit for one child	−1,000
Net tax due after credits	$ 25
Minus federal income tax withheld	−950
Refund	$ 925

Chapter Terms for Review

adjusted gross income (AGI)	levy
assessed valuation	market value
Child Tax Credit	personal exemptions
dependency exemption	property tax
excise tax	sales tax
filing status	tax rate
Form 1040	Tax Rate Schedules
itemized deductions	taxable income

Try Microsoft® Excel

Try working the following problems using the Microsoft Excel templates found on the companion website. Solutions for the problems are also shown on the companion website.

1. Set up the table on next page and complete using Excel formulas to calculate the values in the **Sales Tax Amount** and **Total Sale with Tax** columns using the sales tax rate indicated.

Hint: Use an absolute cell reference for the sales tax rate so that the formula can be copied. Cell references are changed to absolute by adding a $ before both the column letter and the row number. Example: D9

Sales tax rate:	7.25%

Taxable sale	Sales tax amount	Total sale with tax
$12.83		
$81.91		
$20.11		
$111.92		
$0.55		
$7.20		
$328.90		
$1,552.44		
$62.00		

2. Adams Company purchased a new copy machine priced at $2,650 less a 10% discount plus delivery and setup charges of $150. Determine the amount of the discount, the sales tax at 6.5%, and the total amount of the sale including delivery and setup costs. Set up the table below on a Excel worksheet and complete by adding formulas for calculations. *Hint:* Discounts are subtracted before and delivery costs are added after calculating sales tax.

Original price of copy machine	
Discount amount	
Net price after discount	
Sales tax at 6.5%	
Delivery and setup	
Total sale amount	

3. Kingstrom Corporation is located in an area in which assessed valuation is 70% of market value. The current tax rate is 1.35%. Determine Kingstrom's property tax for the year on property with a market value of $652.000. Enter the data below into an Excel worksheet and complete by adding formulas for calculations.

Market value of property	
Assessed valuation at 70%	
Property tax at 1.35%	

THE BOTTOM LINE

Summary of chapter learning objectives:

Learning Objective	Example
11.1 Compute sales taxes, using rate tables and percents.	1. The Farley family lives in a state in which the sales tax rate is 6%. When they purchased a dining room table and chairs regularly priced at $990, they were given a discount of 15%. Shipping charges were $50. What was the total cost to the Farleys? 2. Wanda Green lives in a state in which the state tax on gasoline is $0.22 a gallon. Federal tax is $0.19 a gallon. If she purchased an average of 12 gallons per week during the 52-week year, how much did she pay in state and federal taxes combined?
11.2 Compute assessed valuations and property taxes based on assessed valuation.	3. The Nguyen family lives in a town in which the assessed valuation on property is 65% of market value. The Parker family lives in a town in which the assessed valuation on property is 80% of market value. Each home has a market value of $162,000. How much is the assessed valuation of each home?

11.3
 	
Compute tax rates in percents.
	4. The town of Tyler has a total assessed valuation of $850,000,000. For the coming year the city must raise $11,730,000 for operating expenses.
	  a. What will the tax rate be?
	  b. What will the semiannual taxes be on a home with an assessed valuation of $135,000?

11.4 Compute property tax payments involving special assessments, prorations, and exemptions.	5. A home with annual tax payments of $510 was sold at the end of the tenth month of the taxable year. What was the amount of tax prorated to the buyer? 6. A veteran living in Alameda receives a partial exemption of 10% of regular property taxes. The veteran owns property valued at $312,000. If the property is assessed at 70% of value and the current rate is 1.5%, how much tax is due each six months?

Summary of chapter learning objectives:

Learning Objective	Example
11.5 Make basic computations to determine taxable income for taxpayers who use the standard federal income tax Form 1040.	7. Gilbert Black is 28 years old and single. He claimed one exemption. In 20XX he earned $47,000 in wages and $675 in taxable interest income. During the year he invested $1,800 in an individual retirement account. Because of a change of jobs, he also had $1,200 in moving expenses, which qualified as an adjustment to income. He had qualifying deductions of $1,000 in deductible medical bills, $300 in church donations, and $9,600 in interest on the condominium he owned. He also paid $150 in state taxes. He had $2,500 in federal income tax withheld during the year. What was the amount of tax due with his return? Income: Less adjustments to income: Adjusted gross income Less deductions: Less exemption: Taxable income Tax computation Less tax withheld during the year Tax due with return
11.6 Make basic computations to determine the tax liability for taxpayers who use the standard federal income tax Form 1040.	8. Donald and Judy Mason are 60 and 62 years of age, respectively. They filed as married, filing jointly. Last year they had a total income of $35,000 from investments. They filed a return and claimed the standard deduction. During the year they made quarterly payments of estimated tax totaling $1,000. What was the amount of tax due with their return? Adjusted gross income Less standard deduction Less exemptions: Taxable income Tax computation Less payments made during the year on estimated tax Tax due with return

Review Problems for Chapter 11

1. The Dupree Company is considering the purchase of some equipment from two different suppliers. If the sales tax rate is 6%, which of the following offers should Johnson Company accept?

   Company A: Equipment price of $65,000 plus installation and shipping costs of $1,200.

   Company B: Equipment price of $73,500 less 10% discount, no additional charge for installation or shipping.

2. Georgetown needs to raise $7,800,000 in property taxes on property with a total market value of $650,000,000.

   a. What will the tax rate be if property is assessed at 80% of market value?

   b. Determine the amount of semiannual property tax to be paid by each of the following property owners who live in Georgetown:

   Juan Garcia's home in Georgetown has a market value of $350,000.

   Margaret Smith is a senior citizen who receives a 10% exemption from property tax. Her home in Georgetown has a market value of $215,000.

3. The residents of Hunterville voted to add street lights and sidewalks to their city at a cost per residence of $324 to be spread over 12 years.

   a. If Mary Nowitski, a resident of Hunterville, had an annual tax bill of $860 before the special assessment, how much must she now pay semiannually for her property taxes?

   b. If Mary Nowitski sells her home at the end of the eighth month of the tax year and has already paid the property taxes for the full year, including the special assessment, how much of the prepaid property tax should be allocated to the purchaser?

4. Samantha Jones works as a waitress. Last year she earned $15,800 in wages, $8,600 in tips, and $1,500 catering on weekends. She also received $600 interest from her credit union, $800 from a corporate bond, and an inheritance of $10,000. What was her gross income for federal income tax purposes?

5. Pete and Angel Romero are married and have two children aged 5 and 8. They also support Pete's sister, who lives with them. How much can Pete and Angel subtract from their gross income for exemptions?

6. Jan and Kirsten Bjorg, aged 42 and 40, are married filing a joint tax return. They have itemized deductions totaling $8,500. Should they itemize or use the standard deduction?

7. Eva Jung files as a head of household, has an adjusted gross income of $38,000, claims two exemptions, and uses the standard deduction on her federal return. What is her taxable income?

8. Brad and Justine O'Riley are married, filing a joint return, and have taxable income of $65,000. What is the amount of their income tax?

Answers to the Self-Check can be found in Appendix B at the back of the text.

Assignment 11.1: Sales Tax

Name _____

Date _____ Score _____

A **(50 points) Solve the following problems. (1 point for each correct answer)**

1. The Country Corner store is in a state with a sales tax rate of 7%. Compute the sales tax, the total sale, and the change given for each transaction.

Amount of Sale	Sales Tax	Total Sale	Cash Paid	Amount of Change
$8.37	_____	_____	$10.00	_____
2.35	_____	_____	5.01	_____
34.85	_____	_____	40.00	_____
19.56	_____	_____	25.00	_____
5.12	_____	_____	10.00	_____
16.50	_____	_____	20.00	_____
18.55	_____	_____	20.00	_____
0.98	_____	_____	1.25	_____
9.98	_____	_____	15.00	_____
17.78	_____	_____	20.00	_____

2. Bill's Hardware is in a city where the state sales tax is 3.5% and the city tax is 2%. Determine the sales tax, the total sale, and the change given for each transaction. Then compute the total sales taxes and total sales.

Amount of Sale	Sales Tax	Total Sale	Cash Paid	Amount of Change
$189.50	_____	_____	$200.00	_____
54.21	_____	_____	60.00	_____
22.89	_____	_____	25.00	_____
289.44	_____	_____	320.00	_____
17.00	_____	_____	20.00	_____
99.98	_____	_____	120.00	_____
Total	_____	_____		_____

Score for A (50)

B **(30 points) Solve the following problems. Use Figure 11-1 for problems 3 and 4. (points for correct answers as marked)**

3. A candy store, operating in a state with a sales tax of 4%, made 658 sales at 10¢, 935 sales at 35¢, 720 sales at 49¢, 985 sales at 65¢, 612 sales at 75¢, and 865 sales at 90¢. How much did the store receive in sales taxes? (8 points) _____

4. If the candy store in problem 3 computed the amount of state sales tax submitted to the state based on 4% of gross sales, what would be the difference between the amount of tax the store collected and the amount it submitted to the state? (8 points) _____

5. Discount Carpets Company and Oriental Rugs, Inc., each purchased a new delivery van. Discount Carpets is located in a state that has a 5% sales tax and paid the regular price of $21,800 plus tax. Oriental Rugs is located in a state that has a 6% sales tax and received a special discount of $500 off the regular $21,800 price.

   a. Including sales tax, which company paid more for its van? (8 points) _____

   b. How much more? (6 points) _____

Score for B (30)

C   **(20 points) Solve the following problems. (points for correct answers as marked)**

6. Calico Books has stores in four states. Sales tax rates for the four states are as follows: state A, 8%; state B, 6.2%; state C, $5\frac{1}{2}$%; state D, 3%. Annual sales for the four states last year were as follows: state A, $865,000; state B, $925,000; state C, $539,000; state D, $632,000.

   a. How much did Calico Books pay in sales taxes during the year? (10 points) _____

   b. If all four states had the same lower sales tax rate of 3%, how much would Calico Books have collected in sales taxes during the year? (5 points) _____

   c. If all four states had the same higher tax rate of 8%, how much would Calico Books have collected in sales taxes during the year? (5 points) _____

Score for C (20)

Assignment 11.2: Property Taxes

Name _____

Date _____ Score _____

A **(40 points) Solve the following problems. (4 points for each correct answer)**

1. Find the assessed valuation for each of the following towns.

Town	Property Value	Basis for Tax Billing	Assessed Valuation
A	$625,000,000	100%	_____
B	$862,350,000	85%	_____
C	$516,800,000	70%	_____

2. Find the tax rate for each of the following towns. Show your answer as a percent.

Town	Assessed Valuation	Amount to Be Raised	Tax Rate
F	$860,000,000	$13,932,000	_____
G	$645,000,000	10,965,000	_____
H	$732,000,000	9,150,000	_____

3. Convert the following percentage tax rates into dollars and cents per $100 of assessed valuation.

Tax Rate	Dollars and cents
1.3%	_____
0.98%	_____

4. Convert the following tax rates per $100 of assessed valuation into percents.

Tax Rate	Percent
$1.87	_____
$0.90	_____

Score for A (40)

B **(28 points) Solve the following problems. (7 points for each correct answer)**

5. The Griffin Company is located in a state in which assessed valuation is 100% of market value. The tax rate this year is $1.35 on each $100 of market value. The market value of the company building is $190,000. How much property tax will Griffin pay this year? _____

6. The Balford Corp. is located in an area in which assessed valuation is 80% of market value. The tax rate this year is 1.7%. The market value of Balford's property is $635,000. How much property tax will Balford pay this year? _____

7. Next year, the assessed valuation in Balford's area (problem 6) will decrease to 75% of market value and the tax rate will remain the same as this year. How much less tax will Balford pay next year than it paid this year?

   _____

8. Perez, Inc., is headquartered in an area in which assessed valuation is 80% of market value. The tax rate this year is $1.40 on each $100 of assessed valuation. Its property has a market value of $320,000. How much property tax will Perez pay this year? _____

Score for B (28)

C **(16 points) Solve the following problems. Round to the nearest dollar. (4 points for each correct answer)**

9. There are four towns in Hogan county: Lawton, Johnsville, Dover, and Gault. Using the total assessed valuations given and the amount of money the town must raise for operating expenses, compute the necessary tax rate for each town.

Town	Total Assessed Valuation	Money That Must Be Raised	Tax Rate as a Percent
Lawton	$200,000,000	$3,400,000	_____
Johnsville	$340,000,000	$5,100,000	_____
Dover	$280,000,000	$3,780,000	_____
Gault	$620,000,000	$12,400,000	_____

Score for C (16)

D **(16 points) Solve the following problems. Round to the nearest dollar. (8 points for each correct answer)**

10. A home with annual tax payments of $624 was sold at the end of the fifth month of the taxable year. The seller had already paid the entire tax for the year. How much tax was the seller reimbursed on proration of taxes at the time of the sale? _____

11. A senior citizen lives in a state that grants a 20% exemption on property taxes. Her property is valued at $290,000 and is assessed at 75% of value. The current tax rate is 1.6%. How much tax is due each six months? _____

_____

Score for D (16)

Assignment 11.3: Federal Income Tax

Name _____

Date _____ Score _____

Learning Objectives 5 6

A (52 points) Complete all problems, using the exemptions, deductions, and tax rates given in the chapter. Round all amounts to the nearest dollar. (Rounding is allowed so long as it is done consistently.) (12 points for correct answers to 2a and 3a; 4 points for other correct answers)

1. Determine the taxable income for each of the following taxpayers.

Adjusted Gross Income	Number of Exemptions	Type of Return	Deductions	Taxable Income
a. $28,700	1	Single	Standard	_____
b. $52,450	4	Head of household	Standard	_____
c. $34,700	2	Joint	Standard	_____
d. $16,452	1	Single	$5,960	_____
e. $43,700	6	Joint	$12,218	_____

2. Sadie Gilford is single, age 30, with no dependents. She takes the standard deduction. Her income during the year was $28,700.

   a. What is Sadie's taxable income? _____

   _____

   _____

   b. What is Sadie's tax? _____

3. George Sampson is 52 years old. His wife Marcia is 49. They have $34,300 total income. They file a joint return and take the standard deduction.

   a. What is the Sampsons' taxable income? _____

   _____

   _____

   b. What is the Sampsons' income tax? _____

   _____
   Score for A (52)

B (48 points) Solve the following problems. (12 points for correct taxable income; 4 points for correct income tax)

4. Alfred Wild is 32 years old; his wife Silvia is 34. They file a joint return. Alfred's salary for the year was $45,000. Silvia's salary was $47,000. They paid mortgage interest of $10,400 and property tax of $1,200 on their home. They paid state income tax of $3,800 during the year. They itemize their deductions.

   a. What is their taxable income? _____   **b.** What is their income tax? _____

   _____ _____

   _____

5. Michael and Martha Miller are married and have three dependents living with them: their children, aged 17 and 19, and Martha's mother. Michael's salary for the year was $30,000, and Martha's salary was $32,000. They received taxable interest of $1,250 and $500 interest from a state bond. They take the standard deduction and file a joint return.

   a. What is their taxable income? _____   **b.** What is their net tax after credits? _____

   _____

   _____

6. Renaldo and Rita Hernandez have three children aged 17, 18, and 12. Renaldo's father lives with them and has no income. Renaldo earned a salary of $46,000 during the year. Rita is not employed. They paid $3,100 property tax and $6,200 mortgage interest on their home. They paid $2,600 principal on their mortgage. They paid state income tax of $2,175. They donated $500 to their church and $500 to the Salvation Army. They spent $5,600 on groceries and $1,100 on utilities. They itemize their deductions.

   a. What is their taxable income? _____   **b.** What is their net income tax after credits? _____

   _____

   _____ _____

   _____

   Score for B (48) _____

Insurance

12

Learning Objectives

By studying this chapter and completing all assignments, you will be able to:

Learning Objective 1   Compute costs and savings for auto insurance.

Learning Objective 2   Compute auto insurance premium rates for high- and low-risk drivers.

Learning Objective 3   Compute short-rate refunds.

Learning Objective 4   Compute coinsurance on property losses.

Learning Objective 5   Compute life insurance premiums.

Learning Objective 6   Compute cash surrender and loan values.

Learning Objective 7   Compute medical insurance contributions and reimbursements.

Computing Auto Insurance Costs

Learning Objective 1

Compute costs and savings for auto insurance.

Auto insurance falls into three categories: liability and property damage, comprehensive, and collision. A policy that fully protects the insured will contain all three types.

Auto liability and property damage insurance protects the insured against claims resulting from personal injuries and property damage. Some states require all drivers to carry auto liability and property damage insurance. The amount of protection generally ranges from $50,000 to $1,000,000 per accident.

Auto comprehensive insurance protects the vehicle of the insured against water, theft, vandalism, falling objects, and other damage not caused by collision.

Auto collision insurance protects the vehicle of the insured against collision damage. Such damage may result from a collision with another vehicle or a one-car accident, such as hitting a tree.

The payment for an insurance policy is called a **premium.** Premium rates for auto insurance depend primarily on the coverage included in the policy, the driving record of the insured, the geographical area where the driver lives, and government laws and regulations.

Auto collision insurance policies usually contain a **deductible clause,** which stipulates that the insured will pay the first portion of collision damage, usually $50 to $500, and that the insurance company will pay the remainder up to the value of the insured vehicle. A deductible clause not only reduces the amount of damages for which the insurance company must pay but also keeps the insurance company from having to get involved in and do paperwork for small repairs costing less than the deductible. Therefore, a deductible clause lowers the premium for collision insurance.

EXAMPLE A

Fred Baker's car was insured for collision damage with a $250 deductible. The premium was $1,750 per year. Fred hit a tree, causing $2,530 damage to his car. How much more did he receive than he paid in premiums for that year?

$2,530 damage − $250 deductible = $2,280 paid by insurance
$2,280 received by insured − $1,750 premium paid = $530.

EXAMPLE B

The driver of car A carried auto liability and property damage insurance only. She struck car B, causing $1,400 damage to car B and $700 in injuries to the driver. Car A suffered $940 damage.

a. How much did the insurance company pay for this accident?
   $1,400 for damage to car B + $700 for injuries to driver = $2,100

b. How much did this accident cost the driver of car A?
   $940 in uncovered damage to her own car

No-fault insurance is a term that is used to describe an auto insurance system that requires drivers to carry insurance for their own protection and that limits their ability to sue other drivers for damages. No-fault insurance requires that the driver of each vehicle involved in an injury accident submit a claim to *his or her own insurance company* to cover medical costs for injuries to the driver and passengers in that person's own vehicle. No-fault insurance is mandatory in some states. No-fault insurance doesn't cover damage to either vehicle involved in an accident.

VUK VUKMIROVIC / SHUTTERSTOCK.COM

Drivers A and B live in a state in which no-fault insurance is mandatory. Their two cars collided. Driver A and his passengers incurred medical expenses of $3,500. Driver B and her passengers incurred $1,700 in medical expenses. Car A required $1,400 in repairs. Car B required $948 in repairs. How much did the insurance companies pay under the no-fault insurance coverage?

Driver A's insurance company paid $3,500 in medical expenses.

Driver B's insurance company paid $1,700 in medical expenses.

Car repairs are not covered under no-fault insurance.

✔ CONCEPT CHECK 12.1

Driver A lives in a state in which no-fault insurance is mandatory. He carries all three classifications of insurance to be fully protected. His total insurance premium is $2,400, with a collision deductible of $500. Driver A is involved in a major accident when he loses control of his car and hits two parked cars (cars B and C) before colliding with an oncoming car (car D) containing a driver and three passengers. Driver A is alone.

Damage to driver A's car is $3,200.
Damages to cars B, C, and D total $8,600.
Medical expenses for driver A are $2,800.
Medical expenses for the driver and passengers of car D are $7,300.

a. How much does driver A's insurance company pay?
   Damage to car A: $3,200 − $500 deductible = $2,700 covered by collision
   Damage to cars B, C, and D: $8,600 covered by liability
   Medical expenses for driver A under no-fault: $2,800
   $2,700 + $8,600 + $2,800 = $14,100 paid by driver A's insurance
b. How much does driver D's insurance company pay?
   Medical expenses paid for driver D and passengers (no-fault): $7,300
c. How much more did driver A's insurance company pay to him and on his behalf for this accident than he paid in insurance expenses for the year? (This is the amount driver A saved this year by being fully insured.)
   $2,400 premium + $500 deductible for repairs in this accident = $2,900 paid by driver A
   $14,100 from insurance − $2,900 = $11,200
   Driver A saved $11,200 this year by being fully insured with a $500 deductible clause.

Computing Low-Risk and High-Risk Rates

Auto insurance premium rates reflect the risk involved. Insurance companies study the statistics on automobile accidents relative to driving records. Premium rates are adjusted according to the driving record of the insured. A driver with a clear record of long standing is considered to be a **low-risk driver** and may be rewarded with a discount in the premium rate. Conversely, a driver with a record of numerous citations or accidents is considered to be a **high-risk driver** and may pay double, triple, or even a higher multiple than the normal premium rate.

Learning Objective **2**

Compute auto insurance premium rates for high- and low-risk drivers.

Drivers A and B have identical automobiles and amounts of insurance coverage. The normal premium rate for each is $2,000 per year. Driver A is a low-risk driver and receives a 15% discount on the premium rate. Driver B is a high-risk driver and must pay double the normal rate. How much more does driver B pay for insurance than driver A?

Driver A pays $2,000 × 85% = $1,700 (100% − 15% discount)

Driver B pays $2,000 × 2 = $4,000

Driver B pays $4,000 − $1,700 = $2,300 more

✔ CONCEPT CHECK 12.2

Alice, a very careful driver, has had the same insurance company for 5 years and has not had a ticket during that 5-year period. Each year, she has received a 10% reduction in her premium. Bob has a record of speeding tickets. He has had one or more every year for 5 years. His premium for year 1 was normal, for years 2 and 3 it was 150%, and for years 4 and 5 it was 200%. The normal annual premium rate for each driver would be $980.

a. How much did Alice pay in premiums over the 5-year period?

$980 × 90% = $882

$882 × 5 = $4,410

b. How much did Bob pay in premiums over the 5-year period?

Year 1: $980

Years 2 and 3: $980 × 1.5 × 2 = $2,940

Years 4 and 5: $980 × 2 × 2 = $3,920

$980 + $2,940 + $3,920 = $7,840

c. How much more did Bob pay during the 5-year period than Alice?

$7,840 − $4,410 = $3,430

Computing Short Rates

Short rates are rates charged for less than a full term of insurance. If an insurance policy is canceled by the **insured** (the person who receives the benefit of the insurance) before the policy's full term is complete, the insured will receive a short-rate return of premium. If a policy is canceled by the insurance company rather than by the insured, the company must refund the entire unused premium.

● EXAMPLE E

A driver paid an annual premium of $1,960 for auto insurance. After 3 months, the vehicle was sold and the insurance canceled. The insurance company refunded the remaining portion of the premium at the short rate, based on a penalty of 10% of the full-year premium. What was the refund?

Unused premium: $1,960 × $\dfrac{3}{4}$ = $1,470   (9 months canceled = $\frac{9}{12} = \frac{3}{4}$ year)

Penalty: $1,960 × 10% = $196

Short-rate refund: $1,470 − $196 = $1,274

Davis Company purchased two cars. Each car was insured at an annual premium of $1,780. At the end of 6 months, Davis Company sold one car and canceled the insurance on that car. The insurance company imposes a 10% penalty on the premium for short-rate premiums. At the end of 9 months, the insurance company decided to cancel the insurance on the second car. Compute the refunds the insurance company paid for car 1 and car 2.

Car 1: $1,780 \times \frac{1}{2}$ year = $890 unused premium

$1,780 \times 10\%$ = $178 penalty
$890 - $178 = $712 refunded

Car 2: $1,780 \times \frac{1}{4}$ year = $445 unused and refunded premium
(3 months canceled = $\frac{3}{12} = \frac{1}{4}$ year)

COMPLETE ASSIGNMENT 12.1.

Computing Coinsurance on Property Losses

Property insurance is insurance against loss of or damage to property. A policy can be written to protect the insured against loss from fire, casualty, liability, and theft.

Premium rates, which are quoted in terms of dollars per $1,000 of insurance, depend on the nature of the risk, the location of the property, and the length of time covered by the policy. Short rates and short-rate penalties for less than a full term of insurance apply to property insurance as they do to auto insurance.

Learning Objective **4**

Compute coinsurance on property losses.

● **EXAMPLE F**

A building worth $350,000 is insured for $210,000. The annual premium for the policy is $5,000. A fire causes $80,000 in damage.

a. How much does the insurance company pay?
$80,000 in damage is less than the $210,000 policy. The insurance company pays the entire $80,000.

b. How much does the property owner pay?
The property owner does not pay for damages.

c. How much does the property owner pay that year in damages and insurance?
$5,000 for the insurance premium only.

In an ordinary fire insurance policy, the insured will be paid for the loss up to the amount of the insurance. Policies may be obtained at lower rates if they contain a **coinsurance clause.** This clause specifies that if a property is not insured up to a specified percentage of its value, the owner is responsible for part of the loss and will not be covered for the full amount of damages.

It is common practice for a fire insurance policy to have an 80% coinsurance clause. Under this clause, the full amount of the loss will be paid by the insurance company only if the policy amount equals at least 80% of the property value.

1. Compute the amount of insurance required by multiplying the entire value of the property by the percentage of coinsurance specified.
2. Compute the **recovery amount,** the maximum amount the insurance company will pay, by using the formula

   $$\frac{\text{Amount of insurance carried}}{\text{Amount of insurance required}} \times \text{Loss} = \text{Recovery amount}.$$

3. Compare the recovery amount with the amount of the insurance policy.
   a. If the recovery amount is greater than the amount of the policy, the insurance company will limit its payment to the amount of the policy.
   b. If the recovery amount is less than the amount of the policy, the insurance company will pay the recovery amount.

   Note: The insurance company will never pay more than the amount of the loss.

4. Determine the owner's share of the property loss by subtracting the amount the insurance company will pay from the loss amount.

EXAMPLE G

A building valued at $400,000 is insured for $200,000 under a policy with an 80% coinsurance clause. The annual premium is $2,800. A fire causes $100,000 damage to the building.

a. How much will the insurance company pay the insured?

STEP 1 $400,000 \times 80\% = \$320,000$ insurance required

STEPS 2 & 3 $\dfrac{\$200,000 \text{ amount of insurance carried}}{\$320,000 \text{ amount of insurance required}} \times \$100,000 = \$62,500$ insurance pays

b. How much must the owner pay if the building is repaired for $100,000?

STEP 4 $\$100,000 - \$62,500 = \$37,500$ paid by owner

c. How much does the property owner pay that year for damages and insurance?
   $37,500 damages + $2,800 premium = $40,300

d. How much would the insurance company pay if the fire caused $300,000 damage to the building?
   $\dfrac{\$200,000}{\$320,000} \times \$300,000 = \$187,500$ recovery amount

The insurance company would pay $187,500 (because the recovery amount is within the policy's coverage).

e. How much would the insurance company pay if the fire caused $360,000 damage to the building?
   $\dfrac{\$200,000}{\$320,000} \times \$360,000 = \$225,000$

The insurance company would pay $200,000, the maximum coverage.

EXAMPLE H

If the amount of insurance carried in example G had been $320,000, how much would the insured have paid for damages and insurance that year?

$2,800 premium only (the 80% coinsurance requirement would have been met)

CONCEPT CHECK 12.4

A building worth $100,000 is insured for $60,000 with an 80% coinsurance clause. A fire causes $70,000 in damage. How much of the repair cost will the insurance company pay, and how much will the insured pay?

$100,000 × 80% = $80,000 insurance required

$\dfrac{\$60,000}{\$80,000} \times \$70,000 = \$52,500$ insurance pays

$70,000 − $52,500 = $17,500 insured pays

COMPLETE ASSIGNMENT 12.2.

Computing Life Insurance Premiums

The policies most commonly issued by life insurance companies are term insurance, straight life (sometimes called ordinary life), limited-payment life, endowment, and annuity.

Learning Objective 5

Compute life insurance premiums.

Term insurance is protection issued for a limited time. A certain premium is paid every year *during the specified time period,* or term. The policy is payable only in case of death of the insured during the term. Otherwise, neither the insured nor the specified beneficiaries receive any payment, and the protection stops at the end of the term.

For **straight (ordinary) life insurance** coverage, a certain premium, or fee, is paid every year *until the death of the insured.* The policy then becomes payable to the **beneficiary.** A policy beneficiary can be a person, a company, or an organization.

Limited-payment life insurance (such as 20-payment life) requires the payment of a specified premium each year for a certain number of years or until the death of the insured, whichever comes first. Should the insured live longer than the specified number of years, the policy requires no further payments for the remainder of the insured's life and is payable to the beneficiary on the death of the insured.

Endowment insurance provides insurance payable on the insured's death if it occurs within a specified period. If the insured is alive at the end of the specified period, an endowment of the same amount as the policy is payable.

Annuity insurance pays a certain sum of money to the insured every year after the insured reaches a specified age, until the insured's death.

An **additional death benefit (ADB)**, sometimes referred to as an *accidental death benefit*, accompanies some policies. ADB allows the insured to purchase, at a low rate per thousand dollars of coverage, additional insurance up to the full face value of the policy. In case of death of the insured by accident, both the full value of the policy and the ADB are paid to the beneficiaries. If death occurs other than by accident, the full value of the policy is paid, but no ADB is paid.

BRONWYN KIDD/PHOTODISC/GETTY IMAGES

Chapter 12 Insurance 225

Figure 12-1 shows typical annual, semiannual, and quarterly premiums (ages 25–28) for straight life, 20-payment life, and 20-year endowment policies.

Figure 12-1	Insurance Premium per $1,000								
	Straight Life			**20-Payment Life**			**20-Year Endowment**		
Age	Annual	Semi-annual	Quarterly	Annual	Semi-annual	Quarterly	Annual	Semi-annual	Quarterly
25	$17.20	$ 8.94	$4.73	$31.20	$16.26	$8.26	$52.00	$27.04	$14.30
26	17.85	9.28	4.91	31.81	16.52	8.45	52.60	27.35	14.47
27	18.60	9.67	5.11	32.41	16.83	8.64	53.20	27.66	14.63
28	19.30	10.04	5.31	33.06	17.31	8.85	53.86	28.01	14.81

EXAMPLE I

Using the premiums shown in Figure 12-1, determine the yearly premiums for each of the following $50,000 life insurance policies purchased at age 27. First find the age, 27. Then read across the table to the type of insurance and frequency of payment. Finally, multiply the table amount of 50 ($50,000 ÷ 1,000) to determine the premium.

Type of Insurance	Method of Payment	Premium Computation
Straight Life	Annual	$18.60 × 50 = $930
20-Year Endowment	Quarterly	$14.63 × 4 × 50 = $2,926
20-Payment Life	Semiannual	$16.83 × 2 × 50 = $1,683
20-Year Endowment	Semiannual	$27.66 × 2 × 50 = $2,766
Straight Life	Quarterly	$ 5.11 × 4 × 50 = $1,022

 CONCEPT CHECK 12.5

(Use the premiums in Figure 12-1.)

a. If a person at age 28 purchases a straight life insurance policy having a face value of $150,000 with quarterly premiums, what is the yearly premium?
$5.31 × 4 × 150 = $3,186

b. If a person at age 25 purchases a 20-payment life insurance policy having a face value of $100,000 with semiannual premiums, what is the yearly premium?
$16.26 × 2 × 100 = $3,252

c. If a person at age 25 purchases a 20-year endowment insurance policy having a face value of $75,000 with annual premiums, what is the yearly premium?
$52 × 75 = $3,900

Computing Cash Surrender and Loan Values

Learning Objective 6

Compute cash surrender and loan values.

Except for term insurance, insurance usually has a **cash surrender value,** which is the amount of cash that the company will pay the insured on the surrender, or "cashing in," of the policy. The **loan value** of a policy is the amount that the insured may borrow on the policy from the insurance company. Interest is charged on such loans. The values, often quoted after the third year of the policy, are stated in the policy and increase every year. Figure 12-2 shows typical cash surrender and loan values for policies issued at age 25 per $1,000 of life insurance.

Figure 12-2	Insurance Values per $1,000		
End of Policy Year	**Cash Surrender and Loan Values**		
	Straight Life	**20-Payment Life**	**20-Year Endowment**
3	$ 10	$ 43	$ 88
4	22	68	130
5	35	93	173
10	104	228	411
15	181	380	684
20	264	552	1,000

EXAMPLE J

Use the values shown in Figure 12-2 to determine the cash surrender or loan value for each of the following policies.

Policy Year	Type of Policy	Amount of Policy	Cash Surrender or Loan Value
10	Straight Life	$ 75,000	75 × $104 = $ 7,800
5	20-Year Endowment	$ 15,000	15 × $173 = $ 2,595
10	20-Payment Life	$ 50,000	50 × $228 = $11,400
20	Straight Life	$200,000	200 × $264 = $52,800
15	20-Year Endowment	$ 50,000	50 × $684 = $34,200

✔ CONCEPT CHECK 12.6

Use the values shown in Figure 12-2 to determine the cash surrender or loan value for each of the following policies.

a. Third policy year of a $50,000 20-year endowment policy
   50 × $88 = $4,400

b. Twentieth policy year of a $100,000 straight life policy
   100 × $264 = $26,400

c. Tenth policy year of a $25,000 20-payment life policy
   25 × $228 = $5,700

Computing Medical Insurance Contributions and Reimbursements

Most large employers and many small employers subscribe to a group plan on behalf of their employees. **Group insurance** plans provide medical insurance coverage to large numbers of people at lower premium rates than individuals could obtain separately. Employers generally pay most of the premium for employees and a smaller portion of

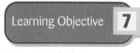

Learning Objective **7**

Compute medical insurance contributions and reimbursements.

the premium for family members of employees. Many employers now use group plans known as a **health maintenance organization (HMO)** or a **preferred provider organization (PPO).**

EXAMPLE K

Employer A selected a basic health care plan to cover employees who want to participate. Monthly premiums are as follows: employee only, $520; employee with one dependent, $680; and employee with multiple dependents, $740. Employees pay a portion of the premium as follows: employee only, $0; employee with one dependent, $80; and employee with multiple dependents, $120. How much does the employer pay during the year for each category of employee?

Employee only: $520 × 12 = $6,240
Employee with one dependent: ($680 − $80) × 12 = $7,200
Employee with multiple dependents: ($740 − $120) × 12 = $7,440

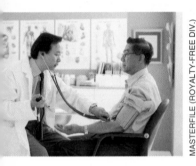

EXAMPLE L

Employer B selected a total care health plan to cover employees who want to participate. Monthly premiums are as follows: employee only, $400; employee with one dependent, $500; and employee with multiple dependents, $580. The employer pays most of the premium, but employees pay a portion as follows: employee only, $60; employee with one dependent, $160; and employee with multiple dependents, $240. What percent of the premium will be paid by a single employee, an employee with one dependent, and an employee with six dependents?

A single employee: $60 ÷ 400 = 0.15, or 15%
An employee with 1 dependent: $160 ÷ 500 = 0.32, or 32%
An employee with 6 dependents: $240 ÷ 580 = 0.41, or 41%

Many group plans include a provision for an annual deductible, which is the cost that must be paid by the employee before any cost is paid by the insurance company. Group medical plans also frequently provide for the payment by the insurance company of a percent of costs over the deductible, usually 70% to 90%, with the remaining 30% to 10% paid by the insured.

EXAMPLE M

Employer C provides group health coverage that includes a $500 annual deductible per family and payment of 70% of the medical charges exceeding the deductible. How much would an employee with three dependents pay if her medical bills for the year were $1,500?

$1,500 − $500 deductible = $1,000
$1,000 × 30% paid by employee = $300
$500 deductible + $300 payments = $800 paid by the employee

An employer provides group health coverage that includes a $300 annual deductible per family and payment of 80% of costs over the deductible.

a. How much would an employee with two dependents pay if his medical bills for the year were $460?

$460 − $300 deductible = $160

$160 × 20% = $32

$300 deductible + $32 = $332 paid by the employee

b. How much would that employee have paid if his total medical bills for the year had been $4,300?

$4,300 medical costs − $300 deductible = $4,000

$4,000 × 20% = $800

$300 deductible + $800 = $1,100

c. How much of the $4,300 in medical bills would that employee have paid if his employer did not provide medical insurance and he did not have other coverage?

$4,300

d. How much would the employer pay if the monthly premium for an employee with multiple dependents was $480?

$480 × 12 = $5,760

COMPLETE ASSIGNMENT 12.3.

Chapter Terms for Review

additional death benefit (ADB)

annuity insurance

auto collision insurance

auto comprehensive insurance

auto liability and property damage insurance

beneficiary

cash surrender value

coinsurance clause

deductible clause

endowment insurance

group insurance

health maintenance organization (HMO)

high-risk driver

insured

limited-payment life insurance

loan value

low-risk driver

no-fault insurance

preferred provider organization (PPO)

premium

property insurance

recovery amount

short rates

straight (ordinary) life insurance

term insurance

Try Microsoft® Excel

Try working the problems using the Microsoft Excel templates found on the companion website. Solutions for the problems are also shown on the companion website.

Summary of chapter learning objectives:

Learning Objective	Example
12.1 Compute costs and savings for auto insurance.	Drivers A and B live in a state in which no-fault insurance is mandatory. Both drivers carry all three classifications of insurance. Driver A has a deductible of $500; driver B has a deductible of $200. Driver A crashes into driver B. Neither auto has any passengers. Car A has $1,800 in damages; car B has $2,000 in damages. Driver A is not hurt; driver B has $900 in medical bills. 1. How much does driver A's insurance company pay? 2. How much does driver B's insurance company pay?
12.2 Compute auto insurance premium rates for high- and low-risk drivers.	3. Juan has an excellent driving record and receives a 20% discount on his annual premium. Dave has a record of numerous tickets and must pay 2 times the normal annual premium rate. If the normal premium for each driver is $1,500, how much more does Dave pay for his insurance than Juan pays?
12.3 Compute short-rate refunds.	4. XYZ company purchased a delivery truck and paid an annual insurance premium of $3,600. XYZ company sold the truck at the end of 8 months and canceled the policy. The insurance company charges a 10% penalty for short-rate refunds. What was the amount of the short-rate refund to XYZ company?
12.4 Compute coinsurance on property losses.	5. A building worth $400,000 is insured for $300,000 with an 80% coinsurance clause. Fire causes $200,000 in damage. How much does the insurance company pay?
12.5 Compute life insurance premiums.	6. Premiums per $1,000 of straight life insurance at the age of 25 are as follows: annual, $17.20; semiannual, $8.94; and quarterly, $4.73. What will be the total yearly premiums for the following three policies: $50,000, annual; $25,000, semiannual; and $20,000, quarterly?

Answers: 1. $3,300 2. $900 3. $1,800 4. $840 5. $187,500 6. $1,685.40

THE BOTTOM LINE

Summary of chapter learning objectives:

Learning Objective	Example
12.6 Compute cash surrender and loan values.	7. If cash surrender values for year 15 of a policy are $200 per thousand dollars of coverage for straight life and $380 per thousand dollars of coverage for 20-payment life, what is the total cash surrender value of these two policies: $50,000 straight life and $50,000 20-payment life?
12.7 Compute medical insurance contributions and reimbursements.	8a. An employer provides group health coverage that includes a $200 annual deductible per family and payment of 80% of costs over deductible. How much would an employee with four dependents pay if his medical bills for the year were as follows: self, $240; dependent 1, $170; dependent 2, $30; dependent 3, $460; and dependent 4, $2,200? b. How much would the employee pay if the annual deductible were $50 per person?

Review Problems for Chapter 12

1. Drivers Jim Olson and Joshua Stein live in a state having no-fault auto insurance. Joshua causes an accident by hitting Jim's car. Joshua isn't hurt. Jim spends 3 days in the hospital at a cost of $5,300. Compute the amount that each driver's insurance company pays toward medical expenses. _____

2. IXP insured an office building for $290,000 for 1 year at a premium rate of $7.20 per thousand. At the end of 9 months, IXP sold the building and canceled the policy. If the insurance company has a short-rate refund policy that includes a 10% penalty, how much refund did IXP receive? _____

3. Driver Devon Cooper has a poor driving record and pays double the usual premium as a high-risk driver. The regular premium would be $490 for a year. If Devon must pay the high-risk premium every year for 5 years, how much more will he pay for insurance premiums than a low-risk driver receiving a 10% discount over the same 5-year period? _____

4. Insurance company A has a standard 90% coinsurance clause for all fire insurance coverage. Insurance company B has a standard 75% coinsurance clause for all fire insurance coverage. A building is valued at $195,000. How much more insurance coverage would insurance company A require than insurance company B for full coinsurance coverage? _____

5. The Morgan Company warehouse was valued at $425,000. The building was insured for $170,000. The policy contained an 80% coinsurance clause. A fire caused $60,000 in damages. Compute the amount of the fire damage The Morgan Company had to pay. _____

6. Mike Jankowski, age 27, purchased a $35,000, 20-payment life policy with premiums payable annually. John Jamison, also age 27, purchased a $35,000 straight life policy with premiums payable semiannually. Both Mike and John lived 40 more years. How much more in premiums did John pay the insurance company during his lifetime than Mike paid during his? (Use values from Figure 12-1.) _____

7. Sally Munson, age 25, purchased a $35,000, 20-payment life policy. Five years later she needed cash. Compute the maximum amount she could borrow on the policy. (Use values from Figure 12-2.)

    _____

8. An employer provides group health coverage that includes a $600 annual deductible per family and payment of 80% of costs exceeding the deductible amount. An employee with no dependents incurs $4,800 in medical expenses during the year. How much of the medical costs must the employee pay?

    _____

Answers to the Self-Check can be found in Appendix B at the back of the text.

Assignment 12.1: Auto Insurance

Name _____

Date _____ Score _____

A **(50 points) Solve the following problems. (5 points for each correct answer)**

1. Susan Li had full insurance coverage. Her liability and property damage coverage was $100,000 per accident. Her collision insurance had a $500 deductible clause. She struck two cars. Damages to the cars were $640 and $320. Damage to her own car was $470. Her annual insurance premium was $1,180.

   a. What are the total costs to the insurance company for Susan's accident? _____

   b. If this was the only accident that Susan had this year, did the insurance company profit after paying for Susan's accident? _____

   c. What are Susan's total costs this year for insurance and the accident? _____

   d. What would Susan's total costs for the accident have been without insurance? _____

2. Renaldo Garcia paid an annual premium of $2,700 for auto collision insurance with a $500 deductible clause. His steering went out and he hit a tree, causing $4,000 damage to his car. How much did he save this year by having insurance? _____

3. Sean O'Day received his driver's license 1 year ago. He has had three citations for speeding, but no accidents. His insurance premium last year was $1,800. This year his premium will be 100% higher because of his driving record.

   a. What will be the amount of his premium this year? _____

   b. Four months into the next year, Sean has continued his unsafe driving habits. The insurance company is canceling his policy. What will be the amount of the refund? _____

   c. Sean O'Day has found an insurance company that will insure him as a high-risk driver at triple the standard annual rate of $1,600. What will be his average monthly insurance premium for the first 28 months of his driving career? (Round your answer to the nearest dollar.) _____

   d. If Sean had been a careful driver and kept the amount of his premium unchanged, how much would he have saved in these first 28 months? (Round your computations to the nearest dollar.) _____

4. Drivers A and B have identical insurance coverage. Driver A has an excellent driving record and receives a 15% discount on the standard premium. Driver B has numerous citations and pays 50% above the standard rate. The standard rate in both cases is $1,800. How much more does driver B pay for insurance than driver A? _____

_____

Score for A (50)

B **(50 points) Solve the following problems. (5 points for each correct answer)**

5. Tom Barton carries liability and property damage insurance coverage up to $50,000 per accident, comprehensive insurance, and collision insurance with a $100 deductible clause. He lost control of his car and drove through the display window of a furniture store. Damage to the building was $17,200 and the damage to the inventory was $34,300. Damage to a bike rack on the sidewalk and three bicycles in the rack was $1,840. Damage to his own car was $6,100.

   a. What was the total property damage, excluding damage to Tom's car? _____

   b. How much did the insurance company pay for property damage, excluding damage to Tom's car? _____

   c. How much did the insurance company pay for damage to Tom Barton's car? _____

   d. How much did the accident cost Tom Barton? _____

   e. If Tom Barton had been in a previous accident this year in which there had been property damage to a parked car of $12,700, how much would the insurance company have paid for damages to everything in the current accident, including Tom Barton's car? _____

6. Amy Tan and John Rogers live in a state in which no-fault insurance is mandatory. They have identical full coverage of $50,000 liability and property damage per accident, comprehensive insurance, and collision insurance with a $350 deductible. John lost control of his car on an icy street and struck Amy's car, a parked motorcycle, and a fence. Amy had medical expenses of $780. John had medical expenses of $560. Amy's car had damages of $1,350. John's car had damages of $1,750. Damage to the parked motorcycle was $650 and damage to the fence was $320.

   a. What did Amy's insurance company pay under the no-fault provision? _____

   b. What did John's insurance company pay under the no-fault provision? _____

   c. How much did John's insurance company pay under his liability and property damage coverage? _____

   d. How much did John's insurance company pay under his comprehensive coverage? _____

   e. How much would John's insurance company have paid under his liability and property damage if he had hit Amy's car and five parked cars, with total damage to the six cars of $56,700? _____

_____

Score for B (50)

Assignment 12.2: Property Insurance

Name

Date   Score

A   **(42 points) Solve the following problems. (6 points for each correct answer)**

1. A building valued at $380,000 is insured for its full value. The annual premium is $9.80 per thousand dollars of coverage.

   a. How much does the insured pay to insure his building? _____

   b. If the insurance company cancels the policy at the end of 3 months, how much refund does the insured receive? _____

   c. If the insurance company has a 10% penalty clause for short-rate refunds and the insured cancels the policy after 9 months, how much refund does the insured receive? _____

2. If a company pays an annual premium of $6,000 and the insurance company charges $30 per thousand dollars of insurance, how much insurance does the company carry? _____

3. A company carries property insurance of $200,000 with no coinsurance clause. A fire causes $210,000 in damage. How much does the insurance company pay the insured? _____

4. A company carries property insurance of $300,000 with a premium of $13.10 per thousand dollars of coverage. A fire causes $120,000 in damage.

   a. How much does the insurance company pay the insured? _____

   b. What did the company save by carrying insurance? _____

                                                    _____
                                                    Score for A (42)

B   **(58 points) Solve the following problems. (points for correct answers as marked)**

5. A building worth $300,000 is insured for $180,000, and the policy carries an 80% coinsurance clause. A fire causes $220,000 in damage.

   a. How much will the insurance company pay? (10 points) _____

   b. How much will the insured pay if the building is repaired for $220,000? (6 points) _____

   c. How much would the insurance company pay if damage to the building totaled $300,000? (10 points)

   _____

   d. If the damage totaled $300,000, how much would the insured pay if the building were rebuilt for $300,000? (6 points) _____

6. A building worth $1,800,000 is insured for $1,200,000, and the policy carries an 80% coinsurance clause. A fire causes $300,000 in damage. (Round to the nearest dollar.)

   a. How much does the insurance company pay if the building is repaired for $300,000? (10 points) _____

   b. How much of the repair cost must the insured pay? (6 points) _____

7. If an insurance company issues insurance on property valued at $400,000 with a 90% coinsurance clause, what is the amount required to be carried by the insured? (5 points) _____

8. If an insurance company issues insurance on property valued at $3,000,000 with a 75% coinsurance clause, what is the amount required to be carried by the insured? (5 points) _____

_____

Score for B (58)

Assignment 12.3: Life and Medical Insurance

Name

Date   Score

A **(50 points) Refer to Figures 12-1 and 12-2 for the premium and surrender rates in solving the following problems. Assume that every year is a full 12 months long. (points for correct answers as marked)**

1. Find the rates per thousand dollars and the premiums for the following policies. (1 point for each correct answer)

Age	Type	Payments Made	Face Value of Policy	Rate per $1,000	Premium Paid Each Year
28	Straight Life	Annually	$200,000	_____	_____
25	20-Payment Life	Quarterly	80,000	_____	_____
25	20-Year Endowment	Semiannually	10,000	_____	_____
26	Straight Life	Quarterly	120,000	_____	_____
27	20-Payment Life	Semiannually	100,000	_____	_____
28	20-Year Endowment	Annually	85,000	_____	_____

2. Find the cash surrender or loan value for each of the following policies issued at age 25. (1 point for each correct answer)

Policy Year	Type of Policy	Amount of Policy	Cash Surrender or Loan Value
10	Straight Life	$50,000	_____
15	20-Payment Life	$25,000	_____
10	20-Year Endowment	$50,000	_____
3	Straight Life	$20,000	_____
5	20-Payment Life	$75,000	_____
4	20-Year Endowment	$60,000	_____

3. When Jo Yager was 27 years old, she took out a $80,000, 20-year endowment policy. She paid the premiums annually and survived the endowment period. How much more did she pay in annual premiums than she received from the insurance company at the end of 20 years? (4 points) _____

4. Roy Boatman purchased a $50,000 ordinary life policy and an ADB for 50% of the value of the policy. In addition, he purchased a 5-year, $50,000 term policy. He died in an accident 3 years later.
   a. How much money did Roy's beneficiaries receive? (4 points) _____

   b. How much money would Roy's beneficiaries have received if he had died in an accident 7 years after purchasing the policies? (4 points) _____

   c. How much money would Roy's beneficiaries have received if he had died of natural causes 10 years after purchasing the policies? (4 points) _____

5. At the age of 25, Carlos Baker purchased a $50,000 straight life policy, with premiums payable annually. He also purchased a $25,000 20-payment life policy, with premiums payable semiannually. At the end of 15 years, he decided to cash in both policies.

   a. How much did Carlos receive for the straight life policy? (4 points) _____

   b. How much did Carlos receive for the 20-payment life policy? (4 points) _____

   c. How much more did Carlos pay in premiums than the total amount received for both policies? (8 points) _____

Score for A (50)

B **(50 points) Solve the following problems. (10 points for a correct answer to problem 6; 8 points for each other correct answer)**

6. An employer provides group health coverage that includes a $250 annual deductible per family and payment of 80% of costs exceeding the deductible. How much would an employee with two dependents pay if her medical bills for the year were $550 for herself; $920 for dependent 1; and $230 for dependent 2? _____

7. An employer provides group health coverage that includes a $500 annual deductible per family and 80% of costs over the deductible.

   a. How much would an employee with no dependents pay if his medical bills were $2,850 this year? _____

   b. How much would that employee have paid this year if his medical bills were $7,480? _____

8. An employer provides group health coverage with the following monthly premiums: employee only, $450; employee with one dependent, $550; and employee with multiple dependents, $650.

   a. How much does the employer pay over a 5-year period for an employee with multiple dependents? _____

   b. If that employee had a dependent with a catastrophic illness that cost $97,000 for hospitalization and treatments during that 5-year period, how much would the insurance company lose on that employee, assuming that she had no other medical claims? _____

   c. If an employee with no dependents had no illnesses during that same 5-year period, how much would the insurance company make on that employee? _____

Score for B (50)

Simple Interest

13

Learning Objectives

By studying this chapter and completing all assignments, you will be able to:

Learning Objective 1 Compute simple interest with time in years or months.

Learning Objective 2 Compute ordinary simple interest, using a 360-day year.

Learning Objective 3 Compute exact simple interest, using a 365-day year.

Learning Objective 4 Compare ordinary simple interest and exact simple interest.

Learning Objective 5 Estimate exact simple interest computations.

Learning Objective 6 Compute the Principal, Rate, and Time from the basic interest formula.

Most businesses and individuals buy at least some assets without making full payment at the time of the purchase. The seller gives immediate possession to the buyer but does not require payment until some later date. For example, large retailers such as Macy's Department Store may receive merchandise for the Christmas season but may not be required to pay the seller until January. The seller, who *extends credit* to the buyer, may or may not charge for this privilege. The charge is called **interest,** and it is usually quoted as a percent of the amount of credit extended (the principal). When part of the price is paid at the time of purchase, that part is called a **down payment.**

If the seller charges too much interest or does not extend credit, the buyer might borrow money from a third party, such as a bank. The buyer would then sell the merchandise to repay the bank loan. The amount borrowed is called the **principal,** and the interest charged is a percent of the principal. The bank will charge interest between the loan date and the repayment date. This period of **time** is called the **interest period** or the **term of the loan.**

The promise to repay a loan or pay for merchandise may be oral or written. If it is written, it may be in the form of a letter or it could be one of several special documents known collectively as **commercial paper. Short-term credit** transactions are those whose term is between 1 day and 1 year. **Long-term credit** transactions are those for longer than 1 year. Normally, long-term credit transactions involve major items such as new buildings or equipment rather than supplies or merchandise for sale.

Computing Simple Interest

Learning Objective 1

Compute simple interest with time in years or months.

The easiest type of interest to calculate is called **simple interest.** The calculations are the same for both a loan and a purchase on credit. The interest rate is a percent of the principal for the period of the loan or credit. The quoted percent usually is an *annual* (yearly) rate. An interest rate of 10% means that the interest payment for 1 year will be 10% of the principal.

To compute the amount of simple interest on a 1-year loan, simply multiply the Principal by the Rate.

EXAMPLE A

Don Bunyard borrowed $1,000 for 1 year at a rate of 8% simple interest. Compute the interest.

The principal is $1,000. The interest for 1 year is 8% of $1,000, or 0.08 × $1,000 = $80.

Most loans, however, are not for a period of exactly 1 year. Loans for longer periods will require the borrower to pay more interest. Likewise, loans for shorter periods will require less interest. To compute the simple interest on loans of any period, multiply the Principal by the Rate and then multiply by the Time, with Time stated in years or in fractions of years. The fundamental formula for simple interest is

Interest = Principal × Rate × Time
abbreviated as $I = P \times R \times T$ or, even more simply, $I = PRT.$

EXAMPLE B

Find the amounts of simple interest on loans of $1,200 when the rate is 6% and the loan periods are $\frac{3}{4}$ year and 4 years.

$\frac{3}{4}$ **year**

$I = P \times R \times T$

$\quad = \$1{,}200 \times 0.06 \times \dfrac{3}{4}$

$\quad = \$54$

4 years

$I = P \times R \times T$

$\quad = \$1{,}200 \times 0.06 \times 4$

$\quad = \$288$

The time period often will be measured in months instead of years. Before computing the interest, change the time into years by dividing the number of months by 12 (the number of months in 1 year).

EXAMPLE C

Compute the interest on credit purchases of $3,000 at 5% for periods of 8 months and 30 months.

8 months

$I = P \times R \times T$

$\quad = \$3{,}000 \times 0.05 \times \dfrac{8}{12}$

$\quad = \$100$

30 months

$I = P \times R \times T$

$\quad = \$3{,}000 \times 0.05 \times \dfrac{30}{12}$

$\quad = \$375$

USING CALCULATORS

Today, calculators or computers are used in almost every interest application. The numbers are often large and are always important. The steps are performed on the calculator in the same order as they are written in the formula.

EXAMPLE D

Write the calculator steps for computing the simple interest on $8,000,000 at 9% for 18 months.

$I = P \times R \times T = \$8{,}000{,}000 \times 0.09 \times \dfrac{18}{12}$

8 000 000 $\boxed{\times}$ .09 $\boxed{\times}$ 18 $\boxed{\div}$ 12 $\boxed{=}$

The display will show 1,080,000, which means $1,080,000.

Using the percent key $\boxed{\%}$, the steps would be

8 000 000 $\boxed{\times}$ 9 $\boxed{\%}$ $\boxed{\times}$ 18 $\boxed{\div}$ 12 $\boxed{=}$

The display will again show 1,080,000, or $1,080,000.

✔ CONCEPT CHECK 13.1

The Principal is $2,500, the Rate is 10%, and Interest = Principal × Rate × Time, or $I = P \times R \times T$. Find the interest both for 5 years and for 6 months.

a. For Time = 5 years: $I = P \times R \times T = \$2{,}500 \times 0.10 \times 5 = \$1{,}250$

b. For Time = 6 months: $I = P \times R \times T = \$2{,}500 \times 0.10 \times \frac{6}{12} = \$125$

Computing Ordinary Interest

Learning Objective 2

Compute ordinary simple interest, using a 360-day year.

If the term of the loan is stated as a certain number of days, computing interest involves dividing the number of days by the number of days in 1 year—either 360 or 365. Before computers and calculators, interest was easier to compute by assuming that every year had 360 days and that every month had 30 days. The 360-day method, called the **ordinary interest method,** is still used by some businesses and individuals.

MONARX3D/SHUTTERSTOCK.COM

EXAMPLE E

Compute the ordinary simple interest on $900 at 9% for 120 days.

$$I = P \times R \times T$$

$$= \$900 \times 0.09 \times \frac{120}{360}$$

$$= \$27$$

✔ CONCEPT CHECK 13.2

The Principal is $4,000, the Rate is 7%, and the Time is 180 days. Compute the ordinary simple interest.

Use a 360-day year: $I = P \times R \times T = \$4,000 \times 0.07 \times \frac{180}{360} = \$140$

Computing Exact Interest

Learning Objective 3

Compute exact simple interest, using a 365-day year.

Banks, savings and loan institutions, credit unions, and the federal government use a 365-day year (366 days for leap years) to compute interest. This method is called the **exact interest method.** The computations are the same as for ordinary simple interest, except that 365 days is used instead of 360 days.

EXAMPLE F

Compute the exact simple interest on $900 at 9% for 120 days.

$$I = P \times R \times T$$

$$= \$900 \times 0.09 \times \frac{120}{365}$$

$$= \$26.6301, \text{ or } \$26.63$$

The Principal is $4,000, the Rate is 7%, and the Time is 180 days. Compute the exact simple interest.

Use a 365-day year: $I = P \times R \times T = \$4,000 \times 0.07 \times \frac{180}{365} = \$138.0822$, or $138.08

Comparing Ordinary Interest and Exact Interest

The 360-day year was very useful before the advent of calculators and computers, so there is a long tradition of using it. However, the 365-day year is realistic. Also, the 365-day year is financially better for the borrower because the interest amounts are always smaller. (Why? Because a denominator of 365 gives a smaller quotient than a denominator of 360.)

Reexamine examples E and F. The difference between ordinary interest and exact simple interest is only $27.00 − $26.63, or $0.37. When businesses borrow money, the principal may be very large and then the difference will be more significant. Example G is similar to examples E and F, except that the principal is in millions of dollars rather than hundreds.

Learning Objective **4**

Compare ordinary simple interest and exact simple interest.

EXAMPLE G

Find the difference between the amounts of ordinary simple interest and exact simple interest on $8,000,000 at 9% for 120 days.

Ordinary Interest	**Exact Interest**
$I = P \times R \times T$	$I = P \times R \times T$
$= \$8,000,000 \times 0.09 \times \dfrac{120}{360}$	$= \$8,000,000 \times 0.09 \times \dfrac{120}{365}$
$= \$240,000$	$= \$236,712.3288$, or $236,712.33

The difference is $240,000.00 − $236,712.33 = $3,287.67.

The Principal is $6,000, the Rate is 12%, and the Time is 120 days. Find the difference between the amounts of simple interest calculated by using the ordinary method (360-day year) and the exact method (365-day year).

Ordinary interest: $I = P \times R \times T = \$6,000 \times 0.12 \times \frac{120}{360} = \$240.00$

Exact interest: $I = P \times R \times T = \$6,000 \times 0.12 \times \frac{120}{365} = \$236.7123$, or $236.71

Difference = Ordinary interest − Exact interest = $240.00 − $236.71 = $3.29

Estimating Exact Simple Interest

Learning Objective **5**

Estimate exact simple interest computations.

Although calculators are used to compute exact interest, approximation remains very useful. The following calculator solution requires a minimum of 20 key entries.

8 000 000 $\times$ .09 $\times$ 120 $\div$ 365 $=$
The display will show 236,712.3288.

Pressing any one of the 20 keys incorrectly could result in a large error. By making an estimate of the interest amount in advance, you may discover a significant calculator error.

COMBINATIONS OF TIME AND INTEREST THAT YIELD 1%

To simplify mental estimates, you can round the rate and time to numbers that are easy to compute mentally. Also, use 360 days instead of 365 because it cancels more often. For ordinary interest, several combinations of rate and time are very easy to use because their product is 1%. For example, $12\% \times \frac{30}{360} = 12\% \times \frac{1}{12} = 1\%$ and $6\% \times \frac{60}{360} = 6\% \times \frac{1}{6} = 1\%$.

EXAMPLE H

Approximate the ordinary simple interest on $2,500 at 6.15% for 59 days. Then calculate the actual ordinary simple interest.

Round   6.15% to 6% and 59 days to 60 days.

Estimate: $\$2,500 \times 0.06 \times \frac{60}{360} = \$2,500 \times 0.01 = \$25.00$

Actual interest: $\$2,500 \times 0.0615 \times \frac{59}{360} = \$25.1979$, or $25.20

OTHER RATES AND TIMES

Table 13-1 shows several combinations of Rate and Time whose products are useful for estimating simple interest.

Table 13-1	Rate and Time		
$4\% \times \dfrac{90}{360} = 4\% \times \dfrac{1}{4} = 1\%$		$10\% \times \dfrac{36}{360} = 10\% \times \dfrac{1}{10} = 1\%$	
$6\% \times \dfrac{60}{360} = 6\% \times \dfrac{1}{6} = 1\%$		$12\% \times \dfrac{30}{360} = 12\% \times \dfrac{1}{12} = 1\%$	
$8\% \times \dfrac{45}{360} = 8\% \times \dfrac{1}{8} = 1\%$		$18\% \times \dfrac{20}{360} = 18\% \times \dfrac{1}{18} = 1\%$	
$9\% \times \dfrac{40}{360} = 9\% \times \dfrac{1}{9} = 1\%$		$6\% \times \dfrac{120}{360} = 6\% \times \dfrac{1}{3} = 2\%$	
$12\% \times \dfrac{60}{360} = 12\% \times \dfrac{1}{6} = 2\%$		$12\% \times \dfrac{90}{360} = 12\% \times \dfrac{1}{4} = 3\%$	
$8\% \times \dfrac{90}{360} = 8\% \times \dfrac{1}{4} = 2\%$		$9\% \times \dfrac{120}{360} = 9\% \times \dfrac{1}{3} = 3\%$	

ESTIMATING EXACT INTEREST

The goal in approximating interest is just to get an estimate. Even though exact interest requires 365 days in a year, you can make a reasonable estimate by assuming that the number of days in a year is 360. This permits the use of all of the shortcut combinations from Table 13-1.

● **EXAMPLE I**

First, compute the actual exact simple interest on $1,200 at 11.8% for 62 days.

Actual interest: $1,200 \times 0.118 \times \dfrac{62}{365} = \$24.0526$, or $24.05

Second, estimate the amount of interest by using 12% instead of 11.8%, 60 days instead of 62 days, and 360 instead of 365.

Estimate: $1,200 \times 0.12 \times \dfrac{60}{360} = \$1,200 \times 0.02 = \$24$

The difference is $24.05 − $24 = $0.05.

✔ **CONCEPT CHECK 13.5**

The Principal is $3,750, the Rate is 9.1%, and the Time is 39 days. Calculate the actual exact simple interest. Then make an estimate by using a 360-day year and simpler values for *R* and *T*. Compare the results.

Actual interest: $I = P \times R \times T = \$3,750 \times 0.091 \times \frac{39}{365} = \$36.4623$, or $36.46

Estimate: $I = P \times R \times T = \$3,750 \times 0.09 \ \times \frac{40}{360} = \$3,750 \times 0.01 = \$37.50$

Difference: Estimate − Actual = $37.50 − $36.46 = $1.04

Computing the Interest Variables

Every simple interest problem has four variables: Interest, Principal, Rate, and Time. Thus far, you have solved for the Interest Amount *(I)* when the Principal *(P)*, Rate *(R)*, and Time *(T)* were all given. However, as long as any three variables are given, you can always compute the fourth by just changing the formula $I = P \times R \times T$ into one of its possible variations, as shown in Table 13-2.

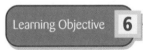
Learning Objective **6**

Compute the Principal, Rate, and Time from the basic interest formula.

Table 13-2	PRT formulas	
To find	**You must know**	**Use this formula**
I	*P, R*, and *T*	$I = P \times R \times T$
P	*I, R*, and *T*	$P = \dfrac{I}{(R \times T)}$
R	*I, P*, and *T*	$R = \dfrac{I}{(P \times T)}$
T	*I, P*, and *R*	$T = \dfrac{I}{(P \times R)}$

Assume the use of ordinary simple interest (a 360-day year) unless the use of exact interest (a 365-day year) is indicated. The stated or computed interest rate is the rate for 1 full year. Also, the length of time used for computing interest dollars must be stated in terms of all or part of a year.

FINDING THE INTEREST AMOUNT, PRINCIPAL, RATE, OR TIME

When any three variables are known, you can solve for the fourth variable. The previous examples in this chapter all solved for I. To find the other three variables, use the other formulas from Table 13-2. All rates are ordinary simple interest (360-day year).

● EXAMPLE J

Find the Principal if the Interest is $75, the Rate is 6%, and the Time is 30 days.

$$P = ?; \quad I = \$75; \quad R = 6\%; \quad T = \frac{30}{360} \text{ year}$$

$$P = \frac{I}{(R \times T)} = \frac{\$75}{\left(0.06 \times \dfrac{30}{360}\right)} = \frac{\$75}{0.005} = \$15,000$$

● EXAMPLE K

JUICE IMAGES/PHOTO LIBRARY

Find the Rate if the Interest is $22, the Principal is $2,000, and the Time is 30 days. Round the Rate to the nearest $\frac{1}{10}\%$.

$$R = ?; \quad I = \$22; \quad P = \$2,000; \quad T = \frac{30}{360} \text{ year}$$

$$R = \frac{I}{(P \times T)} = \frac{\$22}{\left(\$2,000 \times \dfrac{30}{360}\right)} = \frac{\$22}{\$166.67} = 0.132, \text{ or } 13.2\%$$

● EXAMPLE L

Find the Time if the Interest is $324, the Principal is $4,800, and the Rate is 9%. Round Time to the nearest whole day, based on a 360-day year.

$$T = ?; \quad I = \$324; \quad P = \$4,800; \quad R = 9\%$$

$$T = \frac{I}{(P \times R)} = \frac{\$324}{(\$4,800 \times 0.09)} = \frac{\$324}{\$432} = 0.75 \text{ year}$$

Based on a 360-day year, 0.75 year = 0.75 × 360 days = 270 days.

Each of the following problems gives three of the four variables. Compute the missing variable. All rates are ordinary simple interest (360-day year). Round P and I to the nearest cent; round R to the nearest $\frac{1}{10}$%; round T to the nearest whole day, assuming that 1 year has 360 days. Use one of the four formulas:

$$I = P \times R \times T, \quad P = \frac{I}{(R \times T)}, \quad R = \frac{I}{(P \times T)}, \quad \text{and} \quad T = \frac{I}{(P \times R)}$$

a. Principal = \$1,240; Rate = 6%; Time = 270 days
   Find Interest:

   $$I = P \times R \times T = \$1,240 \times 0.06 \times \frac{270}{360} = \$55.80$$

b. Principal = \$8,000; Interest = \$50; Time = 45 days
   Find Rate:

   $$R = \frac{I}{(P \times T)} = \frac{\$50}{\left(\$8,000 \times \dfrac{45}{360}\right)} = 0.05, \text{ or } 5\%$$

c. Principal = \$1,280; Interest = \$64; Rate = 10%
   Find Time:

   $$T = \frac{I}{(P \times R)} = \frac{\$64}{(\$1,280 \times 0.10)} = 0.5 \text{ year}$$

   In a 360-day year, $T = 0.5$ year $= 0.5 \times 360$ days $= 180$ days.

d. Interest = \$90; Rate = 9%; Time = 60 days
   Find Principal:

   $$P = \frac{I}{(R \times T)} = \frac{\$90}{\left(0.09 \times \dfrac{60}{360}\right)} = \$6,000$$

COMPLETE ASSIGNMENTS 13.1 AND 13.2.

Chapter Terms for Review

commercial paper

down payment

exact interest method

interest

interest period

long-term credit

ordinary interest method

principal

short-term credit

simple interest

term of the loan

time

Try Microsoft® Excel

Try working the problems using the Microsoft Excel templates found on the companion website. Solutions for the problems are also shown on the companion website.

THE BOTTOM LINE

Summary of chapter learning objectives:

Learning Objective	Example
13.1 Compute simple interest with time in years or months.	Find the simple interest using the basic formula: **Interest = Principal × Rate × Time**, or $I = P \times R \times T$ 1. Principal = \$3,500; Rate = 9%; Time = 2.5 years 2. Principal = \$975; Rate = 8%; Time = 9 months
13.2 Compute ordinary simple interest, using a 360-day year.	3. Find the ordinary simple interest for a 360-day year: Principal = \$5,000; Rate = 6%; Time = 150 days
13.3 Compute exact simple interest, using a 365-day year.	4. Find the exact simple interest for a 365-day year: Principal = \$2,800; Rate = 7%; Time = 75 days
13.4 Compare ordinary simple interest and exact simple interest.	5. Find the difference between ordinary simple interest and exact simple interest: Principal = \$5,000; Rate = 6%; Time = 75 days
13.5 Estimate exact simple interest computations.	6. Estimate the exact interest by using a 360-day year and simpler values for Rate and Time: Principal = \$2,100; Rate = 5.8%; Time = 62 days
13.6 Compute the Principal, Rate, and Time from the basic interest formula.	Solve for Principal, Rate, and Time using a 360-day year and the formulas $$P = \frac{I}{(R \times T)}, \quad R = \frac{I}{(P \times T)}, \text{ and } T = \frac{I}{(P \times R)}$$ 7. Interest = \$42; Rate = 6%; Time = 105 days 8. Principal = \$1,600; Interest = \$30; Time = 75 days 9. Principal = \$7,200; Interest = \$135; Rate = 15% (express Time in days)

Answers: 1. \$787.50   2. \$58.50   3. \$125.00   4. \$40.27   5. \$62.50 − \$61.64 = \$0.86
6. \$2,100 × 0.06 × $\frac{60}{360}$ = \$21   7. \$2,400   8. 0.09, or 9%   9. 45 days

Review Problems for Chapter 13

In problems 1 and 2, compute the amount of (a) ordinary simple interest and (b) exact simple interest. Then compute (c) the difference between the two interest amounts.

	Principal	Rate	Time	Ordinary Interest	Exact Interest	Difference
1	$1,680	6%	270 Days	a. _____	b. _____	c. _____
2	$10,500	8%	60 Days	a. _____	b. _____	c. _____

In problems 3 and 4, first compute (a) the actual exact simple interest. Then, change each rate and time to the closest numbers that permit use of the shortcuts shown in Table 13-1 and compute (b) the *estimated* amount of exact interest. Finally, compute (c) the difference between the actual and estimated exact interest.

	Principal	Rate	Time	Actual Exact Interest	Estimated Exact Interest	Difference
3	$12,000	3.8%	92 Days	a. _____	b. _____	c. _____
4	$2,000	9.2%	117 Days	a. _____	b. _____	c. _____

5 Dick Liebelt borrowed money for 240 days at a rate of 9% ordinary simple interest. How much did Dick borrow if he paid $90 in interest? _____

6 Rose Chavez loaned $1,000 to one of her employees for 90 days. If the employee's interest amount was $12.50, what was the ordinary simple interest rate? _____

7 Erinn Kelley loaned $8,000 to a machine shop owner who was buying a piece of used equipment. The interest rate was 6% ordinary simple interest, and the interest amount was $360. Compute the number of days of the loan. _____

8 Julie Horton loaned $2,500 to Kathy Lee a good friend since childhood. Because of their friendship, Julie charged only 3% ordinary simple interest. Two months later, when Kathy received her annual bonus, she repaid the entire loan and all the interest. What was the total amount that Kathy paid? _____

9 Cynthia Chu and her sister Martha have a home decorating and design business. They often buy antiques and fine art objects and then resell the items to their clients. They have a line of credit at their bank to provide short-term financing for these purchases. The bank always charges exact simple interest, but the rate varies depending on the economy. Cynthia and Martha need to borrow $22,400 for 90 days to buy a collection of antique furniture at an estate sale. If the bank charges 5.25%, how much interest would they pay? _____

Answers to the Self-Check can be found in Appendix B at the back of the text.

Assignment 13.1: Simple Interest

Name _____

Date _____ Score _____

A (20 points) Compute the simple interest. If the time is given in months, let 1 month be $\frac{1}{12}$ of a year. If the time is in days, let 1 year be 360 days. (2 points for each correct answer)

Principal	Rate	Time	Interest		Principal	Rate	Time	Interest
1. $500	6.0%	1 year	_____		**2.** $4,000	8%	3 years	_____
3. $1,800	8%	4 months	_____		**4.** $1,025	4.5%	16 months	_____
5. $7,500	5%	180 days	_____		**6.** $3,600	12%	30 months	_____
7. $12,800	7%	2.5 years	_____		**8.** $1,250	6%	$1\frac{3}{4}$ years	_____
9. $5,200	10%	90 days	_____		**10.** $20,000	7.5%	8 months	_____

_____

Score for A (20)

B (30 points) Compute the ordinary interest, the exact interest, and their difference. Round answers to the nearest cent. (2 points for each correct interest; 1 point for each correct difference)

	Principal	Rate	Time	Ordinary Interest	Exact Interest	Difference
11.	$2,400	4%	180 days	_____	_____	_____
12.	$960	7%	45 days	_____	_____	_____
13.	$12,000	6%	240 days	_____	_____	_____
14.	$2,000	5%	135 days	_____	_____	_____
15.	$7,500	8%	225 days	_____	_____	_____
16.	$365	4%	30 days	_____	_____	_____

Score for B (30)

C **(20 points)** In each problem, first find the actual exact simple interest. Then, estimate the interest by assuming a 360-day year and round each rate and time to the nearest numbers that will permit the shortcuts in Table 13-1. Finally, find the difference. Round answers to the nearest cent. (2 points for each correct estimate and actual interest; 1 point for each correct difference)

	Principal	Rate	Time	Actual Exact Interest	Estimate	Difference
17.	$925	8.1%	47 days	_____	_____	_____
18.	$5,600	3.99%	92 days	_____	_____	_____
19.	$2,000	8.95%	123 days	_____	_____	_____
20.	$12,500	6.3%	117 days	_____	_____	_____

Score for C (20)

D **(30 points)** Determine the missing variable by using one of the following formulas:

$$I = P \times R \times T, \quad P = \frac{I}{(R \times T)}, \quad R = \frac{I}{(P \times T)}, \quad \text{or} \quad T = \frac{I}{(P \times R)}$$

For problems 21–25, use a 360-day year. For problems 26–30, use a 365-day year. Round dollar amounts to the nearest cent. Round interest rates to the nearest $\frac{1}{10}$ of a percent. Find the time in days, rounded to the nearest whole day. (3 points for each correct answer)

	Principal	Rate	Time	Interest
21.	_____	11%	240 days	$352.00
22.	$12,500	5%	_____	$50.00

Principal	Rate	Time	Interest
23. $600	_____	45 days	$6.00
24. $8,840	4.8%	135 days	_____
25. $25,000	4%	_____	$625.00
26. _____	8%	270 days	$510.00
27. $3,650	6.75%	136 days	_____
28. $18,500	5%	_____	$185.00
29. $16,000	_____	90 days	$296.00
30. _____	4.9%	270 days	$50.00

_____

Score for D (30)

Assignment 13.2: Simple Interest Applications

Name _____

Date _____ Score _____

A **(50 points) Solve each of the following ordinary simple interest problems by using a 360-day year. Find both the interest dollars and the total amount (i.e., principal plus interest) of the loan. (7 points for each correct interest; 3 points for each correct amount)**

1. Bruce Sanberg plans to lend $850 to his friend Bill Rice so that Bill can fly with him to Canada for vacation. Bruce is charging Bill only 3% ordinary simple interest. Bill repays everything, interest plus principal, to Bruce 180 days later. How much does Bill pay?

   Interest _____

   Amount _____

2. David and Ellen Cho are planning to start a business that will export American food to China. They estimate that they will need $85,000 to pay for organizational costs, get product samples, and make three trips to Shanghai. They can borrow the money from their relatives for 3 years. The Chos are willing to pay their relatives 6% ordinary simple interest. Compute the total amount that they will owe their relatives in 3 years.

   Interest _____

   Amount _____

3. Carolyn Wilfert owns a temporary services employment agency. Businesses call her when they need to hire various types of workers for a short period of time. The businesses pay a fee to Carolyn, who pays the salaries and benefits to the employees. One benefit is that Carolyn will make small, short-term loans to her employees. After a flood, employee Judy Hillstrom needed to borrow $3,600 to have her house cleaned and repainted. Judy repaid the loan in 6 months. If Carolyn charged 5% ordinary simple interest, how much did Judy repay?

   Interest _____

   Amount _____

4. Several years ago, Ed Velure and Lee Oman formed a partnership to rent musical instruments to school districts that do not want to own and maintain the instruments. In the spring, they investigate borrowing $120,000 to buy some new instruments. Because they collect their rental fees in advance, they anticipate being able to repay the loan in 150 days. How much will they need to repay if the ordinary simple interest rate is 5.5%?

   Interest _____

   Amount _____

5. Buck Williams owns and manages a video game arcade. A manufacturer developed a new line of games and offered very low interest financing to encourage arcade operators such as Buck to install the new games. He was able to finance $60,000 worth of games for 8 months for 5.2% ordinary simple interest. Calculate how much Buck will repay.

   Interest _____

   Amount _____

   _____

   Score for A (50)

B (50 points) Solve each of the following exact simple interest problems by using a 365-day year. Find both the interest dollars and the total amount (i.e., principal plus interest) of the loan. (7 points for each correct interest; 3 points for each correct amount)

6. Don McIntosh, managing partner of a local transportation company, thinks that the company should borrow money to upgrade its truck repair facility. After investigating several sources of short-term loans, Don determines that the company can borrow $300,000 for 180 days at 6% exact simple interest. If his company decides to take out this loan, how much will it need to repay at the end of the 180 days?

Interest _____

Amount _____

7. Dave Engle, a former teacher, now has a business selling supplemetary educational materials such as books and computer software to parents and schools. In June, he borrowed $45,000 from his bank to buy some new educational computer games that he hopes to sell during August and September. The bank's rate is 6.25% exact simple interest as long as the time does not exceed half a year. If Dave pays the principal plus the interest in 120 days, how much will he pay?

Interest _____

Amount _____

8. After working as a food broker for 5 years, Roger Sundahl had saved almost enough money to buy a fishing boat and move to Alaska to open a charter fishing business. He still needed $50,000, which he could borrow until the end of the first fishing season. The lender charged 6.5% exact simple interest, and Roger repaid them after 150 days. How much interest did Roger pay, and what was the total amount?

Interest _____

Amount _____

9. Carol Payne needs to purchase two new saws for her retail lumber yard. The company that sells the saws offers her short-term financing at the relatively high rate of 11% exact simple interest. She decides to accept the financing offer, but only for $5,000 and only for 45 days. How much will Carol pay at the end of the 45 days? What will be the total amount that she pays?

Interest _____

Amount _____

10. After working for a large accounting firm for 10 years, Bette Ryan, C.P.A., decided to open her own office. She borrowed $50,000 at 6.7% exact simple interest. She made enough during the first income tax season to repay the loan in 219 days. How much did Bette pay and what was the total amount?

Interest _____

Amount _____

_____

Score for B (50)

Installment Purchases

14

Learning Objectives

By studying this chapter and completing all assignments, you will be able to:

Learning Objective 1 Convert between annual and monthly interest rates.

Learning Objective 2 Compute simple interest on a monthly basis.

Learning Objective 3 Compute finance charges.

Learning Objective 4 Compute costs of installment purchases.

Learning Objective 5 Compute effective rates.

Learning Objective 6 Amortize a loan.

Learning Objective 7 Compute a monthly mortgage payment.

Most individuals today can purchase goods or services on credit if they choose. The buyer gets immediate possession or immediate service but delays payment. Either the seller extends the credit or the buyer uses a **credit card,** or loan, from a third party.

Credit is usually offered for an interest charge, which is usually computed each month. A summary of the purchases, payments, and interest charges is sent to the borrower (credit purchaser) each month, either by mail or electronically. It may not be simple to compare the methods used to compute interest by competing lenders. Some lenders may charge interest on the **average daily balance.** Although it is a simple concept, and easy for a computer to calculate, it may be difficult for the purchaser to reconcile when he or she makes many purchases and/or merchandise returns in a single month.

In addition to interest, a lender may charge additional fees to extend credit or loan money. These might include items such as loan origination fees, membership fees, credit check fees, administrative fees, and insurance premiums. All of the fees together are called **finance charges.** These additional fees, whether one-time, annual, or monthly, also make it difficult to compare lenders because each lender could be slightly different. It is of some help to consumers that there are laws that mandate that lenders must explain their various fees and rates. In fact, the Consumer Financial Protection Bureau was authorized by Congress in 2010 and began its mission in 2011.

Converting Interest Rates

Learning Objective 1

Convert between annual and monthly interest rates.

The general concept behind charging for credit purchases is to compute finance charges on the remaining unpaid balance each month. The formula can still be $I = P \times R \times T$, where P is the unpaid balance. However, T is not years or a fraction of a year (as in Chapter 13)—T is in months, and R, the rate, is a monthly rate. For example, the rate might be 1.5% *per month*.

Understanding the relationship between monthly and annual rates is important.

> **Rule: To convert an annual rate to a monthly rate, divide the annual rate by 12; to convert a monthly rate to an annual rate, multiply the monthly rate by 12.**

● EXAMPLE A

a. Convert 9% per year to the equivalent monthly rate.

9% annually ÷ 12 = 0.75% monthly

b. Convert 0.5% per month to the equivalent annual rate.

0.5% monthly × 12 = 6% annually

✔ CONCEPT CHECK 14.1

a. Convert an 18% annual rate to the equivalent monthly rate.
Divide the annual rate by 12 to get the monthly rate: 18% ÷ 12 = 1.5% per month

b. Convert a 1.25% monthly rate to the equivalent annual rate.
Multiply the monthly rate by 12 to get the annual rate: 1.25% × 12 = 15% per year

Computing Simple Interest on a Monthly Basis

In terms of single-payment simple interest, 1.5% *per month* is identical to 18% *per year*.

Rule: If the rate is annual, the time must be in years; if the rate is monthly, the time must be in months.

Learning Objective **2**

Compute simple interest on a monthly basis.

EXAMPLE B

Compute the simple interest on $1,000 for 2 months at 18% per year, on an annual basis and on a monthly basis.

Annual: $I = P \times R \times T = \$1,000 \times 0.18 \text{ per year} \times \frac{2}{12} \text{ year} = \$30$

Monthly: $18\% \text{ per year} = 18\% \div 12 = 1.5\% \text{ per month}$

$I = P \times R \times T = \$1,000 \times 0.015 \text{ per month} \times 2 \text{ months}$
$= \$30$

Reminder: Both computations differ from most of those in Chapter 13, where you counted the exact number of days and divided by either 360 or 365.

✔ CONCEPT CHECK 14.2

Compute the simple interest on $800 for 3 months at 0.5% per month.

$I = P \times R \times T = \$800 \times 0.5\% \text{ per month} \times 3 \text{ months} = \$800 \times 0.005 \times 3 = \$12$

Computing Finance Charges

Before a creditor (lender) calculates the "interest on the unpaid monthly balance," it usually determines the amount of any payments, of any credits for returned merchandise, and/or any subsequent purchases. To give you an introduction, Figure 14-1 is the lower portion of a monthly statement that might have come from a retail store which has

Learning Objective **3**

Compute finance charges.

| Figure 14-1 | Retail Statement of Account |

PREVIOUS BALANCE	FINANCE CHARGE	PAYMENTS	CREDITS	PURCHASES	NEW BALANCE	MINIMUM PAYMENT	CLOSING DATE
624.12	9.36	500.00	62.95	364.45	434.98	45.00	10-16-09

IF WE RECEIVE PAYMENT OF THE FULL AMOUNT OF THE NEW BALANCE BEFORE THE NEXT CYCLE'S CLOSING DATE, SHOWN ABOVE, YOU WILL AVOID A FINANCE CHARGE NEXT MONTH. THE FINANCE CHARGE, IF ANY, IS CALCULATED ON THE PREVIOUS BALANCE BEFORE DEDUCTING ANY PAYMENTS OR CREDITS SHOWN ABOVE. THE PERIODIC RATES USED ARE 1.5% OF THE BALANCE ON AMOUNTS UNDER $1,000 AND 1% OF AMOUNTS IN EXCESS OF $1,000, WHICH ARE ANNUAL PERCENTAGE RATES OF 18% AND 12%, RESPECTIVELY.

charge accounts. These stores continue to exist because smaller, local stores such as paint stores, hardware stores, and grocery stores can extend credit to regular customers and not be required to pay the fees that are required by credit card companies. Examples C and D are two very simple methods that might be used to compute finance charges.

● EXAMPLE C

Compute the finance charge and the new balance for the statement shown in Figure 14-1 based on the previous balance, $624.12, ignoring all payments, credits, and purchases.

Finance charge = $624.12 × 1.5% × 1 month = $9.3618, or $9.36
New balance = $624.12 + $9.36 − $500.00 − $62.95 + $364.45 = $434.98

● EXAMPLE D

Assume that the finance charge in Figure 14-1 is based on the previous balance, less any payments or credits, but ignores subsequent purchases. Compute the finance charge and the new balance.

The finance charge is based on $624.12 − $500.00 − $62.95 = $61.17
Finance charge = $61.17 × 1.5% × 1 month = $0.91575, or $0.92
New balance = $624.12 + $0.92 − $500.00 − $62.95 + $364.45 = $426.54

CONSUMER PROTECTION ACTS AND TERMINOLOGY

For more than 40 years, Congress has been active with major legislation to try to protect and educate consumers about the financial world and about borrowing and lending practices. The first major law was in 1968, the Consumer Credit Protection Act, administered by the Federal Reserve System. Then came the Consumer Leasing Act of 1976, administered by the Federal Trade Commission, and the Home Ownership and Equity Protection Act of 1994, administered by the Department of Housing and Urban Development. The most recent major protection legislation is the Wall Street Reform and Consumer Protection Act of 2010 (the Dodd-Frank bill) which has established the Consumer Financial Protection Bureau (CFPB). It is an independent bureau within the Federal Reserve System, officially started in mid-2011, and is expected to consolidate the regulatory responsibilities and some employees of several agencies, including those mentioned. A major objective is to have all the important consumer protection functions controlled from one powerful, independent agency.

Our study in Chapter 14 is an introduction to calculating the costs of borrowing on installment purchases. One part of the earliest legislation still has particular significance for us. Title 1 of the original 1968 act is known as the **Truth in Lending Act (TILA)**. Among several mandates, TILA require creditors (lenders) to tell consumers (borrowers) these three things:

1. The total of all finance charges, including interest, carrying charges, insurance, and special fees
2. The annual percentage rate (APR) of the total finance charge
3. The method by which they compute the finance charge

As noted in the previous section, an annual interest rate is a monthly interest rate multiplied by 12. However, as the term is used in TILA, the **annual percentage rate (APR)** is a specific, defined term that must include all finance charges, not just interest. Furthermore, under TILA, lenders are permitted to use more than one method to compute the APR. Lenders may even use either a 360-day year or a 365-day year. TILA does not set limits on rates.

As mentioned, TILA does require that total finance charges be stated clearly, that the finance charges also be stated as an annual percentage rate, and that the method of computation be given. Although the method that is mentioned may be stated clearly, it may not always be simple for a consumer to calculate. One difficulty might be to determine the account balance that is to be used in the calculation. A wide variety of methods may be applied. For example:

1. The finance charge may be based on the amount owed at the beginning of the current month, ignoring payments and purchases.
2. The finance charge may be based on the amount owed at the beginning of the month, after subtracting any payments during the month and ignoring purchases.
3. The finance charge may be based on the average daily balance. (Add the unpaid balance each day; divide the total by the number of days in the month.) Payments are usually included; new purchases may or may not be included.
4. A variation of the average daily balance method is to compute the interest charge each day, on a daily basis, and then add all the daily interest charges for the month.

Although the total finance charges, and the annual percentage rate, and the method of calculation may all be clearly stated, some consumers will have difficulty reconstructing the interest and finance charges on their bills. A consumer who wants to understand more can write to the creditor to request a more detailed explanation and even an example of how to do the calculations.

✓ CONCEPT CHECK 14.3

The finance terms given in the charge account statement of Figure 14-1 indicate that the finance charge, if any, is charged on the previous balance, before deducting payments or credits or adding purchases. Calculate the finance charge and the unpaid balance if the previous balance was $2,425.90, the payment was $1,200, there were no credits, and there were $572.50 in new purchases.

An interest rate of 1.5% applies to the first $1,000 and 1% applies to the excess:

$2,425.90 − $1,000 = $1,425.90.

$0.015 \times \$1,000 = \$15.00$
$0.01 \times \$1,425.90 = \$14.26$
Finance charge = $15.00 + $14.26 = $29.26
New balance = $2,425.90 − $1,200 + $29.26 + $572.50 = $1,827.66

COMPLETE ASSIGNMENT 14.1.

Computing Costs of Installment Purchases

In a credit sale, the buyer pays the purchase price plus credit charges. Usually, the buyer makes monthly payments called **installments.** Just as you saw in the previous section, the method of computing the interest is just as important as the interest rate. Most often, the interest is based on the unpaid balance and is calculated each month using a monthly interest rate. Sometimes, the interest may be calculated only once at the beginning using an annual interest rate, but the interest might be paid in equal installments along with the principal installments.

Learning Objective **4**

Compute costs of installment purchases.

● **EXAMPLE E**

Nancy Bjonerud purchases $4,000 worth of merchandise. She will repay the principal in four equal monthly payments of $1,000 each. She will also pay interest each month on the unpaid balance for that month, which is calculated at an annual rate of 12%. First, calculate each of the monthly interest payments. Then, display the results in a table.

Given the annual interest of 12%, the monthly rate is 12% ÷ 12 = 1% per month.

Month 1: $4,000 × 1% = $40   Month 3: $2,000 × 1% = $20

Month 2: $3,000 × 1% = $30   Month 4: $1,000 × 1% = $10

Total interest = $40 + $30 + $20 + $10 = $100

Month	Unpaid Balance	Interest Payment	Principal Payment	Total Payment	New Balance
1	$ 4,000	$ 40	$1,000	$1,040	$3,000
2	3,000	30	1,000	1,030	2,000
3	2,000	20	1,000	1,020	1,000
4	1,000	+10	+1,000	+1,010	0
		$100	$4,000	$4,100	

● **EXAMPLE F**

Carmel Dufault purchases $4,000 worth of merchandise. She will pay interest of 12% on $4,000 for four months. First, calculate the total amount of interest. Carmel will repay one-fourth of the interest amount each month. In addition, she will repay the $4,000 in four equal monthly amounts of $1,000 each. Display the results in a table.

$$\$4,000 \times 12\% \times \frac{4}{12} = \$160$$

$160 ÷ 4 = $40 per month for interest

Month	Unpaid Balance	Interest Payment	Principal Payment	Total Payment	New Balance
1	$ 4,000	$ 40	$1,000	$1,040	$3,000
2	3,000	40	1,000	1,040	2,000
3	2,000	40	1,000	1,040	1,000
4	1,000	+ 40	+1,000	+1,040	0
		$160	$4,000	$4,160	

✔ CONCEPT CHECK 14.4

A kitchen stove is priced at $600 and is purchased with a $100 down payment. The $500 remaining balance is paid in two successive monthly payments of $250 each. Compute the total interest using the following methods:

a. Interest of 1.5% is calculated on the unpaid balance each month (18% annual rate).

   Month 1: $500 × 0.015 = $7.50

   Month 2: New balance is $250. $250 × 0.015 = $3.75

   Total interest = $7.50 + $3.75 = $11.25

b. Simple interest is calculated on the entire $500 for 2 months at 1.5% per month (18% annual rate).

   $500 × 0.015 per month × 2 months = $15.00

Computing Effective Interest Rates

Examples E and F are very similar, but not quite identical. The numbers are the same: Both purchases are for $4,000; both repay the $4,000 principal in four equal monthly payments; both use a 12% annual interest rate. The only difference is the method of calculating the interest. In example E, the total amount of interest is $100; in example F, it is $160. In example F, it is more expensive to borrow the same money than in example E. In example F, interest is calculated as if the entire $4,000 were borrowed for 4 months ($4,000 × 0.12 × 4/12). But Carmel repays $1,000 of the money after only 1 month.

Compute effective rates.

The true interest rate, or the **effective interest rate,** cannot be the same in each example because it costs more in example F to borrow the same amount of money for the same length of time. To calculate the effective interest rate, we use the familiar formula from Chapter 13, $R = \dfrac{I}{P \times T}$, where I is the amount of interest in dollars, T is the time of the loan in years, and P is the **average unpaid balance** (or the **average principal**) over the period of the loan. The average unpaid balance is the sum of all of the unpaid monthly balances divided by the number of months. (*Note:* The term *effective interest rate* is also used in other contexts where a different formula is used to find the effective rate.)

● EXAMPLE G

Use the formula $R = \dfrac{I}{P \times T}$ to compute the effective interest rates for (a) example E and (b) example F. In both examples, the time of the loan is $T = \frac{4}{12}$ of a year. Using the preceding tables, for each example, the average unpaid balance is

$$P = \frac{\$4,000 + \$3,000 + \$2,000 + \$1,000}{4} = \frac{\$10,000}{4} = \$2,500.$$ But in example E, $I = \$100$ and in example F, $I = \$160$.

a. Example E: $T = \dfrac{4}{12}$; $P = \$2,500$; $I = \$100$; so that

$$R = \frac{I}{P \times T} = \frac{\$100}{\$2,500 \times \dfrac{4}{12}} = \frac{\$100}{\$833.33} = 0.120000, \text{ or } 12\%$$

b. Example F: $T = \dfrac{4}{12}$; $P = \$2,500$; $I = \$160$; so that

$$R = \frac{I}{P \times T} = \frac{\$160}{\$2,500 \times \dfrac{4}{12}} = \frac{\$160}{\$833.33} = 0.1920008, \text{ or } 19.2\%$$

Rule: When the interest is calculated on the unpaid balance each month, the quoted rate and the effective rate will always be the same. When interest is computed only once on the original principal, but the principal is repaid in installments, then the effective interest rate will always be higher than the quoted rate.

The preceding rule is true even when the principal is not repaid in equal installments each month.

Chapter 14 Installment Purchases 265

Look back at example E where Nancy Bjonerud made four equal principal payments of $1,000 each. Suppose instead that she repays the principal in four monthly payments of $900, $1,200, $1,100, and $800. As in example E, she will also pay interest each month on the unpaid balance for that month, which is calculated at an annual rate of 12%. Compute the interest amount for each month and display the results in a table. Then, compute the average unpaid balance and the effective interest rate using the formula $R = \dfrac{I}{P \times T}$.

Given annual interest of 12%, the monthly rate is 12% ÷ 12 = 1% per month.

Month 1: $4,000 × 1% = $40   Month 3: $1,900 × 1% = $19
Month 2: $3,100 × 1% = $31   Month 4: $800 × 1% = $8
Total interest = $40 + $31 + $19 + $8 = $98

Month	Unpaid Balance	Interest Payment	Principal Payment	Total Payment	New Balance
1	$4,000	$40	$ 900	$ 940	$3,100
2	3,100	31	1,200	1,231	1,900
3	1,900	19	1,100	1,119	800
4	800	+ 8	+ 800	+ 808	0
		$98	$4,000	$4,098	

$$P = \frac{\$4{,}000 + \$3{,}100 + \$1{,}900 + \$800}{4} = \frac{\$9{,}800}{4} = \$2{,}450$$

$$R = \frac{I}{P \times T} = \frac{\$98}{\$2{,}450 \times \dfrac{4}{12}} = \frac{\$98}{\$816.67} = 0.11999951, \text{ or } 12\%$$

INCREASING THE EFFECTIVE RATE

Example F shows how the effective rate in an installment sale can be increased by using a different method to calculate interest. Of course, a reputable lender should indicate the true interest rate in the terms of the agreement. But in installment sales, the interest rate may be only one of several variables in the total cost of purchasing. Any additional fees to make the installment purchase increase the actual cost of borrowing.

Naturally, some businesses will attempt to attract buyers by offering very low purchase prices, even "guaranteeing to match all competitors' advertised prices for 30 days." Others may offer installment purchases at low or even 0% interest rates and no additional fees—but they will charge a higher base price. Different consumers are attracted by different things—some by low prices, some by favorable terms of purchase. For many consumers, buying is simply an emotional response with very little thought given to actual costs.

Lenders and sellers "effectively" increase the cost of borrowing money or buying in installments by charging or suggesting additional fees. If it is a purchase of merchandise, the lender could require that the merchandise be insured for the term of purchase. Or the lender could charge a credit application fee.

Consider the following modification to example G, part a, which had an effective rate of 12%.

Look back at example G, part a, where we used $R = \dfrac{I}{P \times T}$ to calculate the effective rate for example E, with I equal to the total interest charge of $100. Suppose instead that the lender had charged Nancy the interest of $100, and a loan origination fee of 1% of the purchase price, and an insurance premium of $1 per month for the term of the loan. Use the formula $R = \dfrac{I}{P \times T}$ to compute the effective interest rate, but let I be the total finance charge.

The average unpaid balance is still $P = \dfrac{\$4,000 + \$3,000 + \$2,000 + \$1,000}{4} =$

$\dfrac{\$10,000}{4} = \$2,500$.

I = Total finance charge = Interest + Loan origination fee + Insurance

Interest only = $40 + $30 + $20 + $10 = $100

Loan origination fee = 1% of $4,000 = 0.01 × $4,000 = $40

Insurance = $1 × 4 months = $4

Therefore, I = $100 + $40 + $4 = $144

$$R = \frac{I}{P \times T} = \frac{\$144}{\$2,500 \times \dfrac{4}{12}} = \frac{\$144}{\$833.33} = 0.17280069, \text{ or } 17.3\%$$

Because the interest in example E was paid on the unpaid balance, the effective rate was 12%, the same as the quoted interest rate. If the same additional finance charges from example I were applied to example F, the results would be even more dramatic.

✔ CONCEPT CHECK 14.5

From Concept Check 14.4, a kitchen stove priced at $600 is purchased with a $100 down payment. The remaining balance of $500 may be financed over 2 months with either of the following installment payment plans:

Plan 1: Two monthly principal payments of $250 each and a total interest amount of $11.25

Plan 2: Two monthly principal payments of $250 each and a total interest amount of $15.00

Calculate the effective annual rate of each plan, using $R = \dfrac{I}{(P \times T)}$, where P is the average unpaid monthly balance and T is $\dfrac{2}{12}$ year. In each plan, the monthly unpaid balances are $500 in month 1 and $250 in month 2.

The average unpaid balance is $\dfrac{(\$500 + \$250)}{2} = \dfrac{\$750}{2} = \$375$, so $P = \$375$.

Plan 1: $R = \dfrac{I}{(P \times T)} = \dfrac{\$11.25}{(\$375 \times \frac{2}{12})} = \dfrac{\$11.25}{\$62.50} = 0.18$, or 18% effective annual rate

Plan 2: $R = \dfrac{I}{(P \times T)} = \dfrac{\$15.00}{(\$375 \times \frac{2}{12})} = \dfrac{\$15.00}{\$62.50} = 0.24$, or 24% effective annual rate

COMPLETE ASSIGNMENT 14.2.

Amortizing a Loan

In example E, interest was calculated on the unpaid balance, but the total payments were different each month: $1,040, $1,030, $1,020, and $1,010. Equal monthly payments are usually simpler, especially for the borrower. In example F, the total payments were the same each month, always $1,040. However, the interest was not calculated on the unpaid balance. In example E, the effective interest rate was equal to the quoted interest rate of 12%. But in example F, the effective rate was much higher, 19.2%.

Taking the best features of each example, consider a loan where the total payments are equal each month and the interest is calculated on the unpaid balance each month. Such a loan is said to be *amortized;* the method is called **amortization.** (The word *amortize* is also used in different contexts and there is more than one way to amortize a loan.) Although possible for purchases of any length of time, amortization is especially relevant for larger purchases made over longer periods of time. Loans to pay for homes and automobiles are usually amortized. There may or may not be a down payment.

COMPUTING THE MONTHLY PAYMENT

The basic concept to amortize a loan is to multiply the loan amount by an **amortization payment factor.** The product is the amount of the monthly payment. This factor may be derived from a calculator or computer or from a book of financial tables. When lenders amortize loans today, they use computers to do the final calculations. Initial calculations, however, are often made using calculators or tables. In this chapter we will use tables and will get the same results. (You can also go to the Internet, search on "amortization calculations," and find websites that help you do the calculations.)

Table 14-1 illustrates the concept of tables for amortization payment factors. Actual tables would have many pages and would be much more detailed. If you study other courses in business mathematics, accounting or finance, you may use tables that are slightly different than Table 14-1. Regardless of the exact format of the table, the concepts are the same. And, to repeat, with the prerequisite background knowledge, financial calculators and computers completely eliminate the need for any of these tables.

Notice that the title of Table 14-1 is "Amount of Monthly Payment per $1,000 Borrowed." Therefore, you must first determine the amount of the loan in "thousands of dollars," not in the number of dollars. The annual interest rates in Table 14-1 were selected because they are evenly divisible by 12. This will eliminate the necessity to round off interest rates when you convert an annual rate into a monthly rate.

STEPS **to Find the Monthly Payment of an Amortized Loan Using Table 14-1**

1. Divide the loan amount by $1,000 to get the number of thousands of dollars.
2. Locate the amortization payment factor in Table 14-1.
3. Multiply the quotient in Step 1 by the amortization payment factor. The product is the amount of the monthly payment.

Table 14-1	Amortization Payment Factors—Amount of Monthly Payment per $1,000 Borrowed					
Term of Loan	**Annual Interest Rate**					
	3.6%	**4.8%**	**6.0%**	**7.2%**	**8.4%**	**9.6%**
1 month	1003.00000	1004.00000	1005.00000	1006.00000	1007.00000	1008.00000
2 months	502.25112	503.00200	503.75312	504.50449	505.25610	506.00797
3 months	335.33533	336.00355	336.67221	337.34131	338.01085	338.68083
4 months	251.87781	252.50499	253.13279	253.76122	254.39026	255.01992
5 months	201.80359	202.40639	203.00997	203.61436	204.21953	204.82550
6 months	168.42104	169.00776	169.59546	170.18411	170.77374	171.36432
1 year	84.96726	85.51586	86.06643	86.61897	87.17348	87.72996
2 years	43.24711	43.78188	44.32061	44.86330	45.40994	45.96053
3 years	29.34638	29.88118	30.42194	30.96862	31.52122	32.07972
4 years	22.40050	22.93881	23.48503	24.03914	24.60112	25.17092
5 years	18.23656	18.77974	19.33280	19.89569	20.46837	21.05076
10 years	9.93550	10.50906	11.10205	11.71419	12.34515	12.99457
15 years	7.19803	7.80414	8.43857	9.10047	9.78887	10.50267
20 years	5.85111	6.48957	7.16431	7.87349	8.61504	9.38671
25 years	5.06003	5.72997	6.44301	7.19589	7.98499	8.80658
30 years	4.54645	5.24665	5.99551	6.78788	7.61838	8.48160

EXAMPLE J

Find the monthly payment required to amortize a $5,000 loan over 3 months at 8.4% (0.7% per month).

STEP 1 $5,000 ÷ $1,000 = 5 (thousands)

STEP 2   Find the intersection of the 8.4% column and the 3-month row in Table 14-1. The amortization payment factor is $338.01085 per each one thousand dollars.

STEP 3   Multiply the 5 (from Step 1) by the amortization payment factor.
5 × $338.01085 = $1,690.05425, or $1,690.05 per month

EXAMPLE K

Karen Krenz agrees to purchase an automobile for $22,500. Karen will make a $4,000 down payment and amortize the balance with monthly payments over 3 years at 7.2% (0.6% per month). Determine Karen's monthly payment.

$22,500 − $4,000 = $18,500 amount financed

STEP 1 $18,500 ÷ $1,000 = 18.5 (thousands)

STEP 2   Find the intersection of the 7.2% column and the 3-year row in Table 14-1. The amortization payment factor is $30.96862 per thousand.

STEP 3   Multiply the 18.5 (from Step 1) by the amortization payment factor.
18.5 × $30.96862 = $572.91947, or $572.92 per month

LOAN PAYMENT SCHEDULE

After determining the amount of the monthly payments, a lender can prepare a schedule of loan payments called an **amortization schedule.** The payment for the last month is determined in the schedule, and it may be slightly different from the payment in the other months.

STEPS **to Create an Amortization Schedule**

For each row except the last:
1. Interest payment = Unpaid balance × Monthly interest rate
2. Principal payment = Monthly payment − Interest payment
3. New unpaid balance = Old unpaid balance − Principal payment

For the last row (the final payment):
1. Interest payment = Unpaid balance × Monthly interest rate
2. Monthly payment = Unpaid balance + Interest payment
3. Principal payment = Unpaid balance

EXAMPLE L

Create an amortization schedule for the loan in example J, a $5,000 loan amortized at 8.4% over 3 months. The interest rate is 0.7% per month.

Month	Unpaid Balance	Interest Payment	Principal Payment	Total Payment	New Balance
1	$ 5,000.00	$35.00	$1,655.05	$1,690.05	$3,344.95
2	3,344.95	23.41	1,666.64	1,690.05	1,678.31
3	1,678.31	11.75	1,678.31	1,690.06	0.00
Totals	$10,023.26	$70.16	$5,000.00	$5,070.16	

Note: In example L, the last monthly payment is 1 cent larger than the others. Because the interest payments need to be rounded, the final payment usually will be slightly different from the previous payments.

Since amortization implies that interest is paid on the unpaid balance, the formula $R = \dfrac{I}{P \times T}$ should show that the effective rate is the same as the quoted rate of 8.4%. Looking at the table for example L, the average unpaid balance is

$$P = \frac{\$5,000.00 + \$3,344.95 + \$1,678.31}{3} = \frac{\$10,023.26}{3}$$

$$= \$3,341.087, \text{ or } \$3,341.09$$

The total interest paid is $I = \$35.00 + \$23.41 + \$11.75 = \$70.16$. Therefore,

$$R = \frac{I}{P \times T} = \frac{\$70.16}{\$3,341.09 \times \dfrac{3}{12}} = \frac{\$70.16}{\$835.27} = 0.0839968, \text{ or } 8.4\%$$

The reason that the result was 8.39968% instead of 8.4% is that all the payments were rounded to the nearest cent.

A $2,000 purchase is amortized over 2 months at an annual rate of 6%. First use Table 14-1 to calculate the monthly payment for month 1. Then show the calculations to construct a 2-month amortization schedule. *(Remember: In this problem, month 2 is the last month.)*

$2,000 ÷ $1,000 = 2 (thousands)

Amortization payment factor from Table 14-1 is $503.75312.

2 × $503.75312 = $1,007.50624, or $1,007.51 for month 1

Month	1		2	
Unpaid balance	Original principal:	$2,000.00	From end of month 1:	$1,002.49
Monthly rate	0.06 ÷ 12 = 0.005			
Interest payment	$2,000.00 × 0.005 =	$ 10.00	$1,002.49 × 0.005 =	$ 5.01
Total payment	From above:	$1,007.51	$1,002.49 + $5.01	$1,007.50
Principal payment	$1,007.51 − $10.00 =	$ 997.51		$1,002.49
New balance	$2,000.00 − $997.51	$1,002.49	$1,002.49 − $1,002.49 =	$ 0.00

Computing a Monthly Mortgage Payment

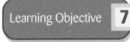
Learning Objective **7**

Compute a monthly mortgage payment.

Persons who decide to purchase a home usually borrow the majority of the money. The amount that is borrowed is usually amortized, and usually for a long time, such as 15, 20, or 30 years. Such a home loan is called a **mortgage.** The interest rate may be **fixed,** which means that it stays the same for the entire length of the loan. Other mortgages are **variable-rate loans,** which permit the lender to periodically adjust the interest rate depending on current financial market conditions. Whether a borrower decides on a fixed or variable rate loan depends on several factors, such as how long he or she plans to remain in that home.

A mortgage loan is still a loan. And amortizing a mortgage is the same as amortizing any other loan: Look up the amortization payment factor in Table 14-1 and multiply by the number of thousands of dollars that are borrowed.

● EXAMPLE M

George and Kathy Jarvis bought a condominium priced at $190,000. They made a $20,000 down payment and took out a 30-year, 6% mortgage on the balance. Find the size of their monthly payment.

$190,000 − $20,000 = $170,000 amount borrowed

STEP 1   Divide $170,000 by $1,000 to get 170 (thousands)

STEP 2   Find the amortization factor in the 6% column and 30-year row of Table 14-1. It is $5.99551.

STEP 3   Multiply the 170 from Step 1 by $5.99551 to get $1,019.2367. The monthly payment will be $1,019.24.

AMORTIZATION SCHEDULE FOR A MORTGAGE

An amortization schedule for a mortgage is computed line by line, just as the amortization schedules are for other loans such as the one in example L. However, a 30-year home mortgage will have 360 lines, one for each month of the loan. This could be about six or seven pages of paper with three calculations per line, or 1,080 calculations. Today, these tables are always produced with a computer. You can create an amortization schedule using Excel or you can find several sources on the Internet to do the calculations for you. However, to review the concept manually, examine example N.

EXAMPLE N

Construct the first three lines of an amortization schedule for the Jarvis's home mortgage loan in example M.

The Jarvis's $170,000 mortgage has a monthly payment of $1,019.24.
For a 6% annual interest rate, the monthly rate is 6% ÷ 12 = 0.5%.
For each row,   1. Monthly interest = Unpaid balance × 0.005
            2. Principal payment = Total payment − Monthly interest
            3. New balance = Unpaid balance − Principal payment

Month	Unpaid Balance	Interest Payment	Principal Payment	Total Payment	New Balance
1	$170,000.00	$850.00	$169.24	$1,019.24	$169,830.76
2	169,830.76	849.15	170.09	1,019.24	169,660.67
3	169,660.67	848.30	170.94	1,019.24	169,489.73

CONCEPT CHECK 14.7

A home cost $280,000. The buyers made a down payment of $30,000. Compute the monthly payment on a 25-year mortgage with an annual interest rate of 4.8%. Use Table 14-1.

The amount borrowed is $280,000 − $30,000 = $250,000.
The amortization payment factor from Table 14-1 is $5.72997.
The amount of the loan in thousands is $250,000 ÷ $1,000 = 250 (thousands).
The monthly mortgage payment is 250 × $5.72997 = $1,432.4925, or $1,432.49.

COMPLETE ASSIGNMENT 14.3.

Chapter Terms for Review

amortization

amortization payment factor

amortization schedule

annual percentage rate (APR)

average daily balance

average principal

average unpaid balance

credit card

effective interest rate

finance charge

fixed interest rate

installments

mortgage

Truth in Lending Act (TILA)

variable-rate loans

THE BOTTOM LINE

Summary of chapter learning objectives:

Learning Objective	Example
14.1 Convert between annual and monthly interest rates.	1. Convert 0.75% per month to an annual rate. 2. Convert 15% per year to a monthly rate
14.2 Compute simple interest on a monthly basis.	3. Compute the simple interest on $2,500 for 7 months at 0.5% per month (6% per year).
14.3 Compute finance charges.	4. Charge account terms apply a 1.25% finance charge to the previous balance, less any payments and credits, but ignoring purchases. Find the finance charge and new balance when the previous balance is $1,683.43, payments plus credits total $942.77, and purchases are $411.48.
14.4 Compute costs of installment purchases.	5. Furniture worth $2,500 is paid for with a $400 down payment and three payments of $700, plus monthly interest of 1% on the unpaid balance. Find the total interest paid. The monthly unpaid balances are $2,100, $1,400, and $700.
14.5 Compute effective rates.	6. A $2,400 purchase is to be repaid in three equal monthly principal payments of $800 each. There will be one interest payment of $60 (10% of $2,400 for three months) and insurance premiums of $1 each month. Calculate the effective rate of interest. The monthly unpaid balances are $2,400, $1,600, and $800.
14.6 Amortize a loan.	7. A $2,000 loan will be amortized over 6 months at an annual rate of 4.8%. Find the payment, using Table 14-1, and calculate the unpaid balance after the first month.
14.7 Compute a monthly mortgage payment.	8. A $180,000 home mortgage is for 20 years at 6% annual interest. Find the monthly payment.

Answers: 1. 9% per year 2. 1.25% per month 3. $87.50 4. Finance charge, $9.26; new balance, $1,161.40 5. $42 6. 15.75% 7. Payment, $338.02; unpaid balance, $1,669.98 8. $1,289.58

Review Problems for Chapter 14

1. Change the monthly rates to annual rates.

   a. 0.75% = _____ **b.** 0.625% = _____ **c.** 1.2% = _____ **d.** $\frac{2}{5}$% = _____

2. Change the annual rates to monthly rates.

   a. 6% = _____ **b.** 15% = _____ **c.** 13.2% = _____ **d.** 9.6% = _____

3. A store offers the following credit terms: "There will be no finance charge if the full amount of the new balance is received on or before the due date. Unpaid balances after the due date will be charged interest based upon the previous balance, less any payments and credits before the due date. The rates are 1.75% on the first $1,000 of the unpaid balance and 1.25% on the part of the unpaid balance that exceeds $1,000."

   Calculate (a) the finance charge and (b) the new balance on an account that had a previous balance of $2,752.88; a payment of $800; credits of $215; and purchases of $622.75.

4. Neta Prefontaine buys $3,000 worth of merchandise. She agrees to pay $1,000 per month on the principal. In addition, she will pay interest of 1% per month (12% annually) on the unpaid balance. Complete the following table.

Month	Unpaid Balance	Interest Payment	Principal Payment	Total Payment	New Balance
1	$3,000.00	a. _____	$1,000.00	b. _____	c. _____
2	d. _____	e. _____	$1,000.00	f. _____	g. _____
3	h. _____	i. _____	$1,000.00	j. _____	$0.00

5. Use the results of problem 4 and compute the effective annual interest rate using the formula $R = \dfrac{I}{P \times T}$, where P is the average unpaid balance, I is the total interest paid, and T is the period of the loan in years.

6. Use Table 14-1 to find the monthly payment of a $225,000 mortgage that is amortized over 15 years at 3.6%. _____

7. A $3,000 loan is amortized over 3 months at 9.6%. The first two monthly payments are $1,016.04; the final payment may differ. Complete the following table.

Month	Unpaid Balance	Interest Payment	Principal Payment	Total Payment	New Balance
1	$3,000.00	a. _____	b. _____	$1,016.04	c. _____
2	d. _____	e. _____	f. _____	$1,016.04	g. _____
3	h. _____	i. _____	j. _____	k. _____	$0.00

Answers to the Self-Check can be found in Appendix B at the back of the text.

Assignment 14.1: Monthly Finance Charges

Name _____

Date _____   Score _____

A   (19 points) Problem 1: Change the rates from annual to monthly. Problem 2: Change the rates from monthly to annual. (1 point for each correct answer)

1a. 18% = _____   **b.** 15% = _____   **c.** 3.6% = _____   **d.** 7.2% = _____

e. 6% = _____   **f.** 4.8% = _____   **g.** 9% = _____   **h.** 8.4% = _____

i. 12% = _____   **j.** 9.6 % = _____

2a. 0.5% = _____   **b.** 0.7% = _____   **c.** 0.3% = _____   **d.** 1.25% = _____

e. 0.8% = _____   **f.** 0.75% = _____   **g.** 0.6% = _____   **h.** 0.4% = _____

i. 1.5% = _____

_____
Score for A (19)

B (33 points) Lakeside Furniture Store offers the credit terms shown below to its retail customers. In problems 3–5 compute the finance charge, if any, and the new balance. Assume that all payments are made within the current billing cycle. (3 points for each correct answer)

TERMS: There will be no finance charge if the full amount of the new balance is received within 25 days after the cycle-closing date. The finance charge, if any, is based upon the entire previous balance *before* any payments or credits are deducted. The rates are 1.5% per month on amounts up to $1,000 and 1.25% on amounts in excess of $1,000. These are annual percentage rates of 18% and 15%, respectively.

Cycle Closing	Previous Balance	Payment Amount	Credits	Finance Charge	Purchases	New Balance
3. 3/20/20– –	$2,147.12	$900.00	$175.50	_____	$647.72	_____
4. 6/20/20– –	$862.42	$375.00	$116.24	_____	$527.40	_____
5. 9/20/20– –	$3,412.27	$3,000.00	$212.98	_____	$907.51	_____

In problems 6 and 7, Lelia McDaniel has an account at Lakeside Furniture Store. Compute the missing values in Lelia's account summary for the months of August and September. The previous balance in September is the same as the new balance in August.

Cycle Closing	Previous Balance	Payment Amount	Credits	Finance Charge	Purchases	New Balance
6. 8/20/20– –	$1,636.55	$900.00	$ 36.00	_____	$966.75	_____
7. 9/20/20– –	_____	$1,200.00	$109.75	_____	$589.41	_____

_____

Score for B (33)

C (48 points) Devlin's Feed & Fuel offers the credit terms shown below to its retail customers. In problems 8–12 compute the missing values in the charge accounts shown. Assume that all payments are made within 30 days of the billing date. (3 points for each correct answer)

TERMS: Finance Charge is based on the Net Balance, if any payment is received within 30 days of the billing date. If payment is made after 30 days, then the Finance Charge is based on the Previous Balance. Net Balance equals Previous Balance less Payments and Credits. In either case, the monthly rate is 1.25% on the first $500 and 1% on any amount over $500. These are annual percentage rates of 15% and 12%, respectively.

Billing Date	Previous Balance	Payment Amount	Credits	Net Balance	Finance Charge	New Purchases	New Balance
8. 4/25/20– –	$2,621.05	$1,900.00	$0.00	_____	_____	$661.28	_____

Billing Date	Previous Balance	Payment Amount	Credits	Net Balance	Finance Charge	New Purchases	New Balance
9. 3/25/20−−	$1,827.15	$700.00	$28.75	_____	_____	$672.39	_____
10. 11/25/20−−	$1,019.63	$325.00	$26.50	_____	_____	$218.75	_____

In problems 11 and 12 compute the missing values in Jimmy Petrasek's charge account summary at Devlin's for the months of June and July. The previous balance in July is the same as the new balance in June.

Billing Date	Previous Balance	Payment Amount	Credits	Net Balance	Finance Charge	New Purchases	New Balance
11. 6/25/20−−	$1,352.12	$500.00	$62.00	_____	_____	$772.35	_____
12. 7/25/20−−	_____	$750.00	$93.02	_____	_____	$324.17	_____

_____

Score for C (48)

Assignment 14.2: Installment Sales and Effective Rates

Name _____

Date _____   Score _____

A **(60 points)** Jill Jensen needed to purchase office equipment costing $4,800. She was able to finance her purchase over 3 months at a 9% annual interest rate. Following are three different payment options under these conditions. Complete the installment purchase table for each payment option. **(2 points for each correct answer)**

1. Jill pays $1,600 per month on the principal and pays interest of 0.75% on the unpaid balance each month (9% annual rate).

Month	Unpaid Balance	Interest Payment	Principal Payment	Total Payment	New Balance
1	$4,800	_____	$1,600	_____	_____
2	_____	_____	1,600	_____	_____
3	_____	_____	+1,600	_____	0
			$4,800		

2. Jill makes monthly payments of $2,000, $1,600, and $1,200 on the principal and pays interest of 0.75% on the unpaid balance each month (9% annual rate).

Month	Unpaid Balance	Interest Payment	Principal Payment	Total Payment	New Balance
1	$4,800	_____	$2,000	_____	_____
2	_____	_____	1,600	_____	_____
3	_____	_____	+1,200	_____	0
			$4,800		

3. Jill pays $1,600 per month on the principal. The total interest charge is 9% of the original principal for 3 months. She pays $\frac{1}{3}$ of the total interest each month.

Month	Unpaid Balance	Interest Payment	Principal Payment	Total Payment	New Balance
1	$4,800	_____	$1,600	_____	_____
2	_____	_____	1,600	_____	_____
3	_____	_____	+1,600	_____	0
			$4,800		

_____

Score for A (60)

B   **(40 points) For each of the following problems calculate the effective rate using the formula** $R = \dfrac{I}{P \times T}$.
(Points for each correct answer as shown)

4. Compute R = effective rate for the table in problem 1 in part A, with P = average unpaid balance, I = total interest charge and $T = \frac{3}{12}$ year.

    a. P = Average unpaid balance _____ (3 pts)

    b. I = Total interest charge _____ (3 pts)

    c. R = Effective interest rate _____ (4 pts)

5. Compute R = effective rate for the table in problem 1 in part A, with P = average unpaid balance, I = total finance charge, and $T = \frac{3}{12}$ year. The finance charge is the total interest, plus a loan origination fee of $\frac{3}{4}$% of the original principal, plus \$7.50 of insurance premiums (\$2.50 per month).

    a. P = Average unpaid balance _____ (3 pts)

    b. I = Total finance charge _____ (3 pts)

    c. R = Effective interest rate _____ (4 pts)

6. Compute R = effective rate for the table in problem 2 in part A, with P = average unpaid balance, I = total interest charge, and $T = \frac{3}{12}$ year.

    a. P = Average unpaid balance _____ (3 pts)

    b. I = Total interest charge _____ (3 pts)

    c. R = Effective interest rate _____ (4 pts)

7. Compute R = effective rate for the table in problem 3 in part A, with P = average unpaid balance, I = total interest charge, and $T = \frac{3}{12}$ year.

    a. P = Average unpaid balance _____ (3 pts)

    b. I = Total interest charge _____ (3 pts)

    c. R = Effective interest rate _____ (4 pts)

Score for B (40)

Assignment 14.3: Amortization and Mortgages

Name _____

Date _____ Score _____

A (16 points) Lincoln Lending Corp. amortizes all of its mortgage loans and many of its personal loans on a monthly basis. The total monthly payments are equal each month and include both interest and principal. Use Table 14-1 to find the amortization payment factor for each loan. Then compute the monthly payment. (2 points for each correct answer)

Loan and Terms of Amortization	Amortization Payment Factor	Monthly Payment
1. $18,000 over 5 months at 9.6%	_____	_____
2. $27,000 over 3 years at 7.2%	_____	_____
3. $275,000 over 20 years at 4.8%	_____	_____
4. $150,000 over 15 years at 6%	_____	_____

Score for A (16)

B (32 points) On April 13, Braunda Johannesen borrowed $6,000 from her bank to help pay her federal income taxes for the previous year. The bank amortized her loan over 4 months at an annual rate of 7.2%. Braunda paid interest of 0.6% on the unpaid balance each month. Find the amortization payment factor in Table 14-1. This factor makes a total payment of $1,522.57 each month except the last. For the last month, the total payment is the interest payment plus the unpaid balance. Complete the following amortization schedule. (2 points for each correct answer)

5. Amortization factor from Table 14-1: _____
   Multiply the amortization factor by 6 to get the total payment shown for months 1, 2, and 3.

	Month	Unpaid Balance	Interest Payment	Principal Payment	Total Payment	New Balance
6.	1	6,000.00	_____	_____	1,522.57	_____
7.	2	_____	_____	_____	1,522.57	_____
8.	3	_____	_____	_____	1,522.57	_____
9.	4	_____	_____	_____	_____	0.00

Score for B (32)

C (30 points) Refer to part B, in which Braunda Johannesen borrowed $6,000 to help pay her federal income taxes. Now suppose that Braunda agreed to make payments of $1,200 in months 1, 2, and 3. The bank will compute the interest on the unpaid balance at a rate of 0.6% (7.2%/12) each month and will deduct the interest from the $1,200. In the last (fourth) month, Braunda will pay all of the remaining unpaid balance plus the interest for the last month. Complete the table, using the same procedure as in part B. (2 points for each correct answer)

	Month	Unpaid Balance	Interest Payment	Principal Payment	Total Payment	New Balance
10.	1	6,000.00	_____	_____	1,200.00	_____
11.	2	_____	_____	_____	1,200.00	_____
12.	3	_____	_____	_____	1,200.00	_____
13.	4	_____	_____	_____	_____	0.00

Score for C (30)

D (22 points) Mr. and Mrs. Paul Yeiter sold their previous home and used the profits as a down payment to buy a new home. They took out a $160,000, 25-year mortgage from Colonial Home Finance. The mortgage had an annual interest rate of 6%. From Table 14-1, the amortization payment factor is $6.44301 and the monthly payment is $1,030.88. Complete the first three rows of the amortization schedule for the Yeiters' mortgage. (2 points for each correct answer)

		Amortization Schedule for Mortgage				
	Month	Unpaid Balance	Interest Payment	Principal Payment	Total Payment	New Balance
14.	1	$160,000.00	_____	_____	$1,030.88	_____
15.	2	_____	_____	_____	1,030.88	_____
16.	3	_____	_____	_____	1,030.88	_____

Score for D (22)

Promissory Notes and Discounting

15

Learning Objectives

By studying this chapter and completing all assignments, you will be able to:

Learning Objective 1 — Compute the number of interest days of a promissory note.

Learning Objective 2 — Determine the due date of a promissory note.

Learning Objective 3 — Compute the maturity value of a promissory note.

Learning Objective 4 — Discount a promissory note.

Learning Objective 5 — Compute the proceeds and actual interest rate on a bank discount loan.

Learning Objective 6 — Compute the savings from borrowing money to take a cash discount.

Businesses and individuals both use long-term loans (more than 1 year) to purchase large items such as equipment or buildings. Likewise, businesses and individuals also use short-term loans when they are convenient and make sense financially. Long-term and short-term loans are written in the form of various financial documents, one of which is called a **promissory note.** It is a promise by a borrower to repay a certain amount of money on a certain date. Sometimes the promissory note can be sold to a third party, in which case the note is called a **negotiable promissory note.** Because the buyer of the note is assuming some risk that the borrower will not repay the original loan, he or she will not likely pay the entire value of the note. Such a note is called a **discounted note.** Similarly, an individual may go to a bank to borrow money, and the bank may deduct the entire amount of the interest in advance. This is called bank discounting, and the loan is called a **bank discount loan.**

Unlike individuals, however, businesses may borrow large amounts of money for only a few days. For example, a retail business buys merchandise from manufacturers and wholesalers. But the retailer may know immediately that it cannot sell enough merchandise in time to pay the supplier's invoice. Perhaps the supplier also offers a cash discount if the buyer pays the invoice within a few days (see Chapter 7). The retailer can often save money by borrowing enough cash to pay the invoice and take advantage of the cash discount. If the amounts are large, the savings can be significant.

Promissory Notes

A promissory note is an unconditional promise by the **maker** of the note (the borrower) to repay money to the **bearer** of the note (the lender) at some time in the future. This date is called the **due date** or the **maturity date.** The dollar amount written on the note is called the **face value** (*FV*) of the note. It is usually the same as the principal (*P* in Chapter 13). Most promissory notes are **interest-bearing,** especially if one or both parties is a business. This means that the maker must also pay interest to the bearer on the maturity date. The sum of the face value and the **interest dollars** (*I*) is the **maturity value** (*MV*) of the note. Figure 15-1 illustrates a simple promissory note.

Figure 15-1	Promissory Note

$ _2,000 00_ _____ ATLANTA, GEORGIA _March 15_ _____ 20 _ _

_____ _— Sixty days —_ _____ AFTER DATE _____ _I, Sylvia Cometta,_ _____ PROMISE TO PAY TO

THE ORDER OF _____ _William Dale Crist_ _____

PAYABLE AT Bank of the South

Two thousand and 00/100 _____ DOLLARS

VALUE RECEIVED WITH EXACT INTEREST AT _____ _10 %_ _____ PER ANNUM

NO. _47_ _____ DUE _May 14, 20--_

_____ _Sylvia Cometta_ _____

Computing the Number of Interest Days of a Note

To define the interest period, or term, of a promissory note, the lender either specifies the due date of the note or states the number of interest days. When the due date is given, the number of interest days must be computed before the interest charge can be computed.

To compute the interest days, you need the number of days in each month, as shown in Table 15-1. Remember that February has 29 days in leap years. A leap year is any year that is evenly divisible by 4, except for certain years ending in 00 (e.g., 1900). In order to be leap years, years ending in 00 must be evenly divisible by 400; thus 2000 was a leap year, but 1900 was not and 2100 will not be either.

STEPS to Compute the Number of Interest Days Between Two Dates

1. Determine the number of interest days in the beginning month.
2. Determine the number of interest days in the middle months.
3. Add the numbers from Steps 1 and 2 to the number of interest days in the final month. (For the final month, the number of interest days is equal to the number of the due date.)

Table 15-1 | Days in Each Month (non-leap years)

Month	Number of Days	Month	Number of Days	Month	Number of Days
January	31 days	May	31 days	September	30 days
February	28 days	June	30 days	October	31 days
March	31 days	July	31 days	November	30 days
April	30 days	August	31 days	December	31 days

● **EXAMPLE A**

A promissory note is made on July 25. The due date is October 8. Use Table 15-1 to help you determine the number of interest days between July 25 and October 8.

STEP 1

31	days in July
−25	date of note
6	days of interest

STEP 2

August has 31 days
September has 30 days

STEP 3

6	days in July
31	days in August
30	days in September
+ 8	days in October (due date)
75	total interest days in the promissory note

A promissory note is dated October 20. The maturity date (due date) is February 20. Determine the number of interest days.

As October has 31 days and the note is dated October 20, there are $31 - 20 = 11$ days of interest in October. Since the note is due on February 20, there are 20 interest days in February. The total can be expressed as

October		November		December		January		February		Total Interest Days
11	+	30	+	31	+	31	+	20	=	123

© R. ALCORN

Determining the Due Date of a Note

When the promissory note explicitly states the number of interest days, then you must determine the due date. The procedure is somewhat the reverse of finding the number of interest days.

STEPS **to Determine the Due Date**

1. Determine the number of interest days in the beginning month.
2. Determine the number of interest days that remain after the first month.
3. Determine the number of interest days remaining at the end of each succeeding month by subtracting. Continue subtracting until less than 1 month remains. The due date is the number of interest days remaining in the final month.

EXAMPLE B

A promissory note is made on July 25. The note is for 75 days. Determine the due date.

STEP 1

```
 31    days in July
−25    date of note
  6    days of interest in July
```

STEP 2

```
 75    days of interest in the note
−  6   days of interest in July
 69    days left in term after end of July
```

STEP 3

```
 69    days of interest left after July
−31    days in August
 38    days of interest left after August
−30    days in September
  8    days of interest left after end of
       September, or 8 days of interest in
       October
```

The due date is October 8.

Although the procedure looks somewhat cumbersome on paper, it goes very quickly on a calculator. You can subtract repeatedly to deduct the days of each month, and after each subtraction, the calculator will display the number of interest days remaining. You don't need to write down all the intermediate results.

When the length of the interest period is expressed in months, the date is advanced by the number of months given. The due date is the same date of the month as the date of the note. For example, a 2-month note dated July 3 will be due on September 3. The exact number of interest days must then be computed, as shown previously. If the note is dated the 31st of a month and the month of maturity is April, June, September, or November, the due date is the 30th. If the month of maturity is February, the due date is the 28th (or 29th in a leap year).

EXAMPLE C

Find the due date of a 3-month note dated January 31 (the last day of the month).

Maturity month: April (count "February, March, April")

Last day: 30 (last day of April)

                   Therefore the due date is April 30.

✔ CONCEPT CHECK 15.2

a. A 90-day promissory note is dated February 5 in a non-leap year. Determine the due date.

```
 28    days in February
− 5    date of note
 23    days of interest in February

 90    days of interest in the note
−23    days of interest in February
 67    days of interest left after February
```

```
 67    days of interest left after February
−31    days in March
 36    days of interest left after March
−30    days in April
  6    days of interest left after April
```
The due date is May 6.

b. A 4-month promissory note is dated April 30. Determine the due date.

Four months after April 30 is August 30. The due date is August 30.

Computing the Maturity Value of a Note

The maturity value (*MV*) of a promissory note is the sum of the face value (principal) of the note and the interest:

Maturity Value = Principal + Interest,   or $MV = P + I$

EXAMPLE D

Compute the maturity value of the interest-bearing promissory note illustrated in Figure 15-1.

The face value (*P*) of the note is $2,000. The interest rate (*R*) is 10% exact interest per year. The loan period of the note is 60 days, so the time in years (*T*) is $\frac{60}{365}$.

$$I = P \times R \times T = \$2,000 \times 0.10 \times \frac{60}{365} = \$32.88$$

$$MV = P + I = \$2,000 + \$32.88 = \$2,032.88$$

✔ CONCEPT CHECK 15.3

A 90-day promissory note has a face value of $2,800 and an exact simple interest rate of 7.5%. Compute the maturity value.

$$I = P \times R \times T = \$2,800 \times 0.075 \times \frac{90}{365} = \$51.78 \quad MV = P + I = \$2,800 + \$51.78 = \$2,851.78$$

COMPLETE ASSIGNMENT 15.1.

Discounting Promissory Notes

Often, when a lender holds a promissory note as security for a loan to a borrower, the lender may need cash before the maturity date of the note. One option is for the lender to "sell" the note to a third party. Such a note is said to be *negotiable*.

However, now the third party is assuming the risk that the original borrower might not pay everything on the maturity date. Therefore, to acquire the note, the third party will pay the original lender less money than the maturity value. The note is said to "sell at a discount."

There are several vocabulary terms involved in discounting promissory notes. The calculations, however, are straightforward and very similar to simple interest calculations. These can be explained by using examples.

On August 19, Telescan Medical Instruments borrows $75,000 from a private investor, Anne Harding. In return, Telescan gives Anne a 120-day promissory note at an ordinary simple interest rate of 8% (360-day year). Compute the due date and the maturity value of the promissory note.

Due date: August 19 + 120 days = December 17

Interest: $I = P \times R \times T = \$75{,}000 \times 0.08 \times \dfrac{120}{360} = \$2{,}000$

Maturity value: $MV = P + I = \$75{,}000 + \$2{,}000 = \$77{,}000$

In example E, Telescan Medical must pay $77,000 to Anne Harding on December 17. During the 120 days, Anne has only the promissory note—no cash. If the note is negotiable, Anne can sell the note to a third party at any time before December 17. Suppose that Anne sells the note on October 5 to Auburn Financial Corporation. October 5 is called the **discount date.** The time between October 5 and December 17 is the **discount period.** The length of the discount period is the number of days between October 5 and December 17. Since the original 8% interest rate was ordinary simple interest (360-day year), we will also use a 360-day year in the discount calculation.

Auburn Financial agrees to buy the note at a discount of 12% of the maturity value. 12% is the **discount rate.** The **discount amount** is calculated using a formula similar to ordinary simple interest:

Discount Amount = Maturity value × Discount rate × Time (Discount period)

Maturity value: $77,000

Discount rate: 12%

Discount period: October 5 to December 17 = (31 − 5) + 30 + 17 = 73 days

Discount Amount $= \$77{,}000 \times 0.12 \times \dfrac{73}{360} = \$1{,}873.67$

The difference between the maturity value and the discount amount is called the **proceeds.** It is the amount that Auburn Financial will pay to Anne Harding for her promissory note from Telescan Medical Instruments.

Proceeds = Maturity value − Discount amount
           = $77,000 − $1,873.67 = $75,126.33

STEPS   **to Discount a Promissory Note**

1. Compute the interest amount (*I*) and maturity value (*MV*) of the promissory note.
2. Determine the maturity (due) date of the note.
3. Compute the number of days in the discount period. The time, *T*, is the number of days in the discount period divided by 360, or by 365.
4. Compute the discount amount, using $D = MV \times R \times T$, where *R* is the discount rate.
5. Compute the proceeds by subtracting the discount amount from the maturity value.

NON-INTEREST-BEARING PROMISSORY NOTES

Sometimes the original lender may not charge any interest at all. In this situation, the maturity value of the note is equal to the face value. Similarly, the original lender may require that all the interest must be completely paid in advance. Therefore, this is another type of promissory note that does not have any interest dollars in the maturity value, so the maturity value is equal to the face value. To find the proceeds of a **non-interest-bearing promissory note,** follow the same steps that were listed above. But, in Step 1, the amount of interest is $0 and the maturity value is the face value.

● EXAMPLE F

C. W. Smith, owner of a True-Value Hardware Store, is holding a 75-day, non-interest-bearing note for $3,500. The note is dated June 21. On August 10, C. W. sells the note to the Millicoma Lending Company, which discounts the note at 11%. Find the discount amount and the proceeds using a 365-day year.

STEP 1   Interest amount = $0; Maturity value = Face value = $3,500

STEP 2   Due date: June 21 + 75 days = September 4

STEP 3   Discount period: August 10 to September 4 = 25 days

STEP 4   Discount amount: Maturity value × Discount rate × Time

$$= \$3,500 \times 0.11 \times \frac{25}{365}$$

$$= \$26.3697, \text{ or } \$26.37$$

STEP 5   Proceeds: Maturity value − Discount amount

$$= \$3,500 − \$26.37$$

$$= \$3,473.63$$

✔ CONCEPT CHECK 15.4

A 75-day promissory note, bearing interest at 10%, is dated December 11 and has a face value of $5,000. On January 24, the note is discounted at 14%. Find the discount amount and the proceeds. *Note:* The interest amount, the maturity value, the maturity date, and the days of discount must first be determined. Use a 365-day year for all interest and discount calculations.

Interest amount: $\$5,000 \times 0.10 \times \dfrac{75}{365} = \$102.7397$, or $102.74

Maturity value: $5,000 + $102.74 = $5,102.74

Maturity date: Dec. 11 + 75 days = Feb. 24

Days of discount: Jan. 24 to Feb. 24 = 31 days

Discount amount: $\$5,102.74 \times 0.14 \times \dfrac{31}{365} = \$60.6737$, or $60.67

Proceeds: $5,102.74 − $60.67 = $5,042.07

COMPLETE ASSIGNMENT 15.2.

Bank Discounting

In Chapter 13 and at the beginning of this chapter, we studied the simple procedure to borrow and repay money: Determine the Principal, Rate, and Time; compute the interest amount; the maturity value (amount due) is the principal plus the interest.

Learning Objective **5**

Compute the proceeds and actual interest rate on a bank discount loan.

EXAMPLE G

Silvia Jiminez, owner/operator of a small restaurant, borrows $50,000 from her bank for 60 days at 9% ordinary simple interest. Using a 360-day year, compute the interest and the maturity value.

$P = \$50,000; R = 9\%; T = \dfrac{60}{360}$

Interest $(I) = P \times R \times T = \$50,000 \times 0.09 \times \dfrac{60}{360} = \$750$

Maturity value $(MV) = P + I = \$50,000 + \$750 = \$50,750$

Please observe: Silvia will keep the entire $50,000 for the entire 60 days and then repay a total of $50,750 on the due date.

In the previous section, we studied promissory notes that were discounted at some date between the date of the loan and the due date. Similarly, sometimes banks will discount loans immediately, at the time they are written. The steps to discount a loan are the same as discounting promissory notes, but even simpler because (a) the face value is equal to the maturity value, (b) the discount date is the same as the loan date, and (3) the number of discount days is the same as the period of the loan.

STEPS **to Discount a Bank Loan**

1. Compute the discount amount, using $D = FV \times R \times T$, where R is the discount rate.
2. Compute the proceeds by subtracting the discount amount from the face value.

EXAMPLE H

Silvia Jiminez, owner/operator of a small restaurant, goes to her bank to borrow money. Silvia signs a 60-day note with a $50,000 face value at a 9% discount rate. Using a 360-day year, compute the discount amount and the proceeds of the loan.

$FV = \$50,000; R = 9\%; T = \dfrac{60}{360}$

STEP 1   Discount amount $(D) = FV \times R \times T = \$50,000 \times 0.09 \times \dfrac{60}{360} = \$750$

STEP 2   Proceeds = Face value − Discount amount = $50,000 − $750 = $49,250

Please observe: In example H, Silvia will keep $49,250 for the entire 60 days and then repay a total of $50,000 on the due date.

As mentioned earlier, some persons refer to this type of discounted loan as "non-interest-bearing" because the amount to be repaid is the "face value." However, the term *non-interest-bearing* is misleading because the loan is *not* "interest-free." There is a charge of $750 to borrow $49,250 for 60 days.

COMPARING A DISCOUNT RATE TO AN INTEREST RATE

Discount rates are less familiar to those consumers who have encountered only interest rates. There is the possibility of misunderstanding or confusion. In example G, Silvia Jiminez borrowed $50,000 for 60 days and paid $750. The ordinary simple interest rate was 9%. In example H, Silvia borrowed $49,250 for 60 days and paid $750. Although a discount rate (9%) was given, a simple interest rate was not given. To compute Silvia's actual simple interest rate in example H, use the formula from Chapter 13:

$$R = \frac{I}{P \times T}, \text{letting } I = \$750, P = \$49,250, \text{ and } T = \frac{60}{360}$$

$$R = \frac{I}{P \times T} = \frac{\$750}{\$49,250 \times \dfrac{60}{360}} = \frac{\$750}{\$8,208.33} = 0.09137, \text{ or } 9.14\%$$

The interest rate in example H is actually 9.14%; the discount rate is 9%. They are different rates, but both lead to a $750 fee to borrow $49,250 for 60 days. A borrower must understand the difference between interest rates and discount rates and how each is used in loan calculations.

✔ CONCEPT CHECK 15.5

A bank made a 90-day loan on a discount basis. The face value was $64,000, and the discount rate was 11%. Compute the discount amount and the proceeds. Then compute the actual interest rate, using the proceeds as the principal of the loan instead of the face value. Use a 360-day year in all calculations.

Discount amount $= FV \times R \times T = \$64,000 \times 0.11 \times \dfrac{90}{360} = \$1,760$

Proceeds $=$ Face value $-$ Discount amount $= \$64,000 - \$1,760 = \$62,240$

Actual interest rate $= \dfrac{I}{(P \times T)} = \dfrac{\$1,760}{\left(\$62,240 \times \dfrac{90}{360}\right)} = 0.1131, \text{ or } 11.31\%$

Borrowing Money to Take a Cash Discount

In Chapter 7, we described how manufacturers and wholesalers use cash discounts to encourage their customers to pay their invoices early. Recall that the terms "2/10, net 30" mean that the buyer will receive a 2% discount by paying the invoice within 10 days and that the entire invoice is due within 30 days. However, it would be normal that a buyer would not have the immediate cash to pay the invoice early. The buyer may need to sell the merchandise to get the cash to pay the invoice. Normally, a buyer can save money by borrowing money to pay the invoice early and earn the cash discount.

Learning Objective **6**

Compute the savings from borrowing money to take a cash discount.

● EXAMPLE I

Mega Media purchased $100,000 worth of CDs and DVDs. The invoice was dated October 4 with terms of 2/10, net 30. Compute the due date, the (cash) discount date, the cash discount, and the total remittance required to get the cash discount. (Review Chapter 7 if necessary. Notice that the terms "discount date" and "due date" had different meanings in Chapter 7 than they have had here in Chapter 15.)

Due date = October 4 + 30 days = November 3

Discount date = October 4 + 10 days = October 14

If paid by October 14:

Cash discount = $100,000 × 0.02 = $2,000

Total remittance = $100,000 − $2,000 = $98,000

Regardless of whether it takes the discount, Mega Media needs to pay $100,000 by November 3. The company may want to save the $2,000, but perhaps it doesn't have the $98,000 now. Or maybe it has the money but wants to spend it on something else. In either situation, Mega Media might be able to borrow the money from October 14 until November 3. Before borrowing, Mega Media should compare the savings from the cash discount with the interest on a loan.

● EXAMPLE J

Mega Media can borrow $98,000 for 20 days (October 14 to November 3) by paying 10% exact simple interest (365-day year). Compute the interest on the loan and the savings for Mega Media if it borrows to take the cash discount.

Interest = $P \times R \times T = \$98,000 \times 0.10 \times \dfrac{20}{365} = \$536.99$

Savings = $2,000 cash discount − $536.99 interest = $1,463.01

The reason for borrowing only between the (cash) discount date and the due date is to delay making payments as long as possible, whether to get cash discounts or to avoid penalties. The (cash) discount date is the latest possible date to pay and get the cash discount; the due date is the latest possible date to pay and avoid a penalty.

Although borrowing and taking the cash discount is almost always cheaper, the actual dollar amount may determine what Mega Media decides. If the original purchase were only $1,000, the savings would be only $14.63. Such an amount may not be worth the effort of getting a loan. However, for borrowing small amounts regularly, businesses often have "revolving lines of credit." These allow them to borrow and repay frequently, without always making a new loan application.

✔ CONCEPT CHECK 15.6

A retailer purchases merchandise under the terms 1.5/20, net 45. The invoice is for $45,000 and is dated July 22. For the cash discount, calculate the due date, the (cash) discount date, the amount of the cash discount, and the total remittance required. The retailer borrows enough money to pay the entire remittance. The interest rate is 12% exact simple interest, and the loan is for the length of time between the last date to take advantage of the cash discount and the due date. Calculate the amount of the interest and the savings gained by borrowing the remittance to take the discount.

Discount: Due date: July 22 + 45 days = September 5
               Discount date: July 22 + 20 days = August 11
               Cash discount: $45,000 × 0.015 = $675
               Remittance: $45,000 − $675 = $44,325
Loan: Interest days: August 11 to September 5 = 25 days

$$\text{Interest} = P \times R \times T = \$44{,}325 \times 0.12 \times \frac{25}{365} = \$364.32$$

Savings: $675 cash discount − $364.32 interest = $310.68

COMPLETE ASSIGNMENT 15.3.

Chapter Terms for Review

bank discount loan	interest dollars
bearer	maker
discounted note	maturity date
discount amount	maturity value
discount date	negotiable promissory note
discount period	
discount rate	non-interest-bearing promissory note
due date	
face value	proceeds
interest-bearing note	promissory note

Summary of chapter learning objectives:

Learning Objective	Example
15.1 Compute the number of interest days of a promissory note.	1. Find the number of days between December 10 and February 27.
15.2 Determine the due date of a promissory note.	2. Find the due date of a 90-day note written on May 20.
15.3 Compute the maturity value of a promissory note.	3. Find the maturity value of a 90-day promissory note with a face value of $6,500 and an exact interest rate of 8%.
15.4 Discount a promissory note.	4a. A 30-day note, bearing an interest rate of 9%, is dated November 6 and has a face value of $8,000. On November 15, the note is discounted at 12%. Use a 365-day year to find the interest amount, the discount amount, and the proceeds. 4b. A 60-day, non-interest-bearing note has a face value of $2,500 and is dated May 13. On June 3, the note is discounted at 11%. Use a 365-day year to find the discount amount and the proceeds.
15.5 Compute the proceeds and actual interest rate on a bank discount loan.	5. A 60-day bank loan with a face value of $3,900 is made on a discount basis at a discount rate of 12%. Use the 360-day year to compute the discount amount and the proceeds. Then find the actual interest rate, based on the proceeds rather than on the face value.
15.6 Compute the savings from borrowing money to take a cash discount.	6. A $20,000 invoice dated March 15 has terms of 2/5, net 25. Find the due date, (cash) discount date, cash discount, and required remittance. Next, calculate the interest amount of borrowing the remittance at 9% exact interest for the time between the last date to take advantage of the cash discount and the due date. Finally, calculate the savings.

Review Problems for Chapter 15

1 A 75-day promissory note for $3,400 is dated December 27, 2013. Find (a) the due date and (b) the maturity value, if the rate is 9% ordinary simple interest.

2 A promissory note for $5,600 is dated April 10, 2012, and has a due date of September 10, 2012. Find (a) the number of interest days and (b) the maturity value, if the rate is 5.5% ordinary simple interest.

3 A 135-day promissory note for $15,000 is dated August 25, 2014. Find (a) the due date and (b) the maturity value, if the rate is 4.6% exact simple interest.

4 A promissory note for $2,980 is dated November 21, 2012, and has a due date of March 21, 2013. Find (a) the number of interest days and (b) the maturity value, if the rate is 6.5% exact simple interest.

5 Vernon Lee holds a 120-day, interest-bearing note for $2,960 that is dated May 15 and has a rate of 8% exact simple interest. On July 15, Vernon sells it at a discount rate of 15%. Using a 365-day year, calculate (a) the interest amount, (b) the maturity value, (c) the maturity date, (d) the days of discount, (e) the discount amount, and (f) the proceeds.

6 Contractor Allen Kimmel is holding a 90-day, non-interest-bearing note for $3,100 dated November 10. On December 10, Mr. Kimmel sells the note to Thrifty Lending Corp. at a discount rate of 12%. Using a 365-day year, calculate (a) the maturity value, (b) the maturity date, (c) the days of discount, (d) the discount amount, and (e) the proceeds.

7 Eastside Bank & Trust Co. made a 120-day loan for $4,500 on a discount basis, using a discount rate of 9%. Using a 360-day year, calculate (a) the discount amount, (b) the proceeds, and (c) the actual interest rate (to two decimal places).

8 VanderBeek Landscape Construction just received an invoice for $1,600 that has cash discount terms of 2/10, net 30. VanderBeek borrows enough money from Eastside Bank & Trust Co. at 10% exact simple interest (365-day year) to take advantage of the cash discount. It borrows the money only for the time period between the due date and the last day to take advantage of the discount. Calculate (a) the amount of the cash discount, (b) the number of interest days, (c) the amount of interest on the loan, and (d) the amount of its savings.

Answers to the Self-Check can be found in Appendix B at the back of the text.

Assignment 15.1: Dates, Times, and Maturity Value

Name

Date   Score

A   **(36 points) Problems 1–6: Find the number of interest days. Problems 7–12: Find the due date. Be sure to check for leap years. (3 points for each correct answer)**

Date of Note	Due Date	Days of Interest
1. April 5, 2013	October 11, 2013	_____
2. June 29, 2015	October 6, 2015	_____
3. February 7, 2014	May 12, 2014	_____
4. June 15, 2012	October 15, 2012	_____
5. November 8, 2013	April 9, 2014	_____
6. July 16, 2015	October 26, 2015	_____

Date of Note	Days of Interest	Due Date
7. October 7, 2014	90 days	_____
8. September 20, 2013	180 days	_____
9. September 18, 2015	75 days	_____
10. May 30, 2013	60 days	_____
11. December 8, 2014	120 days	_____
12. November 30, 2012	3 months	_____

Score for A (36)

B **(64 points)** For each of the following promissory notes, find the missing entry for days of interest or maturity date (due date). Then compute the amount of interest due at maturity and the maturity value. For problems 13–16, use a 360-day year; for problems 17–20, use a 365-day year. (Points indicated at the top of each column)

	Face Value	Date of Note	Days of Interest (3 pts)	Maturity Date (3 pts)	Rate	Interest Amount (3 pts)	Maturity Value (2 pts)
13.	$26,000	Oct. 11, 2013	90	_____	6.2%	_____	_____
14.	$14,500	Mar. 29, 2013	_____	July 8, 2013	8.5%	_____	_____
15.	$35,750	July 16, 2012	105	_____	5.6%	_____	_____
16.	$960	Jan. 23, 2014	_____	Mar. 31, 2014	7.2%	_____	_____
17.	$41,800	Nov. 16, 2012	_____	Mar. 21, 2013	5.1%	_____	_____
18.	$18,400	May 5, 2014	_____	Sept. 5, 2014	6.75%	_____	_____
19.	$52,000	Mar. 14, 2012	180	_____	8.25%	_____	_____
20.	$31,800	Aug. 6, 2015	105	_____	7.5%	_____	_____

Score for B (64)

Assignment 15.2: Discounting Promissory Notes

Name

Date   Score

A **(50 points) Compute the missing information to discount the following interest-bearing and non-interest-bearing promissory notes. Use a 360-day year for all interest and discount calculations. (Points for each correct answer are shown in parentheses)**

1. Bonnie Bomar had been holding a 75-day note for $2,500. The note had a 6% interest rate and had been written on March 1. To pay income taxes, Bonnie sold the note on April 13 to a loan company. The loan company discounted the note at 11%.

   Interest amount (3 pts) _____

   Maturity value (2 pts) _____

   Maturity date (2 pts) _____

   Days of discount (2 pts) _____

   Discount amount (3 pts) _____

   Proceeds (2 pts) _____

2. On July 10, Joe Morrison Financial Services bought a $15,000 promissory note. The note had been written on May 8, was for 120 days, and had an interest rate of 8%. Joe's company discounted the note at 10%.

   Interest amount (3 pts) _____

   Maturity value (2 pts) _____

   Maturity date (2 pts) _____

   Days of discount (2 pts) _____

   Discount amount (3 pts) _____

   Proceeds (2 pts) _____

3. Bob Miles was holding a 105-day, non-interest-bearing note for $4,500. The note was dated October 9. To raise Christmas cash, Bob sold the note to a local finance company on December 14. The company discounted the note at 10%.

   Interest amount (1 pt) _____

   Maturity value (1 pt) _____

   Maturity date (2 pts) _____

   Days of discount (2 pts) _____

   Discount amount (3 pts) _____

   Proceeds (2 pts) _____

4. Barbara Cain owned a finance company. On July 19 she purchased a 180-day, non-interest-bearing promissory note. The note had been written on May 23 for $7,100. Because of the high financial risk involved, Barbara discounted the note at 14%.

   Interest amount (1 pt) _____

   Maturity value (1 pt) _____

   Maturity date (2 pts) _____

   Days of discount (2 pts) _____

   Discount amount (3 pts) _____

   Proceeds (2 pts) _____

Score for A (50)

B **(50 points) Compute the missing information to discount the following interest-bearing and non-interest-bearing promissory notes. Use a 365-day year for all interest and discount calculations. (Points for each correct answer are shown in parentheses)**

5. As payment for services, Pat Chard held a 90-day, 8% note for $3,600 that was dated April 20. On June 5, Pat took the note to a financial services company, which bought the note at a 13% discount rate.

   Interest amount (3 pts) _____
   Maturity value (2 pts) _____
   Maturity date (2 pts) _____
   Days of discount (2 pts) _____
   Discount amount (3 pts) _____
   Proceeds (2 pts) _____

6. Jorgenson Builders accepted a 150-day, 9% negotiable note dated June 17. The face value of the note was $10,700. On August 8, Jorgenson sold the note to Molitor Financial Group, which discounted the note at 11%.

   Interest amount (3 pts) _____
   Maturity value (2 pts) _____
   Maturity date (2 pts) _____
   Days of discount (2 pts) _____
   Discount amount (3 pts) _____
   Proceeds (2 pts) _____

7. Teri Chung loaned $4,000 to a client who gave Teri a non-interest-bearing note dated August 1. The note was for 75 days. On August 31, Teri sold the note to her finance company, which discounted it at 10%.

   Interest amount (1 pt) _____
   Maturity value (1 pt) _____
   Maturity date (2 pts) _____
   Days of discount (2 pts) _____
   Discount amount (3 pts) _____
   Proceeds (2 pts) _____

8. Patti Riddle was holding a 60-day, non-interest-bearing note for $1,700. The note was dated June 22. On July 16, Patti sold the note to a lender who discounted the note at 15%.

   Interest amount (1 pt) _____
   Maturity value (1 pt) _____
   Maturity date (2 pts) _____
   Days of discount (2 pts) _____
   Discount amount (3 pts) _____
   Proceeds (2 pts) _____

Score for B (50)

Assignment 15.3: Bank Discounting and Cash Discounts

Name

Date   Score

A **(36 points)** The Bank of the Southwest made six new loans on a discount basis. Compute the discount amount and the proceeds. Then compute the actual interest rate based on the proceeds rather than the face value. Use a 360-day year for problems 1–3 and use a 365-day year for problems 4–6. Round the actual interest rates to the nearest 1/100 of a percent. **(2 points for each correct answer)**

	Face Value	Discount Rate	Time	Discount Amount	Proceeds	Actual Interest Rate
1.	$7,500	10%	120 days	_____	_____	_____
2.	$6,650	5.5%	75 days	_____	_____	_____
3.	$16,500	12%	150 days	_____	_____	_____
4.	$22,500	6.5%	60 days	_____	_____	_____
5.	$980	7.5%	135 days	_____	_____	_____
6.	$10,120	9.1%	90 days	_____	_____	_____

Score for A (36)

B   (64 points) Atlantic Construction made several purchases from vendors who offered various terms of payment. How much can Atlantic save on each invoice if it borrows the money to pay the invoice early and receive the cash discount? The loan interest rates are all exact simple interest (365-day year). Assume that the number of interest days is the time between the due date and the last day to take advantage of the cash discount. (2 points for each correct answer)

Invoice	Terms	Cash Discount	Interest Rate on Loan	Days of Interest	Interest Amount	Savings
7. $5,000	2/10, n/30	_____	10%	_____	_____	_____
8. $16,200	2.5/10, n/35	_____	7.5%	_____	_____	_____
9. $32,575	1.25/7, n/40	_____	8.75%	_____	_____	_____
10. $34,620	2/10, n/30	_____	9.25%	_____	_____	_____
11. $9,200	1/30, n/60	_____	9.6%	_____	_____	_____
12. $12,500	2/10, n/45	_____	8%	_____	_____	_____
13. $26,000	2.5/5, n/25	_____	8.5%	_____	_____	_____
14. $42,800	3/20, n/45	_____	10%	_____	_____	_____

Score for B (64)

Compound Interest

16

Learning Objectives

By studying this chapter and completing all assignments, you will be able to:

Learning Objective	**1**	Compute future values.
Learning Objective	**2**	Compute present values.
Learning Objective	**3**	Compute using present value factors.

Most Americans will buy at least one item that is financed over one or more years. The product will probably be expensive, such as a car or a home. Likely, the interest on the loan will not be the simple interest you studied in Chapter 13; it will be *compound* interest. Interest on car loans and home loans is normally compounded monthly. Most banks offer savings accounts and certificates of deposit (CDs) for which interest is compounded daily. A credit union may pay interest that is compounded quarterly (four times a year). To evaluate the value of corporate or municipal bonds, an investor uses calculations on interest that is normally compounded semiannually (twice a year).

To understand even the most fundamental financial decisions in today's world, you need to understand the basic concepts of compound interest, future values, and present values.

Compute Future Values

Compute future values from tables and formulas.

Simple interest is computed with the formula $I = P \times R \times T$, which you studied in Chapter 13. For example, the simple interest on $2,000 invested at 6% for 2 years is $I = P \times R \times T = \$2,000 \times 0.06 \times 2 = \$240$. The amount, or future value, of the investment is $A = P + I = \$2,000 + \$240 = \$2,240$.

Compound interest means that the computations of the simple interest formula are performed repeatedly during the term of the investment. The money from the previous interest computation is added to the principal before the next interest computation is performed. If an investment is *compounded annually for 2 years,* the simple interest is computed once at the end of each year. The simple interest earned in year 1 is added to the principal at the beginning of year 2. The total value of an investment is the principal plus all of the compound interest. The total is called the **future value** or the **compound amount.** In finance, the original principal is usually called the present value.

● EXAMPLE A

Kathie Maguire invests $2,000 for 2 years in an investment that pays 6% compounded annually. Compute the total compound interest and future value (compound amount).

$2,000.00	Original principal
× 0.06	Interest rate
$120.0000	First-year interest
+2,000.00	First-year principal
$2,120.00	Second-year principal
× 0.06	Interest rate
$127.2000	Second-year interest
+2,120.00	Second-year principal
$2,247.20	Final compound amount (future value)
−2,000.00	Original principal
$247.20	Total compound interest

On the $2,000 investment in example A, the total amount of compound interest paid is $247.20, compared to $240 simple interest over the same 2 years. Notice that the total compound interest amount, $247.20, is equal to the sum of the first-year interest and the second-year interest: $120 + $127.20. Because you need to be familiar with all the terminology, we will use *compound amount* and *future value* interchangeably and also *principal* and *present value* interchangeably in this chapter. As the chapter progresses, however, we will use the terms *future* value and *present value* more often.

FUTURE VALUE FORMULA

There were many similar computations in example A. There would be twice as many computations if the investment had been for 4 years instead of 2. To eliminate all the tedious computations, compound interest is computed using a single number called the **future value factor,** or FVF. The FVF is used with a shortcut formula called the *Future Value Formula* (also known as *the compound amount* formula) for compound interest calculations:

Future Value (compound amount) = Present Value (principal) × Future Value Factor, or $FV = PV \times FVF$

The total amount of the compound interest earned is equal to the difference between the future value and the present value. As a formula, we can write

Compound Interest = Future Value − Present Value = $FV - PV$

KAREN ROACH/SHUTTERSTOCK.COM

To use the formulas, you first need to find the future value factor (FVF) using a calculator or a future value table. Table 16-1 at the end of this chapter is a partial table of future value factors (FVFs). In modern practice, FVFs are usually computed with a calculator or computer rather than a table. However, using a calculator requires that you (a) understand "exponents," (b) have an appropriate calculator, and (c) know how to compute easily with exponents. Chapter 16 is designed so that you can succeed whether or not you already have the prerequisite knowledge and/or an appropriate calculator available. If you are not using exponents, you easily can use Table 16-1 to find FVFs. If you are using exponents, you can compute the FVFs directly with your calculator. First we will illustrate the solution using tables; then, using calculators. Examine both methods so that subsequent examples will be meaningful.

In example A, the principal was $2,000, the interest rate was 6%, and the time was 2 years. We need the future value factor (FVF). You can find the FVF in Table 16-1. Table 16-1 is organized by rows and columns. The columns represent the interest rate being compounded, *i*. The rows represent the number of times the interest rate is compounded, *n*. The FVF is where the correct row and column intersect. In example A, a 6% interest rate was compounded twice. The FVF is in the 6% column and row 2 and is 1.12360. From the formula, the future value is $FV = PV \times FVF = \$2,000 \times 1.12360 = \$2,247.20$ which agrees with example A. The compound interest is $FV - PV = \$2,247.20 - \$2,000 = \$247.20$ which also agrees with example A.

STEPS **to Calculate the Future Value and Compound Interest Using a Future Value Table**

1. Find *i*, the interest rate, and *n*, the number of times to compound the interest. Locate the future value factor (FVF) in the proper row and column of Table 16-1.

2. Multiply the present value (principal) by the FVF. The product is the future value, or $FV = PV \times FVF$.

3. Subtract the present value (principal) from the future value. The difference is the total amount of compound interest, or compound interest = $FV - PV$.

Ray Wilson loans $5,000 to his cousin for 6 years at 4% compounded annually. Compute the future value and the total compound interest. Use Table 16-1.

STEP 1   The interest rate is $i = 4\%$. Interest is compounded 6 times, once each year for $n = 6$ years. The FVF in the 4% column and row 6 is 1.26532.

STEP 2   Future Value $= PV \times FVF = \$5{,}000 \times 1.26532 = \$6{,}326.60$.

STEP 3   Compound Interest $= FV - PV = \$6{,}326.60 - \$5{,}000 = \$1{,}326.60$.

FINDING THE FUTURE VALUE FACTOR USING A CALCULATOR (OPTIONAL)

Note: This optional section is for those students who understand how to compute using exponents on a calculator. You have the choice of using your calculator or Table 16-1. You can even use Table 16-1 first and then check your work using your calculator. First, review this very brief summary of rules and terminology about exponents.

The expression 2^4 means $2 \times 2 \times 2 \times 2 = 16$. The 2 is called the **base**; the 4 is called the **exponent.** We can say that "2 is raised to the 4th **power.**" Many calculators have a key labeled $\boxed{y^x}$ that is used for exponents. To compute 2^4, you might enter the following keystrokes: 2 $\boxed{y^x}$ 4 $\boxed{=}$. The answer on the calculator display will be 16. Likewise, $(1 + 0.06)^2$ means $1.06^2 = 1.06 \times 1.06 = 1.1236$ and we say that "1.06 is raised to the 2nd power." (We can also say that 1.06^2 means "1.06 *squared.*")

To find the future value factor, the formula is $\boldsymbol{FVF = (1 + i)^n}$, where i is the interest rate being compounded and n the number of times the interest is compounded. *Important: In the formula, the interest rate must be written as a decimal, not as a percent.*

In example A, the interest rate was 6% and it was compounded twice. Therefore, $i = 6\% = 0.06$ and $n = 2$. The future value factor is $FVF = (1 + i)^n = (1 + 0.06)^2 = 1.06^2 = 1.1236$ which is identical to the same value from Table 16-1. Depending upon your calculator, you might be using the calculator keystrokes 1.06 $\boxed{y^x}$ 2 $\boxed{=}$. The exact calculator keystrokes will depend upon your own calculator. Refer to your calculator's manual. Many calculators also have keys for "parentheses," but it is usually faster to mentally add the "$(1 + i)$."

STEPS   **to Calculate the Future Value and Compound Interest Using a Calculator**

1. Find i, the interest rate, and n, the number of times to compound the interest. Compute the FVF using the formula is $FVF = (1 + i)^n$.
2. Multiply the present value (principal) by the FVF. The product is the future value, or $FV = PV \times FVF$.
3. Subtract the present value (principal) from the future value. The difference is the total amount of compound interest, or compound interest $= FV - PV$.

Example C below is the same as example B, except that you are asked to solve the problem using a calculator with an exponent function.

Ray Wilson loans $5,000 to his cousin for 6 years at 4% compounded annually. Compute the future value and the total compound interest. Use a calculator with exponents.

STEP 1   The interest rate is 4%, so $i = 4\%$ or 0.04. Interest is compounded six times, once each year for 6 years, so $n = 6$. The FVF $= (1 + i)^n = (1 + 0.04)^6 = (1.04)^6 = 1.26531902$.

STEP 2   Future Value $= PV \times FVF = \$5,000 \times 1.26531902 = \$6,326.595092$, or $6,326.60.

STEP 3   Compound Interest $= FV - PV = \$6,326.60 - \$5,000 = \$1,326.60$.

Note: In examples B and C, the answers came out identical. However, very often there will be slight difference. The FVFs in Table 16-1 have only five decimal places. However, many calculators have 9 or more decimal places. In example C, we wrote the FVF with eight decimal places. Throughout this chapter, when the FVF has eight decimal places, it came from a calculator. When the FVF has five decimal places, it came from Table 16-1.

In the remainder of Chapter 16, the calculator solutions will be shown in the margins, written in blue ink, next to the solutions that use Table 16-1. You can compare the solutions and decide which you prefer. It is faster for many persons to use a calculator than to look through tables. A calculator is easier to carry than a book of tables. Also, the tables are limited to only certain interest rates and time periods. With a calculator you can use any interest rate and any time period.

VARIOUS COMPOUNDING PERIODS

In examples A, B, and C, the compounding was annual (i.e., done once each year). Compounding is also done semiannually, quarterly, monthly, and daily. The word **period** is the unit of time of the compounding. The letter m represents *the number of compounding periods in one year.* Thus, $m = 1$ for annual compounding; $m = 2$ for semiannual; $m = 4$ for quarterly; $m = 12$ for monthly; and $m = 365$ for daily. Most often, the interest rate of an investment or loan will be *stated* as an annual rate (r) and the total time (t) will be stated in years. However, very often the actual *compounding* will not be done annually.

Examples B and C illustrated that you need i and n to calculate the future value factor (FVF) and the future value, whether you use a calculator or Table 16-1. Steps i, ii, and iii describe how to determine the values of i and n for all the various compounding periods. During the remainder of Chapter 16, i will represent the **periodic interest rate** and n will represent the total **number of compounding periods.**

> **STEPS** **to Determine the Periodic Interest Rate and the Number of Compounding Periods**
>
> **i.** Determine m, the compounding periods in one year: $m = 1, 2, 4, 12, 365$.
>
> **ii.** Determine i, the periodic interest rate: $i = r \div m$.
>   (Divide the stated annual rate, r, by m.)
>
> **iii.** Determine n, the total number of compounding periods: $n = m \times t$.
>   (Multiply the periods per year, m, by the number of years, t.)

For a 3-year, 6% loan: Find i, the periodic interest rate, and n, the total number of compounding periods, when the loan is compounded (a) semiannually; (b) quarterly; and (c) monthly. Each loan is for a total of $t = 3$ years at a stated annual rate of $r = 6\%$, but each loan is compounded differently.

STEP i	STEP ii	STEP iii
Periods per Year	**Periodic Interest Rate**	**Number of Compounding Periods**
a. $m = 2$	$i = 6\% \div 2 = 3\%$	$n = 2 \times 3$ years $= 6$ half-years
b. $m = 4$	$i = 6\% \div 4 = 1.5\%$	$n = 4 \times 3$ years $= 12$ quarters
c. $m = 12$	$i = 6\% \div 12 = 0.5\%$	$n = 12 \times 3$ years $= 36$ months

Carefully study examples E and F below and verify all the calculations. Use Steps i, ii, and iii to find the periodic interest rate and the number of compounding periods. Then use Steps 1, 2, and 3 to find the future value factor (FVF), the future value, and the total amount of compound interest. Computations are shown for both methods: (a) using a calculator with exponents; and (b) using Table 16-1.

● **EXAMPLE E**

$m = 2$

$i = \dfrac{0.04}{2} = 0.02$

$n = 6 \times 2 = 12$

$FVF = (1 + i)^n = (1.02)^{12}$

$= 1.26824179$

$FV = PV \times FVF$

$= \$5{,}000 \times 1.26824179$

$= \$6{,}341.20897$

or $\$6{,}341.21$

Ray Wilson loans $5,000 to his cousin for 6 years at 4% compounded semiannually. Compute the future value and the total compound interest. The stated interest rate of 4% is an annual rate. Determine the periodic rate, i, and the total number of compounding periods, n. Then compute the future value and the total compound interest. Use a calculator with exponents or Table 16-1.

STEP i   There are $m = 2$ compounding periods in 1 year.

STEP ii   Periodic interest rate is $i = r \div m = 4\% \div 2 = 2\%$.

STEP iii   Number of periods is $n = t \times m = 6 \times 2 = 12$ periods.

   With $i = 2\%$ and $n = 12$, use a calculator with exponents or Table 16-1.

STEP 1   Using Table 16-1, in the 2% column and row 12, the FVF is 1.26824.

STEP 2   Future Value $= PV \times FVF = \$5{,}000 \times 1.26824 = \$6{,}341.20$.

STEP 3   Compound interest $= FV - PV = \$6{,}341.20 - \$5{,}000 = \$1{,}341.20$.

$m = 4$

$i = \dfrac{0.05}{4} = 0.0125$

$n = 2.5 \times 4 = 10$

$FVF = (1 + i)^n = (1.0125)^{10}$

$= 1.13227083$

$FV = PV \times FVF$

$= \$20{,}000 \times 1.13227083$

$= \$22{,}645.41660$

or $\$22{,}645.42$

Example E is identical to examples B and C, except the compounding is semiannual instead of annual. Using Table 16-1 with five decimal places, the solution is $1,341.20. With a calculator, using eight decimal places, the answer rounds off to $1,341.21. This discrepancy is normal.

● **EXAMPLE F**

Sharon Sumpter and her husband deposit $20,000 into her credit union, which pays interest at 5% compounded quarterly. Find the future value and the total compound interest after 2.5 years. Use a calculator with exponents or Table 16-1.

STEP i   There are $m = 4$ compounding periods in 1 year.

STEP ii   Periodic interest rate is $i = r \div m = 5\% \div 4 = 1.25\%$.

STEP iii	Number of periods is $n = t \times m = 2.5 \times 4 = 10$ periods.
	With $i = 1.25\%$ and $n = 10$, use a calculator with exponents or Table 16-1.
STEP 1	Using Table 16-1, in the 1.25% column and row 10, the FVF is 1.13227.
STEP 2	Future Value $= PV \times FVF = \$20,000 \times 1.13227 = \$22,645.40$.
STEP 3	Compound interest $= FV - PV = \$22,645.40 - \$20,000 = \$2,645.40$.

DAILY COMPOUNDING (OPTIONAL)

Today, essentially all banks offer daily compounding on several different savings accounts and certificates of deposit. Tables to do daily compounding would be cumbersome and impractical. However, using a calculator with an exponent key, the computation is just as simple as other compounding computations. Assume that there are 365 days in a year.

EXAMPLE G (OPTIONAL)

Use a calculator with exponents to find the future value of $20,000 invested for 2 years at 8% compounded daily. First find the periodic interest rate (i) as a decimal with eight decimal places and find the number of days (n) in two years. Then find the future value factor (FVF) to eight decimal places.

STEP i	Compounding periods in one year: $m = 365$
STEP ii	Periodic interest rate: $i = r \div m = 0.08 \div 365 = 0.00021918$
STEP iii	Number of compounding periods: $n = m \times t = 365 \times 2 = 730$
STEP 1	$FVF = (1 + i)^n = (1 + 0.00021918)^{730} = 1.17349194$
STEP 2	Future value $= \$20,000 \times 1.17349194 = \$23,469.84$

✓ CONCEPT CHECK 16.1

a. If \$2,600 is invested for 5 years at 6% compounded semiannually, compute the future value of the investment. (Use Table 16-1 or a calculator.)

Semiannually means $m = 2$ periods per year.
Periodic rate $= 6\% \div 2 = 3\%$ per half-year
Number of periods $= 2 \times 5$ years $= 10$ periods
The FVF from row 10 of the 3.00% column in Table 16-1 is 1.34392.

$FV = PV \times FVF = \$2,600 \times 1.34392 = \$3,494.192$, or $3,494.19

$$m = 2$$
$$i = \frac{0.06}{2} = 0.03$$
$$n = 2 \times 5 = 10$$
$$FVF = (1 + 0.03)^{10}$$
$$= 1.34391638$$
$$FV = \$2,600 \times 1.34391638$$
$$= \$3,494.18$$

b. If \$3,200 is invested for 1 year at 9% compounded monthly, what is the compound interest on the investment?

Monthly means $m = 12$ periods per year.
Periodic rate $= 9\% \div 12 = 0.75\%$ per month
Number of periods $= 12 \times 1$ year $= 12$ periods
The FVF from row 12 of the 0.75% column in Table 16-1 is 1.09381.

$FV = PV \times FVF = \$3,200 \times 1.09381 = \$3,500.192$, or $3,500.19
Compound interest $=$ Future value $-$ Present value (Principal)
$\qquad\qquad\qquad = \$3,500.19 - \$3,200 = \$300.19$

$$m = 12$$
$$i = \frac{0.09}{12} = 0.0075$$
$$n = 12 \times 1 = 12$$
$$FVF = (1 + 0.0075)^{12}$$
$$= 1.09380690$$
$$FV = \$3,200 \times 1.09380690$$
$$= \$3,500.18$$

COMPLETE ASSIGNMENT 16.1.

Compute Present Values

Learning Objective 2

Compute present values.

In the previous section, the basic investment problem was to compute the value that a given sum of money, invested today, would be worth at some time in the future. Example F was a future value problem. In it, we found that a $20,000 principal (present value) invested today at 5% compounded quarterly would have a future value of $22,645.40 in 2.5 years.

Some savers and investors want to compute future values; others want to compute present values. Consider the following which is a present value problem.

EXAMPLE H

Polly Layer has a 13-year-old grandson when she inherits $175,000 from her father's estate. A financial planner tells Polly that she should plan to have $60,000 cash available for her grandson's college education when he turns 18. She wants to put enough money into an investment account for her grandson so that in 5 years his account will be worth $60,000. Polly found a very safe investment that guaranteed to pay her 4% compounded quarterly. To achieve her objective, how much money should she invest today?

In example H, Polly knows the required future value of her investment for her grandson—$60,000. What Polly wants to calculate is the **present value**—the amount that she needs to invest today.

Like individuals, a business makes investments or savings now, in the present, to provide for future expenses and/or to earn future revenues (the future values). The business will estimate those future amounts and decide how much they must budget today (the present values).

As given earlier, the formula to find future value is

$$FV = PV \times (1 + i)^n$$

> Future Value = Present Value × Future Value Factor, or $FV = PV \times FVF$

Rewriting the formula, we get a formula to find present value:

$$PV = \frac{FV}{(1 + i)^n}$$

> Present Value = Future Value ÷ Future Value Factor, or $PV = FV \div FVF = \dfrac{FV}{FVF}$

EXAMPLE I

$m = 2$

$i = \dfrac{0.08}{2} = 0.04$

$n = 2 \times 3 = 6$

$FVF = (1 + 0.04)^6$

$\quad = 1.26531902$

$PV = \dfrac{\$6,000}{1.26531902}$

$\quad = \$4,741.89$

How much money must be invested today to end up with $6,000 in 3 years? The interest rate is 8% compounded semiannually. Use a calculator or Table 16-1.

The $6,000 is the future value for which we want to find the present value. Interest is computed six times—twice each year for 3 years. The future value factor in Table 16-1 in the 4.00% column and row 6 is 1.26532. Substitute these values into the formula for present value.

Present value = $FV \div FVF = \$6,000 \div 1.26532 = \$4,741.88$

If $4,741.88 is invested today at 8% compounded semiannually, it will be worth $6,000 after 3 years.

Monza Motors estimates that in 2 years it will cost $20,000 replace some diagnostic equipment. Monza Motors wants to know how much to invest today if they can earn a return of 6% compounded monthly. Also, how much money would Monza Motors actually earn on this investment? Use either a calculator with exponents or Table 16-1 to find FVF.

The given future value is $20,000; Monza Motors wants to know the present value.

STEP i	There are $m = 12$ compounding periods in one year.
STEP ii	The periodic interest rate is $i = 6\% \div 12 = 0.5\%$.
STEP iii	The number of compounding periods is $n = 12 \times 2$ years $= 24$.

Using Table 16-1, in row 24 of the 0.5% column, FVF = 1.12716.

Substitute the values in the formula for present value:

Present Value $= FV \div FVF = \$20,000 \div 1.12716 = \$17,743.71$

If Monza Motors invests $17,743.71 today at 6% compounded monthly, it will have $20,000 at the end of 2 years.

The $20,000 is the sum of the amount invested plus the total compound interest earned. To find the interest, subtract the amount invested from $20,000.

Interest = Future value − Present value = $20,000 − $17,743.71 = $2,256.29

$$m = 12$$
$$i = \frac{0.06}{12} = 0.005$$
$$n = 12 \times 2 = 24$$
$$FVF = (1 + 0.005)^{24}$$
$$= 1.12715978$$

$$PV = \frac{FV}{FVF}$$
$$= \frac{\$20,000}{1.12715978}$$
$$= \$17,743.71$$

✔ CONCEPT CHECK 16.2

What present value (principal) invested for 4 years at 6% compounded quarterly will result in a total future value of $8,000? (Use Table 16-1 or a calculator.)

Quarterly means 4 periods per year.
Periodic rate = 6% ÷ 4 = 1.5% per quarter
Number of periods = 4 years × 4 = 16 periods
The future value factor from row 16 of the 1.50% column in Table 16-1 is 1.26899.

Present value = Future value ÷ Future value factor
= $8,000 ÷ 1.26899 = $6,304.226, or $6,304.23

$$m = 2$$
$$i = \frac{0.06}{4} = 0.015$$
$$n = 4 \times 4 = 16$$
$$FVF = (1 + 0.015)^{16}$$
$$= 1.26898555$$
$$PV = \frac{\$8,000}{1.26898555}$$
$$= \$6,304.25$$

Compute Using Present Value Factors

You can solve every present value problem in Chapter 16 with future value factors and the formula $PV = FV \div FVF$, or $PV = \frac{FV}{FVF}$. In a present value problem, the future value, FV, will be given information. Then, use Steps i, ii, and iii to determine i and n; use either a calculator or Table 16-1 to find the FVF; finally, substitute FV and FVF into the formula $PV = FV \div FVF$ and solve for the present value.

Learning Objective **3**

Compute using present value factors.

ALTERNATE PRESENT VALUE FORMULA

Students who plan to study other courses in accounting or finance will also want to learn to use **present value factors (PVF)** and an alternate form of the present value formula. Using the present value factors, the alternate present value formula is written

Present Value = Future Value × Present Value Factor, or $PV = FV \times PVF$

Using this alternate form of the present value formula is essentially an identical process. The future value, FV, is given. Next, find i, the periodic interest rate, and n, the total number of compounding periods. Then, however, use a calculator, or use Table 16-2, to find the present value factor (PVF). Table 16-2 is organized exactly the same as Table 16-1. The column is the periodic interest rate, and the row is the total number of compounding periods. Multiply the future value by the PVF to get the present value.

● EXAMPLE K

$$m = 12$$

$$i = \frac{0.06}{12} = 0.005$$

$$n = 12 \times 2 = 24$$

$$PVF = \frac{1}{(1 + 0.005)^{24}}$$

$$= 0.88718567$$

$$PV = FV \times PVF$$
$$= \$20,000 \times 0.88718567$$
$$= \$17,743.71$$

In example J, Monza Motors needed a future value $20,000 on a 2-year investment earning 6% compounded monthly. Compute the present value using the alternate formula $PV = FV \times PVF$. Use Table 16-2 to find PVF.

STEP i   There are 12 compounding periods in 1 year: $m = 12$

STEP ii   Periodic interest rate $= i = r \div m = 6\% \div 12 = 0.5\%$

STEP iii   Number of compounding periods $= n = m \times t = 12 \times 2 = 24$

Using Table 16-2, in row 24 of the 0.5% column, PVF = 0.88719.

Substitute the values in the alternate formula for present value:

Present Value $= FV \times PVF = \$20,000 \times 0.88719 = \$17,743.80$ to the nearest cent

The present value in example J was $17,743.71. The discrepancy between the results of examples J and K is because Table 16-1 and 16-2 have only five decimal places. The more decimal places you use, the smaller the discrepancy will be.

USING A CALCULATOR TO FIND THE PVF (OPTIONAL)

Recall that using exponents on a calculator, a future value factor is $FVF = (1 + i)^n$. The formula for a present value factor is $PVF = \frac{1}{FVF} = \frac{1}{(1 + i)^n}$.

With $i = 0.5\% = 0.005$ and $n = 24$,

$$PVF = \frac{1}{FVF} = \frac{1}{(1 + i)^n} = \frac{1}{(1 + 0.005)^{24}} = \frac{1}{1.12715978} = 0.88718567, \text{ rounded}$$

to eight places

To solve example K using the alternate present value formula and PVF = 0.88718567, the present value is $PV = FV \times PVF = \$20,000 \times 0.88718567 = \$17,743.71$.

Notice that now the solutions to examples J and K are identical to the nearest cent.

Solve the present value problem from example H using a present value factor (PVF) and the alternate present value formula: $PV = FV \times PVF$. Polly Layer wants to have \$60,000 available five years from now for her grandson's college education. She can earn 4% compounded quarterly on her investment. How much should Polly invest today? Use either a calculator with exponents or Table 16-2 to find PVF.

STEP i   Four compounding periods in 1 year: $m = 4$

STEP ii   Periodic interest rate: $i = r \div m = 4\% \div 4 = 1\%$

STEP iii   Number of compounding periods: $n = m \times t = 4 \times 5 = 20$

Using Table 16-2, in row 20 of the 1% column, PVF = 0.81954.

Present Value = $FV \times PVF = \$60,000 \times 0.81954 = \$49,172.40$.

$m = 4$

$i = \dfrac{0.04}{4} = 0.01$

$n = 4 \times 5 = 20$

$PVF = \dfrac{1}{(1+i)^n} = \dfrac{1}{(1.01)^{20}}$
$= 0.81954447$

$PV = FV \times PVF$
$= \$60,000 \times 0.81954447$
$= \$49,172.67$

If Polly invests \$49,172.40 today, at a rate of 4% compounded quarterly, she will have \$60,000 five years from now.

✓ CONCEPT CHECK 16.3

a. What present value (principal) invested for 3 years at 10% compounded semiannually will result in a total future value of \$4,000? (Use a calculator or Table 16-2.)

Semiannually means 2 periods per year.
Periodic rate = 10% ÷ 2 = 5% per half-year
Number of periods = 2 × 3 years = 6 periods
The present value factor from row 6 of the 5.00% column in Table 16-2 is 0.74622.

$PV = FV \times PVF = \$4,000 \times 0.74622 = \$2,984.88$

b. Four years ago, a woman invested money at 9% compounded monthly. If the investment is now worth \$12,000, how much compound interest did she earn in the 4 years? (Use a calculator or Table 16-2.)

Monthly means 12 periods per year.
Periodic rate = 9% ÷ 12 = 0.75% per month
Number of periods = 12 × 4 years = 48 periods

The present value factor from row 48 of the 0.75% column in Table 16-2 is 0.69861.

$PV = FV \times PVF = \$12,000 \times 0.69861 = \$8,383.32$

Compound interest = Future value − Present value
$= \$12,000 - \$8,383.32 = \$3,616.68$

COMPLETE ASSIGNMENT 16.2.

$m = 2$

$i = \dfrac{0.10}{2} = 0.05$

$n = 2 \times 3 = 6$

$PVF = \dfrac{1}{(1+0.05)^6}$
$= 0.74621540$

$PV = \$4,000 \times 0.74621540$
$= \$2,984.86$

$m = 12$

$i = \dfrac{0.09}{12} = 0.0075$

$n = 12 \times 4 = 48$

$PVF = \dfrac{1}{(1+0.0075)^{48}}$
$= 0.69861414$

$PV = \$12,000 \times 0.69861414$
$= \$8,383.37$

Chapter Terms for Review

base

compound amount

compound interest

exponent

future value

future value factor

number of compounding periods

period (compounding period)

periodic interest rate

power

present value

present value factor

THE BOTTOM LINE

Summary of chapter learning objectives:

Learning Objective	Example
16.1 Compute future values.	Use a calculator with exponents or Table 16-1. 1. Compute the future value of $8,000 invested at 9% compounded monthly for 3 years. 2. Compute the compound interest earned on $5,000 invested at 6% compounded quarterly for 5 years.
16.2 Compute present values.	Use a calculator with exponents or Table 16-1. 3. Compute the present value that has to be invested at 10% compounded semiannually for 6 years to result in $8,000.
16.3 Compute using present value factors.	Use a calculator with exponents or Table 16-2. 4. If $6,000 is the future value after 13 years at 9% compounded annually, compute the principal (present value). 5. An investment made 16 months ago is worth $5,634.95 today. If the interest rate was 9% compounded monthly, what was the amount of compound interest?

Answers: 1. $10,469.20 2. $1,734.30 3. $4,454.69 4. $1,957.08 5. $634.95

Review Problems for Chapter 16

1 Calculate the future value (compound amount) and compound interest. (Use a calculator or Table 16-1.)

Principal	Rate	Time	Future Value		Interest	
$ 4,000	6% compounded monthly	3 yr	a. _____		b. _____	
$12,000	8% compounded quarterly	7 yr	c. _____		d. _____	
$30,000	10% compounded annually	16 yr	e. _____		f. _____	
$ 8,000	10% compounded semiannually	10 yr	g. _____		h. _____	

2 Calculate the present value (principal) and compound interest. (Use a calculator or Table 16-1 or Table 16-2.)

Future Value	Rate	Time	Present Value		Interest	
$25,000	6% compounded annually	9 yr	a. _____		b. _____	
$ 6,000	8% compounded semiannually	12 yr	c. _____		d. _____	
$15,000	9% compounded monthly	4 yr	e. _____		f. _____	
$40,000	6% compounded quarterly	5 yr	g. _____		h. _____	

3 Gary Sharman received a $6,000 bonus from his employer. He can invest it safely in his credit union at 4% compounded quarterly. What will be the value of the investment in 7 years?

4 Martha Butler inherited $26,760. She invested it immediately in an investment fund paying 8% compounded semiannually. How much interest would Martha earn if she left principal and interest invested for 9 years?

5 Toni McSwain was planning to buy a new car in 3 years. She has some money today that she can invest for 3 years in an account that will pay 6% compounded quarterly. How much of it would she need to deposit today so that she will have $8,000 in her account in 3 years?

6 Doug Johnson will need to buy a $25,000 wood lathe in 2 years. He can deposit excess profits from this year in an investment that should pay 9% compounded monthly. If Doug has the $25,000 in 2 years, how much will he earn in interest?

Answers to the Self-Check can be found in Appendix B at the back of the text.

Assignment 16.1: Future Value (Compound Amount)

Name _____

Date _____ Score _____

A **(28 points) Find the future value (compound amount) and the compound interest, as indicated, for each of the following investments. Round answers to the nearest cent. Use a calculator or Table 16-1 to find FVF. (2 points for each correct answer)**

	Present Value	Rate	Term	Future Value	Compound Interest
1.	$6,000	6% compounded monthly	4 years	_____	_____
2.	$960	6% compounded semiannually	11 years	_____	_____
3.	$20,000	8% compounded quarterly	8 years	_____	_____
4.	$12,500	12% compounded annually	30 years	_____	_____
5.	$5,000	9% compounded monthly	18 months	_____	_____
6.	$14,450	6% compounded quarterly	4 years	_____	_____
7.	$4,000	4% compounded semiannually	9 years	_____	_____

Score for A (28) _____

B **(32 points) Find the future value (compound amount) or the compound interest, as indicated, for each of the following investments or loans. Round answers to the nearest cent. Use a calculator or Table 16-1 to find FVF. (4 points for each correct answer)**

8. Compute the future value (compound amount) of $6,200 invested for 12 years at 3% compounded quarterly.

   _____

9. How much compound interest will you pay if you borrow $25,000 for 13 months at 15% compounded monthly?

   _____

10. Calculate the future value (compound amount) on a loan of $38,260 at 8% compounded annually for 13 years.

   _____

11. How much compound interest will you earn if you invest $7,900 for 16.5 years at 12% compounded semiannually?

   _____

12. What total amount (principal and interest) must be repaid in $2\frac{1}{2}$ years on a loan of $15,000 at 9% compounded monthly?

   _____

13. Determine the total compound interest that you will have to pay if you borrow $1,780 at 16% compounded semiannually and don't pay it back for 5 years.

   _____

14. How much compound interest will you earn if you invest $9,650 for 12 years at 5% compounded annually?

   _____

15. Compute the future value (compound amount) of $18,000 invested for 4.5 years at 5% compounded quarterly.

   _____

   _____

   Score for B (32)

C **(40 points) Business Applications. Find the future value (compound amount) or the compound interest, as indicated. Round answers to the nearest cent. Use a calculator or Table 16-1 to find FVF. (4 points for each correct answer)**

16. Steve Wilkins thinks that he needs to borrow $8,800 for 3 years. He doesn't have a very good credit rating, so most finance companies want to charge him a high interest rate. He finally finds a lender that will loan him the money at 9% compounded monthly. How much interest will Steve have to pay to this particular lender?

_____

17. Mary Sousa receives a telephone call from a salesperson who describes "an incredible investment opportunity." The investment promises a return of 16% compounded semiannually for investments of $5,000 or more. One disadvantage is that no money will be paid out for a long time. Another disadvantage is that the investment is very risky. Mary doesn't think that she will need the money for 6 years, so she decides to invest $5,000. If the investment pays what it promises, how much interest will Mary earn in the 6 years?

_____

18. Samuel Tang wants to borrow money from his father to buy a car. Samuel's father is trying to teach him how to manage money, so he agrees to loan him the money, but at 5% compounded quarterly. Samuel borrows $11,200 and repays everything—principal plus all of the interest—in $3\frac{1}{2}$ years. How much does Samuel pay back to his father?

_____

19. Don Hildebrand is trying to decide whether to invest money in a bank or in something a little riskier that will pay a higher return. One very simple investment promises to pay a minimum of 8% compounded annually, but he must leave all of the money and interest invested for 9 years. How much interest will Don earn during the 9 years if he invests $7,150 and the investment pays the minimum?

_____

20. Marcia Juarez and her brother-in-law have a successful business with several employees. They decide to borrow $15,000 to pay their quarterly deposits for payroll taxes and federal income tax. They get the money at 9% compounded monthly and repay all interest and principal after 9 months. How much do they repay?

_____

21. Sammie Crass inherited $16,780. She wants to invest it in something relatively safe so that she can transfer all the money to her children's college fund in about 8 years. One investment brochure (called a prospectus) states that it will pay a return of 8% compounded quarterly. How much will Sammie have in total, principal plus interest, after 8 years?

_____

22. To help his daughter and son-in-law purchase their first new car, David Lo loans them $12,000. They agree on an interest rate of 3% compounded annually, and Mr. Lo tells them that they can pay it all back, the $12,000 plus the interest, in 5 years. How much interest will Mr. Lo receive from them?

_____

23. Sandee Millet owns and operates an art supply store in a suburban shopping center. Sandee learns about an investment that claims to pay a return of 8% compounded semiannually for 4 years. Sandee decides to invest $4,750. Compute the amount of interest that she will earn in the 4 years.

_____

24. Ken Couch is a student at medical school. He borrowed $32,000 for 26 months at the rate of 6% compounded monthly. How much in total, principal plus compound interest, must Ken repay at the end of the 26 months?

_____

25. The County Employees Credit Union pays an interest rate of 8% compounded quarterly on savings accounts of $1,000 or more, with the requirement that the money be deposited for at least 6 months. How much interest will Marilyn Bunnell earn if she deposits $1,800 and leaves it in the credit union for 2 years?

_____

_____

Score for C (40)

Assignment 16.2: Present Value

Name

Date   Score

Learning Objectives **2** **3**

A (28 points) Find the present value (principal) and the compound interest, as indicated, for each of the following investments. (*Hint:* Subtract the present value from the future value to find the compound interest.) Use a calculator or Table 16-1 or Table 16-2 to find FVF or PVF. Round answers to the nearest cent. (2 points for each correct answer)

	Future Value	Rate	Term	Present Value	Compound Interest
1.	$3,900	6% compounded semiannually	3 years	_____	_____
2.	$18,000	6% compounded quarterly	5 years	_____	_____
3.	$23,000	6% compounded annually	11 years	_____	_____
4.	$6,800	9% compounded monthly	4 years	_____	_____
5.	$26,000	8% compounded quarterly	8 years	_____	_____
6.	$50,000	8% compounded semiannually	6 years	_____	_____
7.	$2,500	6% compounded monthly	18 months	_____	_____

Score for A (28)

Chapter 16 Compound Interest **321**

B **(32 points) Find the present value (principal) or the compound interest, as indicated, for each of the following investments or loans. Use a calculator or Table 16-1 or Table 16-2 to find FVF or PVF. Round answers to the nearest cent. (4 points for each correct answer)**

8. Compute the present value (principal) if the future value 16 years from now is $32,000 and if the interest rate is 6% compounded semiannually.

   _____

9. How much compound interest would you pay if you repay a total of $8,425 one and a half years after borrowing the principal at 9% compounded monthly?

   _____

10. Calculate the present value (principal) of a loan made 4 years ago at 12% compounded quarterly if the borrower repays a total of $9,600.

    _____

11. Compute the amount that a company must invest (the present value) at 10% compounded annually if it wants to have $100,000 available (the future value) in 25 years.

    _____

12. How much compound interest is earned on a 6.5-year investment that has a rate of return of 6% compounded quarterly and repays a total compound amount (future value) of $9,600?

    _____

13. Determine the present value (principal) of a single deposit that is worth exactly $4,750 after 15 months at 6% compounded monthly.

    _____

14. Calculate the amount of compound interest that has accrued on an investment that is worth $8,600 after 8 years at 4% compounded semiannually.

    _____

15. Compute the present value (principal) if the future value is $50,000 after 50 years at 6% compounded annually.

_____

_____

Score for B (32)

C **(40 points) Business Applications. Find the present value (principal) or the compound interest, as indicated. Use a calculator or Table 16-1 or Table 16-2 to find FVF or PVF. Round answers to the nearest cent. (4 points for each correct answer)**

16. Bill Starnes needs to buy another used logging truck. His mother will loan him part of the money at 4% compounded quarterly. If Bill estimates that he will be able to repay his mother a total of $27,400 in $1\frac{1}{2}$ years, how much can he borrow from her today?

_____

17. Six years ago, Eleanor Baker invested money at 8% compounded annually. Today she received a check for $6,000 that represented her total payment of principal and interest. Compute the amount of the interest that she earned.

_____

18. John Burnett wants to have $30,000 available at the end of 3 years to help purchase a computerized metal lathe for his machine shop. If John can invest money at 6% compounded semiannually, how much should he invest?

_____

19. As part of their financial planning, Janice Garcia's grandparents made monetary gifts to each of their grandchildren. In addition, Janice's grandfather told her that, if she would save part of her gift for at least a year, he would pay her interest of 9% compounded monthly. Janice decided to save just enough so that she would have $5,000 at the end of 21 months, when she will be 16 years old. How much should she save?

_____

20. Erin Bernstein estimated that she would need $26,000 in $2\frac{1}{2}$ years to buy new equipment for her pottery shop. Having extra cash, she invested money in an extremely safe investment that advertised a return of 4% compounded semiannually. Erin invested just enough money to end up with the $26,000. How much of the $26,000 did Erin earn on her investment?

_____

21. Warren Schulze is a financial advisor. A client would like to have $25,000 in 5 years for possible weddings for her twin daughters who are now 18 years old. After comparing the projected returns with the risk, Warren recommends an investment that will pay 6% compounded quarterly. To end up with the $25,000, how much must the client invest today?

_____

22. A small company estimates that a modest investment today would realize a return of 10% compounded annually. The company wants a total sum of $20,000 in 5 years. If the company invests the appropriate amount to reach the $20,000 objective, how much of the $20,000 will be earned by the investment?

_____

23. Linda Anderson inherited $10,000. She knew that she would need $8,000 in 3 years to pay additional tuition for her children's education. Linda wanted to save enough to have the $8,000 three years from now. She found an incredible, relatively safe investment that would pay 15% compounded monthly for the entire 3 years—if she agreed to leave the money untouched for 3 years. Linda invests just enough of her inheritance to create the $8,000. How much does she have left over from the $10,000?

_____

24. Norman Peterson owns an antique store in the Midwest. He is planning a buying trip to Thailand 15 months from now. Norman estimates the cost of the trip will be $9,000 in 15 months. How much should he set aside today to have $9,000 in 15 months? He can earn 5% compounded quarterly.

_____

25. Technology advances so rapidly that printers for higher-end computer systems are obsolete almost before they come onto the market. Frances Leung thinks that it would be reasonable to budget $2,600 for a high-speed color printer. Frances can make a safe investment paying 12% compounded monthly for 15 months. If she invests the necessary amount of money now, how much of the $2,600 will be paid by the investment at the end of the 15 months?

_____

_____

Score for C (40)

Table 16-1 Future Value (Compound Amount) Factors

Period	0.50%	0.75%	1.00%	1.25%	1.50%	2.00%	3.00%	4.00%	5.00%	6.00%	8.00%	9.00%	10.00%	12.00%
1	1.00500	1.00750	1.01000	1.01250	1.01500	1.02000	1.03000	1.04000	1.05000	1.06000	1.08000	1.09000	1.10000	1.12000
2	1.01003	1.01506	1.02010	1.02516	1.03023	1.04040	1.06090	1.08160	1.10250	1.12360	1.16640	1.18810	1.21000	1.25440
3	1.01508	1.02267	1.03030	1.03797	1.04568	1.06121	1.09273	1.12486	1.15763	1.19102	1.25971	1.29503	1.33100	1.40493
4	1.02015	1.03034	1.04060	1.05095	1.06136	1.08243	1.12551	1.16986	1.21551	1.26248	1.36049	1.41158	1.46410	1.57352
5	1.02525	1.03807	1.05101	1.06408	1.07728	1.10408	1.15927	1.21665	1.27628	1.33823	1.46933	1.53862	1.61051	1.76234
6	1.03038	1.04585	1.06152	1.07738	1.09344	1.12616	1.19405	1.26532	1.34010	1.41852	1.58687	1.67710	1.77156	1.97382
7	1.03553	1.05370	1.07214	1.09085	1.10984	1.14869	1.22987	1.31593	1.40710	1.50363	1.71382	1.82804	1.94872	2.21068
8	1.04071	1.06160	1.08286	1.10449	1.12649	1.17166	1.26677	1.36857	1.47746	1.59385	1.85093	1.99256	2.14359	2.47596
9	1.04591	1.06956	1.09369	1.11829	1.14339	1.19509	1.30477	1.42331	1.55133	1.68948	1.99900	2.17189	2.35795	2.77308
10	1.05114	1.07758	1.10462	1.13227	1.16054	1.21899	1.34392	1.48024	1.62889	1.79085	2.15892	2.36736	2.59374	3.10585
11	1.05640	1.08566	1.11567	1.14642	1.17795	1.24337	1.38423	1.53945	1.71034	1.89830	2.33164	2.58043	2.85312	3.47855
12	1.06168	1.09381	1.12683	1.16075	1.19562	1.26824	1.42576	1.60103	1.79586	2.01220	2.51817	2.81266	3.13843	3.89598
13	1.06699	1.10201	1.13809	1.17526	1.21355	1.29361	1.46853	1.66507	1.88565	2.13293	2.71962	3.06580	3.45227	4.36349
14	1.07232	1.11028	1.14947	1.18995	1.23176	1.31948	1.51259	1.73168	1.97993	2.26090	2.93719	3.34173	3.79750	4.88711
15	1.07768	1.11860	1.16097	1.20483	1.25023	1.34587	1.55797	1.80094	2.07893	2.39656	3.17217	3.64248	4.17725	5.47357
16	1.08307	1.12699	1.17258	1.21989	1.26899	1.37279	1.60471	1.87298	2.18287	2.54035	3.42594	3.97031	4.59497	6.13039
17	1.08849	1.13544	1.18430	1.23514	1.28802	1.40024	1.65285	1.94790	2.29202	2.69277	3.70002	4.32763	5.05447	6.86604
18	1.09393	1.14396	1.19615	1.25058	1.30734	1.42825	1.70243	2.02582	2.40662	2.85434	3.99602	4.71712	5.55992	7.68997
19	1.09940	1.15254	1.20811	1.26621	1.32695	1.45681	1.75351	2.10685	2.52695	3.02560	4.31570	5.14166	6.11591	8.61276
20	1.10490	1.16118	1.22019	1.28204	1.34686	1.48595	1.80611	2.19112	2.65330	3.20714	4.66096	5.60441	6.72750	9.64629
21	1.11042	1.16989	1.23239	1.29806	1.36706	1.51567	1.86029	2.27877	2.78596	3.39956	5.03383	6.10881	7.40025	10.80385
22	1.11597	1.17867	1.24472	1.31429	1.38756	1.54598	1.91610	2.36992	2.92526	3.60354	5.43654	6.65860	8.14027	12.10031
23	1.12155	1.18751	1.25716	1.33072	1.40838	1.57690	1.97359	2.46472	3.07152	3.81975	5.87146	7.25787	8.95430	13.55235
24	1.12716	1.19641	1.26973	1.34735	1.42950	1.60844	2.03279	2.56330	3.22510	4.04893	6.34118	7.91108	9.84973	15.17863
25	1.13280	1.20539	1.28243	1.36419	1.45095	1.64061	2.09378	2.66584	3.38635	4.29187	6.84848	8.62308	10.83471	17.00006

Table 16-1 | Future Value (Compound Amount) Factors (continued)

Period	0.50%	0.75%	1.00%	1.25%	1.50%	2.00%	3.00%	4.00%	5.00%	6.00%	8.00%	9.00%	10.00%	12.00%
26	1.13846	1.21443	1.29526	1.38125	1.47271	1.67342	2.15659	2.77247	3.55567	4.54938	7.39635	9.39916	11.91818	19.04007
27	1.14415	1.22354	1.30821	1.39851	1.49480	1.70689	2.22129	2.88337	3.73346	4.82235	7.98806	10.24508	13.10999	21.32488
28	1.14987	1.23271	1.32129	1.41599	1.51722	1.74102	2.28793	2.99870	3.92013	5.11169	8.62711	11.16714	14.42099	23.88387
29	1.15562	1.24196	1.33450	1.43369	1.53998	1.77584	2.35657	3.11865	4.11614	5.41839	9.31727	12.17218	15.86309	26.74993
30	1.16140	1.25127	1.34785	1.45161	1.56308	1.81136	2.42726	3.24340	4.32194	5.74349	10.06266	13.26768	17.44940	29.95992
31	1.16721	1.26066	1.36133	1.46976	1.58653	1.84759	2.50008	3.37313	4.53804	6.08810	10.86767	14.46177	19.19434	33.55511
32	1.17304	1.27011	1.37494	1.48813	1.61032	1.88454	2.57508	3.50806	4.76494	6.45339	11.73708	15.76333	21.11378	37.58173
33	1.17891	1.27964	1.38869	1.50673	1.63448	1.92223	2.65234	3.64838	5.00319	6.84059	12.67605	17.18203	23.22515	42.09153
34	1.18480	1.28923	1.40258	1.52557	1.65900	1.96068	2.73191	3.79432	5.25335	7.25103	13.69013	18.72841	25.54767	47.14252
35	1.19073	1.29890	1.41660	1.54464	1.68388	1.99989	2.81386	3.94609	5.51602	7.68609	14.78534	20.41397	28.10244	52.79962
36	1.19668	1.30865	1.43077	1.56394	1.70914	2.03989	2.89828	4.10393	5.79182	8.14725	15.96817	22.25123	30.91268	59.13557
37	1.20266	1.31846	1.44508	1.58349	1.73478	2.08069	2.98523	4.26809	6.08141	8.63609	17.24563	24.25384	34.00395	66.23184
38	1.20868	1.32835	1.45953	1.60329	1.76080	2.12230	3.07478	4.43881	6.38548	9.15425	18.62528	26.43668	37.40434	74.17966
39	1.21472	1.33831	1.47412	1.62333	1.78721	2.16474	3.16703	4.61637	6.70475	9.70351	20.11530	28.81598	41.14478	83.08122
40	1.22079	1.34835	1.48886	1.64362	1.81402	2.20804	3.26204	4.80102	7.03999	10.28572	21.72452	31.40942	45.25926	93.05097
41	1.22690	1.35846	1.50375	1.66416	1.84123	2.25220	3.35990	4.99306	7.39199	10.90286	23.46248	34.23627	49.78518	104.21709
42	1.23303	1.36865	1.51879	1.68497	1.86885	2.29724	3.46070	5.19278	7.76159	11.55703	25.33948	37.31753	54.76370	116.72314
43	1.23920	1.37891	1.53398	1.70603	1.89688	2.34319	3.56452	5.40050	8.14967	12.25045	27.36664	40.67611	60.24007	130.72991
44	1.24539	1.38926	1.54932	1.72735	1.92533	2.39005	3.67145	5.61652	8.55715	12.98548	29.55597	44.33696	66.26408	146.41750
45	1.25162	1.39968	1.56481	1.74895	1.95421	2.43785	3.78160	5.84118	8.98501	13.76461	31.92045	48.32729	72.89048	163.98760
46	1.25788	1.41017	1.58046	1.77081	1.98353	2.48661	3.89504	6.07482	9.43426	14.59049	34.47409	52.67674	80.17953	183.66612
47	1.26417	1.42075	1.59626	1.79294	2.01328	2.53634	4.01190	6.31782	9.90597	15.46592	37.23201	57.41765	88.19749	205.70605
48	1.27049	1.43141	1.61223	1.81535	2.04348	2.58707	4.13225	6.57053	10.40127	16.39387	40.21057	62.58524	97.01723	230.39078
49	1.27684	1.44214	1.62835	1.83805	2.07413	2.63881	4.25622	6.83335	10.92133	17.37750	43.42742	68.21791	106.71896	258.03767
50	1.28323	1.45296	1.64463	1.86102	2.10524	2.69159	4.38391	7.10668	11.46740	18.42015	46.90161	74.35752	117.39085	289.00219

Period	0.50%	0.75%	1.00%	1.25%	1.50%	2.00%	3.00%	4.00%	5.00%	6.00%	8.00%	9.00%	10.00%	12.00%
1	0.99502	0.99256	0.99010	0.98765	0.98522	0.98039	0.97087	0.96154	0.95238	0.94340	0.92593	0.91743	0.90909	0.89286
2	0.99007	0.98517	0.98030	0.97546	0.97066	0.96117	0.94260	0.92456	0.90703	0.89000	0.85734	0.84168	0.82645	0.79719
3	0.98515	0.97783	0.97059	0.96342	0.95632	0.94232	0.91514	0.88900	0.86384	0.83962	0.79383	0.77218	0.75131	0.71178
4	0.98025	0.97055	0.96098	0.95152	0.94218	0.92385	0.88849	0.85480	0.82270	0.79209	0.73503	0.70843	0.68301	0.63552
5	0.97537	0.96333	0.95147	0.93978	0.92826	0.90573	0.86261	0.82193	0.78353	0.74726	0.68058	0.64993	0.62092	0.56743
6	0.97052	0.95616	0.94205	0.92817	0.91454	0.88797	0.83748	0.79031	0.74622	0.70496	0.63017	0.59627	0.56447	0.50663
7	0.96569	0.94904	0.93272	0.91672	0.90103	0.87056	0.81309	0.75992	0.71068	0.66506	0.58349	0.54703	0.51316	0.45235
8	0.96089	0.94198	0.92348	0.90540	0.88771	0.85349	0.78941	0.73069	0.67684	0.62741	0.54027	0.50187	0.46651	0.40388
9	0.95610	0.93496	0.91434	0.89422	0.87459	0.83676	0.76642	0.70259	0.64461	0.59190	0.50025	0.46043	0.42410	0.36061
10	0.95135	0.92800	0.90529	0.88318	0.86167	0.82035	0.74409	0.67556	0.61391	0.55839	0.46319	0.42241	0.38554	0.32197
11	0.94661	0.92109	0.89632	0.87228	0.84893	0.80426	0.72242	0.64958	0.58468	0.52679	0.42888	0.38753	0.35049	0.28748
12	0.94191	0.91424	0.88745	0.86151	0.83639	0.78849	0.70138	0.62460	0.55684	0.49697	0.39711	0.35553	0.31863	0.25668
13	0.93722	0.90743	0.87866	0.85087	0.82403	0.77303	0.68095	0.60057	0.53032	0.46884	0.36770	0.32618	0.28966	0.22917
14	0.93256	0.90068	0.86996	0.84037	0.81185	0.75788	0.66112	0.57748	0.50507	0.44230	0.34046	0.29925	0.26333	0.20462
15	0.92792	0.89397	0.86135	0.82999	0.79985	0.74301	0.64186	0.55526	0.48102	0.41727	0.31524	0.27454	0.23939	0.18270
16	0.92330	0.88732	0.85282	0.81975	0.78803	0.72845	0.62317	0.53391	0.45811	0.39365	0.29189	0.25187	0.21763	0.16312
17	0.91871	0.88071	0.84438	0.80963	0.77639	0.71416	0.60502	0.51337	0.43630	0.37136	0.27027	0.23107	0.19784	0.14564
18	0.91414	0.87416	0.83602	0.79963	0.76491	0.70016	0.58739	0.49363	0.41552	0.35034	0.25025	0.21199	0.17986	0.13004
19	0.90959	0.86765	0.82774	0.78976	0.75361	0.68643	0.57029	0.47464	0.39573	0.33051	0.23171	0.19449	0.16351	0.11611
20	0.90506	0.86119	0.81954	0.78001	0.74247	0.67297	0.55368	0.45639	0.37689	0.31180	0.21455	0.17843	0.14864	0.10367
21	0.90056	0.85478	0.81143	0.77038	0.73150	0.65978	0.53755	0.43883	0.35894	0.29416	0.19866	0.16370	0.13513	0.09256
22	0.89608	0.84842	0.80340	0.76087	0.72069	0.64684	0.52189	0.42196	0.34185	0.27751	0.18394	0.15018	0.12285	0.08264
23	0.89162	0.84210	0.79544	0.75147	0.71004	0.63416	0.50669	0.40573	0.32557	0.26180	0.17032	0.13778	0.11168	0.07379
24	0.88719	0.83583	0.78757	0.74220	0.69954	0.62172	0.49193	0.39012	0.31007	0.24698	0.15770	0.12640	0.10153	0.06588
25	0.88277	0.82961	0.77977	0.73303	0.68921	0.60953	0.47761	0.37512	0.29530	0.23300	0.14602	0.11597	0.09230	0.05882

Table 16-2 | Present Value Factors

Table 16-2   Present Value Factors (continued)

Period	0.50%	0.75%	1.00%	1.25%	1.50%	2.00%	3.00%	4.00%	5.00%	6.00%	8.00%	9.00%	10.00%	12.00%
26	0.87838	0.82343	0.77205	0.72398	0.67902	0.59758	0.46369	0.36069	0.28124	0.21981	0.13520	0.10639	0.08391	0.05252
27	0.87401	0.81730	0.76440	0.71505	0.66899	0.58586	0.45019	0.34682	0.26785	0.20737	0.12519	0.09761	0.07628	0.04689
28	0.86966	0.81122	0.75684	0.70622	0.65910	0.57437	0.43708	0.33348	0.25509	0.19563	0.11591	0.08955	0.06934	0.04187
29	0.86533	0.80518	0.74934	0.69750	0.64936	0.56311	0.42435	0.32065	0.24295	0.18456	0.10733	0.08215	0.06304	0.03738
30	0.86103	.079919	0.74192	0.68889	0.63976	0.55207	0.41199	0.30832	0.23138	0.17411	0.09938	0.07537	0.05731	0.03338
31	0.85675	0.79324	0.73458	0.68038	0.63031	0.54125	0.39999	0.29646	0.22036	0.16425	0.09202	0.06915	0.05210	0.02980
32	0.85248	0.78733	0.72730	0.67198	0.62099	0.53063	0.38834	0.28506	0.20987	0.15496	0.08520	0.06344	0.04736	0.02661
33	0.84824	0.78147	0.72010	0.66369	0.61182	0.52023	0.37703	0.27409	0.19987	0.14619	0.07889	0.05820	0.04306	0.02376
34	0.84402	0.77565	0.71297	0.65549	0.60277	0.51003	0.36604	0.26355	0.19035	0.13791	0.07305	0.05339	0.03914	0.02121
35	0.83982	0.76988	0.70591	0.64740	0.59387	0.50003	0.35538	0.25342	0.18129	0.13011	0.06763	0.04899	0.03558	0.01894
36	0.83564	0.76415	0.69892	0.63941	0.58509	0.49022	0.34503	0.24367	0.17266	0.12274	0.06262	0.04494	0.03235	0.01691
37	0.83149	0.75846	0.69200	0.63152	0.57644	0.48061	0.33498	0.23430	0.16444	0.11579	0.05799	0.04123	0.02941	0.01510
38	0.82735	0.75281	0.68515	0.62372	0.56792	0.47119	0.32523	0.22529	0.15661	0.10924	0.05369	0.03783	0.02673	0.01348
39	0.82323	0.74721	0.67837	0.61602	0.55953	0.46195	0.31575	0.21662	0.14915	0.10306	0.04971	0.03470	0.02430	0.01204
40	0.81914	0.74165	0.67165	0.60841	0.55126	0.45289	0.30656	0.20829	0.14205	0.09722	0.04603	0.03184	0.02209	0.01075
41	0.81506	0.73613	0.66500	0.60090	0.54312	0.44401	0.29763	0.20028	0.13528	0.09172	0.04262	0.02921	0.02009	0.00960
42	0.81101	0.73065	0.65842	0.59348	0.53509	0.43530	0.28896	0.19257	0.12884	0.08653	0.03946	0.02680	0.01826	0.00857
43	0.80697	0.72521	0.65190	0.58616	0.52718	0.42677	0.28054	0.18517	0.12270	0.08163	0.03654	0.02458	0.01660	0.00765
44	0.80296	0.71981	0.64545	0.57892	0.51939	0.41840	0.27237	0.17805	0.11686	0.07701	0.03383	0.02255	0.01509	0.00683
45	0.79896	0.71445	0.63905	0.57177	0.51171	0.41020	0.26444	0.17120	0.11130	0.07265	0.03133	0.02069	0.01372	0.00610
46	0.79499	0.70913	0.63273	0.56471	0.50415	0.40215	0.25674	0.16461	0.10600	0.06854	0.02901	0.01898	0.01247	0.00544
47	0.79103	0.70385	0.62646	0.55774	0.49670	0.39427	0.24926	0.15828	0.10095	0.06466	0.02686	0.01742	0.01134	0.00486
48	0.78710	0.69861	0.62026	0.55086	0.48936	0.38654	0.24200	0.15219	0.09614	0.06100	0.02487	0.01598	0.01031	0.00434
49	0.78318	0.69341	0.61412	0.54406	0.48213	0.37896	0.23495	0.14634	0.09156	0.05755	0.02303	0.01466	0.00937	0.00388
50	0.77929	0.68825	0.60804	0.53734	0.47500	0.37153	0.22811	0.14071	0.08720	0.05429	0.02132	0.01345	0.00852	0.00346

Appendix A: Answers to Odd-Numbered Problems

Chapter 1

Assignment 1.1

1. $2\frac{1}{6}$

3. 6

5. $1\frac{10}{13}$

7. $\frac{37}{10}$

9. $\frac{21}{8}$

11. $\frac{33}{5}$

13. $\frac{2}{5}$

15. $\frac{3}{5}$

17. $\frac{2}{3}$

19. $\frac{7}{10}$

21. $\frac{15}{18}$

23. $\frac{15}{24}$

25. $\frac{15}{35}$

27. $\frac{36}{45}$

29. $\frac{10}{10} = 1$

31. $3\frac{17}{12} = 4\frac{5}{12}$

33. $7\frac{12}{6} = 9$

35. $6\frac{58}{45} = 7\frac{13}{45}$

37. $1\frac{2}{12} = 1\frac{1}{6}$

39. $1\frac{8}{12} = 1\frac{2}{3}$

41. $1\frac{17}{20}$

43. $2\frac{17}{30}$

45. $8\frac{5}{12}$ qt

47. $\frac{7}{8}$ in.

Assignment 1.2

1. $\frac{1}{6}$

3. $\frac{5}{8}$

5. 7

7. $6\frac{3}{4}$

9. $1\frac{1}{6}$

11. $1\frac{7}{8}$

13. $1\frac{3}{7}$

15. $4\frac{1}{6}$

17. $13\frac{1}{3}$ cu yd

19. $1\frac{1}{2}$ qt

21. $14\frac{2}{3}$ times

Chapter 2

Assignment 2.1

1. 0.0613
3. 0.64
5. 860.00098
7. three hundred eight and ninety-seven hundredths
9. five hundred ninety-two and three tenths
11. forty-two and four hundred eighty-one ten-thousandths
13. one thousand seven and four tenths
15. 49.0 mi
17. 374.3 lb

19. 6.4 oz
21. $0.10
23. $8.10
25. $53.00
27. 0.005 gal
29. 8.186 in.
31. 0.200 lb
33. $0.16
35. $2.10
37. $0.66
39. 22.2363
41. 104.4996
43. 29.281
45. 249.202
47. 0.364
49. 17.415
51. 3.682
53. 0.4095
55. 0.176
57. 1.677

Assignment 2.2

1. $1,311.58
3. $338.52
5. 79.3354
7. 79.9969128
9. $1.85
11. $45.25
13. 6.12
15. 62.5
17. 470
19. 0.632
21. $21,723.00
23. $720.00
25. $0.43
27. c. 0.04
29. c. 28
31. b. 0.048
33. c. 270
35. d. 120,000
37. a. 0.004
39. b. 1.2
41. a. 70

Assignment 2.3

1. 8.25 ft
3. 16.85 mi
5. $302.13
7. $720
9. $125
11. $0.67
13. 23.6 gal

Chapter 3

Assignment 3.1

1. $25,600
3. AUTO
5. $47.40
7. $44.85
9. 10
11. $400
13. $310
15. $21
17. $62.50
19. $114
21. 22
23. 385
25. 7
27. 3
29. 3
31. **a.** 30, 25
    b. 46, 41
    c. 66, 60
33. **a.** 25, 5
    b. 9, 3
    c. 100, 20

Assignment 3.2

1. $1.44
3. $6.12
5. 103 lb
7. $1.50
9. 1,170 mi
11. $23.88
13. $79.92
15. $14.85
17. $23.70
19. $760
21. $801
23. $799.60
25. $240
27. $55.79
29. $89.40
31. 6 + 4 + 2 = 17 − 5
33. 9 − 3 − 1 = 2 + 3
35. 20 + 1 + 2 = 16 + 7
37. 12 + 3 − 3 = 7 + 5
39. 64 − 32 − 8 = 8 + 16

Chapter 4

Assignment 4.1

Prefix	Symbol	Value
kilo	k	1000
centi	c	0.01
deci	d	0.1
deka	da	10
milli	m	0.001

3. **a.** 4000
   b. 0.04
   c. 40000
   d. 5000
   e. 5000000
5. **a.** meters
   b. 54.9 m
7. **a.** 88 km/h
   b. 56 km/h
9. **a.** 0.78 inch
   b. 1.17 inches
   c. 1.56 inches
11. **a.** kiloliter (kL)
    b. liter (L)
    c. milliliter (mL)
    d. liter (L)
    e. kiloliter (kL)

Assignment 4.2

1. $2.36
3. 60.56 L
5. 12¢
7. **a.** kilogram (kg)
   b. gram (g)
   c. metric ton (t)
   d. kilogram (kg)
   e. milligram (mg)
9. $0.73 per kg; $1.17 per kg
11. 11906 g or 11.906 kg
13. **a.** liter
    b. kilogram
    c. gram
    d. milliliter
    e. gram

Chapter 5

Assignment 5.1

1. 0.31
3. 0.0333
5. 300%
7. 15%
9. 175%
11. 2.245
13. 52%
15. 8.25%
17. 400%
19. 0.0001
21. 0.21
23. 11.17
25. 0.34
27. $0.29
29. $1.65
31. 16
33. 75
35. 0.96
37. 20%
39. 200%
41. $1.20
43. 150%
45. $48
47. $8,000
49. 56
51. 480
53. 40%
55. $21.00
57. 160%
59. 25

Assignment 5.2

1. 210
3. 30
5. $8,320
7. 544
9. $170
11. 16%
13. 25%
15. 20%
17. (25); (4.6%)
19. +230; +12.7%
21. (1,318); (8.9%)
23. +156; +14.6%
25. +310; +17.2%
27. ($63.53); (9.4%)
29. +55.60; +14.9%
31. +22.74; +15.0%
33. +193.39; +4.0%
35. +259.01; +5.8%

Assignment 5.3

1. 220
3. 6,500
5. 38%
7. 280,000
9. $720
11. $3,250
13. $52,942
15. 10%
17. $62,500
19. 100%

Assignment 5.4

1. **a.** 1,200; 16%; $2,400
   b. 1,800; 24%; 3,600
   c. 2,100; 28%; 4,200
   d. 2,400; 32%; 4,800
3. $6,400; $3,200; $4,800;
   $5,600
5. $8,840; $6,760; $4,940;
   $5,460

Chapter 6

Assignment 6.1
1. $6,760; $6,760
3. $2,100; $5,850
5. $3,840; $5,640
7. $6,420
9. $7,100
11. $4,900
13. $1,152; $36,997
15. $504; $7,612
17. $987; $12,841
19. $539; $5,634
21. $388; $5,456

Assignment 6.2
1. $6,275
3. $3,750
5. $2,620
7. $1,834.20
9. $1,205
11. $10,800

Chapter 7

Assignment 7.1
1. $441; $819
3. $2,120; $6,360
5. 80%; $5,592
7. $720; $420; —; $1,260
9. 60%; 80%; —; $864
11. 70%; 80%; 95%; 46.8%
13. $466

Assignment 7.2
1. June 1; June 21; $86.25; $2,788.87
3. Sept. 4; Oct. 4; $6.75; $443.25
5. Apr. 8; 98%; $570.85
7. $625.00; $356.94

Chapter 8

Assignment 8.1
1. $655.95
3. $455.48
5. $280.99
7. $340; $1,190
9. $1,050; $2,550
11. $480; $1,120
13. $2,250; $4,750
15. 160%; $775
17. 220%; $50
19. 135%; $440

21. 150%; $1,500
23. $1,575; $3,675
25. $1,116; 55%

Assignment 8.2
1. $149.49
3. $1,819
5. $37.49
7. $66; $54
9. $144; $216
11. $999; $999
13. $494.40; $329.60
15. 60%; $1,425
17. 55%; $260
19. 70%; $3,600
21. 65%; $820
23. $174; $174
25. $72.96; 60%

Chapter 9

Assignment 9.1
1. 585.00; 4,782.50; 3,262.50; 2,272.50; 2,207.20; 1,917.50; 5,762.75; 5,636.33; 4,671.33; 4,021.33
3. 1,190.85; 1,190.85; 1,190.85; 878.05
5. 877.76; 3,037.76; 3,037.76; 1,837.49
7. $1,669.35
9. 2,141.70; 1,993.50; 2,970.30; 2,156.30; $1,871.13
11. 3,020.10; 2,754.38; 2,668.68; 3,604.30; $2,374.16

Assignment 9.2
1. 802.50; 752.90; 678.71; 904.21; 791.89; 758.56; 746.56; 678.79; 466.79; 328.79; 422.79
3. a. $728.47 b. $1,630.27
   c. $951.41 d. $737.40
   e. $664.68

Assignment 9.3
1. Cogswell Cooling, Inc.
   Reconciliation of Bank Statement, November 30

Checkbook balance	$ 480.77
Minus unrecorded bank charges:	
Service charge	− 9.50
	$ 471.27
Plus bank interest credit	+ 12.00
Adjusted checkbook balance	$ 483.27
Bank balance on statement	$1,050.82

Minus outstanding checks:

No. 148	$ 13.90	
No. 156	235.10	
No. 161	96.35	
No. 165	$222.20	−567.55
Adjusted bank balance		$ 483.27

3. Linberg Floors
   Reconciliation of Bank Statement, May 31

Checkbook balance		$19,512.54
Plus bank interest credited		+ 35.20
		$19,547.74
Minus unrecorded bank charges:		
ATM withdrawal	$ 80.00	
Service charge	$ 18.00	
Automatic transfer— insurance	1,765.00	
Returned check	920.00	
Debit card charges	444.90	−3,227.90
Adjusted checkbook balance		$16,319.84
Bank balance on statement		$17,595.26
Plus deposit not recorded by bank		+2,004.35
		$19,599.61

Minus outstanding checks:

No. 730	$ 85.17	
No. 749	1,216.20	
No. 753	462.95	
No. 757	512.80	
No. 761	19.75	
No. 768	982.90	−3,279.77
Adjusted bank balance		$16,319.84

Chapter 10

Assignment 10.1
1. $512.00; $153.60; $25.60; $691.20
   624.00; —; —; 624.00
   540.00; 162.00; 54.00; 756.00
   720.00; 162.00; —; 882.00
   696.00; —; —; 696.00
   540.00; —; —; 540.00
   512.00; 134.40; —; 646.40
   480.00; 18.00; —; 498.00
   720.00; 216.00; 36.00; 972.00
   540.00; —; —; 540.00
   512.00; 57.60; —; 569.60
   696.00; 208.80; 69.60; 974.40
   $7,092.00; $1,112.40; $185.20; $8,389.60
3. $2,868.33
5. $639.54
7. $7.96; $8.00; $0.04
9. $59.98; $60.00; $0.02

Assignment 10.2

1. $596.00; $596.00; $36.95;
$8.64; $64.00; $124.50;
$471.41
568.00; 2; 21.30; 42.60;
610.60; 37.86; 8.85;
32.00; 90.71; 519.89
432.00; 432.00; 26.78; 6.26;
51.00; 96.04; 335.96
600.00; 600.00; 37.20; 8.70;
24.00; 87.90; 512.10
620.00; 5; 23.25; 116.25;
736.25; 45.65; 10.68;
50.00; 124.33; 611.92
592.00; 3; 22.20; 66.60;
658.60; 40.83; 9.55; 22.00;
90.38; 568.22
580.00; 580.00; 35.96; 8.41;
63.00; 119.37; 460.63
720.00; 2; 27.00; 54.00;
774.00; 47.99; 11.22;
27.00; 98.21; 675.79
672.00; 672.00; 41.66;
9.74; 51.00; 117.40;
554.60
$5,380.00; $279.45;
$5,659.45; $350.88;
$82.05; $384.00; $948.93;
$4,710.52

3. $36.93; $8.64; $53.80;
$104.37; $491.28
38.44; 8.99; 57.46; 109.89;
510.11
34.10; 7.98; 46.96; 94.04;
455.96
39.42; 9.22; 59.83; 113.47;
522.33
34.10; 7.98; 46.96; 94.04;
455.96
37.09; 8.67; 54.20; 104.96;
493.31
38.44; 8.99; 57.46; 109.89;
510.11
37.05; 8.66; 54.08; 104.79;
492.71
42.04; 9.83; 66.16; 123.03;
554.97
40.30; 9.43; 61.96; 116.69;
533.31
36.14; 8.45; 51.89; 101.48;
481.42
38.44; 8.99; 57.46; 109.89;
510.11
34.10; 7.98; 46.96;
94.04, 455.96

$486.59; $113.81; $715.18;
$1,380.58; $6,467.54

5. **a.** $22,528.40
b. $1,396.75
c. $326.67
d. $2,500.95
e. $4,224.37

7. **a.** $19,500;
$7,000
b. $56
c. $378
d. $434

Chapter 11

Assignment 11.1

1. $0.59; $8.96; $1.04
0.16; 2.51; 2.50
2.44; 37.29; 2.71
1.37; 20.93; 4.07
0.36; 5.48; 4.52
1.16; 17.66; 2.34
1.30; 19.85; 0.15
0.07; 1.05; 0.20
0.70; 10.68; 4.32
1.24; 19.02; 0.98

3. $106.26

5. **a.** Discount Carpets
b. $312

Assignment 11.2

1. **a.** $625,000,000
b. $732,997,500
c. $361,760,000

3. $1.30
$0.98

5. $2,565

7. $539.75

9. 1.7% (0.017)
1.5% (0.015)
1.35% (0.0135)
2.0% (0.02)

11. $1,392

Assignment 11.3

1. **a.** $19,350
b. $29,450
c. $16,000
d. $7,102
e. $10,400

3. **a.** $15,600
b. $1,560

5. **a.** $33,600
b. $4,203

Chapter 12

Assignment 12.1

1. **a.** $960
b. $220
c. $1,650
d. $1,430

3. **a.** $3,600
b. $2,400
c. $279
d. $3,600

5. **a.** $53,340
b. $50,000
c. $6,000
d. $3,440
e. $56,000

Assignment 12.2

1. **a.** $3,724
b. $2,793
c. $558.60

3. $200,000

5. **a.** $165,000
b. $55,000
c. $180,000
d. $120,000

7. $360,000

Assignment 12.3

1. $19.30; $3,860.00
$8.26; $2,643.20
$27.04; $540.80
$4.91; $2,356.80
$16.83; $3,366.00
$53.86; $4,578.10

3. $5,120

5. **a.** $9,050
b. $9,500
c. $6,545

7. **a.** $970
b. $1,896

Chapter 13

Assignment 13.1

1. $30.00
3. $48.00
5. $187.50
7. $2,240.00
9. $130.00
11. $48.00; $47.34; $0.66
13. $480.00; $473.42; $6.58
15. $375.00; $369.86; $5.14
17. $9.65; $9.25; $0.40

19. $60.32; $60.00; $0.32
21. $4,800
23. 8%
25. 225 days
27. $91.80
29. 7.5%

Assignment 13.2
1. $12.75
$862.75
3. $90
$3,690
5. $2,080
$62,080
7. $924.66
$45,924.66
9. $67.81
$5,067.81

Chapter 14

Assignment 14.1
1. **a.** 1.5%
b. 1.25%
c. 0.3%
d. 0.6%
e. 0.5%
f. 0.4%
g. 0.75%
h. 0.7%
i. 1%
j. 0.8%
3. $29.34; $1,748.68
5. $45.15; $1,151.95
7. $1,690.26; $23.63; $993.55
9. $1,098.40; $12.23;
$1,783.02
11. $790.12; $9.15; $1,571.62

Assignment 14.2
1. $36; $1,636;
$3,200
3,200; 24; 1,624;
1,600
1,600; 12; 1,612
3. $36; $1,636;
$3,200
3,200; 36; 1,636;
1,600
1,600; 36; 1,636
5. **a.** $3,200
b. $115.50
c. 14.4%

7. **a.** $3,200
b. $108
c. 13.5%

Assignment 14.3
1. $204.82550; $3,686.86
3. $6.48957; $1,784.63
5. $253.76122
7. 4,513.43; 27.08;
1,495.49; 3,017.94
9. 1,513.48; 9.08;
1,513.48; 1,522.56
11. 4,836.00; 29.02; 1,170.98;
3,665.02
13. 2,487.01; 14.92; 2,487.01;
2,501.93
15. 159,769.12; 798.85;
232.03; 159,537.09

Chapter 15

Assignment 15.1
1. 189
3. 94
5. 152
7. January 5, 2015
9. December 2, 2015
11. April 7, 2015
13. Jan. 9, 2014; $403.00;
$26,403.00
15. Oct. 29, 2012; $583.92;
$36,333.92
17. 125; $730.07; $42,530.07
19. Sept. 10, 2012; $2,115.62;
$54,115.62

Assignment 15.2
1. $31.25
$2,531.25
May 15
32
$24.75
$2,506.50
3. $0
$4,500
Jan. 22
39
$48.75
$4,451.25
5. $71.01
$3,671.01
July 19
44

$57.53
$3,613.48
7. $0
$4,000
Oct. 15
45
$49.32
$3,950.68

Assignment 15.3
1. $250; $7,250; 10.34%
3. $825; $15,675; 12.63%
5. $27.18; $952.82; 7.71%
7. $100.00; 20; $26.85;
$73.15
9. $407.19; 33; $254.48;
$152.71
11. $92.00; 30; $71.87;
$20.13
13. $650.00; 20; $118.07;
$531.93

Chapter 16

Assignment 16.1
1. $7,622.94; $1,622.94
3. $37,690.80; $17,690.80
5. $5,719.80; $719.80
7. $5,713.00; $1,713.00
9. $4,381.50
11. $46,140.66
13. $2,062.88
15. $22,510.44
17. $7,590.85
19. $7,142.85
21. $31,622.58
23. $1,750.71
25. $308.99

Assignment 16.2
1. $3,266.17; $633.83
3. $12,116.17; $10,883.83
5. $13,796.38; $12,203.62
7. $2,285.35; $214.65
9. $1,060.20
11. $9,230.00
13. $4,407.62
15. $2,714.50
17. $2,218.98
19. $4,273.90
21. $18,561.75
23. $4,884.72
25. $360.49

Appendix B: Answers to Self-Check Review Problems

Chapter 1

1. $\dfrac{17}{6}$
2. $7\dfrac{1}{2}$
3. $\dfrac{6}{7}$
4. $\dfrac{40}{56}$
5. $1\dfrac{17}{30}$
6. $1\dfrac{19}{24}$
7. $7\dfrac{11}{20}$
8. $\dfrac{7}{15}$
9. $1\dfrac{17}{18}$
10. $1\dfrac{34}{45}$
11. $\dfrac{2}{7}$
12. $1\dfrac{1}{20}$
13. $2\dfrac{1}{3}$
14. $2\dfrac{1}{4}$
15. $2\dfrac{1}{10}$
16. $1\dfrac{1}{5}$
17. $8\dfrac{1}{4}$ qt
18. $2\dfrac{1}{12}$ ft
19. $6\dfrac{1}{8}$ tbsp
20. 9 pieces; $\dfrac{1}{3}$ in.

Chapter 2

1. 116.0014
2. six thousand four hundred thirty-one and seven hundred nineteen thousandths
3. 3.5
4. $12.67
5. 743.64475
6. 20.807
7. 2.717
8. 122.4881
9. 1.797726
10. $443.39
11. 3.23
12. $0.74
13. 8,649.30, or 8,649.3
14. $2.76
15. d. 500
16. c. $0.80
17. $3,825.75
18. $281,971.57
19. 590.8 cubic feet
20. 21.88 cu yd

Chapter 3

1. $35.94
2. $7.44
3. $47.76
4. $80.80
5. $31,256
6. $43,244
7. 427 miles
8. $400
9. $404.25
10. $250
11. 23 hours
12. 19 hours
13. 300
14. 8
15. 156
16. 3
17. 3
18. 13
19. 20
20. $2.00; $0.01

Chapter 4

1. decimal; 10
2. a. G; billion or 1,000,000
   b. d; one tenth or 1/10
   c. k; thousand or 1,000
3. 12
4. 720
5. 25.744
6. 12.7
7. 45.948
8. 50
9. 4.488
10. 15.855
11. $3.125 per kilogram
12. 7.666
13. 1.892
14. 1 700.964
15. 78.74 inches;
    118.11 inches;
    157.48 inches

Chapter 5

1. 0.1475
2. 62.5%
3. 1.5
4. $\dfrac{3}{4}$%
5. 0.0006
6. 40%
7. 11.2
8. 150
9. 180
10. 70
11. 87.5%
12. 160%
13. $120,000
14. $96,000
15. 100%
16. 50%
17. 1,625 rose bushes
18. 225%
19. $3,440
20. 64%

Chapter 6

1. a. $3,480
   b. $6,480
2. a. $4,300
   b. $6,800
3. a. $3,114
   b. $6,714
4. a. $6,926
   b. $6,926
5. $6,000
6. $2,550
7. $7,750
8. $3,300
9. $1,400
10. $6,900

11. $3,750
12. $5,500
13. $8,550
14. $33,910
15. $3,210
16. $25,256

Chapter 7

1. a. $190
   b. $570
2. a. $360
   b. $168
   c. $672
3. a. 60%
   b. $525
4. a. 70%
   b. 85%
   c. $1,071
5. a. 60%
   b. 80%
   c. 90%
   d. 56.8%
6. a. Aug. 4
   b. Aug. 24
   c. $17.49
   d. $857.06
7. a. Jan. 2
   b. Feb. 11
   c. 97%
   d. $1,787.15
8. a. $10,204.08
   b. $6,335.92

Chapter 8

1. a. $43.35
   b. $211.83
   c. $1,570
   d. $572.63
2. a. $250
   b. $750
3. a. $23.40
   b. $59.40
4. a. 160%
   b. $360
5. a. 175%
   b. $420
6. a. 200%
   b. $506
7. a. 140%
   b. $70
8. a. $300
   b. 125%

9. a. $400
   b. 25%
10. a. $72
    b. $168
11. a. $36
    b. $108
12. a. 60%
    b. $744
13. a. 25%
    b. $132
14. a. 40%
    b. $2,400
15. a. 75%
    b. $48
16. a. $320
    b. 40%
17. a. $2,250
    b. 60%
18. a. $10
    b. 25%
    c. 20%

Chapter 9

1. a. B
   b. D
   c. A
   d. D
   e. C
   f. C
   g. D
   h. D
   i. D
2. Bank Balance $10,961.65
   + Deposit
     in transit   1,850.15
     Subtotal   12,811.80
   − O/S checks   342.90
   Adj. Bank
     Balance $12,468.90
   Book Balance $12,583.40
   + Interest   52.50
   + Error   3.00
   Subtotal   12,638.90
   − Svc Chg   20.00
   − NSF CK   150.00
   Adj. Book
     Balance $12,468.90

Chapter 10

1. a. Gross pay = $950.00
   b. Social Security = $ 58.90
        Medicare = $ 13.78

   c. FIT withheld = $135.11
   d. Net pay = $742.21
2. a. Percentage
      method = $ 37.01
      Wage-bracket
      method = $ 38.00
   b. Percentage
      method = $ 53.88
      Wage-bracket
      method = $ 54.00
3. Jan. $1,260.35;
   Feb. $1,198.35;
   Mar. $888.35
4. Social Security, $7,688;
   Medicare, $1,798,
   Federal income tax,
   $7,800; Total,
   $17,286
5. Social Security, $440.20;
   Medicare, $142.10;
   Total, $582.30
6. $614.08; $868.00;
   $464.40

Chapter 11

1. Choose A because the cost
   is less than B.
2. a. 1.5%
   b. $2,100; $1,161
3. a. $443.50
   b. 295.67
4. $27,300
5. $17,000 (5 exemptions ×
   $3,400)
6. Standard deduction
7. $23,350 ($38,000 − $7,850
   − $6,800)
8. $9,098 ($8,772.50 + 25% of
   excess over $63,700)

Chapter 12

1. Jim's insurance pays $5,300,
   Jim's medical expenses.
   Joshua's insurance
   pays -0-.
2. $313.20
3. $2,695
4. $29.250
5. $30,000
6. $4,389
7. $3,255
8. $1,440

Chapter 13

1. a. $75.60
   b. $74.56
   c. $1.04
2. a. $140.00
   b. $138.08
   c. $1.92
3. a. $114.94
   b. $120.00
   c. $5.06
4. a. $58.98
   b. $60.00
   c. $1.02
5. $1,500
6. 5%
7. 270 days
8. $2,512.50
9. $289.97

Chapter 14

1. a. 9.0%
   b. 7.5%
   c. 14.4%
   d. 4.8%
2. a. 0.5%
   b. 1.25%
   c. 1.1%
   d. 0.8%
3. a. $26.72
   b. $2,387.35
4. a. $30.00
   b. $1,030.00
   c. $2,000.00
   d. $2,000.00

   e. $20.00
   f. $1,020.00
   g. $1,000.00
   h. $1,000.00
   i. $10.00
   j. $1,010.00
5. 12%
6. $1,619.56
7. a. $24.00
   b. $992.04
   c. $2,007.96
   d. $2,007.96
   e. $16.06
   f. $999.98
   g. $1,007.98
   h. $1,007.98
   i. $8.06
   j. $1,007.98
   k. $1,016.04

Chapter 15

1. a. Mar. 12, 2014
   b. $3,463.75
2. a. 153 days
   b. $5,730.90
3. a. Jan. 7, 2015
   b. $15,255.21
4. a. 120 days
   b. $3,043.68
5. a. $77.85
   b. $3,037.85
   c. September 12
   d. 59 days
   e. $73.66
   f. $2,964.19

6. a. $3,100
   b. February 8
   c. 60 days
   d. $61.15
   e. $3,038.85
7. a. $135.00
   b. $4,365
   c. 9.28%
8. a. $32.00
   b. 20 days
   c. $8.59
   d. $23.41

Chapter 16

1. a. $4,786.72
   b. $786.72
   c. $20,892.24
   d. $8,892.24
   e. $137,849.10
   f. $107,849.10
   g. $21,226.40
   h. $13,226.40
2. a. $14,797.50
   b. $10,202.50
   c. $2,340.72
   d. $3,659.28
   e. $10,479.15
   f. $4,520.85
   g. $29,698.80
   h. $10,301.20
3. $7,927.74
4. $27,450.94
5. $6,691.12
6. $4,104.25

Appendix C: Fundamental Concepts

This appendix is a reference for some of the fundamental concepts and vocabulary of basic mathematics for whole numbers. The concepts and vocabulary of fractions and decimals are contained in Chapters 1 and 2 of the text. Many students may remember some or all of this material from elementary school. This is not a complete review or set of instructions. It is a reminder of what you studied in earlier classes.

Adding pairs of one-digit numbers

The basis of all arithmetic is adding two one-digit numbers such as $5 + 3 = 8$, or $6 + 7 = 13$. The numbers being added are all called **addends**. The result is called the **total**, or the **sum**. You can have several addends, each with multiple digits, such as examples A, B, and C. After addition, subtraction is the reverse of addition; multiplication is "repeated addition;" and division is the reverse of multiplication. In all mathematics, it is useful to recognize the various combinations of digits that add up to 10. Below are some examples:

$$
\begin{array}{cccccccccccc}
1 & 2 & 3 & 4 & 5 & 1 & 1 & 1 & 1 & 2 & 2 & 2 & 3 \\
+9 & +8 & +7 & +6 & +5 & 1 & 2 & 3 & 4 & 2 & 3 & 4 & 3 \\
\hline
10 & 10 & 10 & 10 & 10 & +8 & +7 & +6 & +5 & +6 & +5 & +4 & +4 \\
& & & & & \hline & \hline & \hline & \hline & \hline & \hline & \hline & \hline \\
& & & & & 10 & 10 & 10 & 10 & 10 & 10 & 10 & 10
\end{array}
$$

Interpreting whole numbers with more than one digit

The number 346 is read "three hundred forty-six." Three hundred, written as 300, is 3×100. Forty, written as 40, is 4×10. In mathematics, 346 means $3 \times 100 + 4 \times 10 + 6$.

The column of the digit indicates its value. Starting from the right end of 346, the digit 6 represents the number 6 because 6 is in the "ones column" or "units column" and "6 ones equals 6." Next is the digit 4, which represents the number 40 because 4 is in the "tens column" and "4 tens equals 40." Finally, the digit 3 represents the number 300 because 3 is in the "hundreds column" and "3 hundreds equals 300."

Adding whole numbers containing more than one digit

To add two or more whole numbers, write them neatly, aligned in columns, starting with the right column of each number. Then add each column, from right to left. Examine example A. The steps of the solution are shown in Figures A-1, A-2, A-3, and A-4. The final answer is 689.

EXAMPLE A

Add 215, 42 and 432.

$$
\begin{array}{cccc}
215 & 215 & 215 & 215 \\
42 & 42 & 42 & 42 \\
+432 & +432 & +432 & +432 \\
\hline
 & 9 & 89 & 689 \\
\text{Fig. A-1} & \text{Fig. A-2} & \text{Fig. A-3} & \text{Fig. A-4}
\end{array}
$$

"Carrying" a digit to the next column to the left

In example A, each column had a total with only one digit. Most often, some columns may have a total with more than one digit. In that case, you must "carry" one digit over to the next column to the left. It may be helpful to write that digit above the next column. In example B, every column has a total with more than a single digit.

Add 365, 51, and 797.

$$
\begin{array}{cccc}
 & \overset{1}{} & \overset{2\,1}{} & \overset{2\,1}{} \\
365 & 365 & 365 & 365 \\
51 & 51 & 51 & 51 \\
\underline{+797} & \underline{+797} & \underline{+797} & \underline{+797} \\
 & 3 & 13 & 1{,}213
\end{array}
$$

Fig. B-1   Fig. B-2   Fig. B-3   Fig. B-4

In Fig. B-2, the sum of the ones column is 13; write 3 in the ones column and "carry 1" to the tens column. In Fig. B-3, the sum of the tens column is 21; write 1 in the tens column and "carry 2" to the hundreds column. In Fig. B-4, the sum of the hundreds column is 12; write 2 in the hundreds column and 1 in the thousands column.

Checking your answer in addition

The simplest way to check your answer in addition is to add the numbers again, but in the opposite direction. In the example B, we added *down*. To check, we can add from the bottom *up*. In the ones column, adding up, $7 + 1 + 5 = 13$; and so on. The total will be the same: 1,213.

Another way to check is by adding each column separately and then using the place value of each column.

Ones column: $5 + 1 + 7 = 13$. And 13 ones = 13.

Tens column: $6 + 5 + 9 = 20$. And 20 tens = 20×10, or 200.

Hundreds column: $3 + 7 = 10$. And 10 hundreds = 10×100, or 1,000.

The final total is $1{,}000 + 200 + 13 = 1{,}213$, which checks.

Adding and checking addition of numbers arranged in tables

Very often in business, numbers will be organized into a table and you need to get a grand total for the entire table. You can add each column, and then add the column totals. To check your work, you can add each row, and then add the row totals.

● EXAMPLE C

Tables C-1 and C-2 give the number of minutes that seven different employees spent answering the telephone every day last week. First find the weekly total for each employee (Table C-1) and then find the company total for the week. Check your answer by finding the total for each day (Table C-2) and then the company total. Both solutions give the grand total for the company of 769 minutes.

Telephone Minutes, by Employee

	MB	JR	AT	TF	EJ	KN	HS
Mon	14	15	29	24	23	24	19
Tue	25	26	15	21	15	22	22
Wed	18	28	15	29	17	28	26
Thu	28	19	37	18	21	21	15
Fri	23	21	17	25	19	25	25
Week	108	109	113	117	95	120	107

Total $= 108 + 109 + 113 + 117 + 95 + 120 + 107$
    $= \underline{769}$

Table C-1 – Add Columns First

Check: Telephone Minutes, by Day

	MB	JR	AT	TF	EJ	KN	HS	Day
Mon	14	15	29	24	23	24	19	148
Tue	25	26	15	21	15	22	22	146
Wed	18	28	15	29	17	28	26	161
Thu	28	19	37	18	21	21	15	159
Fri	23	21	17	25	19	25	25	155
Total								769

Table C-2 – Check: Add Rows First

Important! Always check your work, even if you are using a calculator. Each digit must pressed correctly. Sometimes a calculator button will not work properly. Sometimes, if you hold a button down too long, it will enter the digit twice. Sometimes you can press two buttons at the same time. If you are using the calculator on your cell phone it may even be more difficult to accurately press every single digit. Take the time to check your work.

Subtraction

Subtraction is the *inverse* of addition. In addition, we *increase* one number by another number. When we add 3 to 5, we increase 5 by 3 to get 8. In subtraction, we *decrease* one number by another number. When we subtract 4 from 6, we decrease 6 by 4 to get 2. The number being subtracted is called the **subtrahend**. The number being reduced is called the **minuend**. The result is called the **difference**. Here, 4 is the subtrahend; 6 is the minuend; and 2 is the difference. We can write the problem as $6 - 4 = 2$.

When the numbers have more than one digit, arrange the numbers vertically with the minuend at the top. Align the columns at the right – the ones column. Then subtract the subtrahend, one column at a time, starting at the right. Examine example D. The steps of the solution are shown in Figures D-1, D-2, D-3, D-4, and D-5. The final answer is 1,205.

● EXAMPLE D

Subtract 563 from 1,768.

1,768	1,768	1,768	1,768	1,768	minuend
-563	-563	-563	-563	-563	subtrahend
	5	05	205	1,205	difference
Fig. D-1	Fig. D-2	Fig. D-3	Fig. D-4	Fig. D-5	

"Borrowing 1" from the next digit to the left

In example D, the minuend digit in every column was larger than, or equal to, the subtrahend digit below it. That makes the subtraction simple. Often, the minuend digit is smaller than the subtrahend digit below it. When that happens, it is necessary to "borrow a 1" from the adjacent minuend digit at the left. And, the minuend digit at the left must be reduced by 1. Examine example E and the steps in the solution – especially the "borrowing" in Figures E-2 and E-4. It may be helpful to show the borrowing and reducing with small digits above the minuend. The final answer is 3,819.

● EXAMPLE E

Subtract 563 from 4,382.

	$^{7\,1}$	$^{7\,1}$	$^{3\ \ 1}$	$^{3\ \ 1}$	
4,382	4,382	4,382	4,382	4,382	minuend
-563	-563	-563	-563	-563	subtrahend
	9	19	819	3,819	difference
Fig. E-1	Fig. E-2	Fig. E-3	Fig. E-4	Fig. E-5	

Checking your answer in subtraction

To check your answer, always *add* the difference and the subtrahend. The sum should be the original minuend. Examples D and E and their checks are shown below.

Ex. D	Check for Ex. D		Ex. E	Check for Ex. E	
1,768	1,205	1,205	4,382	3,819	3,819
−563	+563	+563	−563	+563	+563
1,205		1,768	3,819		4,382

Negative differences, or negative balances

In business, expenses are normally deducted from revenue to find the profit. Suppose that you have a business that has July revenues of $20,000; and that your business has July expenses of $6,000. Your July profit is $20,000 − $6,000 = $14,000.

But what if your August revenue is $18,000 and you have unexpected expenses totaling $22,000? Subtracting expenses from revenue, August profit = $18,000 − $22,000. In August, your business might say that it has a "loss of $4,000." When you do the subtraction with a calculator, you get "18,000 − 22,000 = −4,000." Mathematically, we can say that "profit was a *negative* $4,000." In accounting, this difference might be written within parentheses, as "$18,000 − $22,000 = ($4,000). Or, it might be written in red ink, as "$18,000 − $22,000 = $4,000." The EXCEL spreadsheet allows negative numbers to be written in four different formats: −4,000; (4,000); 4,000; or (4,000). If the negative numbers are amounts of money, then EXCEL would allow them to be written as −$4,000; ($4,000); $4,000; or ($4,000).

Multiplication

Multiplication, simply stated, is *repeated addition*. You may have learned multiplication from seeing a rectangle that is 3 units high by 5 units wide. When you count all of the squares inside of the rectangle, there are 15 squares. You can add up 5 + 5 + 5 = 15; or 3 + 3 + 3 + 3 + 3 = 15. Either way, 5 × 3 = 3 × 5 = 15. The 5 and the 3 are both **factors**. 15 is the **product**.

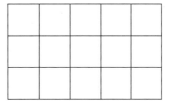

Multiplying whole numbers containing more than one digit

Students practice multiplying two one-digit numbers so often in school that they have memorized the various combinations. When the numbers have more than one digit, they are arranged in columns just as in addition or subtraction. It is more convenient to put the number with the most digits on the top. It is called the **multiplicand**. Underneath it, aligned by the right column, is the shorter number, called the **multiplier**. When using a calculator, distinguishing between the multiplicand and multiplier is not as necessary. They are both factors.

After writing the multiplicand and multiplier, mentally multiply the multiplicand by each digit in the multiplier, starting from the right. Write each of these *partial product*s in separate rows, aligned by the digit in the multiplier. (When two digits have a product of more than one digit, you will need to mentally "carry" the second digit.)

Multiply 45 and 57

57	57	57	57	multiplicand
×45	×45	×45	×45	multiplier
	285	285	285	partial product 1
		2 280	+2 280	partial product 2
			2,565	final product

Fig. F-1 Fig. F-2 Fig. F-3 Fig. F-4

The "trailing 0s" in partial products, as in partial product #2, can often be omitted. (See example G.) They are there as "place-holders. In partial product #2, we multiplied 57 by 4 in the tens column, meaning it was actually a 40. 40 × 57 = 2,280.

Multiply 346 and 1,758. (No "trailing 0s" are used in the partial products.)

1,758	1,758	1,758	1,758	1,758	multiplicand
×346	×346	×346	×346	×346	multiplier
	10 548	10 548	10 548	10 548	partial product 1
		70 32	70 32	70 32	partial product 2
			527 4	+527 4	partial product 3
				608,268	final product

Fig. G-1 Fig. G-2 Fig. G-3 Fig. G-4 Fig. G-5

Multiplying when a digit in the multiplier is zero
When a digit in the multiplier is zero, the partial product for that digit would be all zeros. A shortcut is to write a zero in that column and then move to the next digit to the left.

Multiply 304 and 1,768.

1,768	1,768	1,768	1,768	1,768	multiplicand
×304	×304	×304	×304	×304	multiplier
	7 072	7 072	7 072	7 072	partial product 1
		0	530 40	+530 40	partial product 2&3
				537,472	final product

Fig. H-1 Fig. H-2 Fig. H-3 Fig. H-4 Fig. H-5

Checking your answer in multiplication
The best method to check a multiplication problem is with division. We will illustrate this procedure during the review of division concepts below.

Division
Division is the process of finding how many times one number (the **divisor**) is contained in another number (the **dividend**). The result is called the **quotient**. If anything is remains after the dividing has finished, it is called the **remainder**. For example, 15 ÷ 5 = 3. The

dividend is 15; the divisor is 5; the quotient is 3. The remainder is 0; or, we say that "there is no remainder." But 19 ÷ 5 = 3, with a remainder of 4.

Recall that "multiplication is repeated addition." Similarly, division is essentially "repeated subtraction. We can subtract the divisor 5 from the dividend 19 three times (the quotient), leaving 4 remaining:

$$19 - 5 = 14; \qquad 14 - 5 = 9; \qquad 9 - 5 = 4.$$

Subtracting 5 from 19 three times leaves a remainder of 4

● EXAMPLE I

Divide 2,565 by 57

Division is done manually by first writing the divisor in front of a division bracket $(57\overline{)}\,)$, and writing the dividend inside the bracket: $(57\overline{)2,565})$ The quotient and any remainder are written above the division bracket, with the remainder in parentheses.

Just as there were *partial products* in multiplication, there are *partial dividends* in division. In Fig. I-1, examine the dividend 2,565, starting from the *left* digit (2) There are no 57s in 2; next, there are no 57s in 25. But there are four 57s in 256 (a partial dividend). Write a 4 above the 6 on top of the division bracket; then multiply the divisor 57 by 4 and write the product, 228, under the partial dividend 256 (Fig. I-2). Subtract 228 from 256, leaving 28; then bring down the 5 from the original dividend to make a new partial dividend of 285 (Fig. I-3). There are five 57s in 285. Write a 5 in the quotient above the 5 in the dividend; then multiply the divisor 57 by the 5 and write the product, 285, under the partial dividend 285 (Fig. I-4). Subtract 285 from 285. The remainder is 0 (Fig. I-5).

$57\overline{)2,565}$	$\begin{array}{r} 4 \\ 57\overline{)2,565} \\ -2\ 28 \end{array}$	$\begin{array}{r} 4 \\ 57\overline{)2,565} \\ -2\ 28 \\ \hline 285 \end{array}$	$\begin{array}{r} 45 \\ 57\overline{)2,565} \\ -2\ 28 \\ \hline 285 \\ -285 \end{array}$	$\begin{array}{r} 45 \\ 57\overline{)2,565} \\ -2\ 28 \\ \hline 285 \\ -285 \\ \hline 0 \end{array}$
Fig. I-1	Fig. I-2	Fig. I-3	Fig. I-4	Fig. I-5

Note about "repeated subtraction:" The 4 in the quotient is in the tens column, meaning it represents 4 tens, or 40. 40 × 57 = 2,280. Subtracting 2,280 from 2,565 leaves 285. The 5 in the quotient is in the ones column, meaning it represents 5 ones. 5 × 57 = 285. Subtracting 285 from 285 leaves a remainder of 0. The "repeated subtraction" is 2,565 − 2,280 − 285 = 0.

Examine the arrangement of the partial products in the multiplication of 57 × 45 from example F and the arrangement of the partial dividends from example I. The "zeros" representing the column value of the multiplier are shown. Example F illustrates repeated addition; example I illustrates repeated subtraction. Together, examples F and I illustrate that you can check multiplication by division, and vice-versa.

$\begin{array}{r} 57 \\ \times 45 \\ \hline 285 \end{array}$	$\begin{array}{r} 57 \\ \times\ 45 \\ \hline 285 \\ +2\ 280 \\ \hline 2,565 \end{array}$		$\begin{array}{r} 4 \\ 57\overline{)2,565} \\ -2\ 280 \\ \hline 285 \end{array}$	$\begin{array}{r} 45 \\ 57\overline{)2,565} \\ -2\ 280 \\ \hline 285 \\ -285 \\ \hline 0 \end{array}$
	Example F		Example I	

Checking your answers in multiplication and division

The above illustration shows that you can check your multiplication answers by division. Divide the dividend by either multiplication factor. The quotient will be the other multiplication factor. Inversely, to check a division answer, multiply the quotient and the divisor. If there was not remainder, the product will be the dividend. If the division problem did have a remainder, then multiply the quotient and the divisor. Add the remainder to the product; the sum will be the dividend.

● EXAMPLE J

Divide 2,572 by 57. Check the answer by multiplying the divisor and the quotient; then add the remainder. Examine the similarity of the various numbers in the two calculations.

$$
\begin{array}{r}
4 \\
57\overline{)2{,}572} \\
-2\,280 \\
\hline
292 \\
-285 \\
\hline
\end{array}
\qquad
\begin{array}{r}
45 \\
57\overline{)2{,}572} \\
-2\,280 \\
\hline
292 \\
285 \\
\hline
7
\end{array}
\qquad
\begin{array}{r}
45\ (7) \\
57\overline{)2{,}572} \\
-2\,280 \\
\hline
292 \\
285 \\
\hline
7
\end{array}
\qquad
\begin{array}{r}
57 \\
\times\,45 \\
\hline
285 \\
\end{array}
\qquad
\begin{array}{r}
57 \\
\times\,45 \\
\hline
285 \\
+2\,280 \\
\hline
2{,}565 \\
+\quad 7 \\
\hline
2{,}572
\end{array}
$$

Divide 2572 by 57   Check the answer

A

Account purchase. A detailed statement from the commission merchant to the principal.

Account sales. A detailed statement of the amount of the sales and the various deductions sent by the commission merchant to the consignor.

Addend. Any of a set of numbers to be added together.

Additional death benefit (ADB). Benefits, available with some life insurance policies, that allow the insured to purchase, at a low rate per thousand dollars of coverage, additional insurance up to the full face value of the policy. In case of death of the insured by accident, both the full value of the policy and the ADB would be paid to the beneficiaries of the insured. If death occurs other than by accident, the full value of the policy is paid but no ADB is paid. Sometimes referred to as accidental death benefit.

Adjusted bank balance. The dollar amount obtained by adding to or subtracting from the bank statement balance checkbook activities not yet known to the bank. This amount should equal the adjusted checkbook balance.

Adjusted checkbook balance. The dollar amount obtained by adding to or subtracting from the checkbook balance those activities appearing on the bank statement that do not yet appear in the checkbook. This amount should equal the adjusted bank statement balance.

Adjusted gross income (AGI). Gross income minus certain income adjustments.

Allocate. Assign representative proportions of a business expense to the different departments of a company.

Amortization. The process by which a loan's monthly payments are always equal in dollar amount while the interest amount, which is calculated on the unpaid balance, always varies.

Amortization payment factor. A number which, when multiplied by the per $1,000 loan amount, calculates the amount of each loan payment.

Amortization schedule. A schedule of payments; the schedule shows the amount of interest and the amount of principal in each payment.

Amount credited. The total amount paid plus the amount of cash discount.

Amount of decrease. The rate of decrease times the base amount.

Amount of increase. The rate of increase times the base amount.

Annual percentage rate (APR). The annual equivalent interest rate charged.

Annuity insurance. Life insurance that pays a certain sum of money to the insured every year after the insured reaches a specified age or until the insured's death.

Assessed valuation. A property value determined by a representative of the local or state government.

Auto collision insurance. Insurance that protects the vehicle of the insured against collision damage.

Auto comprehensive insurance. Insurance that protects the vehicle of the insured against fire, water, theft, vandalism, falling objects, and other damage not caused by collision.

Auto liability and property damage insurance. Insurance that protects the insured against claims resulting from personal injuries and property damage.

Automatic teller machine (ATM). A computerized electronic machine, many of which are located outside of banks and in numerous other locations, that allows customers to perform various banking functions, such as checking balances, making deposits, and withdrawing funds.

Average daily balance. The sum of each day's balance divided by the number of days in the month. Payments are usually included; new purchases may or may not be included.

Average principal. The average unpaid balance of a note or loan.

Average unpaid balance. The sum of all of the unpaid monthly balances divided by the number of months.

B

Bank charge. A fee for services performed by the bank.

Bank discount loan. Bank loan for which the interest is subtracted from the face value at the time the loan is made.

Bank statement. A formal accounting by a bank of the adding and subtracting activities that have occurred in one bank account over a stated period of time (usually a month).

Base (B). The whole quantity, or 100%, of an amount.

Bearer. The lender of a note.

Beneficiary. A person, a company, or an organization that benefits from an insurance policy.

Broker. A person who performs services of buying and/or selling for a commission.

C

Cancel. "Divide out" common factors that occur in both the numerator and denominator.

Cancellation. Process of dividing out common factors.

Cash discount. A reduction in an invoice amount available to the buyer for paying all or part of the amount due within a stated period of time.

Cash surrender value. The amount of cash that a company will pay the insured on the surrender, or "cashing-in," of an insurance policy.

Charges. The commission and any other sales expenses, such as transportation, advertising, storage, and insurance.

Check. A written order directing the bank to pay a certain sum to a designated party.

Checkbook. Checks and check stubs to record deposits, withdrawals, check numbers, dates of transactions, other additions or subtractions, and the account balance.

Check register. A place for recording important information about each transaction.

Child Tax Credit. Taxpayers with dependent children under age 17 can receive a credit of $1,000 per qualifying child. The credit phases out at higher income levels.

Coinsurance clause. An insurance policy clause specifying that, if a property is not insured up to a certain percentage of its value, the owner is the bearer of part of the insurance and will not be covered for the full amount of damages.

Commercial paper. Documentation of a promise to repay a loan or pay for merchandise.

Commission. Payment to an employee or to an agent for performing or helping to perform a business transaction or service.

Commission merchant. A person who performs services of buying and/or selling for a commission.

Common denominator. A denominator that is shared by two or more fractions. The product of the denominators of two or more fractions is always a common denominator.

Complement method. Method of computing the net price directly, using the complement of the trade discount rate.

Complement rate. A rate equal to 100% minus the discount rate; used with the complement method in determining trade or cash discounts.

Compound amount. Also known as the future value, the total value of an investment; equal to the principal plus all the compound interest.

Compound amount factor. The number from a calculator or future value table used to compute the future value from a given principal (present value) earning compound interest; also known as a future value factor.

Compound interest. Interest computed by performing the simple interest formula periodically during the term of the investment.

Consignee. The party to whom a consignment shipment is sent.

Consignment. Goods from a producer to a commission merchant for sale at the best possible price.

Consignor. The party who sends a consignment.

Cost of goods sold (CGS). The seller's cost of items (goods) that have been sold during a certain time.

Credit. A deposit to a bank account.

Credit balance. A negative difference.

Credit card. Credit extended by a third party.

Cross-checking. Adding columns vertically and then adding those totals horizontally.

D

Decimal equivalent. The presentation of a non-decimal number in decimal form.

Decimal places. The places for digits to the right of the decimal point, representing tenths, hundredths, thousandths, and so forth.

Decimal point. The period between two numerals.

Declining-balance depreciation rate. A multiple of the basic depreciation rate, such as two (double-declining-balance) or 1.5 (150%-declining-balance).

Declining-balance (DB) method. A method to depreciate assets based on the theory that depreciation is greatest in the first year and less in each succeeding year.

Deductible clause. An insurance policy clause that stipulates that the insured will pay the first portion of collision damage and that the insurance company will pay the remainder up to the value of the insured vehicle.

Denominator. In a fraction, the number below the line.

Dependency exemptions. Reductions to taxable income for each of one or more dependents.

Deposit slip. A written form that lists cash and checks being deposited in a bank account and cash received from the amount being deposited.

Difference. The result of subtracting the subtrahend from the minuend.

Discount. A fee charged when someone buys a note before maturity. With regard to bonds, a bond sells at a discount if the market value becomes less than the face value.

Discount amount. The decrease in value of a discounted note.

Discount date. The last day on which a cash discount may be taken. The day on which a note is discounted (sold).

Discount method. Method of computing the net price using the trade discount rate to calculate the amount of trade discount, and, subsequently, the net price.

Discount period. A certain number of days after the invoice date, during which a buyer may receive a cash discount. The time between a note's discount date and its maturity date.

Discount rate. The percent used for calculating a trade or cash discount. The percent interest charged by the buyer of a discounted note. The percent interest charged by a bank making a loan under the discount method.

Discounted note. A loan that the original lender has sold to a new lender, at a price that is less than the loan's original maturity value.

Dividend. The number being divided.

Divisor. The number used to divide another number.

Dollar markup. The total of operating expenses and net profit. Markup expressed as an amount rather than as a percent.

Down payment. A partial payment made at the time of a purchase with the balance due at a later time.

Due date. The final day an invoice is to be paid. After that day the buyer may be charged interest. Also the date by which a loan is to be repaid.

E

Effective interest rate. The actual annual rate of interest.

Electronic fund transfer (EFT). Money that is transmitted electronically, primarily via computers and automatic teller machines.

Employee's earnings record. Summary by quarter of the employee's gross earnings, deductions, and net pay.

Employer's Quarterly Federal Tax Return. A tax report, filed on Form 941 every three months by all employers, that provides the IRS with details about the number of employees, total wages paid, income and FICA taxes withheld, and other figures that determine whether a tax balance is due from the company.

Endowment insurance. Insurance payable upon the insured's death if it occurs within a specified period, and an endowment of the same amount as the policy, payable if the insured is alive at the end of that period.

Equation. A sentence consisting of numbers and/or letters that represent numbers, divided into two sections by an equal sign (=).

Equivalent single discount rate. A single trade discount rate that can be used in place of two or more trade discount rates to determine the same discount amount.

Exact interest method. The calculation of simple interest based on the assumption that a year is 365 (or 366) days long.

Excise tax. A tax assessed on each unit, such as is levied on the sale of gasoline, cigarettes, and alcoholic beverages.

Exponent. A number written above and to the right of a number used to indicate raising to the power.

F

Face value. The dollar amount written on a note; it is the same as the amount borrowed, or the principal (P). With regard to corporate and government bonds, the amount that will be paid to the holder when a bond is redeemed at maturity.

Factors. Any of a set of numbers to be multiplied together.

Federal Insurance Contributions Act (FICA). Provides for a federal system of old-age, survivors, disability, and hospital insurance.

Federal Unemployment Tax Act (FUTA). Law that requires employers to pay the IRS an annual tax of 6.2% on the first $7,000 paid to each employee. The federal government uses the money to help fund State Employment Security Agencies, which administer unemployment insurance and job service programs.

Filing status. One of five conditions, including single, married, and married filing separate returns, that a taxpayer qualifies for on Form 1040 that will determine such factors as tax rates and allowable deductions.

Finance charge. The fee that the seller charges for the privilege of buying on credit.

Fixed interest rate. An interest rate that stays the same for the entire length of the loan.

Form 1040. One of the basic income tax return forms filed by taxpayers.

Form W-4. The form used to inform the government of a person's marital status and to claim withholding allowances.

Fractions. Number expressions of one or more equal parts of whole units.

Future value. The total value of an investment equal to the principal plus all the compound interest; also called the compounded amount.

Future value factor. The number from a calculator or future value table used to compute the future value from a given principal (present value) earning compound interest; also known as a compound amount factor.

G

Graduated commission rates. A system of rates by which graduated commissions increase as the level of sales increase.

Gross cost. The prime cost and all charges paid by the principal.

Gross proceeds. The price that a commission merchant gets for a consignment.

Gross sales. Total sales before deducting any returns, cancelled orders, or sales expenses.

Group insurance. Health insurance coverage extended to a group of people. The cost for each person's coverage is less expensive than it would be under an individual policy.

H

Health maintenance organization (HMO). Group health insurance coverage with limited options as a means of keeping health insurance costs lower than that of regular group policies.

Higher terms. A fraction in which both the numerator and denominator have been multiplied by the same number.

High-risk driver. A driver with a record of numerous citations or accidents.

I

Improper fraction. A fraction in which the numerator is greater than or equal to the denominator.

Installments. Monthly payments, which for a credit sale typically include the purchase price plus all finance charges.

Insured. For life insurance, the person whose life is being insured; for other types of insurance, the person who receives the benefit of the insurance.

Interest. A fee, usually charged for the use of money or credit.

Interest-bearing note. A note that has a maturity value greater than its face value.

Interest dollars. The interest stated as an amount of money rather than as a percent.

Interest period. The period of time between the loan date and the repayment date.

Invoice. A document from a seller requesting payment from the buyer; the supplier's bill.

Invoice date. The date stated on an invoice; the beginning of the discount period.

Itemized deductions. Potential reductions to income allowed for certain payments made during the tax year.

L

Least common denominator. The lowest shared multiple of two or more denominators.

Levy. A government charge or fee.

Limited-payment life insurance. A certain premium to be paid every year for a certain number of years specified at the time of insuring, or until the death of the insured, should that occur during the specified period. The policy is payable on the death of the insured, although there may be some options available at the end of the payment period.

List price. The price amount listed in a catalog.

Loan value. The amount that an insured may borrow on a policy from the insurance company.

Long-term credit. Loans that are for longer than 1 year.

Lower terms. A fraction that has been reduced by a common divisor.

Lowest terms. A fraction that cannot be reduced by any common divisor.

Low-risk driver. A driver with a long-standing, clear driving record.

M

Maker. With regard to a note, the borrower.

Market value. The dollar amount required to replace the inventory as of the inventory date.

Markup. The difference between price and a seller's cost of an item for sale. In dollars it is the amount added to the cost of the goods in order to have a gross profit high enough to cover operating expenses and to make a net profit.

Markup percent. A percent that is used to compute the amount of dollar markup by multiplication. It could be a percent that multiplies the cost to find the dollar markup; or, it could be a percent that multiplies the selling price to find that dollar markup.

Markup percent based on cost. The percent that is calculated by dividing the desired amount of dollar markup by the cost.

Markup percent based on selling price. The percent that is calculated by dividing the desired amount of dollar markup by the selling price.

Markup rate. Markup percent.

Maturity date. The final day of a note on which the borrower (the maker of the note) pays the face value and any interest due to the holder of the note. The due date.

Maturity value. For an interest-bearing note, it is the sum of the face value (principal) and the interest dollars: MV = P + I.

Metric system. The decimal system of weights (grams, kilograms, etc.) and measures (meters, kilometers, etc.) used in most countries of the world, with the major exception of the U.S.

Mill. One tenth of one cent, or $0.001; a tax rate may be expressed in mills.

Minuend. Number from which subtraction is being made.

Mixed decimal. A number containing a decimal point and both a whole-number part and a decimal part.

Mixed number. A number that represents more than one whole unit by combining a whole number and a proper fraction.

Mortgage. A loan, usually amortized over 15 to 30 years, used to purchase a home.

Multiplicand. The factor that is multiplied.

Multiplier. The factor that indicates how many times to multiply.

N

Negotiable promissory note. A promissory note that may be sold to a third party.

Net price. The price that a distributor will charge a customer after any trade discounts have been subtracted from the list price.

Net proceeds. The amount sent to the consignor as a result of consignment sales; gross proceeds minus charges.

Net purchase amount. The price of the merchandise actually purchased, including allowances for returns but excluding handling and other costs.

Net sales. Total sales for the time period minus sales returned and adjustments made during the same time.

No-fault insurance. Insurance coverage under which the driver of each vehicle involved in an injury accident submits a claim to his or her own insurance company to cover medical costs for injuries to the driver and passengers in that person's own vehicle. The insurance does not cover damage to either vehicle involved in an accident.

Non-interest-bearing promissory note. A note having a maturity value equal to its face value.

Number of compounding periods. The number of compounding periods per year times the number of years of the loan.

Numerator. In a fraction, the number above the line.

Numerical sentence. A mathematical or logical statement, such as an equation, expressed in numbers and symbols.

O

Of. "Multiply," particularly when "of" is preceded by the Rate and followed by the Base.

Ordinary interest method. The calculation of simple interest based on the assumption that a year is 360 days long.

Outstanding check. One that has been written but hasn't yet cleared the bank and been charged to the customer's account.

Outstanding deposit. A credit that hasn't yet been recorded by the bank.

Overhead costs. General costs not directly related to sales merchandise.

P

Payee. Party to whom a check is written.

Payroll register. A summary of wages earned, payroll deductions, and final take-home pay.

Percent. Word and symbol used to communicate a fraction or decimal number, verbally or in writing, as a numerator whose denominator is 100.

Percentage (P). A portion of the Base.

Percentage method. One of two primary methods for calculating the amount of income tax to withhold from employee paychecks. After the total withholding allowance is subtracted from an employee's gross earnings, the amount to be withheld is determined by taking a percentage of the balance. The percentage to be used is specified by the IRS.

Period (compounding period). The unit of time of the compounding.

Periodic interest rate. The rate of interest charged each period.

Personal exemptions. Reductions to taxable income for the primary taxpayer and a spouse.

Power. The number of times as indicated by an exponent that a number is multiplied by itself.

Preferred provider organization (PPO). Group health insurance coverage with benefits based on use of contracted providers as a means of keeping health insurance costs lower than that of regular group policies.

Premium. Fee for insurance coverage, usually paid every year by the insured person. The difference between a bond's par value and its market value when the market value is more.

When bonds are sold at a premium, the yield rate will be lower than the stated (face) rate.

Present value. The amount needed to invest today to reach a stated future goal, given a certain rate of return.

Present value factor. The number from a calculator or present value table used to compute the present value (principal) from a given future value (compound amount).

Prime cost. The price that commission merchants pay for the merchandise when they purchase goods for their principals.

Principal. The person (client) for whom a service is performed. Amount that is borrowed using credit.

Proceeds. The amount that a seller receives from the buyer of a note being discounted; the difference between the maturity value and the discount amount.

Proceeds (from sale of stock). The amount of money received by the seller of stock, which is the price minus commission.

Product. The answer to a multiplication problem.

Promissory note. An agreement signed by the borrower that states the conditions of a loan.

Proper fraction. Smaller than one whole unit. The numerator is smaller than the denominator.

Property insurance. Insurance against loss of or damage to property.

Property tax. A tax on real estate or other property owned by the business or an individual.

Pure decimal. A number with no whole-number part.

Q

Quotient. The answer to a division problem.

R

Rate (R). The stated or calculated percent of interest.

Rate of decrease. The negative change in two values stated as a percent.

Rate of increase. The positive change in two values stated as a percent.

Reconciliation of the bank balance. Comparison of the check stubs or check register with the bank statement to determine the adjusted bank balance.

Recovery amount. The maximum amount that an insurance company will pay on a claim.

Remainder. A part of a dividend that is left after even division is complete. The leftover part of division into which the divisor cannot go a whole number of times.

Remittance. Amount that a buyer actually pays after deducting a cash discount.

Rounding off. Rounding up or down.

S

Sales tax. A government charge on retail sales of certain goods and services.

Series of discounts. Two or more trade discount rates available to a buyer for different volume purchases.

Short rates. Insurance premium rates charged for less than a full term of insurance.

Short-term credit. Loans that are 1 year or less in length.

Short-term credit. Loans that are 1 year or less in length.

Simple interest. The fundamental interest calculation: Interest = Principal $\times$ Rate $\times$ Time.

State Unemployment Tax Act (SUTA). Any of various laws passed by states that require the employer to pay a tax, such as 5.4% on the first $7,000 paid to each employee, used to help fund unemployment programs.

Stockbroker. An agent who handles stock transactions for clients.

Straight (ordinary) life insurance. Insurance requiring a certain premium to be paid every year until the death of the insured person. The policy then becomes payable to the beneficiary.

Subtrahend. Number being subtracted.

Sum. The total of two or more numbers being added together.

T

Tax rate. The percent used to calculate a tax.

Tax Rate Schedules. Tables formulated by the IRS to compute, depending upon filing status, the tax owed for various levels of taxable income.

Taxable income. The amount of income on which the income tax is determined.

Term insurance. Insurance protection issued for a limited time. A certain premium is paid every year during the specified time period, or term. The policy is payable only in the case of death of the insured during the term. Otherwise, neither the insured nor the specified beneficiaries receive any payment, and the protection stops at the end of the term.

Term of a loan. The period of time between the loan date and the due date.

Terms of payment. A statement on the invoice that informs the buyer of any available discount rate and discount date as well as the due date.

Time. Stated in years or part of a year, the length of time used in simple interest calculations.

Trade discounts. Discounts given to buyers that generally are based on the quantity purchased.

Truth in Lending Act (TILA). A federal law to assist consumers in knowing the total cost of credit.

V

Variable-rate loans. Loans that permit the lender to periodically adjust the interest rate depending on current financial market conditions.

W

Wage-bracket method. One of two primary methods for calculating the amount of income tax to withhold from employee paychecks. This method starts by granting a deduction for each withholding allowance claimed. The amount for each withholding allowance is provided by the IRS. This method involves use of a series of wage-bracket tables published by the IRS.

Withholding allowance. An amount claimed on tax Form W-4 that determines how much income tax the employer will withhold from each paycheck. Each allowance claimed (as for a spouse or dependents) reduces the amount of income tax withheld.

Note: Page numbers referencing figures are italicized and followed by an *f* . Page numbers referencing tables are italicized and followed by a *t*.